Biopolitics of the
More-Than-Human

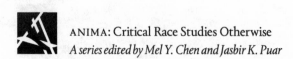 ANIMA: Critical Race Studies Otherwise
A series edited by Mel Y. Chen and Jasbir K. Puar

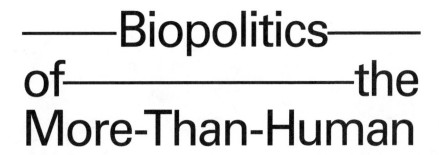

Biopolitics of the More-Than-Human

Forensic Ecologies of Violence

Joseph Pugliese

Duke University Press
Durham and London
2020

Designed by Drew Sisk
Typeset in Portrait Text and Univers by Westchester Publishing
    Services

Library of Congress Cataloging-in-Publication Data
Names: Pugliese, Joseph, [date] author.
Title: Biopolitics of the more-than-human : forensic ecologies of
    violence / Joseph Pugliese.
Other titles: ANIMA (Duke University Press)
Description: Durham : Duke University Press, 2020. | Series:
    ANIMA : critical race studies otherwise | Includes bibliographical
    references and index.
Identifiers: LCCN 2020015354 (print)
LCCN 2020015355 (ebook)
ISBN 9781478007678 (hardcover)
ISBN 9781478008026 (paperback)
ISBN 9781478009078 (ebook)
Subjects: LCSH: War—Environmental aspects. | Geopolitics—
    Environmental aspects. | Biopolitics. | Nature—Effect of human
    beings on. | Political violence—Environmental aspects.
Classification: LCC TD195.W29 P845 2020 (print) | LCC TD195.W29
    (ebook) | DDC 172/.42—dc23
LC record available at https://lccn.loc.gov/2020015354
LC ebook record available at https://lccn.loc.gov/2020015355

Duke University Press gratefully acknowledges Macquarie University,
    which provided funds toward the publication of this book.

CONTENTS

Acknowledgments——vii

Introduction——1

1——Zoopolitics of the Cage——39

2——Biopolitical Modalities of the
More-Than-Human
and Their Forensic Ecologies——81

3——Animal Excendence and
Inanimal Torture——124

4——Drone Sparagmos——166

Afterword——203

Notes——217

Bibliography——255

Index——279

ACKNOWLEDGMENTS

I acknowledge the unceded sovereignty of the Gadigal people of the Eora Nation and the Wattamattagal clan of the Darug Nation on whose lands this book was written: their cultures and customs have nurtured, and continue to nurture, these lands since time immemorial; they have literally made this book possible.

Susan Stryker has been unsparing in her support of this book: my profound thanks for your engaged friendship and for being there when all seemed lost. *Grazie*, Leo Davis, *per la tua amicizia e solidarietà nei momenti più difficili*. I'm particularly grateful to Jasbir Puar and Mel Chen for their strong belief in this book and to Courtney Berger for her care, support, and constructive guidance: it made all the difference. My thanks to the anonymous referees who reviewed the manuscript and who offered invaluable feedback.

Nicole Anderson, both as dear friend and head of department, has been exemplary in her instantiation of an ethics of care when things were most difficult: thank you. Thank you, Tess and Ruben Allas, for being there when it really counted. My thanks to Iqbal Barkat, Bronwyn Carlson, Maria Giannacopoulos, Derek Gregory, Bridget Griffin-Foley, Julian Knowles, Catharine Lumby, Catriona Mackenzie, Lara Palombo, Marilena Parlati, Holly Randall-Moon, Kate Rossmanith, and Adrian Stimson. I'm grateful to Nadera Shalhoub-Kevorkian for her generous hospitality in occupied East Jerusalem and for showing me the occupation "through her eyes," and to Rema Hammami for sharing her insights and irreverent humor. Constance Owen has been a fellow traveler for many years: thank you for your brilliant and enduring research assistance. There are, quite simply, no words with which I can thank Suvendrini Perera: no inventory can do justice.

My late mother and father taught me the beauty of *nu cori sciancatu*. To the late, great Uncle Ray Jackson, president of the Indigenous Social Justice Association, irreplaceable friend and mentor: *FKJ!* Thank you, Raffaella and Larry, for your profound commitment and unwavering support throughout all the tribulations. For Sebastian: the joy of animal excendence. My heartfelt gratitude to Trish: in the face of two health crises, you maintained extraordinary courage, unstinting care, strength, and fearlessness, and in the face of an unending saga, you never gave up hope: you have been inspirational.

Inscribed in the fabric of this book are my more-than-human collaborators, including the venerable golden locust tree, my magpie friends—who sing the most beautiful songs of the earth—and the ravens who have continued to gift me their black raven stones. Special thanks to the two magisterial ravens who, while roosting on the railing of the veranda, oversaw the writing of this book with a sharp and critical eye and who have rightly disowned all the errors that I have no doubt perpetrated despite their expert guidance.

ACKNOWLEDGMENTS

Writing in the midst of the unfolding militarized violence unleashed on Gaza by the Israeli state through its Operation Protective Edge in July 2014, Atef Abu Saif, a citizen of Gaza, documented the breadth of the destruction he was compelled to witness. In the fraught context of the relentless military assault, he repeatedly negotiated the wreckage of his bombed neighborhood to put on public record the enormity of the devastation wreaked by the Israeli Defence Forces (IDF). In one account, Saif describes the corpses of donkeys killed by the IDF's strikes: "Half a dozen lie in the road in front of the school. Their stomachs and intestines hang from their bellies. A seventh donkey is still alive, though critically injured."[1] As he walks away from the site of this killing, he encounters a tree that is also a victim of the strike: "The fig tree in front of the homes is painted white with dust. Branches lie on the ground with fruit still on them."[2] Then, entering one of the bombed homes of his neighborhood, he is confronted by "one boy [who] is still hysterical after seeing the flesh of his father and uncle, mixed together like meat in a butcher's shop."[3] Saif's testimony encapsulates the concerns of this book.

At this opening juncture, Saif's testimony serves to provoke a number of questions, which establish the interrogative coordinates of this project: Is it possible to begin to enlarge the concepts of biopolitics and forensics beyond their anthropocentric frames so that they work to encompass more-than-human entities who are also victims of military violence—such as the disemboweled donkeys and the fig tree with its lopped-off limbs? What if I were to attempt to resignify the traditional disciplinary understanding of "forensic ecology," which presently focuses exclusively on mapping the causes of only human deaths, so that it would work to make the death of other-than-human victims a justiciable issue? What forms of law would begin to do justice to the heterogeneous entities caught in the violent matrix of forensic ecologies of militarized violence and occupation—as the focal sites of this text? I deploy, in this book, two concepts through which I attempt to answer these questions: biopolitics and forensic ecology. I will presently discuss these concepts in some detail, but I offer here synoptic definitions to orient the reader with regard to the approach that informs the analytical framework of this book.

In his theorizing of biopolitics, Michel Foucault raises the ontological question of who is allowed by the state to flourish and who may be left to die or be killed with impunity.[4] Biopolitics, in its on-the-ground deployment by a state, pivots on the governmentalized management of life and death. Forensics is a discipline of law. It is a discipline concerned with interpreting material found in a crime scene and in establishing the evidentiary dimensions of this material; forensic material—a shard of glass or an item of clothing—is mobilized by a forensic expert in the court of law as a form of demonstrative evidence that will speak truth to the crime by disclosing how the criminal act was perpetrated. Ecology refers to the matrix of relations that binds living entities with the complex infrastructure of their environment. The key term here is *relationality*: a rupture of one relational link invariably produces other effects across the broad spectrum of entities that constitute a given ecology.

In my analysis of sites of saturated violence, I deploy the concept of forensic ecologies in an attempt to *articulate* and to bring into *relational visibility* phenomena that would otherwise remain outside the domains of either biopolitics or law—except in the most circumscribed or token ways: for example, the rendering of more-than-human entities as worthy of legal consideration only after they have been processed through the Eurocentric grid of property law.[5] My focus on the operations of biopolitics on both human and more-than-human entities is critically informed by the forensic ecologies that constitute their conditions of survival and that, in death, work to proffer evidence of the criminal violence that transpired in those sites of destruction.

The possibility of making visible the different phenomena that inhabit the fractured terrain violated by military violence—to attend to their articulations as modes of evidentiary testimony and to begin to situate them as entities worthy of ethical consideration—is what animates this study. The shattered and dispersed fragments that remain in the wake of the military assault Saif documents in his wartime diary emerge from the rubble as something more than mere dead matter. The fig tree with its truncated limbs and its mineralized coating of concrete dust, the donkeys with their gaping bellies and hanging entrails, and the butchered bodies of a father and uncle whose intermixed remains appear as so much meat disgorged from the shambles—they are what charged me to become attentive to the agentic and ethical articulations of a host of human and more-than-human entities calling for justice in the face of military violence.

My analytical attention to the victims of military violence and occupation encompasses both the categories of the human and the more-than-human because I see the two as inextricably entangled; indeed, as I discuss in the context of a number of military strikes, the two categories often become so enmeshed as to make it impossible to separate one from the other. Throughout the book, I deploy both the categories of more-than-human and other-than-human, rather than nonhuman and posthuman, for the following reasons: the category of the nonhuman is visibly and conceptually marked by the negative prefix *non-* that functions to define its other (animals, rocks, water, or plants) through a series of tacit or explicit deficits (they do not have language, emotion, culture, and so on); it thus reproduces, by semantic default, yet another form of anthropocentrism. By contrast, the category of the more-than-human refers to that which is other to the human without reproducing an attendant positive/negative hierarchy. The adjective *more* affirms the way more-than-human entities exceed human qualities and conceptual parameters, while the phrase itself visibly marks, through its hyphenated formation, the relational ecologies that constitute the very conditions of possibility for both human and more-than-human entities. Moreover, the hyphenated formation *more-than-human* effectively brings into focus my refusal, in this book, to view either human or other-than-human entities as categorically separated from each other. On the contrary, I work to challenge the sort of human exceptionalism that returns, often by sleight of hand, in seemingly progressive environmental and animal studies when they declare the need for the categorical isolation of the one from the other. As I demonstrate throughout the book, this is a conceptually and physically untenable position once situated in the context of Indigenous cosmo-epistemologies, and it thereby works to reproduce a distinctly Eurocentric position.

I also draw on the category of the *other*-than-human as a way of materializing the constitutive alterity that inscribes animals, plants, rocks, and so on and that continues to defy my definitional and categorical maneuvers. Furthermore, my analysis reflexively refuses to draw on the category of the posthuman. As has transpired with so many other categories inscribed with the prefix *post-* (postcolonialism, postracial, and so on), the conceptual marking of a moment of supersession has, after the fact, too often proven to be premature. This is strikingly so with the category of the posthuman: if the era of the Anthropocene evidences anything, it is that not only has the figure of the human *not* been superseded but also its power and influence will continue to have global effects for millennia.

In sum, my discussion of the impact of military violence and occupation on the human and more-than-human world is foundationally grounded in *forensic ecologies* precisely because the concept evinces the following: as a modality of law, forensics valorizes precisely what has otherwise been dispatched as beyond the purview of the justiciable—here the more-than-human. As a concept predicated on inextricable lines of relationality, ecology foregrounds those zones of determinacy and indeterminacy within which human and more-than-human lives are entangled: they remain determinate in their distinct alterities, even as they are relationally bound in zones of indistinction in the wake of acts of military slaughter that often fuse the flesh of one with that of the other. Borrowing a term from Maurice Merleau-Ponty, I call this fused flesh of animal, vegetal, and mineral entities the *flesh of the world*.[6] As this book unfolds, I traverse a terrain harrowed by military violence and occupation, and I examine the forensic remainders of the flesh of the world. I attend to these remainders precisely to do justice to their forensic testimonies of militarized violence.

Biopolitics of the More-Than-Human and Its Differential and Interlocking Elements

My concentration on biopolitics throughout this book pivots on examining the caesura that divides the human from that which is cast as altogether other-than-human and is thus categorized as lawfully killable. Within the context of this biopolitical schema, law plays a foundational role in determining where diverse subjects are placed along the life–death continuum. Within formations of biopolitical state power, I argue, law becomes yet another adjunct to the ensemble of governmentalities oriented toward expanding and consolidating statist ends. My focus on forensic ecologies will be oriented by a concern to delineate the complex assemblage of biopolitical forces mobilized by the Israeli state and the United States in their respective militarized campaigns. Understood in Foucauldian terms, I analyze these military campaigns as biopolitically oriented by statist objectives "to *foster* life or *disallow* it to the point of death."[7]

In designating the domain of biopolitics as effectively driven by the concern to gather "information on the state's environment, its population, its resources,"[8] Foucault establishes the ground to investigate the *different* modalities of biopolitics that are deployed across a range of contexts and that have diverse targets. I emphasize "different" because, in my work on the Israeli state's militarized occupation of the Palestine territories, it became increasingly evident to me that the homogeneous term *biopolitics* could not do justice to the material specificities that distinguish different modalities of biopolitics as they operate in terms of situated practices.

Both Israel and the United States evidence, in their exercise of biopolitical regimes, what Neel Ahuja terms the "government of species," with its focus on "how interspecies relations and the public hopes and fears they generate shape the living form and affective lineaments of settler societies, in the process determining the possibilities and foreclosures of political life."[9] Drawing on Ahuja's conceptualization of the government of species, I delineate how the possibilities of political life for the settler subject are indissociably predicated on infrastructural foreclosures of political life for the broad spectrum of more-than-human entities attempting to survive within regimes of settler occupation and militarized violence. Inscribing these infrastructural foreclosures of political life is a speciesist logic that designates, in the context of the biopolitical continuum, both targeted Indigenous and more-than-human subjects as eliminable. These infrastructural foreclosures are essential in reproducing the settler state's biopolitical "elimination" and "replacement" of the Indigenous people who have never formally ceded sovereignty over their lands.[10] The settler apparatuses of biopolitical attempted elimination, segregation, and subjugation that I analyze all function to evidence, I underscore, the undiminished resistance of the targeted Indigenous subjects in their contestation of settler rule.

Writing on the historical emergence of biopolitics, Foucault marks the epistemic shift that brings a "new technology" into view, one that is "addressed to a multiplicity of men, not to the extent that they are nothing more than their individual bodies, but to the extent that they form, on the contrary, a global mass that is affected by overall processes characteristic of birth, death, production, illness and so on."[11] Foucault registers the epistemic recalibration that ensues from this shift:

> So after a first seizure of power over the body in an individualizing mode, we have a second seizure of power that is not individualizing but, if you like, massifying, that is directed not at man-as-body but man-as-species. After the anatomo-politics of the human body established in the course of the eighteenth century, we have, at the end of the century, the emergence of something that is no longer an anatomo-politics of the human body, but what I would call a "biopolitics" of the human race.[12]

At this very juncture Foucault offers an opening to disrupt the massifying effects of thinking about biopolitics in exclusively anthropocentric terms and to disaggregate his biopolitical analytics by bringing into focus the range of more-than-human entities that stand beyond the speciesist figuration of that "global mass" of the "human race." Underpinning the biopolitics of the human race is the category's foundational, but unspoken, dependence on speciesism. Foucault elaborates on the centrality of the (anthropocentric) concept of the human race in the operations of the "race struggle":

> It [the discourse of race struggle] will become the discourse of a centered, centralized, and centralizing power. It will become the discourse of battle that has to be waged not between races, but by a race that is portrayed as the one true race, the race that holds power and is entitled to define the norm, and against those who deviate from that norm. . . . At this point, we have all those biological-racist discourses of degeneracy, but also all those institutions within the social body which make the discourse of race struggle function as a principle of exclusion and segregation.[13]

The discourses of biological-racist degeneracy and the institutionalized apparatuses of exclusion and segregation are all conceptually enabled by the concept-specter of speciesism and the superordinate category of anthropocentrism that transmute the race struggle into distinct racio-anthropocentric registers designed to impact diverse targets that are scripted as deviating from the norm. Racio-speciesism is what enables the inversion of human/animal categories according to the biopolitical expediencies operative in a given context. It enables the "putting to death as denegation of murder. The putting to death of the animal, says this denegation, is not murder."[14] In the fraught war-torn terrains that I examine, I track concrete instantiations of this racio-speciesist denegation of murder. In marking the question of the animal as "not one question among others" but, in fact, the "decisive" question "in itself and for its strategic value," Jacques Derrida discloses how a number of other questions ensues from this pivotal question "because, while it is difficult and enigmatic in itself, it also represents the limit upon which all the great questions are formed and determined, as well as the concepts that attempt to delimit what is 'proper to man,' the essence and future of humanity, ethics, politics, law, 'human rights,' 'crimes against humanity,' 'genocide,' etc."[15]

As I discuss across the chapters of the book, the question of the animal effectively establishes the onto-epistemological ground that determines the cultural intelligibility of the human/animal binary[16] and that, moreover, establishes what can be executed on the body of the animal other (and, concomitantly, those humans designated as "mere animals") as lawful practice. To bring into visibility the otherwise disavowed way that various modalities of violence are predicated on the question of the animal, in chapter 4 I coin the term *inanimality*. Inanimality, I contend, is the zoopolitical phantom that beckons from the very limits of the Euro-anthropocentric discursive field, even as, from its bestial and outlaw locus, it supplies the epistemological ground for what can be lawfully perpetrated against whatever is designated by the category of "the animal." For the epistemic and physical violence that underpins the practices of inanimality to register as violence, I argue that Euro-anthropocentric language and thought would have to drop the dogma of human exceptionalism and its attendant reductionism, a reductionism insistently animated, as I remarked above, by a series of speciesist negatives: animals do not have language, subjecthood, society, law, play, altruism, and so on. In this zoopolitical schema, the stripping away of any of these attributes from captive human subjects initiates the vertical descent toward the state of a purely immanent animal biologism that stands as the baseline for the opposite of "the human."

By refracting the seemingly singular concept of biopolitics through a non-anthropocentric prism, a spectrum of otherwise invisibilized biopolitical modalities come into view and the homogenizing effects of anthropocentric massification are fractured to disclose the operations of biopolitics on trees, soil, air, water, rocks, and other-than-human entities. These different modalities of statist operation must be seen as operating within inextricable systems of relation that are nested in the superordinate matrix of the biopolitical. Furthermore, these different modalities of statist operation are tributaries that flow from the governing category of biopolitics. As tributaries, they affirm, consolidate, and extend biopolitical relations of power in a capillary manner through grounded, site-specific modalities. They are at once its adjuncts and its site-specific, on-the-ground operatives designed to target specific ecological entities: water, animals, soil, air, and vegetal life. Collectively, they delineate the contours of the forensic ecologies that I investigate in this book, and in the context of the occupied Palestinian territories, for example, they evidence the Israeli state's differential and diffuse operations of biopolitical war by other means, including the bulldozing of orchards, the contamination of aquifers, the poisoning of soil, and the military shooting of cows and sheep. Even as they emerge as differential categories, they simultaneously evidence interlocking relations of site-specific modalities of biopower that work to intensify biopolitical outcomes.

Occupied Palestine and Indigenous Theories and Alliances

In my analysis of the biopolitical operations of Israeli settler colonialism in the context of the occupied Palestinian territories, I draw on a number of Indigenous decolonizing and deanthropomorphizing cosmo-epistemologies. I do this for two interconnected reasons: they work effectively to illuminate the structural forces at work in the consolidation and expansion of the occupation, and they also underscore the profound political and philosophical alliances that have been established between Palestinian and First Nations peoples. The infrastructural resonances among Native American, Aboriginal and Torres Strait Island peoples, First Nations in Canada, and Palestinian experiences of settler colonialism have been formally acknowledged across a number of statements of solidarity.[17] The Native American and Indigenous Studies Association, for example, has formally declared its support for the Boycott, Divestment, Sanctions movement, refusing to legitimate Israeli moves that appear to support Native American rights while Israel continues the settler colonial occupation of Palestinian lands: "As the elected council of an international community of Indigenous and allied non-Indigenous scholars, students and public intellectuals who have studied and resisted the colonization and domination of Indigenous lands via settler state structures throughout the world, we strongly protest the illegal occupation of Palestinian lands and the legal structures of the Israeli state that systematically discriminate against Palestinians and other Indigenous peoples."[18] These statements of solidarity include, from the Palestinian position, an acknowledgment of the parallel structures of colonial violence endured by Native Americans, First Nations peoples, and Palestinians and the militarization of Indigenous lands to secure settler colonial occupation: "As an indigenous people whose lands have been robbed and pillaged, and face existential settler colonial expansion in Palestine, we recognize that Native Americans and First Nation peoples have endured centuries of violent settler colonialism that has dismantled and robbed them of home, heritage, dignity, security, narrative, land, language, identity, family, trees, cemeteries, animals, livelihoods and life."[19] In naming, in this catalog of violent dispossession and extermination, the loss of land, trees, and animals, the Palestinian signatories to this statement of solidarity with Native Americans acknowledge the critical valence of Indigenous cosmo-epistemologies that refuse Euro-anthropocentric perspectives and that encompass the gamut of more-than-human entities within their eco-ethical worldviews. The Palestinian signatories write: "We also heed the wise leadership of a people who first conceived of mountains and rivers as sacred, who look upon a prairie with reverence, who consider trees as family and who risk their lives to protect the water and the integrity of their ancestral lands."[20] As I demonstrate in my two chapters on the occupied Palestinian territories, it is precisely these more-than-human entities—trees, water, soil, and so on—that are exposed to practices of destruction due to the various biopolitical campaigns deployed by the Israeli settler state.

My concern in this book is to examine the rich intersectional qualities that emerge from the deployment of Indigenous theories of decolonization and their interconnected cosmo-epistemologies of the more-than-human in contexts of settler colonial domination and occupation. As I discuss in some detail below, the power of Indigenous theories resides in how they insistently bind the issues of decolonization with deanthropocentrizing understandings of ecology and life—revealing, in the process, how more-than-human entities are invested with their own cultures, languages, and laws and how, by definition, they are a priori political and always already possess ethico-jural standing. In contrast to a number of Western disciplines—such as critical animal studies and the new materialisms that largely neglect the issue of decolonization— Indigenous positions insist that the instantiation and nurturance of ecological worldviews can be realized only through the nonnegotiable deployment of decolonizing practices. At the close of their extensive historical documentation of Indigenous decolonizing movements that have been inextricably linked to ecocentric concerns, Donald Grindle and Bruce Johansen succinctly sum up this indissociable relation: "Liberation of the environment involves liberation of Native American people."[21]

Law

Across the chapters of this book, I focus on the entrenched Euro-anthropocentrism that inscribes both international environmental law and the laws of war and the environment to underscore the inadequacy of current laws either to address or deliver justice to other-than-human victims of armed conflict. I mark this infrastructural Euro-anthropocentrism not only because it inscribes the key branches of international law that are of concern to this study but also because, as I discuss in the concluding section of my introduction, it continues to generate laws that, in their anthropocentrism, stand in contradistinction to Indigenous law and its relational conceptualization of the law/environment nexus.[22] Furthermore, I qualify the anthropocentrism that inscribes these two fields of international law with the racial prefix *Euro-* because the anthropocentrism that supplies the conceptual infrastructure for the various laws that I discuss is a product of a particular geopolitical legal history fundamentally informed by Eurocentric values.[23] For example, the very point of origin of international environmental law, the London Convention Designed to Ensure the Conservation of Various Species of Wild Animals in Africa, Which Are Useful to Man or Inoffensive (1900),[24] is marked by asymmetrical relations of imperial domination that dictate the "protection" of wildlife in Africa to make it readily available for "sustainable" extermination by European hunters and traders: "Its primary goal was to preserve supplies for trophy hunters and traders and dealers in ivory and skins."[25] Nature, in this foundational moment of international environmental law, is instrumentalized into another form of "livestock" and property, where the ostensible "protection" of nature is in fact underpinned by predatory imperial relations of power that transmute wildlife into a gaming and market resource for European hunters and traders.

This first international environmental agreement is, in other words, based on the expansion of European power into yet another domain, wildlife, of an already imperially subjugated and exploited continent, Africa. European imperial politics, in this instance, was instrumental in the formulation of what would count as the legal values of international environmental law: *the commodification of nature in law*. And European imperial economic interests, and the prospective regulation of competition and attendant conflict, were foundational in establishing the legal norms of international environmental law. Cast in a materialist register, "[international] law is the regulatory mechanism generalised in an economy based on commodity production. The legal form is that form which regulates the legal relationship: dispute is central, because without dispute there would be no need of regulation."[26] Without the disputes between the imperial European powers that centered on the trade in wildlife there would have been, in this foundational instance, no need for an international environmental law.

In the epilogue to his extended analysis of the animal/property/law nexus, Gary Francione writes: "Given that the treatment of animals raises moral questions, one would think that animal welfarism, our current legal framework for resolving human/animal conflicts, would reflect, however imperfectly, some *moral* theory. That, however, is the problem. There is no moral theory that even attempts to justify the present level of abuse permitted under the law."[27] While no explicitly articulated moral theory attempts to justify the abuse of animals permitted under Western law and its various international law embodiments, a type of sublimated moral theory animates and orients it. Precisely as Francione illustrates in the early stages of his analysis, the animal/property nexus finds its originary locus in the orthodox Judeo-Christian view that humans have, according to Genesis, dominion over the earth and all its other-than-human entities.[28] The moral basis of this right of dominion is founded on the culture/nature binary and the theo-onto-epistemological view that only humans possess the cognitive faculties for moral reasoning and that animals (and all other-than-human entities) are congenitally devoid of such a capacity and are thus lesser beings on the biopolitical hierarchy—with all the attendant noncriminal practices against animals that this thus licenses. As I discuss in detail in chapters 3 and 4, at the heart of Western law and its various international law incarnations there is a "theological phantasm or concept" of noncriminal animal sacrifice. It is what animates the 1900 London Convention.

"Theological phantasm," coined by Derrida in his discussion of sovereignty, can be effectively transposed to illuminate the operations of Euro-anthropocentric law. Western society secularizes theological concepts: "That is what it means that our culture lives on secularized sacred concepts, secularized theological concepts."[29] Francione, although he does not cast his discussion in these terms, offers a genealogical tracking of the conversion of the theological into the secularized by delineating the key figures—including Thomas Aquinas, René Descartes, John Locke, and so on—who were foundational in theorizing a Euro-anthropocentric jurisprudence of animals as property. The forces of European imperial expansion and the concomitant hegemonic rise of extractive capitalism worked to intensify the juridical instrumentalization of animals into property and their commodification into what Nicole Shukin calls "animal capital."[30] The transmutation of animal life into animal capital achieved its cogent articulation in a form of law that articulates and governs capitalist modes of production and exchange "between inherently uneven polities, with unequal coercive violence implied in the very commodity form. This unequal coercion is what forces particular content [here animals as property] into the legal form."[31]

Western environmental law and its international incarnations make both animals and the environment coextensive with the concept of property; it is only thus that they can achieve the minimal conditions of possibility for jural standing. As Sean Coyle and Karen Morrow succinctly put it: "Most of [Western] environmental law is, of course, a set of restrictions and limitations on the use of property."[32] The question of property, indeed, is critically aligned, in the annals of Euro-anthropocentric epistemologies, with the question of propriety in terms of the right and proper properties of the human subject. Vinciane Despret terms this the "proprietary rights of properties," which insistently arrogate the very attributes that must be "confiscated" from animals so that humans may continue to make their claim to human exceptionalism.[33] Zoopolitical practices of confiscation ensure the consequent scripting of animals as marked by a series of congenital deficits—they lack language, reason, or emotion—that render them into fungible biological matter that can be liquidated in a noncriminal manner.

That the London Convention, as the first piece of international environmental law, was drafted in the geopolitical context of the European imperial domination of Africa is not surprising when situated in the colonial genealogy of international law. Indeed, as Antony Anghie has demonstrated, this is precisely in keeping with international law's colonial moment of foundation. "Colonialism," he writes, "was central to the constitution of international law," shaping "many basic doctrines of international law" and creating, in turn, "a set of structures that continually repeated themselves at various stages in the history of international law."[34] The undiminished power of this imperial re-iteration of Eurocentric values is evidenced across diverse branches of inter-national law. "Western nations," notes Carl Bruch, "have driven much of the development of international law, including the law of war, humanitarian law, and international environmental law."[35]

Prior to the Vietnam War, the law of war developed, in Richard Falk's tell-ing words, "against a background of virtual environmental unconsciousness."[36] This is graphically evidenced by the way the military campaigns of World Wars I and II produced unprecedented levels of ecological devastation that culmi-nated in the atomic obliteration of both Hiroshima and Nagasaki.[37] Following the enormity of environmental destruction caused by the US military in its use of Agent Orange toxic defoliants during the Vietnam War, a number of interna-tional conventions and protocols were developed to address the environment and the laws of war.[38] Two of the key texts on the laws of war and environmen-tal damage to emerge in the aftermath of the Vietnam War are the Convention on the Prohibition of Military or Any Other Hostile Use of Environmental Modification Techniques (ENMOD) (1976) and the Protocol Additional to the Geneva Conventions of 12 August 1949, and relating to the Protection of Vic-tims of International Armed Conflicts (Protocol I), 8 June 1977. Article 35 (3) of Additional Protocol I states: "It is prohibited to employ methods or means which are intended, or may be expected, to cause widespread, long-term and severe damage to the environment."[39] A number of commentators have re-marked on the "inadequacy of the threshold set in Additional Protocol I to protect the 'environment,'"[40] precisely because "the threshold of damage is set at the causation of 'widespread, long-term and severe damage to the natural environment.'"[41] Despite their avowed commitment to the protection of the environment in times of war, the seemingly environmentally focused articles of Additional Protocol I are Euro-anthropocentric in their orientation, riven with "loopholes," lacking in "authoritativeness" and "coherence," and marred by a "difficulty of implementation."[42]

In the conclusion to his analysis of the law of armed conflict and the envi-ronment, U. C. Jha places the topic in the context of the ecological devastation wreaked by the Gulf War and argues that "the contention that the present en-vironmental law of war is adequate is not reasonable. It is an imprecise law that is full of gaps and open to different interpretations. . . . It is apparent from this example that international systems to deter and redress wartime environmental damage remain ad hoc."[43] The UN International Law Commission appears to be cognizant of these critical failings, as it recently initiated a "Preliminary Report on the Protection of the Environment in Relation to Armed Conflicts" to be included in "its long-term programme of work."[44] Significantly, however, the report concentrates exclusively on "the relevant rules and principles applicable to a potential armed conflict" within the frame of "*peacetime obligations*," and as such, "it will not address measures to be taken *during an armed conflict* or post-conflict measures per se, even if preparatory acts necessary to implement such measures may need to be undertaken prior to the outbreak of an armed conflict."[45] The possibility of drafting new UN rules and principles concerned with protecting the environment during armed conflict has been placed on indefinite hold—as have calls to establish "a 'Fifth Geneva Convention,' an environmental law-of-war treaty in the tradition of the four Geneva Conventions of 1949, or an 'Ecocide Convention,' similar to the Genocide Convention,"[46] in which the crime of ecocide would signify the "destruction of the environment for military purposes."[47] Thus, ecocide is not recognized as a crime within the statutes of international law, and acts of ecocide in the context of armed conflict can be perpetrated with impunity.

In her review of existing laws of armed conflict and environmental protection, Karen Hulme soberly observes: "The simple truth is that environmental damage cannot be enforced. Whilst signature states remain bound to suppress any such violations, the obligation to conduct criminal prosecution of individual violators is absent. If such acts do not constitute war crimes they cannot be tried and punished by international tribunals."[48] I would add that more is at stake than the key problematic of "enforceability." Questions concerning the enforceability of international law are, in realpolitik terms, often determined by the geopolitical standing of a state and the attendant double standards that may ensue. Outlined here is what China Miéville identifies as the "paradoxical form" of international law: "It is simultaneously a *genuine relation between equals*, and a form that the weakest states *cannot hope to win*," precisely because "for a decision to be authoritative—for a particular interpretation to defeat rivals—it must be backed up by the more powerful coercive force in a particular legal relationship."[49] This is clearly evident across a number of the military campaigns that both the United States and Israel conduct and that I examine across the chapters of the book.

The entrenched Euro-anthropocentrism that continues to inscribe laws of war, of the environment, and so on and the consequent failure effectively to prohibit crimes against the environment in the context of militarized zones have driven me to develop the concept of forensic ecologies. Again, I deploy this concept to examine the physical remains, in particular, of more-than-human entities left in the aftermath of the violence and destruction unleashed in zones of militarized occupation. I treat these remains as though they were evidence of culpable war crimes that must be brought to justice, even though currently they are not necessarily proscribed by law. The concept of forensic ecologies, then, is at once outside law, as it covers the gaps and deficiencies not covered by existing law, and inflected by law, precisely through the application of an enlarged sense of forensics.

Forensics: Rhetoric, Narrative, and Tropology

In this book, I attempt to listen to the voices of the rubble in Gaza, a lemon tree in occupied East Jerusalem, the ants of Guantánamo, and in the wake of a drone missile strike, the leaves and rocks that fuse with human and animal flesh in a field in Yemen. In attending to these more-than-human voices and testimonies, my concern is to account for the other victims of militarized violence and occupation that traditional forensic approaches fail to acknowledge and that yet unquestionably constitute the violated entities of a forensic ecology. My aim is to articulate both the relational ecologies that constitute such sites and the sentient expressiveness of the heterogeneous actors that animate these ecological assemblages. Listening to the material actors of these sites entails the deployment of the concept of *distributed cognition*. Distributed cognition means, in Edwin Hutchins's words, "locating cognitive activity in context, where context is not a fixed set of surrounding conditions but a wider dynamical process of which the cognition of the individual is only a small part."[50] As I discuss below, Hutchins's theorization of distributed cognition is antedated by Indigenous cosmo-epistemologies that both understand and appreciate the constitutive role of more-than-human actors in any relational process of meaning production and attendant biocultural exchange.

Forensics signifies a type of legal evidence. When conjoined with the discipline of science, forensics promises to deliver the science of ascertaining the legal evidence of a crime or an accident. Built into the concept of forensics is the notion that an evidentiary truth can be revealed about the identity of a suspect or crime victim, how a crime was committed, or what caused a fatal accident. The term *forensics* can be etymologically traced to the Latin root *forensis*: "The definition," Suzanne Bell notes, "roughly translates as, 'to speak the truth in public.'"[51] Inscribed in the term are the concepts of truth, evidence, and a performative rhetoric of speech that encompass both the expert witness who testifies in court and the material artifacts that speak to the truth of a crime. Always already embedded in the concept of forensics, then, is a combination of rhetorical, performative, and narratological techniques that are deployed to convince the jury and the courtroom audience to adopt a particular point of view.

In this book, I transpose this analytical model of forensics to sites marked by the operations of military violence and occupation. Yet even as I transpose the model of forensics to a gamut of fraught contexts, I refuse to reproduce the discipline's insistence on deploying a scientistic and objectifying lens in the analysis of its "objects" of inquiry. Rather, I inscribe my forensic analyses with the very elements and techniques that the discipline outlaws and disavows: namely, the animating and inescapable influence of embodied affect, rhetoric, tropology, and narrativity. My analysis of forensic ecologies can be seen, for example, as enacting the forensic scientist's equivalent of attempting to constitute a "chain of custody" precisely by materializing the discipline's disavowed *narratological* assemblage of trace evidence; simultaneously, my forensic analysis works to bring to the fore the disavowed, because embodied, *affects* that ineluctably inscribe the production of this same trace evidence. These embodied affects, I contend, cannot be wholly eliminated from the operations of any rational or objective analysis.[52] The seemingly neutral and unemotive style of Western scientific discourse is, after all, just another textual style constituted by a series of effaced rhetorical elements that work metonymically to displace the markers of affective engagement and emotional investment constitutive of scientific knowledge production.[53]

Against Western science's disavowal of the constitutive role of affect in its processes of meaning production, Gregory Cajete counterposes a Native American understanding of science that views affect and tropology as constitutive of the field: "To understand the foundations of Native science one must be open to the roles of sensation, perception, imagination, emotion, symbols, and spirit as well as that of concept, logic, and rational empiricism." Native science is, moreover, "both ecological and integrative."[54] *Forensic evidence*, as I deploy the term, is constituted by a narrator, spatiotemporal markers, affective and rhetorical elements, and the complex interplay between an ecological site and the material actors that enable an entity to assume its veridictional status. My focus on the diverse actors that compose an ecology of military occupation and war will be oriented by what forensics terms "the remnants, or proxy data, of those events [that] are left behind" in the wake of a violent event.[55] I will thus be analyzing, in the process, "evidence of past criminal events to interpret the actions of the perpetrator(s) and victim(s)."[56] "Forensic scientists," Bell notes, "are archaeologists of the recent past."[57]

Eyal Weizman, founder of the group Forensic Architecture, illuminates the key attributes that inscribe architecture and the built environment within the domain of forensics and that enable the "considering of buildings as historical documents": they are, he writes, "both storage and inscription devices," and "they sense or *prehend* their environment, they hold this information in their formal mutations, and they can later *diffuse* and externalize effects latent in their form."[58] In his work on forensic architecture and the built environment, Weizman mobilizes a form of "counterforensics" (drawing on Thomas Keenan's term) to turn "the state's own means against the violence it commits." Counterforensics, he notes, "is a civil practice that aims to interrogate the built environment to uncover political violence undertaken by states."[59] Weizman's acute analyses of forensic architecture in the Palestinian occupied territories demonstrate the deployment, in practice, of counterforensics to document and indict state violence.

In analyzing my selected crime scenes of militarized occupation and violence, I draw on three categories of legal evidence: written and oral testimonies of survivors and detainees; textual documents, such as official reports, that investigate particular criminal actions and crime scenes; and the materiality of physical evidence. I expand the semantic boundaries of forensic evidence by viewing my selected evidence through a *geobiophysical* prism. I take this term from the discipline of physical science and resignify it so as to bring to light the way physical evidence is, at any one time, shot through with both geopolitical and biopolitical vectors.

In the chapters that follow, I situate the concept of forensics within specific ecologies harrowed by regimes of biopolitical violence. My choice of the term *ecology*, rather than *environment*, is one way of attempting to overcome the untenable separation between human subjects and the larger ecological context within which they are situated and which must be preserved in its own right. The concept of ecology, as I use it, is sourced from Ernst Haeckel's first formulation of the term in 1866 in his *Generelle Morphologie*. Drawing on the etymology of the Greek word οἶκος, which he glosses as "household," "living relations," and "dwelling place," Haeckel writes: "By ecology, we mean the whole science of the relations of the organism to the environment including, in the broad sense, all the 'conditions of existence.' These are partly organic, partly inorganic in nature."[60] Already embedded, then, in the etymology of *ecology* is an indissociable relation between nature and culture, as clearly evidenced by Haeckel's inscription of a household within a system of living relations: his ecological attention is on "the relations of the organism to the environment, in the household of nature, in the economy of all nature."[61]

Furthermore, it is precisely Haeckel's expansive conceptualization of *ecology*, encompassing both the organic and the inorganic, that resonates with my use of the term. The concept of ecology, thus, draws attention to the inextricable relations that, in a specific time and place, bind an assemblage of more-than-human entities. As I discuss below, this is a view that has been prefigured, and continues to be *embodied as lived practice*, in many Indigenous cultures. And I emphasize *embodied as lived practice* to preclude the understanding of ecology as a reified scientific category. As Grindle and Johansen note, "While 'ecology' has become a relatively new abstract slice of reality in the Western mind, to Native Americans (including the Navajo) ecology was, and remains, an integral part of living and knowing."[62]

An ecology, crucially, generates the very conditions of possibility for life as such. Situated in this Haeckelian context, I do not view ecology as something that can be found only in "wilderness" or "nature." Rather, I deploy the term *ecology* in the most expansive sense, so that it embraces a range of ecosystems, including urban and rural settings. Moreover, as I discuss in detail below, I draw on Indigenous cosmo-epistemologies of relationality and animism to do justice to the enlarged sense of *ecology* that I propose to deploy, in which a collectivity of different entities are bound within inextricably relational formations: in the words of Ambelin Kwaymullina and Blaze Kwaymullina, "All life—and everything is alive in an Aboriginal worldview—exists in *relationship* to everything else."[63] Before I proceed further, however, I want to underscore that I do not envision Indigenous cosmo-epistemologies of relationality as somehow homogeneous and essentialized in terms of their address of the more-than-human and related ecological concerns, thereby constructing, by default, yet another iteration of the trope of the "noble savage" in harmony with the environment.[64] Indigenous nations are, it goes without saying, inscribed by internal differences and contradictory positions on these matters, including positions that advocate such things as mining.[65]

Indigenous Epistemologies of Relationality and Forensics' Disavowed Animism

The flesh, stones, trees, ants, and rubble that I discuss in my forensic analyses of zones of militarized violence and occupation are not reducible, I emphasize, to an ensemble of narratological and rhetorical constructions or to a series of anthropomorphically animated tropes. On the contrary, they are embedded within the very materiality of the ecological relations that inflect and orient their significations. In the words of Daniel Wildcat, Euchee member of the

Muscogee Nation, these other-than-human entities demand that one exercise what he terms "attentive living," that is, a modality of being-in-the-world that is acutely responsive to and respectful of "the relationships and relatives that constitute the complex web of life."[66] In a similar vein, Linda Hogan, Chickasaw Indian, writes that only in this way can one actually "hear what the material has to say to you."[67] And by material, Hogan includes "the corner of a house, the shaking of leaves on a wind-blown tree, the solid voice of bricks. A fence post talks back. . . . A wall sings out its presences."[68] This animist vision of the world is precisely what underpins, in a disavowed and occluded form, the practice of the forensic scientist, who is taught to listen attentively to the very material signification of the trace evidence of a crime scene—from the pattern of blood-splatter evidence, which indicates the specificity of the weapon used in a homicide, to a clothing fiber, which may identify either the victim or the perpetrator of a crime. The disavowed animist vision that underpins forensics is exemplified by one of the canonical quotes of the discipline by Paul Leland Kirk, founder of the subdiscipline of criminalistics (the use of the androcentric pronoun *he* is in the original):

> Wherever he steps, whatever he touches, whatever he leaves, even unconsciously, will serve as a silent witness against him. Not only his fingerprints or his footprints, but his hair, the fibers from his clothes, the glass he breaks, the tool marks he leaves, the paint he scratches, the blood or semen he deposits or collects. All of these and more, bear mute witness against him. This is evidence that does not forget. It is not confused by the excitement of the moment. It is not absent because human witnesses are. It is factual evidence. Physical evidence cannot be wrong, it cannot perjure itself, it cannot be wholly absent. Only human failure to find it, study and understand it, can diminish its value.[69]

Here numerous forensic materials—including footprints, paint, blood, and so on—is invested with an animism that at once bears witness to the agents of the crime and that refuses to forget what it has witnessed—precisely because the event in question has left an indelible imprint on the material entity. Animated by its own uncanny "aliveness" and obdurate facticity, forensic material bespeaks an evidentiary truth. In Kirk's iconic quotation, forensic evidence is represented as very much fulfilling Bruno Latour's actorial vision, with blood, footprints, and shards of glass *articulating* a series of *propositions* to the forensic expert. "Articulation," Latour writes, "is not a property of human speech but an ontological property of the universe."[70] "Instead of being the privilege of a human mind surrounded by mute things," he contends, "articulation becomes a very common property of propositions, in which many kinds of entities can participate."[71] Propositions "rely on the articulation of differences that make new phenomena visible in the cracks that distinguish them."[72] Kirk presents an understanding of forensic evidence that transcends the fallibilities of the human subject and endures, as trace evidence, regardless of the absence of a human subject. Forensic evidence is, in this Latourian scene, represented as speaking through the idiom of its own material medium—glass, blood, or paint—and offering, in turn, a series of propositions to the analyst in question. Moreover, in Kirk's schema, forensic evidence is invested with a moral rectitude and verdictional status that enable it to make judicative statements on what is in fact the truth of the crime: "It cannot perjure itself."

At this scientifico-animist juncture, I want to take a moment to unpack the denegatory logics that inscribe Kirk's canonical quote. In his text, the evidentiary truth status of forensic material is rendered possible through a circumlocutionary movement that denegates, through the deployment of the strict and rigorous protocols of forensic scientificity, any nonscientific, anthropomorphic, and animist projection onto the material in question. At the same time, however, the forensic evidence is invested with a disavowed animism that is presented as inherent in the empirical object in question and that, in effect, can come to voice only through the attentive use of the same scientific protocols. Here, in this disavowed animist vision of forensic physical evidence, we have what could be called *partial* actors whose conditions of enunciation can be fully realized only through the performative (scientific, rhetorical, and narratological) procedures of the forensic scientist as, by definition, *disclaimed animist*. As Latour sardonically remarks, "Being a matter of fact is not a 'natural' mode of existence but, strangely enough, an *anthropomorphism*. . . . 'Inanimism' is just as much a figuration as 'animism.'"[73] This realization, I would add, appears strange only in the domain of a science that forgets the foundational tropes that constitute its conditions of possibility and that, ipso facto, condition how its objects of inquiry may speak and what they have to say. In the disciplinary space of Western forensics the latent metaphysics that inflect this animist scene are occulted by a set of scientific procedures that conjure up a type of rebus, where the objects in the crime scene constitute an ensemble of cryptic indexes (for example, the pattern of the blood spatter or the angle of a puncture wound) that can be brought to intelligible speech and resolved only through the disciplinary interventions of the forensic scientist.

Despite its avowed scientific undergirding, Western forensic science is shadowed by a disavowed animism. Forensics, indeed, is a field where the epistemology of Western science unreflexively crosses over into the domain of animist cosmologies and epistemologies. The discipline's dependency on (disavowed) animism generates a cognitive contradiction that can be reconciled only through the deployment of a number of disciplinary strategies, including anthropocentric ableism predicated on the deficit model of disability (the forensic object is rendered into a "*mute* witness"); rhetorical effacement (the animating tropes that constitute a forensic object as "witness" must be airbrushed); and human-centered inflation (only the scientist can bring the "mute witness" to speech). As I have discussed elsewhere, the field of Western science is inscribed by the constitutive operations of denegated tropes that work to animate everything from particle matter to genes.[74] By contrast, Cajete underscores, Native science openly draws on symbols and tropes, and language is viewed as what "choreographs" one's engagement with the entities of the world; and, critically, it does not view the diverse entities of the world as "mute objects" that dumbly await the scientist to be brought to speaking life; rather, "Native science continually relates to and speaks of the world as full of *active* entities with which people engage."[75] In Indigenous "cosmopolitical theory," Eduardo Viveiros de Castro notes, the "distinction between society and nature is internal to the social world," thereby overturning the Eurocentric nature/culture binary that relegates nature to an external nonsocial world from which science extracts its truths and facts. In this worldview the "diverse type of actants or subjective agents" include "gods, animals, the dead, plants, meteorological phenomena, and often objects or artifacts as well."[76]

In the context of Western forensic science, the legendary ability of Indigenous trackers to read accurately a forensic ecology for the plenitude of signs that inscribe it is rendered "uncanny" through the occlusion and/or dismissal of their avowedly animist understanding of the land and all its entities. The crossing of forensic science with Indigenous animist cosmo-epistemologies that I stage here is neither fortuitous nor arbitrary. On the contrary, it is grounded in the historical practice of Western colonial police forces employing Indigenous trackers to find escaped criminals or lost civilians in the bush precisely because of their unerring capacity to be acutely attentive to the trace evidence inscribed in the landscape when tracking their subjects.[77] In the words of David Mowaljarlai, Wandjina elder, "When you touch them, all things talk to you, give you their story."[78] Mowaljarlai elaborates on the deep resonances he experiences between the entities of the earth and himself: "These things recognise you. They give their wisdom and their understanding to you when you come close to them."[79] In this worldview, forensic entities are not mute objects awaiting the animating intervention of the human subject; rather, they acknowledge the presence of the human subject, and through the relational practice of haptic exchange ("when you touch them"), they speak and offer, in the idiom of their materiality, their own understanding of what has transpired through "their story." Ludwig Leichhardt, who was dependent on Aboriginal guides and trackers as he explored the Australian continent in the mid-nineteenth century, wrote in his journal: "The impressions on their retina seem more intense than on that of the European; and their recollections are remarkably exact, even to the minutest details. Trees peculiarly formed, broken branches, slight elevations of the ground—in fact, a hundred things, which we should remark only when paying great attention to place—seem to form a Daguerreotype impression on their minds, every part of which is readily recollected."[80] I read scores of Western histories of forensic science in my research for this book, but nowhere are Indigenous trackers mentioned or acknowledged as key players in the field of forensics, despite their celebrated abilities to read the land for its forensic traces. In the state of New South Wales alone, between 1862 (when the state's police force was established) and 1973, more than two hundred police stations employed Aboriginal trackers because of their outstanding forensic skills.[81] During the Boer War, "about 50 Aboriginal trackers were summoned by the British forces in South Africa to join the war to locate Boer fighters. When Australian forces withdraw later that year [1902], the trackers are thought to have been left behind."[82] Regardless of the crucial role of Indigenous forensic expertise across both domestic and international contexts, Indigenous forensic science simply fails to figure in the annals of Western forensic histories. The effacement of Indigenous forensics from the Western canon is crucial in enabling Western science to secure the scientificity of its own practices precisely by categorizing Indigenous forensics as little more than (un)canny folk know-how, animist superstitions, or infra-epistemologies that are dispatched beyond the policed domains of certified scientific knowledge; what becomes unthinkable in such a dichotomous schema, thus, is the very possibility of Native science. This is a familiar colonial move that cuts across diverse disciplinary practices and categories, not the least law, where Western law is represented as the Law, whereas Indigenous law is categorized as a proto-form of "customary law."[83]

Furthermore, the critical intersection of Western forensic science, colonialism, and Indigenous histories that I am staging here must be located at the very historical point of origin of the discipline: Western forensic science was born in the charged context of empire, race, and colonialism. The forensic practice of fingerprint identification, often presented as the foundational forensic practice, emerged in British colonial India and the need of its white administrators to identify, track, and monitor insurgent Indian tribes.[84] Moreover, the discipline of forensic pathology established its medico-legal epistemological grounding on the study of, and traffic in, expropriated Indigenous and enslaved African American bodies.[85] Consequently, Western forensic pathology's epistemologies were founded on the criminal expropriation and violation of Indigenous corpo-ontologies and the dismissal, if not attempted obliteration, of their epistemologies.

In what follows, I want to flesh out in some detail the disavowed animism that haunts the field of forensic science. In the discipline of forensics, material evidence is inscribed by its own animating force and the attendant exchange of properties between seemingly inanimate entities, including soil, dust, or fibers, that come into contact with each other. Matter, even apparently inorganic or mineral matter, is never simply inert. On the contrary, it is enlivened by an exchange of particles between the various entities that constitute a designated forensic context. There would, in fact, be no forensics as such without this process of animated particle exchange. In forensic science, Locard's exchange principle exemplifies this vision of animist exchange: "'Every contact leaves a trace.' This principle reflects the belief that every contact between a person and a person or a person and a place results in the transfer of materials between them."[86] Forensic testimony is what is produced by deploying a relational methodology: "A goal of forensic science is to link a potential offender to a crime scene by way of testimony as to individual characteristics, connecting a physical sample obtained from the suspect with a similar sample from the crime scene."[87] Testimony, in this forensic scene of animist exchange, emerges as a relational assemblage of heterogeneous materials that, collectively, is mobilized to speak an evidentiary truth.

Forensic Ecologies' Flesh of the World

Indigenous relational cosmo-epistemologies, with their distributed and heterogeneous sense of agentic entities, closely resonate, as Cajete contends, with "a number of the central premises of phenomenology (the philosophical study of phenomena)" and, in particular, he adds, with Merleau-Ponty's call to "return to things themselves" in order to make sense of the world.[88] Merleau-Ponty, moreover, insistently overturns anthropocentric hierarchies by positioning the earth and nature as constitutive of human perception, cognition, speech, and so on: "Nature," he writes, "must be our interlocutor in a sort of dialogue."[89] These points of intersection are also clearly evidenced in the resonance between Indigenous and Merleau-Pontian philosophies of embodiment and intercorporeality. In conceptualizing our relation to the world,

Merleau-Ponty posits the flesh as that which conjoins one to the other: "The presence of the world is precisely the presence of its flesh to my flesh."[90] This intercorporeal understanding of the world meshes, as Robert Yazzie, chief justice of the Navajo Nation, notes, with "Native philosophy," which he describes as "the practice of an epistemology in which the mind embodies itself in a particular relationship with all other aspects of the world."[91] In accord with Indigenous philosophies, Merleau-Ponty's theorizing of flesh disrupts the circumscriptions of the anthropocentric frame. Flesh emerges, for him, as both a general and a specific modality of being in the world. It is a general modality as flesh signifies the condition of possibility of being in the world. It is a specific modality because flesh is always already situated in the particularity of its worldly locus.

In the field of forensics, the discipline of forensic ecology refers to the gathering and analysis of soil, entomological samples, plants, and other material to provide evidence about a suspect and the time and place of death of a human victim.[92] In the doxic understanding of forensic ecology, animals, plants, and land are equivalent to negative space in a painting: they are mere background to the positive figures (the human victims of criminal acts) that are seen to dominate the setting. Animals, plants, and soil are mere supplements that are mobilized to offer up the physical evidence that will help solve the crime. They are not themselves seen as the victims, for example, of a military strike. My intention is to challenge and overturn this relationship of (human) figure to ground (all other-than-human entities) and to bring into focus the broad spectrum of entities that may lay claim to speaking an evidentiary truth about a particular crime. In broad terms, my aim is to map suffering's communal dimensions by situating it beyond traditional anthropocentric delimitations and by locating it within ecologies of relationality. In the forensic ecology schema I deploy in this book, human and more-than-human subjects emerge, in Cajete's words, "as dynamic bodies intimately cradled in the body of the world" and thus inextricably inscribed in the "flesh of the world."[93] My attention will center on the destruction that results from militarized assaults, violating and scarring what Hogan calls "this body of earth."[94]

In attempting to theorize a communal and ecological understanding of the experience of suffering that challenges anthropocentric circumscriptions, I want to underscore the critical necessity to articulate a different order of entities that evidences not a binarized subject/object world but a world of differential and yet mutually constitutive actors.[95] As I demonstrate in the chapters that follow, more-than-human entities speak through their own embodied media and through the specificity of their own semiosis, including zoosemiotics (animal languages) and phytosemiotics (plant languages). Biocultural networks of relationality enable mediative and transitive lines of exchange between human and more-than-human entities. In my conceptualization of more-than-human entities as actors, I no doubt will be accused of indulging in acts of anthropomorphism. I would argue that, from a deconstructionist point of view, there can be no zero degree of anthropomorphism for anyone who inhabits the locus inscribed by the figure of "the human"—as a category critically dependent for its cultural intelligibility on its definitional opposition to whatever is deemed to be other-than-human. Any theory, scientific or otherwise, that claims to speak outside a position not inflected to some degree by the operations of anthropomorphism can do so only through an act of disavowal.[96] Furthermore, I am not sure what it means to write outside the inescapable frames of rhetoric and its constitutive repertoire of tropes—metaphor, prosopopoeia (personification), and so on—except by lapsing into catachrestic forms that found their very facticity and literality on the denegated bodies of dead metaphors, where, for example, through customary use we forget that the "leg" of a chair is just another anthropomorphic trope. The charge of projecting anthropomorphic values onto more-than-human entities is yet another instantiation of an untenable human exceptionalism that insists on denying speech, thought, intentionality, emotion, and so on to the other-than-human. Standing at the juncture of tropology and catachresis, I can avow only one thing: that outside the frames of my anthropomorphizing language there still reside entities that are not reducible to the narcissism of the Same.

New Materialisms, Old Eurocentrisms

The relational, animist, and ecocentric Indigenous cosmo-epistemologies I have been invoking resonate with a cluster of relatively new Western theoretical formations, including the new materialisms, critical animal studies, the new ethology, and nonhuman studies. In what follows, I want to focus on the field of the new materialisms. As I discussed above, many Indigenous cosmo-epistemologies are foundationally underpinned by a "kincentric" view of the world, in which all entities are inscribed within ecologies of relationality.[97] Jane Bennett, one of the leading theorists of the new materialisms, defines her approach as one that "emphasizes the shared material basis, the kinship, of all things, regardless of their status as human, animal, vegetable, or mineral."[98] The isomorphism between the key principles of Indigenous cosmo-epistemologies and the new materialisms is striking. Bennett's concept of "vibrant matter," in which all matter is viewed as animate, reproduces Hogan's view of a "vibrant land" scored by the "old, slow pulse of things."[99] Bennett's belief that "*all* forces and flows (materialities) are or can become lively, affective, and signaling" echoes Leroy Little Bear's mapping of the "Native American paradigm," which "is comprised of and includes ideas of constant motion and flux, existence consisting of energy waves, interrelationships, all things being animate, space/place, renewal, and all things imbued with spirit. . . . What Native Americans call 'spirit' and energy waves are the same thing."[100] In a Native American context, Cajete notes, "cosmology" means the "lived story of place, kinship, and environmental knowledge."[101] In Indigenous cosmologies, kinship stands in contradistinction to Western understandings of the term that restrict kinship relations solely to human bio-genealogies. In Indigenous cultures, kinship cuts across and beyond human categories to encompass rocks, water, trees, and so on. Rebecca Adamson, Cherokee, founder and president of First Peoples Worldwide, amplifies this cosmology of the lived and vibrantly alive environment as what is "perceived as a sensate, conscious entity" in which

> all particles of matter, property, position, and velocity are influenced by the intention or presence of other particles. Stated in simpler terms, atoms are aware of other atoms. According to this law of nature, a people rooted in the land over time have exchanged their tears, their breath, their bones, their elements, oxygen, carbon, nitrogen, hydrogen, phosphorous, sulfur, all of their elements with their habitat many times over. In the words of the Diné traditionalist Ruth Benally, "Our history cannot be told without naming the cliffs and the mountains that have witnessed our people."[102]

In Benally's vision, the cliffs and mountains are not inert and mute objects in the landscape; on the contrary, they are agentic witnesses inextricably enmeshed in the everyday life of her people. "Modern science," Adamson adds, "is just beginning to catch up with such ancient wisdom."[103] Despite the manifold ways in which such Indigenous cosmo-epistemologies at once antedate and are contemporary with the theories of the new materialisms, the field is largely marked by the very absence of any mention of their work. Reproduced across a number of the foundational texts of the new materialisms is a Eurocentric erasure of the Indigenous knowledges that, seemingly, can inscribe the field only through their absence.[104] For example, Bennett begins the introduction to her book *Vibrant Matter* with this statement: "The idea of vibrant matter also has a long (and if not latent, at least not dominant) philosophical history in the West. I will reinvoke this history too, drawing in particular on the concepts and claims of Baruch Spinoza, Friedrich Nietzsche, Henry David Thoreau, Charles Darwin, Theodor Adorno, Gilles Deleuze, and the early twentieth-century vitalisms of Bergson and Hans Driesch."[105] Circumscribed by the seemingly sealed epistemological borders of the West, even when this history is stretched back to ancient cultures, the catalog of names can only, tautologically, remain Eurocentric: "I pursue a materialism in the tradition of Democritus-Epicurus-Spinoza-Diderot-Deleuze more than Hegel-Marx-Adorno. It is important to follow the trail of human power to expose social hegemonies (as historical materialists do)."[106] A double logic is operative here. On the one hand, this autotelic genealogy is informed by an apparently impermeable concept of the West, as though this geopolitical configuration is uniquely capable of operating outside any of the structuring influences of the various lands and cultures it colonizes and imperially occupies. On the other hand, through the invocation of "human power," a sleight of hand is performed in which the West is universalized as "the human," as a seemingly racially unmarked subject that is inscribed by a denegated (because white), a priori raciality. In following this distinctly Eurocentric trail of "human power," Bennett effectively reproduces one of the key "social hegemonies" of the very nation-state from within which she thinks and writes: settler colonialism and its ongoing erasure of the very Native American cosmo-epistemologies that are critically relevant to both her new materialism project and her desire to expose social hegemonies as such.

In her coruscating analysis of the way Western thinkers repeatedly "talk *around* themes shared in Indigenous thought without giving Indigenous people credit or a nod," Zoe Todd, Indigenous feminist, Red River Métis, Otipemisi-wak, asks: "So why does this all matter? Why am I so fired up at the realisation that (some) European thinkers are replicating Indigenous thought, seemingly with no awareness? Well, it's this little matter of *colonialism*, see."[107] Todd's sardonic line on "this little matter of *colonialism*" profoundly resonates. In her work, she exposes how the erasure of Indigenous cosmo-epistemologies in much Western thought concerned with "animals, the climate, water, 'atmospheres' and non-human presences like ancestors and spirits are *sentient* and *possess agency*, that 'nature' and 'culture,' 'human' and 'animal' may not be so separate after all" reproduces forms of epistemic violence and injustice by "perpetuating the exploitation of Indigenous peoples."[108]

Following Todd's critical call for a decolonizing practice, in my reading of the fields of the new materialisms and critical animal and plant studies, I discern maneuvers that have clear colonial resonances. Much that is presented in these fields is largely oriented by Eurocentric frames and genealogies that work to represent any innovations in thought in terms of self-referential "discoveries": it is thus, for example, that the new materialisms become "new." In Bennett's text, relevant Native American cosmo-epistemologies (that actually antedate and would productively inform and amplify new materialist theories) remain as "absent referents," to draw on an apposite term coined by Carol Adams.[109] It is the scripting of Indigenous peoples and their knowledges as absent referents in the colonized lands of the United States and Australia that enables both the reproduction and consolidation of the settler colonial project along all the key axes of economic, cultural, political, and academic activity.

Whereas Aboriginal people and Native Americans, for example, call for a decolonizing practice that is indissociable from an ecocentric worldview, many of the new materialists focus solely on the need to deanthropocentrize European thought, thereby leaving intact the originary and unfolding violence of settler colonialism that effectively works to reproduce racio-speciesist relations that themselves continue to impact Indigenous peoples, the more-than-human world, and its diverse entities. The liberatory and antihegemonic potential of a field such as the new materialisms cannot be fully realized without the nonnegotiable address of settler colonialism in the context of such states as Australia, the locus from which I write, and the United States. In my analysis, I insistently interlink a decolonizing methodology with a deanthropocentrizing one because, when viewed in the context of Indigenous cosmo-epistemologies, the two approaches are intertwined in their operations.

Even as I cast a critical eye on Bennett's new materialist work, I want to affirm its generative poetics of matter and its call to reenvision the world otherwise. Furthermore, I inscribe myself within the same, if geographically and historically differentiated, settler configuration of power that transnationally binds our respective positions. My own personal and academic labor of decolonization is a strictly *unfinished* business. To rework Patrick Wolfe's now-canonical formulation of settler colonialism, self-decolonization is *a process and not an event*.[110] Moreover, even as I draw on Indigenous knowledges, I do so with the critical qualification that my understanding is delimited by my own embodied positionality as a non-Indigenous subject. Todd, drawing on Vanessa Watts's work, underscores the fact that "there is a very real risk to Indigenous thinking being used by non-Indigenous scholars who apply it to Actor Network Theory, cosmopolitics, ontological and posthumanist threads without contending with the embodied expressions of stories, laws, and songs bound within Indigenous-Place Thought."[111] Thus, even as I celebrate Indigenous understandings of "attentive living" that enable me to catch a glimpse of the sentient world of the more-than-human and its ecology of relationality and negotiation, I respectfully mark the ethical and embodied circumscriptions that preclude me from the locus of Indigenous-Place Thought and its lived and generative matrix of stories, laws, and songs.

Bennett concludes her book on the new materialisms with what she calls "a kind of Nicene Creed" that leads her to "believe in one matter-energy, the maker of things seen and unseen. . . . I believe it is wrong to deny vitality to nonhuman bodies, forces, and forms."[112] Absent from this animist creed is the very Native American referent that constitutes both the expropriated physical ground from which this creed can be enunciated and the Indigenous cosmo-epistemologies that antedate and contemporize this vitalist, new materialist epistemology. "In Native science," Cajete explains, "there is an inclusive definition of 'being alive.' Everything is viewed as having energy and its own unique intelligence and creative process, not only obviously animate entities such as plants, animals, and microorganisms, but also rocks, mountains, rivers, and places large and small."[113] "The conclusion," writes Vine Deloria Jr., "reached by contemporary physicists, biologists, and near death scholars are a result of a long, tedious path from the Greek atomists and philosophers, through the European struggles with the false mind/body dichotomy, to the achievements in physics in the twentieth century."[114] To this list, one can add the West's new materialists, animal ethicists, and new ethologists.

"Perhaps," Hogan ironically remarks, "as these fields come to understand that all matter has life, spirit, and even consciousness" and that "every particle of the universe is alive," "ours will no longer be a 'primitive' way of looking at the world."[115] Situated in this context, it is the West that has been "primitive" in its reductive way of looking at the world; it has thus, to invoke Latour's titular phrase, "never been modern."[116] The ramifications that follow from the spatiotemporal anteriority of the Indigenous cosmo-epistemologies discussed above are profound. On the one hand, they rupture, through their spatiotemporal anteriority, the driving telos of the colonial project, thereby exposing the delusional myths on which it has been predicated: if colonialism is characterized by the way it violently inscribes Indigenous nations within a Eurocentric teleology oriented toward the acquisition of civilizational culture, then the anteriority of these Indigenous knowledges works to destructure this teleological movement and to overtake it through its very anachronic status. The anachronic, in its definitional sense, is precisely that temporal vector that can topologically conjoin both flashbacks (analepsis) and flash-forwards (prolepsis). Indigenous knowledges remain, in this anachronic topology, at the vanguard, both epistemologically and civilizationally, both before and after the imposition of colonial regimes on Indigenous lands. What the colonizers had relegated to the "archaic," "primitive," and "pre-modern" is what always already constituted the futural horizon toward which the West laboriously slouched. It is the laggardness of the West that now comes into focus as it attempts to play catch-up. Within this anachronic schema, the colonial project emerges as a violent interchronic phase, inscribed with an autoimmune expiry date, that is situated between the enduring past and protentive present of Indigenous peoples and their cultures.

Moreover, the enduring nature of these Indigenous knowledges evidences the failure of the obliterative process of settler colonialism: as they have continued to survive in the face of relentless regimes of destruction, they signal the nonsuccess of that other teleological movement—the process of settler colonial elimination and replacement. They are inscribed in what Shino Konishi terms "extra-colonial histories" that evidence, "most significantly," that "Indigenous people have been agentic in evading and resisting the logic of elimination."[117] The indissociable temporality of both before (precolonial) *and* after (the colonial present) marks the alterity of Indigenous cosmo-epistemologies that could not be vanquished by the imperialism of the Same.

Western scholars, writes Deloria, are slowly coming to the realization that we inhabit "a world in which everything [is] alive and related."[118] And the ethical corollary of this view, he concludes, is that we are compelled to "take up responsibilities for all livings things."[119] Deloria here offers an affirmative answer to the urgent question that Derrida raises and answers in the negative: "Do we have a responsibility to the living in general? The answer is still 'no.'" With characteristic reflexivity, Derrida outlines why this is so, as he locates his negative answer within a Eurocentrically circumscribed religio-metaphysical domain: "The answer is still 'no,' and this may be because the question is formed, asked in such a way that the answer must necessarily be 'no' according to the whole canonized or hegemonic discourse of Western metaphysics or religions, including the most original forms that this discourse might assume today, for example, in Heidegger and Levinas."[120]

Unrequited Ecological Justice

The militarized zones of violence and occupation that I examine in the book might be best characterized as ecologies of unrequited justice: in the wake of militarized campaigns of killing and destruction, justice has not been served to either the victims or survivors of the crimes perpetrated in these locations. The militarized zones that I examine exemplify the operations of state military apparatuses in the targeted destruction of a number of different ecologies and the various entities that inhabit and constitute them. Writing in the context of the Anthropocene, which marks the global scale of human-induced changes to the environment, my concern is to contribute to the address of a lacuna in the international debates on the potentially catastrophic effects of climate change. As Oliver Belcher, Patrick Bigger, Ben Neimark, and Cara Kennelly argue, what is consistently missing from these debates on the cumulative global forces that are generating global warming is the constitutive role of the military. The work of Belcher and colleagues and of Bigger and Benjamin Neimark sheds critical light on the role of the US military, in particular, in accelerating anthropogenic climate change precisely by situating military operations within the theoretical framework of *geopolitical ecology*. Geopolitical ecology is a "conceptual framework that combines the strengths of political ecology with those of geopolitics in order to account for, and gain a deeper understanding of, the role of large geopolitical institutions, like the U.S. military, in environmental change."[121] Moreover, a geopolitical ecology approach brings to the fore "the hydrocarbon logistical infrastructure that makes U.S. imperialism possible."[122]

The urgency of addressing this nexus of political ecology with critical geopolitics in the context of anthropogenic climate change is brought into sharp focus by the fact that, even as the Pentagon has begun to deploy a number of strategies that are designed to contribute to the "greening" of the military, in practice the US military remains the world's largest institutional consumer of natural resources. It is "one of the largest climate polluters in history" and the world's largest polluter in terms of its production of greenhouse gases and its ongoing destruction of global ecologies through its production and dumping of toxic wastes.[123] Through the ruse of "national security," however, the US military, like the armed forces of many other sovereign states, is largely exempt from environmental protection legislation. "The armed forces of the world," Jha underlines, "are both 'normal' and 'special' polluters producing toxic and radioactive wastes. They are also 'protected' polluters because there are no environmental legislations to control their activities. The overall and worldwide pollution by the armed forces could be as high as 30 percent."[124]

Furthermore, I insistently intertwine ecological and social justice concerns because I see the two as entangled. The category of the Anthropocene, for example, must be seen as always already racialized, constitutively inscribed by European histories of empire and colonialism, and riven by asymmetrical axes of geopolitical and economic power. Two anthropocenic points illustrate this. First, the year 1492, as enunciating the "collision of the Old and New Worlds," has been suggested as the historical marker, or "golden spike," to determine the beginning of the Anthropocene. This is due to the seismic impact that the European colonization of the New World had on geohistory through the mass genocides of the Indigenous peoples of the Americas and the cluster of ecological flow-on effects that proceeded from this momentous date.[125] Second, the bulk of carbon emissions are Anglocentric: "In cumulative terms from 1800 to 1950, 65 per cent of carbon emissions were emitted by Great Britain and the United States alone. Historically speaking, the Anthropocene could well be called the Anglocene."[126]

Inscribed in this anthropocenic history are the racialized forces that constitute the lethal assemblage of imperialism, settler colonialism, and extractive capitalism. This toxic assemblage is responsible for Indigenous genocides; expropriation of Indigenous lands; ecocidal practices of land clearing; serial species extinction; the enslavement of people of color, including Aboriginals, Africans, and Native Americans; the slave plantations of North America, the Spanish Americas, and the Caribbean; the indentured labor of colonial Africa and Asia; the establishment of crop monocultures; and so on—that were instrumental in generating the Industrial Revolution. Reflecting on this violent history and its unfolding anthropocenic impacts, Tony Birch underscores how "within the Anthropocene narrative Indigenous nations are too often relegated to the state of non-existence, producing an intellectual equivalent of the *terra nullius* narrative of the late eighteenth and nineteenth centuries, a white mythology that continues to allow colonial powers to mask their histories of violence."[127] Furthermore, as numerous scholars have noted, anthropogenic change, including extreme weather and rising sea levels, is reproducing yet another form of environmental racism, since it is largely Indigenous peoples and communities of color that are at the front line of climate change.[128]

As the sites that I examine are inscribed by the inextricable relation of human and other-than-human entities, the concept of ecological justice best captures how "the interplay between nature and humans is such that social justice is equally important and inextricably bound to issues of ecology."[129] Rob White offers a succinct definition of the concept: "Ecological justice demands that how humans interact with their environment be evaluated in relation to potential harms and risks to specific creatures and specific locales as well as the biosphere generally."[130] Ecological justice is what can be realized, in both international and domestic law, through the development of what Cormac Cullinan calls "Earth jurisprudence," which ensures that legal systems are oriented by ecophilosophical values.[131] The centrality of law within these urgent debates resides in the fact that it not only serves a regulative function but also "plays an equally important role in constituting and forming society itself"[132] and, as a corollary, in determining a society's impact on the ecological context within which that society is situated.

Drawing on Indigenous understandings of justice as encompassing "all our relations,"[133] including plants, animals, mountains, and so on, and interlacing this expansive view of justice with the concept of ecological justice, this book attempts to interrogate dominant Euro-anthropocentric conceptualizations of justice exemplified by this leading justice philosopher: "Taking Aristotle's lead by seeking the distinctiveness of justice as a moral value, we should note that justice does not arise in our treatment of inanimate things, and possibly not in our treatment of animals."[134] Encapsulated here, in the excising of our treatment of the more-than-human from the purview of justice, is the license to continue business as usual in the ongoing destruction of the earth. Outside existing Indigenous laws, with their long-established frameworks of ecological justice that have been consistently marginalized from the Western legal systems that have set the terms of reference for international law, an Earth jurisprudence can be seen to be in a *status nascendi*.[135] Three recent and significant examples of Earth jurisprudence include the constitution of Ecuador; the Universal Declaration of the Rights of Mother Earth/Pachamama; and the Aotearoa–New Zealand government's legal recognition of the Te Urewera National Park as an entity with its own "legal personhood."[136] The Aotearoa–New Zealand's government's recognition of the legal standing of Te Urewera was driven by the Māori people of the region, and it was their cosmo-epistemologies and language that enabled the process of legal recognition to take place: "[The act] uses the Māori language about [Te Urewera] having its own *mana*—its own authority, having its own *mauri*—its own life force, and that Te Urewera has an identity in and of itself. . . . It is its own person, it cannot be owned."[137] The constitution of Ecuador has established a framework that "goes beyond issues of legal standing [of more-than-human entities] and includes mandates to public officials about how to interpret and apply them [the rights of nature]."[138] These jurisprudential breakthroughs are underpinned by Indigenous legal frameworks that at once challenge and reorient Eurocentric schemas that foreclose the possibility to envision other-than-human entities, such as mountains and rivers, as having ethical and jural status. Gary Steiner, for example, who articulates an impassioned case for the extension of rights to animals, appears to balk at extending ethical status to, in Western terms, "non-sentient" entities, marking, in the process, the clear limits of Eurocentric thinking: "But we do not know what it would mean to extend moral status to all life, whether sentient or nonsentient—unless, of course, we embrace biocentrism rather than zoocentrism, and even then it is extremely difficult if not impossible to articulate what it would mean to have a direct moral obligation to a nonsentient being."[139]

A number of Indigenous cosmo-epistemologies articulate with compelling lucidity precisely what it means to have an ethical obligation to rocks, trees, rivers, mountains, and so on, predicating this understanding on a kincentric vision in which both sentient and nonsentient entities are inscribed in an affective and ethical ecology. Understood in this expansive and relational context, ecological justice is what enables me to call attention to the multidimensional and interleaved levels of violence that armed conflict generates in the context of a forensic ecology. Ecological justice is what works to bring into focus different entities (soil, water, trees, animals) that, under existing forms of Euro-anthropocentric law, possess no jural life and thus remain outside the purview of justiciability.[140] Such entities are, in Cullinan's terms, "outlaws, and are treated as such. They are not part of the community or society that the legal systems concern themselves with, and have no inherent right to existence or to have a habitat in which to live."[141]

In the context of ecological justice, Deloria articulates what is essentially at stake: "The sole question is, who has standing to be heard?"[142] Deloria's question is, critically, directed at Western law and its entrenched anthropocentrism, in contrast to ecocentric Indigenous law. When Derrida, for example, decries that there is no "'crime against animality' nor crime of genocide against nonhuman living beings,"[143] this is so only in the anthropocentrically circumscribed, yet hegemonic, domain of Western law. By contrast, Indigenous laws name and condemn animal and tree genocides, such as "the great massacres" of the bison by settler colonial Americans, mass killings of what Winona LaDuke calls the "Buffalo Nations."[144] "The genocide of trees in Australia," write Gladys Idjirrimoonya Milroy and Jill Milroy, Palyku peoples, "leaves a bloodied landscape."[145]

Whereas in Western understandings law is seen to issue in a unidirectional vector from humans to animals, in Indigenous systems of law, animals are seen to possess their own law, and this in turn determines human actions and behavior. In the Yarralin people's law, for example, "all species have a Law and culture, free will; the burden of responsibility is shared among all living things."[146] In her writing on Aboriginal law, Irene Watson notes: "Our [Nunga] law embraces all things in the universe, a different idea to the states' concept of sovereignty. . . . As law holds no outer or inner place, it is in all things"; thus, in Nunga law, all other-than-human entities have jural life and standing.[147] Overturning Euro-anthropocentric understandings of law as what governs demarcated entities ordered along speciesist hierarchies, Aboriginal law pivots on maintaining and nurturing relational networks: "Law," Kwaymullina and Kwaymullina underscore, "extends beyond human beings to all life in country, *with the relationship—rather than the species—being the primary creator of legal categories.*"[148]

Indigenous biocultural understandings of law not only refuse the nature/culture binary, but they also overturn the Euro-anthropocentric locus from which law is made, issued, and deployed. "Thus habitats and ecosystems are better understood," Vanessa Watts explains, "as societies from an Indigenous point of view; meaning that they have ethical structures, inter-species treaties and agreements, and further their ability to interpret, understand and implement. Non-human beings are active members of society. Not only are they active, they also directly influence how humans organize themselves into that society."[149] Animals, soil, water, and plants, in this Indigenous view, are coconstitutive of human subjectivities and cultures, rather than passive matter that is only ever acted on by humans. "The shape and pattern of this Law of Relationship," writes C. F. Black, Aboriginal scholar of Indigenous jurisprudence, "creates a body of law which, in Australia's case, 'vibrates in song' and is 'woven across' *Corpus Australis*."[150]

In the chapters that follow, I trace the agentic role of more-than-human entities in the forensic ecologies of militarized zones. In the context of these lethal zones, more-than-human entities bear witness to the destruction they are compelled to endure, and they offer their own evidentiary testimony to the violence that has transpired.

Chapters

Across all four chapters of the book, I delineate acts of violence produced by the forces of armed conflict and/or occupation—forces that are, tautologically and by definition, violent—and discuss the forensic ecologies left in the wake of these acts of violence. My concern in focusing on violent acts of armed conflict and/or occupation is to make visible the more-than-human entities that are either the targets of this violence or ensnared in violence largely directed at human subjects. I concentrate not on the violence per se but, rather, on its impact on a number of more-than-human entities (and their human relations) and the way they largely fail to register as material victims of armed conflict and/or occupation in traditional anthropocentric accounts of violence. In the face of the violence that either obliterates them or that they strive to survive, more-than-human entities emerge, in the context of a reenvisioning of forensic ecologies, as subjects that continue to assert their call for ethical consideration and jural standing.

Chapters 1 and 2 primarily address the forensic ecologies left in the wake of the Israeli Defense Forces' Operation Protective Edge, July–August 2014, in Gaza. I focus on this military campaign in particular as it evidences the widespread impact of military violence on the more-than-human entities caught in its crossfire. As many Palestinian commentators have remarked, this particular military operation was unprecedented in the scale of destruction, "target[ing] the whole . . . life of Gaza": "The Israeli attacks deliberately and systematically targeted the trees, stones, people, and even animals and birds."[151]

Chapter 1 begins with a scene of destruction in one of Gaza's neighborhoods following a lethal strike by the Israeli Defense Forces during Operation Protective Edge. This scene of destruction establishes the conceptual coordinates that constitute my analysis of the impact of military violence on both human and more-than-human entities and the forensic ecologies that remain in the wake of this violence. The chapter is primarily concerned with the concept of zoopolitics. As I discussed above, the question of "the animal" is not, as Derrida underscores, merely one question among others, as it critically inflects a number of foundational categories, including law, justice, human and animal rights, and so on—all key concerns of the later chapters. The chapter focuses on, and develops in detail, the analytical dimensions of a specific modality of biopolitics, zoopolitics, as it inscribes the life of Gaza's human and animal subjects—all effectively entrapped in the open-air prison, "the Cage," that is Gaza. Zoopolitics shapes and determines the key spatial configurations and apparatuses, including the checkpoints and the casting of Gaza as a "zoo" and an "experimental laboratory," that enable the biopolitical governance of the human and more-than-human entities of Gaza. I conclude the chapter by discussing the relations of zoopolitical power that are instantiated in a meme that circulated on social media of a Palestinian youth juxtaposed with a pig. The onto-epistemological rendering of Palestinian life in terms of nonhuman animal life is underpinned, I disclose, by a zoopolitical framework that enables and legitimates the racio-speciesist military-industrial-prison-surveillance complex and its regime of ongoing occupation.

After chapter 1's expansive analysis of how one modality of biopolitics, zoopolitics, works to extend, consolidate, and reproduce the Israeli state's settler occupation of Palestine, chapter 2 opens with a detailed discussion of how settler biopolitical practices of ecological destruction emerge as intersectionally linked with settler colonial ambitions of territorial expropriation and expansion. The chapter then enlarges the biopolitical aperture and brings into focus all the other biopolitical modalities that are deployed toward this same end. Elaborating my discussion of the Israeli Defense Forces' military campaign in Gaza in July 2014, in this chapter I examine how Operation Protective Edge effectively destroyed orchards, aquifers, animals, and large swaths of agricultural fields. In my analysis of the ongoing environmental health effects of these forensic ecologies on both human and more-than-human entities, I deploy the concept of the "atomization of biopolitics" to demonstrate the distributed and attenuated relations of toxic biopolitical power that operate in such sites. The atomization of biopolitics that is unfolding in Gaza in particular, following the ecocidal effects of Operation Protective Edge, are generating, I contend, a form of transboundary biopolitics of autoimmunity that is now asymmetrically ensnaring both Palestinians and Israelis. I also examine, in the context of the occupied Palestinian territories, the concept of *phytopolitics*, which is specifically concerned with the biopolitics of plant life. I deploy the concept of phytopolitics to examine the Israeli state's war on Palestinian trees and the complex and affective relations between Palestinians and trees.

In chapter 3, I transpose the zoopolitical question concerning "the animal" to Guantánamo Bay military prison to bring to light its lethal effects in the context of this gulag. The chapter begins with an analysis of the legal transmutation of Guantánamo's detainees into "nonpersons" and the consequent death of one of the detainees, Adnan Latif. By focusing on the official forensic report into his death and its footnoted documentation of Latif's relations with the animals in the camp, I discuss his attempt to survive the military prison's regime of torture and abuse through interspecies relations that were in fact prohibited under the standard operating procedures of the camp. Drawing on Heideggerian and Agambenian understandings of the Open, I proceed to re-signify the term. In my reading, the Open in the cage establishes the heterotopic contours of a moment of intimate contact between one (the animal) and the other (the detainee), who has been legally categorized as a "nonperson." I track complex relations of acknowledgment, hospitality, and ethical engagement between the detainees and the camp's resident animals, including feral cats, iguanas, and banana rats. In chapter 3 I also examine the way various experimental torture practices first performed on nonhuman animals were effectively transposed to the torture of human subjects in Guantánamo. I then flesh out how the UN Convention against Torture and Other Cruel, Inhuman or Degrading Treatment or Punishment tacitly codifies and enshrines the human/animal caesura in both the title and substance of its text. Animating the lexico-discursive logics of "inhuman" treatment, as outlined in the convention, is the speciesist knowledge of its absolute nonhuman animal other as an entity that can be tortured and killed with impunity. I coin the term *inanimal* as a way of identifying and naming this modality of zoopolitical violence.

The zoopolitical question as to who can be tortured or killed with impunity is further elaborated in chapter 4. There I discuss the United States' drone campaigns in Afghanistan, Pakistan, Somalia, and Yemen, and I examine how the destruction of civilians, more-than-human entities, and their respective ecologies is now being facilitated by semiautomated technologies of war that generate "death by metadata," that is, a telemediated form of extrajudicial killing-at-a-distance that entails targeted liquidation by drones. I situate my analysis in the context of the US military's use of metadata to conduct drone kills and its reliance on advanced mathematical formulas to track drone targets on kill lists and to establish a calculus of probability of "hostile intent." My interest is in examining the interlocking of the National Security Agency's metadata with the algorithmic formulas that underpin the Department of Defense's (DoD) drone program in order to conduct drone kills in which the identities of those killed often are not known. I situate what I term the *bioinformationalization* of life within the United States' drone killing fields to disclose the transliteration of abstract metadata to flesh. In analyzing the bioinformationalization of life, I examine the ways in which the DoD's increasing reliance on death by metadata is inscribed by a zoopolitics predicated on anthropocentric hierarchies of life. The harrowing human-animal detritus of US drone kills, I argue, throws into crisis categorical understandings of "the human" and "the animal" as delineated by anthropocentric law. I conclude by arguing that what is instantiated in these sites of drone-enabled military violence is the practice of *sparagmos*, the Greek term naming the ritualized dismemberment and dispersal of bodies. In ancient Greek culture, sparagmos identified the performative of ritualized murder in terms of an aesthetico-political art of the kill that dispersed and attenuated the role of any individual in the act of murder. Sparagmos names the militarized dismemberment of the targeted flesh of the lands of Afghanistan, Pakistan, Somalia, and Yemen and the attendant structural failure to hold accountable those culpable of the extrajudicial assassination of civilians and their more-than-human relations.

1————Zoopolitics of the Cage

Forensic Ecologies of Zoopolitical Death

The 2014 military campaign dubbed Operation Protective Edge was the latest iteration of Israel's recursive wars on Gaza.[1] Operation Protective Edge reproduced Israel's "strategy of managed attrition" and "deterrence"; these military campaigns of "managed attrition" and "deterrence" are punctuated by a "subsequent duration of relative calm before Israel is pressured to mow the grass again."[2] As one commentator observes, "To succeed, a grass-mowing operation must inflict a certain level of pain on the enemy."[3] The "enemy" in the context of Operation Protective Edge, as I will demonstrate, encompassed both human and more-than-human entities caught in the crosshairs of the military campaign. Atef Abu Saif, a Gazan journalist and writer, describes the scene he encountered in Shujai'iya neighborhood, Gaza City, as Operation Protective Edge unfolded:

> A dozen or so cows have been killed near a farm on the edge of the neighborhood. Even cows have failed to escape this war. Each one lies on its side; its tongue lolling out of its mouth, its belly starting to inflate with decay. One cow seems to be split in half. We're delighted, eventually, to see that one cow is still alive. It's standing in a small square of rubble—presumably

the remains of what was its barn—and we approach it carefully. It keeps its face close to one remaining part of the wall; it looks pale and appears to have a leg wound. As we get near it limps away, clearly in pain, but too scared to let us help it.

Old women sit helplessly in the debris of their homes. A few kids can be seen searching for toys. Ambulances and medical teams work through the day to find people still alive under these ruins. Today, some 151 corpses have been found in this rubble. Some of them have started to decay already. You can smell the dead bodies on every corner of Shujai'iya. One of the corpses found was of a woman: she had been carrying her children, one in each arm, when the tank shell hit her home.[4]

Delineated in this scene of destruction is the broad spectrum of the victims of war: animals, barns, humans, and houses. Linda Hogan's compelling vision of the landscape—in which "everything answers," including "the corner of a house . . . the solid voice of bricks. A fence post talks back. . . . A wall sings out its presence"[5]—is here cast in an entirely different register. If the ecology of Shujai'iya neighborhood can be said to sing, it is in the modality of a dirge, a lamentation over the death and destruction of all its relations. Corpses and carcasses, the living and the dead, humans and animals, bricks and rubble—all answer back in the unique cadence of their material specificity to the militarized violence of this onslaught. The author of this account of the Israeli military's assault on Gaza does not neglect to name and identify the animal victims of this violence. Saif, indeed, offers a profoundly affecting forensic account of the violence inflicted on the cows caught in the military assault on Gaza. The wounded cow evidences clear signs of posttraumatic stress, a disorder now recognized as also afflicting nonhuman animals that manage to survive the horrors of war.[6] The doleful stare of the wounded cow instantiates an interlocutionary relation between this victim of military assault and the narrator-witness. The violence unleashed by the Israeli Defense Forces (IDF) is clarified through this dialogic line of sight, which is effectively triangulated to interpellate the reader.

This chapter is principally concerned with the zoopolitical dimensions of biopolitical violence in the specific context of the IDF's Operation Protective Edge campaign in Gaza. As I discussed in the introduction, the zoopolitical question of "the animal" occupies a central position in the overall framework of this book's conceptual apparatus because it informs such foundational categories as human rights, animal rights, and jural standing. A zoopolitics of power is not an autonomous domain within the biopolitical assemblage;

rather, it operates within inextricable systems of relation that are nested in the superordinate matrix of the biopolitical. In this chapter, I focus specifically on zoopolitical relations of power that frame Palestinian people as effectively nonhuman animal forms of life that can be caged, experimented on, and killed with impunity, precisely because they are regarded as outside the purview of the legal category of human personhood and all the attendant rights this confers. Furthermore, I underline the capacity for diverse biopolitical categories—such as zoopolitics—to be recalibrated by the biopolitical state in its exercise of violence. As I discuss below, Palestinian life can at one moment be categorized zoopolitically as nonhuman animal life, only to be reassigned yet another status on the biopolitical hierarchy—for example, as a purely disposable vegetal form of life that can be repeatedly "mowed" down to keep it in check. Across this chapter, I place in relation both human and animal subjects caught in the forensic ecologies of war and military experimentation to bring into visibility the way key apparatuses of zoopolitical power—including the cage, the animal holding pen, the laboratory, and the military test range—work to secure the consolidation and expansion of the Israeli settler state.[7]

The overwhelming scale of the destruction inflicted on the neighborhood of Shujai'iya by the IDF led one journalist, who inspected the area immediately after the assault, to declare that it was tantamount to entering "a vast crime scene."[8] Saif, in his account, forensically documents the various elements of this crime scene. Couched in the relevant forensic terms, he identifies the *geolocation* of the crime, Gaza, and the area of the *primary crime scene*, Shujai'iya. He names the *modus operandi* of the crime, or, in forensic terms, what reveals "criminal repeat behavior" and represents a criminal's "signature or preferred method of operation."[9] In the context of this crime scene, the IDF's modus operandi is the indiscriminate shelling by tanks of Gaza's civilian neighborhoods. Saif offers what in forensics would be described as the *taphonomic context*, that is, the immediate environment in which the body of a victim is located.[10]

In this taphonomic context of destruction, rubble and debris bear testimony to the aftermath of military violence. The remains of what was presumably a barn evidence the scale of the destruction. The one remaining part of the wall offers comfort to the wounded cow: morphologically and olfactorily, it bespeaks the enduring presence of a past that has been virtually obliterated. Articulated here is a bovine epistemology of place and its vital experiential dimensions. The remainder of the wall and the complex ensemble of scents that it exudes synchronize the diachronic traces of what was this wounded cow's abode, its site of nourishment, and its locus of belonging. Inscribing this site and its multiple actors is an assemblage of distributed cognition and affect. For some animals, Vicki Hearne writes, the olfactory sense works as "a metonymy for knowledge."[11] There is, she argues, an epistemology of scent that makes available a particular knowledge of the world that is inaccessible to the other senses. The wall *speaks with* the cow in the enunciation of survivor testimony: together they evidence the lethal blows of the IDF's tank shells and the scene of a crime that will have been perpetrated with impunity. These dead bodies remain outside the concerns of law and beyond the purview of accountability jurisprudence: they possess, in fact, no jural standing. There will be no necropsies performed on the animal victims to determine the cause of death and to establish criminal proceedings for this slaughter. They will not be categorized as innocent victims of war under the aegis of either the laws of war or the laws of armed conflict and the environment. And the cow's manifest pain, fear, and desire to seek comfort in the ruins of a familiar wall will not be rendered as instantiations of what Vinciane Despret terms "cultural behavior." Animals, by Euro-anthropocentric definition, are incapable of expressing anything other than raw instinct embedded in unmediated nature.[12]

The proximity of the dead cows and the body of the mother carrying her two children in her arms when she was killed establish binding relations of consanguinity in both life and death. In life, the cows offered nourishment and life to their human subjects; their human subjects, in turn, offered care, nourishment, and a home for the cows. In death, this profound relationality endures. At a nucleic level, an exchange of mediated blood binds the one to other: the sweat of labor transmuted into feed and milk transformed into blood and bone. The proximity of flesh with flesh signals not a simple substitution of one with the other but, rather, a relational ecology of flesh that, from its own unique identity and from the specificity of its geopolitical locus, testifies to the outrages of a military campaign that, as I document below, was inscribed by acts of indiscriminate military violence.

The scene of destruction that I cite above is repeated across a number of survivor and media accounts. Robert Tait, journalist for the *Telegraph*, begins one of his reports thus:

> The bile-inducing, overpowering smell was the first sign that something was very wrong. Then came the truly distressing sight: dozens of dead cows, some with open infested wounds, strewn across the grounds of a partially devastated farm yard. One lonely beast had managed to survive, mooing plaintively in distress beside its stricken fellow animals. Nearby

lay a solitary dead horse, again dead from its injuries, in a sight eerily reminiscent of Pablo Picasso's Guernica painting, in which the artist depicted the aerial bombing of a civilian population by Fascist forces during the Spanish civil war.[13]

Jeremy Bentham's impassioned question on the sentient capacities of animals—"Can they *suffer*?"—is here answered in an inarguable manner.[14] In the context of this bombed farmyard, the answer to this question is articulated by the surviving cow vocalizing her loss and trauma in the midst of the corpses of her fellow cows. Her plaintive mooing ruptures the narcissistic soliloquy of human-sentience-as-exceptionalism. The dead horse that conjures up the iconic *Guernica* emerges from this devastated site as the embodied emblem of indiscriminate military destruction. The dead horse fleshes out in their decomposing contemporaneity a genealogy of animal victims caught in the maelstroms of human wars. Another reporter describes how a Palestinian farmer's apiary "had been crushed. Bees were buzzing everywhere. He told me his orange trees had been bulldozed five years before by the Israeli military. He had been reduced to nothing."[15] These accounts of the forensic ecologies of war identify a broad range of more-than-human victims that, as I discuss in detail in chapter 2, evidence the interlinking of diverse biopolitical modalities in the IDF's campaign of the destruction of Palestinian ecologies of life.

In the wake of the IDF's shelling of the UN's Abu Hussein school, which killed fifteen civilian refugees who had sought refuge in a site officially designated by the UN as a safe sanctuary, Saif describes the scene that confronts him when he enters the school grounds: "Many of the donkeys brought by the refugees were killed by the strike. Half a dozen lie in the road in front of the school. Their stomachs and intestines hang from their bellies. A seventh donkey is still alive, though critically injured."[16] In this account, animal finitude is violently splayed across the road. The inner organs of donkeys disemboweled by the explosive force of the shells mark the visceral morphology and decomposing temporality of war-fueled necrosis. This is the physical evidence of animal suffering and death caught in the crosshairs of war: the line of entrails confirms the violence of the military assault. Across the street from this scene, Saif writes of seeing a boy who is "still hysterical after seeing the flesh of his father and his uncle, mixed together like meat in a butcher's shop."[17] Delineated here is the undifferentiated realm of the carcass, where there is no body or corpse but only butchered meat. Asked to help collect the dismembered bodies of the victims of a missile strike, Saif writes: "I see everything: scattered organs, severed limbs. I have to pick them up. I touch them. I see how a human can be sliced into pieces like a cow in a butcher's shop. How bodies can become indistinguishable when divided into so many parts."[18] In the context of this shambles, Saif names the blurring of the lines between the different entities caught in the carnage of war. He draws attention to the otherwise forgotten lines of consanguineous connection that bind one victim with the otherwise wholly other: "The long black hair of a woman is carried, all in one clump, with part of her head still attached. The hair is matted with blood like the hind of a sheep when it's just been skinned."[19]

Operative in the context of Operation Protective Edge, I contend, is an expanded zoopolitical understanding of the slaughterhouse that encompasses a heterogeneity of lives, intermixing the dead flesh of different subjects. What comes to mind here are Francis Bacon's uncompromising pictures of carcasses and transhuman-animal entities that, with gaping mouths, howl silently from his canvases, insistently shadowed by the specter of the shambles. Reflecting on the arbitrary juridico-ethical divisions that work to separate human from nonhuman animal, Bacon declares, "We are meat, we are potential carcasses. If I go into a butcher's shop I always think it's surprising that I wasn't there instead of the animal."[20] Glossing the significance of the transhuman animals that haunt Bacon's pictures, Gilles Deleuze notes: "This is not an arrangement of [hu]man and beast, nor a resemblance; it is a deep identity, a zone of indiscernibility ... the [hu]man who suffers is a beast, the beast that suffers is a [hu]man."[21] Deleuze anticipates here, as I discuss in detail below, the invertible logics of zoopolitics.

In the scene of animal-human killing documented above, the zone of indiscernibility between the suffering of animal and human is emblematized by the shredded flesh of both entities. The depth of identity that binds one to the other is materialized in the intermixed entrails and blood that result from this act of butchery. In this site of militarized violence, the one becomes the other in a relation of lacerated consanguinity. The consanguinity between the different victims of war also finds its proof in the IDF's bombing of a Palestinian cemetery in the Jabalia neighborhood. Saif continues his testimony of the destruction unleashed by Operation Protection Edge: "The shell that fell two nights ago landed 150 metres away, smack in the middle of the Jabalia cemetery. The dead do not fight wars, but on this occasion they were forced to participate in the suffering of the living. The next morning dirty, grey bones lay scattered about the broken gravestones."[22] The enforced participation of the dead in the suffering of the living evidences the transition from biopolitics to thanatopolitics. In her deployment of the term in the context of occupied Palestine, Honaida Ghanim examines how thanatopolitics shifts the focus "from managing life to managing death" and simultaneously materializes the move "from the politicization of life to the politicization of death."[23] As I examine below and in keeping with Foucault's thesis on the unintended effects of power (necro- or otherwise), this politicization of death generates a number of significations that challenge any univocal reading of this scene of double death in the context of a Palestinian necropolis.

In this account of violent military excess, the dwellings of the living and of the dead become inverted. The living subjects of Gaza are bombed, buried, and encrypted in the rubble of their collapsed houses, and the dead of Gaza are exteriorized and tumultuously uplifted from their subterranean graves into the violent light of day. The thread that ties the living and the dead is now one of a thanatopolitical kinship that works to erase the ontological differ-ence between the two: the living are now the dead, and the dead are now vio-lently resurrected into the domain of the living. Unceremoniously disinterred by the shelling, the bones of the Palestinian dead emerge as ossified actors in this drama of military violence. They attest to the violation of the sacrality of their past burial. Catapulted from the peace of their underworld existence into the harrowed fields of their bombed cemetery, the bones of the dead emerge as forensic indexes of a type of double death. The broken graves, in con-cert with the bones of the dead, testify to military tactics that work to en-sure that the living are reduced to the dead and that the dead are doubly dead. Saif, in his war journal, reports on "the strange fate of the corpses interred there—many of whom were killed in previous bombings—finding themselves once more under attack."[24] Those killed by a previous Israeli war are disinterred so that they may be killed again. Despite the double death imposed on the Palestinian dead, as revenants they refuse to die or to be silenced. Exposed to the light of day, they resolutely insinuate themselves into the world of the living. In this way, they defy their own finitude and the nullity of their double death.

In her work on the postmortem violence inflicted on the Palestinian dead by Israeli authorities, Nadera Shalhoub-Kevorkian draws attention to the "modes of denial silence" that are imposed on the dead, precisely as she also calls for "the ability to learn from and listen to their stories."[25] Documenting the violation of Palestinian graves and the removal and erasure of these graves by Israeli authorities, she views these practices of elimination as coextensive with the logic of the settler colonial state and "the conquest and permanent occupation" of Palestinian land.[26] Focusing on the "removal and obliteration of Palestinian graves in East Jerusalem," she describes the city as "under colo-nial occupation" and as "a space in which even a body in a cemetery is subject to violence, displacement, and eviction. Defining the dead and spaces of the dead as requiring colonial power, surveillance, and eviction, allows the colonizer to further fabricate narratives of past and future, strengthening and affirming a right to land, and sovereignty over this land."[27] The obliteration of Palestinian cemeteries by the Israeli state is, Shalhoub-Kevorkian underscores, yet another "practice of 'rooting out,' of severing ties between [Palestinian] land, body and history."[28]

How to "Verify a Neutralization": Palestinian Double Death

The issue of Palestinian double death resonates along two related necropolitical axes. Even after a Palestinian has been fatally shot, the IDF, in the words of one battalion commander, deploys a policy that clarifies how a soldier can make sure the body is unquestionably dead: "You go up to the body, put the barrel between the teeth, and shoot."[29] The IDF views this practice of double killing as what will finally "verify a neutralization."[30] The apparently revenant and necromantic power of Palestinian defiance demands that the death status of the Palestinian dead be verified by a double execution. The veridictional status of the corpse's deadness can be categorically proven only by shooting a bullet between its teeth. This practice aims to ensure that nothing but a definitively terminal silence will now issue from the dead mouth of a dead Palestinian. For the IDF, the inordinate power of a dead Palestinian often requires more than just firing a bullet between the teeth to verify the death status of the dead. An IDF soldier describes the "verification procedure" that was enacted after the killing of an innocent civilian:

> Guys from the team, according to the verification procedure they know—they threw a grenade and then put a bullet in his head. Turns out the guy was holding a drum. What did we learn later? That there's a custom during Ramadan, at four in the morning people go out and start drumming to wake everyone up for breakfast, before the fast. . . . No one in the IDF bothered to tell us that during Ramadan, at such and such an hour people go around holding something, with a drum in their hands, and maybe you need to tone down the rule of engagement, maybe you need to be more careful. No one bothered to tell us, and because of that this man died. Because of our ignorance.[31]

Even the deadly force of a grenade fails to ensure the categorical death of the Palestinian dead. The exploded corpse must also submit to having a bullet put in his head.

Forensic Assemblages of More-Than-Human Witnesses

At one point in his extended chronicle on the impact of Operation Protective Edge on Gaza, Saif pauses in his narrative and offers a detailed catalog of the material entities left in the wake of the bombing of a Palestinian school by the Israeli military: "The pair of shoes in the corner, the blackboard, the huge tree in front of the school, the clothes hanging out to dry in the playground, the benches under the tree, the notice board in the school assembly point, the clay pot in the front room, the blankets, the toilets, the broken tiles, the paintings on the walls of every classroom, the kids' toys—each and every one of these has the imprint of death on it."[32] Saif's testimony is shaped by an inventory of mourning that is materialized by the heterogeneous more-than-human entities that constitute the practices of everyday life. These diverse entities, however, have now been transformed from artifacts that enable the practices of everyday life into the stilled witnesses of death and destruction. They are now survivor entities that gesture toward absence, loss, and mourning. These forensic assemblages of other-than-human witnesses—shoes, broken tiles, blankets—compel the articulation of these questions: What are the limits of the category of the witness? Can the category be enlarged to encompass other-than-human entities, such as animals and a broken tile? What modalities of speech do these other-than-human entities deploy? These questions, I contend, can be answered by attending to that range of Indigenous cosmoepistemologies that, as I discussed in my introduction, effectively configure a world in which attributes such as agency and speech are not delimited to the category of the human but, rather, are distributed across the spectrum of more-than-human entities, including rocks, plants, and water. As I also mentioned in the introduction, the discipline of Western forensics views an entity such as a broken tile as being invested with the capacity to bear witness to a crime and to offer up, through the intermediary operations of the forensic scientist, evidentiary truths. Underpinning Western forensics, I suggested, is a denegated animism that, should it be broached and named, would ostensibly undermine the scientificity of the discipline. My concern, in what follows, is to attend to the animate testimonies of the more-than-human entities that survive the act of militarized destruction that Saif traces in his narrative and to situate them within forensic ecologies of relationality and distributed cognition that, collectively, speak to the aftermath of an act of militarized violence.

The diverse entities that Saif identifies—shoes, blankets, broken tiles, clothes—bespeak testimonies of violence, severed relationships, grieving silences, and materially congealed trauma. They at once name and constitute the physical evidence of forensic ecologies. This disparate assemblage of entities materializes the temporal dimensions of suffering. In the context of the bombed and now-deserted school, they testify to the perduration of loss and pain, as that which continues long after the death or disappearance of the subject. Shoes, clothes, blankets, and broken tiles emerge as different indexes of suffering within forensic ecologies of state violence. They evidence suffering's diffusiveness as it imbues an array of entities situated within sites of saturated violence.

These diverse entities embody the forensic modality of the survivor testimony. This testimony, though, is not cast in a linguistic register. The survivor is not the human subject but instead the domestic remainders that have witnessed and survived acts of catastrophic violence and now evidence an ecology of the dead. As such, they constitute a material semantics comprising shoes, clothes, blankets, and broken tiles. The explosive violence they have survived rearranges these disparate entities into frozen syntagms. In the wake of the moment of explosive violence, the living have been violently disappeared, and the domestic shards that remain are now immobilized in their shattered quotidian habitus: no further dispositions will be assumed; they will no longer be actors in the differential and shifting routines of the everyday. Marked with the impress of lethal violence, as arrested fragments they attest to lives that have been either dispersed or terminated. The absent dead are materially indexed by the charged perturbations of these shattered remainders. These fragments act as relay points that continue to configure what has been rendered void by the violence of the military assault: they temporarily magnetize the affective circuits of ruptured lives.

Saif elaborates on the scene of destruction that confronts him as he walks through the school bombed by the IDF:

> Dust covers everything and everyone, making displaced people still inhabiting it look white-haired and ancient. The water tanks that ought to be up on the roof now squat in the street. Water pipes dangle down from the walls like figures on a gallows. The mattresses that people had been sleeping on look like great sponges, dyed deep red, soaked. Each mattress could just as well be another body part. The cooking pot from which these people had been serving their dinner sits exactly as it was, with good food still in it. But no one will eat from it now.[33]

This is a picture of a deranged landscape. The order of life has been violently upended: what was up is now down; what was a site of repose is now a mattress seeping blood; body parts are now interchangeable with the dismembered parts of all the other entities that cohabited in this space. The survivor-entities that remain after the bombing of this school in Gaza have been exiled from the flux of life. The semantics of shattered entities, now caught in a violently contorted syntax, embody a language of the dead. As frozen assemblages, they can enunciate only a dead narrative, as they can no longer be reconfigured and recontextualized to narrate the ever-changing stories of the living: clothes will not be donned, shoes will not be removed, and the food in the pot will not be eaten. As the principal actors of a drama from which the human agents have been violently removed, these diverse entities—shoes, blankets, a cooking pot—bespeak forensic ecologies of the aftermath. Collectively, these domestic survivors constitute intimate cenotaphs to the civilian dead. The blood spatters and twisted forms of these grieving remainders enunciate the unsettling murmur of the disappeared. They are expert witnesses of the horror that unfolded in the sight of their unblinking stare. These are not forensic assemblages of temporal unfolding; rather, they are configurations of termination without succession, final witnesses of their owners' end-time.

Zoopolitics of the Cage

Following the cessation of Operation Protective Edge, journalists began to file reports on the destruction of Gaza City's zoo. One report begins thus:

> The lions sit dazed in the shade of their damaged pen, while nearby the decayed carcasses of two vervet monkeys lie contorted on the grass of a Gaza zoo. The animals were caught in the crossfire in over a month of fighting between Israel and Hamas. In one enclosure at the zoo a fly-covered pelican huddles in the corner with a duck. Opposite, a small crocodile sits motionless in an inch of stagnant water, next to the rotting corpse of a stork. . . . Everywhere, there is a sickly stench from the animals' cages, which have not been cleaned for weeks . . . the wire of its [the zoo's] enclosures twisted and crushed, debris and dead animals strewn around.[34]

In this site of destruction, dead and live animals are entangled. The cages and enclosures of this bombed zoo emanate the stench of death and accumulated excreta. The double meaning of *zoo* is, in this locus of captive animal trauma and death, brutally realized: we have here a caged display of animals and a situation of total disorder. Inscribed in this particular zoological site is a layered biopolitical history, as well as an attendant zoopolitical regime, that effectively encompasses both the animals in Gaza's zoo and the Palestinian subjects of Gaza. This palimpsestic history captures humans and animals alike and encloses them in a relation of nested cages in which Gaza's zoo becomes coextensive with

Gaza-as-zoo. As Irus Braverman remarks in her analysis of human and nonhuman animal relations in the context of Gaza and its zoos, "In Gaza, captivity occurs on multiple geographic scales, species' registers, temporalities."[35] Reflecting on how "the whole nation is imprisoned . . . in a prison called Gaza," Saif focuses on the complicity of the international community and humanitarian organizations in producing, sanctioning, and maintaining this superordinate prison called Gaza: "With each new refugee center, they've made a new prison—UN-sanctioned prison-within-a-prison. And even there, they're bombed and shelled and murdered."[36]

In his history of the Palestinian struggle for statehood, Rashid Khalidi names Gaza "the iron cage," "the vast prison of the Gaza Strip," built, surveiled, bombed, and patrolled by "Israel's military-security establishment."[37] A Palestinian NGO report "highlights that the continuing Israeli measures aim at the institutionalization of the closure [of the Gaza Strip]" and thereby stand to violate "international law, including international humanitarian law and human rights law. . . . As a result, 2 million people have been denied their right to the freedom of movement."[38] Deema El Ghoul describes life in Gaza as tantamount to being enclosed in "animal pens."[39] Nowhere is this analogy more graphically realized than in the caged corridors and turnstiles that Palestinians are compelled to negotiate at Israeli checkpoints (figures 1.1 and 1.2). Through their "ubiquity and constancy," Rema Hammami writes, "checkpoints materialize the wider logics of Israeli necropolitics at the level of the everyday for wide swathes of the population." For Hammami, the checkpoints are informed by the "biopolitical management" of Palestinians.[40] Situated in the context of the biopolitical management and control of Palestinians, the checkpoints emerge, in Ron Smith's words, as "the microgeographies of graduated incarceration," which, he underscores, must be understood as operating within the frame of the "larger processes of incarceration, central to the overall project of settler colonialism."[41]

The carceral logic that inscribes the checkpoints produces both the lived effects of graduated incarceration and, on occasion, the death of Palestinians trapped in the strictures of the checkpoints' technologies of control. Reflecting on the combined effects of Israeli checkpoints and what she terms "chokepoints" in the Gaza Strip, Jasbir Puar writes: "Clearly the capacity to asphyxiate is not a metaphor" but, as I discuss below, a physical literality.[42]

Corralled into suffocating caged corridors that lead to a series of turnstiles, metal detectors, and inspection stations, Palestinians often die from being crushed by the overcrowding of bodies in these carceral enclosures. An IDF officer at Erez Checkpoint, Gaza Strip, describes the lethal architecture

Figure 1.1 Tulkarem, Ephraim/Tabeh checkpoint, West Bank, occupied Palestine. EAPPI/David Heap.

of the checkpoints and the death that he witnessed: "The checkpoint is built like this: here's the bars, there's the revolving door ... where you can't exit or enter, and then there's the direction to exit. They wait for them to open the crossing, and they push one another from the pressure, and one of them was just crushed by the bars."[43] The checkpoints, in other words, interrogate facile understandings of more-than-human actors that risk generating an untenable binary in which more-than-human actors are intrinsically "good" in contrast to the nefarious operations of the state. The ethico-political role of more-than-human actors, such as the checkpoints or the Wall, is always context dependent in terms of networked relations of power. Couched in Latourian terms, the checkpoints emerge as *delegates* of the Israeli state. In the context of the checkpoints, the Israeli state's sovereignty is "delegated in concrete,"[44] steel, and razor wire. Transposing Latour's analysis of concrete speed bumps to the checkpoints, one can identify the concrete and steel apparatus of the checkpoints as a mineralogical barrier that interdicts, segregates, and constrains freedom of movement along interlocking spatio-temporal axes: the checkpoints divide space and people; the checkpoints are also inscribed with a temporal dimension—they are there, as Latour would say, "night and day."[45] As such, the checkpoints are the steel and concrete delegates of the Israeli settler state, stopping, surveilling, sorting, and dividing its targeted Palestinian subjects. As mineralogical delegates, the checkpoints embody the panoply of state and non-state actors crucial to the exercise and maintenance of settler power. Continuing to transpose Latour's analysis of speed bumps, we can say that the checkpoints are "full of engineers . . . and lawmakers, commingling their storylines *with* those of gravel, concrete."[46] I have emphasized Latour's use of the preposition *with* precisely because what is operative here is a concrete assemblage of agents, forces, and materials working in association. Even as the engineers and lawmakers mobilize the conditions of possibility for the building of these segregationist apparatuses, the checkpoints cannot come into being without the material agencies of gravel, concrete, steel, and razor wire. The distributed cognition of the checkpoints—as barriers, boundary markers, and graphic symbols of Israeli state sovereignty—is instantiated by this collective assemblage.

In what follows, I superimpose the architectonics of the abattoir's animal forcing and holding pens on the Israeli checkpoints in order to expose the zoopolitical relations of power that order both structures. In her theorization of the symbolic codes that organize the different sectors of the abattoir, Noëli Vialles articulates the significance of the space in the complex that she calls the "dirty sector": this "is the realm of the warm, the moist, the living, of smells and secretions, of the biological threat that needs constantly to be contained and cleaned up."[47] The "forcing pens" of the "dirty sector" of an abattoir, which forcefully channel animals through caged corridors and turnstiles, are reproduced in almost exact detail in the design of the IDF's checkpoints. Israel's reproduction of the architectonics of the forcing pens at the checkpoints works to produce a number of embodied zoopolitical effects. It spells out to Palestinians that they are little more than captive flesh that can be killed by zoopolitical practices of noncriminal putting to death. It reminds Palestinians that they are perceived as biological threats that need constantly to be surveilled, contained, and neutralized by operatives of the Israeli military-security-surveillance complex.

In their collectivity, the checkpoints generate the abject reality of the colonist's dirty sector as envisaged by Frantz Fanon: it is the space, he writes, of "the hordes, the stink, the swarming, the seething, and the gesticulations." It is, he adds, what "the colonist refers constantly to [as] the bestiary" in which the colonized are forcefully held captive.[48] The bestiary defines the zoopolitical space in which the colonized can be both quartered and executed, like nonhuman animals, in acts of noncriminal putting to death. The dust, the rubbish, the sweat, the stink, the swarming, the seething anger, and the crush of the bestiary checkpoints are the product of a militarized surveillance power of zoocolonial subjugation. As an instantiation of the colonist's dirty sector, the checkpoints signal to the Palestinian subjects that they are "biological threats" that need to be contained and screened in order to be evaluated in terms of their "risk index." Israel's epidemiological framing of Palestinians in terms of biological threats, whose native locus is the dirty sector, is further evidenced by the IDF's name for those areas designated as off-limits to Palestinians: "sterile zones."[49] Voided of the contaminating presence of Palestinians-as-pathogens, these sterile zones re-elaborate, in specifically spatial terms, the Israeli practice of "neutralizing" the targeted Palestinian subject.

The checkpoint forcing pens compel Palestinians to embody their subjugated status by materially controlling their freedom of movement. The design of the checkpoints must be understood as a mnemonic architecture of control that daily reminds Palestinians of the nonnegotiable reality of their captive status. Operative here is a violent mnemonics of law that violates the principles of just law. The architecture of the checkpoints is such that it demands that Palestinians daily undergo, as they negotiate its carceral disposition of space, embodied acts of ritualized subjection and recursive criminalization. The daily channeling of Palestinians through these surveillance-identity checkpoints is grounded on policing the a priori criminality of every Palestinian compelled to run this steel cage and razor wire gauntlet. It articulates, precisely through the prison bars of checkpoint cages, the notion that Palestinians are always already guilty until proven innocent through the compulsory checking of their identity papers. The checkpoints, then, function as localized auxiliaries of Israel's military-industrial-prison-surveillance complex. They materially evidence the networked distribution of the carceral modality of power through which that complex exercises its biopolitical governance of Palestinians; as such, the checkpoints reproduce at the local level the settler colonial state's punitive economies of penalties, petty retributions, and graduated incarceration.

Furthermore, given that the checkpoints are located on the liminal space of the threshold between Palestinian and Israeli land and subjects, they reproduce, both architecturally and through embodied practice, what Jacques Derrida terms *limitrophy*, as "what abuts onto limits but also what feeds" the very categorical marking of the limit.[50] Situated in a limitrophe context, Palestinians at once face and abut the borders of the Israeli state as they are processed through the zoopolitical apparatus of the checkpoints; simultaneously, through their embodiment of the category of nonhuman animals, they work to constitute the very intelligibility and the conceptual borders of the Israeli

Figure 1.2 Tulkarem, Tay'be checkpoint, West Bank, occupied Palestine.
EAPPI/David Heap.

citizen subject. This limitrophy is inscribed by the violence of the biopolitical caesura that divides the human from the animal. The violent practices of
zoopolitical subjection inflicted on Palestinians by the Israeli state are legitimated, as I discussed in the introduction, by their racio-speciesist branding as
the absolute other of the tautological human citizen subject.

In keeping with the zoopolitical instrumentalization of animal life in the
shambles, the forcing pens of the checkpoints corral, enclose, and compress
Palestinian bodies into an undifferentiated corporeal mass. In other words,
despite the ostensible rationale that the checkpoints are merely security-
surveillance structures designed to check individual identity papers, the violent architectonics of the forcing pens works to generate a homogeneous corpus that, in zoopolitical terms, can be named the Palestinian *species body*. The
disciplinary architectonics of the checkpoints collapses individual identities
and discrete bodies into an abject entanglement of limbs and lives, compress-
ing them into an undifferentiated cellular mass where, in typical herd formation, the one becomes serially interchangeable with the other. As biopolitical
technologies of racio-speciesist boundary marking, the forcing pens of the

checkpoints visibly and materially produce for the benefit of the Israeli state the spectacle of the bestial Palestinian that needs to be ritually domesticated and contained by a disciplinary architecture that spatially and corporeally enacts the *speciation of the Palestinian* as the animal other. And I use the definite article here as it reproduces the very genericity, homogenization, and fungibility that inscribe the anthropocentric figuration of "the animal."

The speciation of the Palestinian as nonhuman-animal other is materially achieved through the combination of architectural design—the use of turnstiles and carceral technologies of steel bars and razor wire—and the attendant disposition of space that reproduces the shambles' forcing pens. The electronically controlled turnstiles that control the flow of movement through the checkpoints' forcing pens are often abruptly locked by the soldiers as Palestinians are actually attempting to pass through, thereby trapping them like livestock between the bars. The zoopolitical effects of the checkpoints as holding pens are, simultaneously, inscribed by racio-gendered dimensions of necropolitical violence. In her analysis of the impact of various carceral regimes on pregnant Palestinian women, Ronit Lentin writes: "Palestinian women's birthing agonies are compounded by the fact that between the years 2000 and 2007, 69 Palestinian babies were born at West Bank checkpoints where 34 babies and five mothers died."[51] Hagar Kotef and Merav Amir mention one such checkpoint death in their discussion of the case of Rula, a pregnant Palestinian woman. Rula recounts the trauma she was compelled to endure at a checkpoint: "I was in pain and felt I was going to deliver the baby there. . . . I lay down on the ground, in the dirt, and crawled behind a concrete block to get some privacy, and there I had the baby, in the dirt, like an animal. I held the baby, she moved a little, but a few minutes later she died in my arms."[52]

In the process of their enforced passage through the animal vestibularity of the holding pens, Palestinian women and their babies experience what Hortense Spillers terms the "theft of the body" as they are "reduced to a thing, to *being* for the captor."[53] For the parturitional Palestinian women and their babies who have died in the holding pens of the checkpoints, being for the captor engenders the terminal theft of their bodies. There is, in zoopolitical terms, no body for the animal; rather, in the vestibular zone of the holding pens, there is either the live animal or the carcass. The very moment of genesis, in these checkpoint deaths, is transmuted into the trauma of necrogenesis and the commencement of grieving for the surviving Palestinian family members as they are left to mourn a scene of violated natality.

The expropriative nature of the checkpoint holding pens can be elaborated along yet another axis of "theft." As holding pens, they literally hold Palestinians in a state of extended abeyance, compelling them to wait for hours in queues to be processed—thereby producing, in effect, the "theft of time."[54] As such, the exorbitant spatiotemporal logics of these structures can be seen to work in tandem: they work both spatially to enact relations of subjugating power and temporally to extract time from the lives of their captive subjects. The Israeli state thus captures the living bodies of Palestinians, even as it coercively extracts their irreplaceable lived time, transforming their forcibly seized time into a form of immaterial waste, as yet another index of the state's sovereign power. The hyperbolic vortices of razor wire that surmount the steel cages of the checkpoints are the material signs of absolute excess and overkill: they emblematize the state's sovereign exercise of "*surplus* violence."[55]

The Vestibularity of Israel's "Animal Kingdom"

In its pursuit of Palestinians, the IDF terms its predatory exploits "turkey hunts," and once Palestinians have been captured, blindfolded, and shackled, they are transported by IDF personnel in "Safari" trucks.[56] Categorized as nonhuman animals, Palestinian civilians can be assaulted and killed by the IDF with a sense of impunity. The testimony of one IDF soldier demonstrates this point: "First, that it doesn't matter what you do, you always come out okay. Meaning, I could slap people, hit them, shoot someone in the leg. I can't see any situation where I'd be responsible, because I could always say it was in self-defense. Second, the lives of ordinary [Palestinian] civilians matter less than the needs of the army. Meaning, either they're not important, or they're less important to the military objective, or to the force."[57] Returning to my analysis above of the zoopolitical homologies between Gaza's zoo-jail and Gaza-as-zoo-jail, I want to underscore that the two sites are not symmetrically homologous. There are clear political, ethical, cultural, and economic differences. Braverman, in her analysis of this configuration, notes how "animal captivity in Gaza . . . serves to exhibit the perceived normal conditions: that of noncaptive humans displaying captive animals. In other words, both the establishment of zoos and the pastoral care of zoo animals are zoometric tactics used by Gazans to reassert their categorization as humans in the face of their continued oppression."[58] In my analysis, I want to map the binding zoopolitical relations between these two superposed modalities of the zoo and the topological means by which they effectively enfold the lives of the different entities encaged in their respective cages. Deleuze elaborates on the logics of this topological formation: "The 'duplicity' of the fold has to be reproduced from the two sides that it distinguishes, but it relates one to the other by distinguishing them:

a severing by which each term casts the other forward, a tension by which each fold is pulled into the other."[59] The topology of the fold marks the inextricable relation between the human and the other-than-human in Gaza's layered series of cages. The power of the biopolitical caesura works to hold both human and other-than-human subjects in a binding tension through which each different entity is pulled into the other. The very "factors of segregation and social hierarchization" that Foucault identifies as constitutive of the operations of biopolitics, and their attendant "exerting of influence on the respective forces of both these movements, guarantees relations of domination and effects of hegemony" across the speciesist divide, thereby asymmetrically encompassing both animals and humans.[60]

Spillers, in her work on how the apparatus of colonial violence was constitutive in the production of US slavery, draws attention to how the exercise of violence on the enslaved Black subject served, through "lacerations, woundings, fissures, tears, scars, openings, ruptures, lesions, rendings, punctures of the flesh [to] create the distance between a cultural *vestibularity* and the *culture*, whose state apparatus includ[ed] judges, attorneys, 'owners,' 'soul drivers,' 'overseers,' and 'men of God.'"[61] The cultural vestibularity that Spillers identifies functions as the antechamber of the human, even as it marks the limitrophe area that guarantees the cultural intelligibility of the one, the human, and the other, the animal. As such, it must be seen as the racio-speciesist cage of animal subjugation, enslavement, torture, and execution that simultaneously guarantees the white master his status as (civilized) human. Racio-speciesism never operates as an autonomous couplet. On the contrary, its power and resilience testify to a history of permutations inscribed by combinatory possibilities that encompass all the other descriptors constitutive of epistemic and physical violence, including the racio-gendered and -sexualized speciesism that, for example, violently inscribes the many Palestinian women caught in the brutality of Operation Protective Edge and the other serial wars waged on Palestine.[62] Nadera Shalhoub-Kevorkian, Sarah Ihmoud, and Suhad Dahir-Nashif document the violence inflicted on Palestinian women during Operation Protective Edge and situate it within the frame of settler colonial violence. "Sexual and gender violence," they write, "are not merely a tool of patriarchal control, the byproduct of war or intensified conflict. Colonial relationships are themselves gendered and sexualized. We contend that sexual violence [is] a logic embedded in the Israeli settler project."[63]

I introduce this discussion on the operations of the biopolitical caesura, its power-in-spacing carceral enclosures, such as graphically evidenced by the checkpoints, to begin to flesh out its material ramifications in the context of Gaza. Across the spectrum of Israeli political statements and the discourses and visual imageries of Israeli popular culture, the biopolitical caesura is what often frames, renders intelligible, and legitimates violence against Palestinians. I reproduce here a representative sampling of the enframing of Palestinians as nonhuman animals: "Palestinians were 'grasshoppers' compared with the Israelis" (former prime minister Yitzhak Shamir);[64] Palestinians are "drugged cockroaches in a bottle" (Rafael Eitan, former Israeli chief of staff and government minister);[65] "while discussing the resumption of peace talks in a radio interview in 2013, Eli Ben Dahan [former deputy defense minister] said that: 'To me, they [Palestinians] are like animals, they aren't human.'"[66]

These statements evidence, as Elia Zureik documents in *Israel's Colonial Project in Palestine*, that "racism in Israel . . . permeates the institutional structure of the state, such as the Knesset and government policies."[67] What is operative in these statements, however, is a form of racism that is zoopolitically inflected by racio-speciesism. The zoopolitical transmutation, by these representatives of the Israeli state, of Palestinians into nonhuman animals is crucial in the Israeli state's production of Gaza as both iron cage and zoo. The framing of Gaza-as-zoo brings into focus the colonial history that attends the emergence and reproduction of zoos as such. This is a history, as Eric Baratay and Elizabeth Hardouin-Fugier have documented, in which the zoo has operated as a microcosm that is "linked to vast parallel histories of colonization, ethnocentrism and the discovery of the other."[68] Former Israeli prime minister Ehud Barak's description of Israel as "a villa in the middle of the jungle" critically amplifies Spillers's thesis.[69] In her use of the metaphor of the vestibule, Spillers effectively spatializes the distance between slave and human, thereby mapping the coordinates of the space that will quarter animal life, in contrast to the civic space of *the culture*. Once held captive in the vestibule, the subject can be exposed to a number of violent and lethal practices because the captor knows that such practices can be exercised with no penalty. In Spillers's terms, Israel, as the villa, emblematizes *the culture*, in contrast to the vestibularity of the Palestinian jungle. The critical purchase that Spillers's theory possesses resides in the way it discloses the spatializing dimensions of zoopolitical power and the attendant biopolitical need to deploy a military-prison-security-surveillance apparatus crucial to protecting the sovereign's villa from the bestial savagery of the jungle. The master metaphor of the "jungle" derives its signifying force from the colonial imaginary of Africa as the "savage" "heart of darkness" and all the attendant relations of violence and subjugation this licensed. Its undiminished and mobile power is evidenced by the nickname of the French refugee camp on the outskirts of Calais, "The Jungle," which marks it as a zoopolitical site of savage animal life in contradistinction to the culture of Calais.

In mapping the inextricable relation between raciality and embodied spatiality, Spillers draws attention to the manner in which the "captive body" is rendered as "property" that is both "movable by nature" and "immovable by the operation of law."[70] Once situated within the Israeli settler-racial-capitalism assemblage, the Palestinian captive body becomes coextensive with moveable colonized "property" (its mobility ensures that it can be exploited according to the exigencies of the market and that maximum profit can be extracted), while also being positioned as immovable in terms of its ontological fixity as propertied "object" devoid of rights. Through the deployment of a raft of racialized labor laws, the Israeli state has established what Ilan Pappé terms "a modern-day slave market"—in which Palestinians are compelled to "work with no social rights or health insurance, no unions or labour rights."[71]

The settler colonial construction and cultural intelligibility of the vestibularity as the quartering space of the nonhuman other (Black animal-slave or Palestinian beast-terrorist) is undergirded by the intertwining of speciesism and the racism of anti-Blackness. In his tracing of the "entanglements of slavery and settler colonialism" in the context of "black history in the occupied territories," Justin Leroy elucidates how "it is through the language of anti-blackness—apartheid, open-air prison, ghetto—that the ongoing occupation of the West Bank and Gaza have been legible to anti-Zionist activists around the globe."[72] He tracks the contemporary history of anti-Black racism in Israel (including anti-African race riots and threats of deportation of African Jewish migrants) while, critically, complicating and qualifying its texture by situating it within the specificity of the racial schemas operative in Israel-Palestine.[73] As Leroy notes, the history of Black solidarity between Palestinians and African Americans found one of its most acute points of crossover in the wake of Operation Protective Edge in Gaza and the protests in Ferguson, Missouri, and the attendant exchange of tactics of resistance, encapsulated in the refrain "Occupation is a crime, from Ferguson to Palestine."[74]

Benny Morris, "dean of Israeli 'new historians,'" pondering the question of how to deal with the Palestinians, invokes the racio-speciesism of the biopolitical caesura to categorize them as "a species of animal not yet inducted into full humanity."[75] Having already encaged them in their animal vestibularity, Morris then rhetorically asks: "To fence them in? To place them under closure? Something like a cage has to be built for them. I know that sounds terrible. It is really cruel. But there is no choice. There is a wild animal there that has to be locked up in one way or another."[76] The cage designed to hold captive the Palestinian wild animal has, of course, already been built. It is, as Khalidi emphasizes, an iron cage within which are nested multiple other cages. The zoopolitical configurations of the Israeli villa and the Palestinian jungle exemplify what Fanon describes as the colonist's "compartmentalized world, this world divided in two, inhabited by different *species*."[77] Throughout the corpus of his work, Fanon never loses sight of the foundational use by the colonist of zoopolitical language in enabling the colonial practices of expropriation, exploitation, and extermination. He clearly anticipates, moreover, the biopolitical interlocking of race and speciesism: "Looking at the immediacies of the colonial context," he writes, "it is clear that what divides this world is first and foremost what species, what race one belongs to."[78] And the culture of the villa and the vestibularity of the jungle clearly determine where a species will be quartered and whether one can be biopolitically enabled to flourish or will be left to die. Just prior to the launch of Operation Protective Edge, Israel's foreign minister, Avigdor Lieberman, advocated for the "reoccupation of Gaza and a clean-out of the stables there."[79] Gaza was here cast as the animal vestibularity that would be necropolitically "cleansed" by yet another military operation. Here I invoke Achille Mbembe's concept of necropolitics as it clarifies the operations of this form of biopolitics in this context: "The most accomplished form of necropower," he writes, "is the contemporary colonial occupation of Palestine."[80]

Zoopolitics of the Beast and the Sovereign

As I have discussed thus far, operative in the Israeli state's exercise of sovereign power and violence against its Palestinian human and other-than-human targets is a form of biopolitics that can be identified in its specific embodiment as *zoopolitics*. Zoopolitics is not separate from biopolitics. On the contrary, it draws its violent metaphysics and operational logics from biopolitics and its attendant concerns with the management of the life and death of its subjects. I deploy the concept of zoopolitics as, at its very etymological level, it visibly marks the question of the *zōon* or the animal, while, philosophically, it "binds together . . . the beast, power, knowledge, seeing, and having."[81] An analysis of the interlinking of the zoopolitical categories of the beast, power, knowledge, seeing, and having are what will preoccupy the remainder of this chapter.

In his theorization of the link between sovereignty and the animal, Derrida fleshes out the specific inflections that distinguish the concept of zoopolitics. He identifies the crucial nexus between economy and sovereignty in the exercise of zoopolitics: "*Oikonomia*," he notes, is the "general condition of this *ipseity* as sovereign mastery over the beast."[82] Israel's rule over Gaza is predicated on its sovereign control of Gaza's economy, understood in its broadest sense, including control over the supply of food, water, electricity, medicine, and so on. Operative here is the state's exercise of a zoopolitical sovereignty "as animal machine, living machine and death machine."[83] It is a zoopolitical machine, understood in Derrida's tripartite sense, that, in the context of Operation Protective Edge, saw the deployment of the "Israeli policy of the calorie regulation or the 'starvation diet'" to keep Palestinians barely alive: "The policy . . . was described as a 'meeting with a dietician' where the goal would be to 'make them [Palestinians] much thinner, but not enough to die.'"[84] In one sense, what is operative in this regime of calorie restriction is a zoopolitical inversion of the fattening of the nonhuman animal for slaughter. The Palestinian is, under this inverted regime, rendered as a nonhuman animal that, in Puar's terms, is "stunted" into a state of "debilitation."[85] This biopolitical regime of debilitation, she asserts, "tests the framing of settler colonialism as a project of elimination of the indigenous through either genocide or assimilation."[86] As she elaborates, this biopolitical regime of debilitation "is extremely profitable economically and ideologically for Israel's settler colonial regime" along a number of axes, including corporate economies of humanitarianism and reconstruction.[87]

The Israeli state's construction of Gaza as an iron cage within which to pen its Palestinian inhabitants, framed as "wild beasts of the desert" that understand only the "language [of] force,"[88] exemplifies the operational logic of zoopolitics. The iron cage, however, extends well beyond Gaza's borders, encompassing the Wall, built largely on expropriated land in the occupied Palestinian territories.[89] Prime Minister Benjamin Netanyahu has initiated plans to expand the cage's parameters: "At the end, in the State of Israel, as I see it, there will be a fence that spans it all. . . . Will we surround all the State of Israel with fences and barriers? The answer is yes. In the area that we live in, we must defend ourselves against the wild beasts."[90] The Israeli state's continued expansion of the Palestinian cage within which to imprison its wild beasts, and the consequent denial of Palestinians' liberty, implies, in zoopolitical terms, "something of that indivisible sovereignty accorded to what is proper to [the hu]man and denied the beast."[91] Instantiated in Israel's exercise of zoopolitics is that hierarchized binarism identified by Fanon as crucial to the operations of a colonizing state: "Sometimes this Manicheanism reaches its logical conclusion and dehumanizes the colonized subject. In plain talk, he is reduced to the state of an animal. And consequently, when the colonist speaks of the colonized he uses zoological terms. . . . In his endeavours at description and finding the right word, the colonist refers constantly to the bestiary."[92]

The zoological rendition of Palestinians as nonhuman animals and their quartering in its quarantined bestiary work to legitimate the Israeli state's practices of containment and collective punishment as deployed against its captive targets. I part company with Fanon, however, in condemning this zoological branding as a process of dehumanization. I appreciate Fanon's intention here in disclosing how a human subject is rendered into a form of disposable life through the process of zoopolitical inscription, which works, in terms of this dehumanizing logic, to divest colonized subjects of whatever human attributes they may possess and thereby disenfranchise them of the attendant human rights enabled by this juridical category. The logic of this move, however, is ineluctably entrenched in the locus of an unthought anthropocentrism that effectively operates to reproduce the very epistemic violence it desires to expose, failing to acknowledge that the process of zoopolitical inscription has operated a priori in the colonizer/colonized nexus. The category of "dehumanization" can maintain its cultural intelligibility only by referencing the essentialized concept of "the human"—as the idealized subject invested with all the attendant rights and privileged anthropologocentric attributes: reason, language, speech, soul, conscience, and so on. Critically, its definitional essence is based on its absolute animal other. Consequently, the category of "dehumanization" can maintain its ethico-juridical coherency and valency only by drawing on its denegated, but constitutive, animal other. It silently yet insistently reproduces the hegemonic schema of anthropocentrism and thereby unreflexively continues to generate, by default, its disavowed violent effects (a point I elaborate in some detail in chapter 3). It is a move, moreover, that is mired in what Foucault would term "the permanent anthropologism of Western thought," with its insistence on maintaining, through either positive or negative forms of anthropologism, the fiction of a self-identical human essence.[93]

As soon as one has exclusive purchase on the privileged category of "the human," one is potentially armed to dispatch one's targeted other to the vestibularity of the bestiary. The human/inhuman binary is predicated on the reproduction of the subject/object dichotomy, which structurally leaves itself open to systemic processes of inversion. Reflecting on the dangers of this problematic, Latour remarks: "Inhumanity was thus always the inaccessible joker in the *other* stack of cards. . . . It is surely possible to do better, to locate inhumanity somewhere else: in the gesture that produced the subject-object dichotomy in the first place."[94] In other words, the Manichaean gesture identified by Fanon can be short-circuited only through a deconstructive move that (1) refuses to sustain the self-identity of the human through a disavowed process of animal othering; (2) thwarts the process of merely inverting the devalorized category, thereby leaving the violent logics of the structure intact; and (3) proceeds, instead, to displace the hierarchized binary categories and horizontally redistribute essentialized essences across genera and species. As I discussed in the introduction, this practice is exactly what is exemplified in a number of the Indigenous cosmo-epistemologies, where rocks, plants, animals, and humans are understood as jural subjects that are always already cultural, political, sentient, and situated within distributed and multilateral networks of law, ethical relations, negotiation, and respect.

Critically, in his deconstruction of zoopolitics, Derrida refuses to stop at the human/animal divide that informs the exercise of this particular modality of biopolitical power. His deconstructive move entails an exposure of the lines of inextricable connection between the sovereign and the animal, of the ways, indeed, in which the sovereign/human is also indissociably animal/beast. Having marked the a priori politicality of the animal, Derrida deconstructs the lines of force that inscribe the beast/sovereign binary. The "relations between the beast and sovereign," he writes, "are also relations between an animal, a *zōon* supposed to be without reason, and a *zōon* supposed to be rational, the sovereign being posited human."[95] What is of critical significance in this theorization of the sovereign as also constitutively beast, as animal, is that it brings to light the denegated bestiality that animates the exercise of zoopolitical violence. Rather than doxically reproducing the seeming line of absolute difference that separates one, the human sovereign, from the other, the animal, Derrida exposes the parallel qualities that inscribe both categories.[96] At every turn, he insists on unsettling the anthropocentrisms that continue to animate the operational logics of zoopolitics: "We should never be content to say, in spite of temptations, something like: the social, the political, and in them the value or exercise of sovereignty are merely disguised manifestations of animal force, or conflicts of pure force, the truth of which is given to us by zoology, that is to say at bottom bestiality or barbarity or inhuman cruelty."[97] Zoopolitics operates as though the figure of the beast or wild animal were somehow outside the structuring purview of political figuration and its charged tropologies, as though it were thus capable of self-evidently inhabiting the pure and unmediated locus of its own naturally inherent savagery—in which the animal's natural savagery would be tautologically guaranteed by the scientific truths of zoology. Refusing this anthropocentric schema, Derrida insists on acknowledging that: "on the contrary, not that political man is still animal but that the animal is already political, and exhibit[ing], as is easy to do, in many examples of what are called animal societies, the appearance of refined, complicated organizations, with hierarchical structures, attributes of authority and power, phenomena of symbolic credit, so many things that are so often attributed to and so naïvely reserved for so-called human *culture*, in opposition to *nature*."[98]

Antedating Derrida's zoopolitical schema are a number of Indigenous cosmo-epistemologies that situate nonhuman animals as sociopolitical actors in culture. Eduardo Viveiros de Castro talks, for example, of Amerindian "cosmopolitics" in which nonhuman animals "perceive themselves as (or become) anthropomorphic beings when they are in their houses or villages, and apprehend their behaviour and characteristics through a cultural form . . . and they even organize their social systems in the same way as human institutions."[99] The Amerindian cosmopolitics of nonhuman animal cultures underscores the belatedness of Western philosophy's attempt to think through the question of the animal as a being that is always already sociopolitical.

In his theorization of zoopolitics, and in contradistinction to the work of Giorgio Agamben, who argues for the separation of *bios* from *zoē* in his conceptualization of biopolitics,[100] Derrida articulates the conceptual impossibility of this division. By returning to the Aristotelian text that Agamben cites as the originary source of this division, Derrida notes, "This distinction is never so clear and secure, and . . . Agamben himself has to admit that there are exceptions." It is thus impossible to determine and maintain a historical periodization and indivisible conceptual categorization on the basis of "such an insecure semantic distinction."[101] Drawing on the work of Derrida and Fabián Ludueña, Idelber Avelar underscores the untenability of Agamben's position by bringing into focus the a priori politicality of *zoē*: "There is no politics that transcends the biological fact of life itself or remains uncontaminated by it. Politics is always already the managing of *zoé*."[102] Avelar discloses what continues to be effaced in efforts to erase the a priori politicality of *zoē*: that the very figure of the human is predicated on the untenable separation of *zoē* and *bios* and the attendant subordination of animality.[103] One can further extend this understanding of the a priori politicality of the animal to the superordinate category of "nature" by drawing on "Darwin's most fundamental ecological concept": "that of the economics and sociology of organisms as a system—the economy or polity of nature."[104] The concept of the *polity of nature* clearly enunciates its always already political dimensions, as there are no ecologies of economics or sociology without an attendant politics. The reinscription of the politicality of the animal effectively opens up that otherwise effaced, yet insistently operative, space that Neel Ahuja terms "the interspecies zone of the political."[105]

Zoopolitics, then, in the light of this reevaluated schema, exposes what biopolitics continues to elide and disavow: that the conditions of possibility of the very concept of the "the human" are founded on the occlusive operations of this originary ruse. By contrast, in a number of Australian Aboriginal and Native American cosmo-epistemologies the constitutive power of animals in the production of humans is what is avowed and ethically acknowledged. Gregory Cajete notes that Native Americans believe "that animal nature helped to create humans and that animals have always served as humanity's mentors in coming to know the nature of the world."[106] In her discussion of Aboriginal cosmo-epistemologies, Deborah Bird Rose succinctly articulates the Yarralin people's position in the animal/human nexus. In Yarralin culture, it is the dingo that "makes us human": the dingo "opens us up to the world, requiring that we come to an understanding of our place in it."[107] The dingo, in other words, is the subject that anachronically enables the constitution of the human and activates the very possibility of ethico-juridical relations between the one and the other.

Zoopolitical Regimes of Visuality

On July 6, 2014, two days before Israel launched Operation Protective Edge in Gaza, a photo of the injured face of a young Palestinian American, Tariq Abu Khdeir, was posted on social media. Khdeir had been savagely beaten by Israeli police officers in riot gear. A video of his beating shows the police officers punching, kicking, and stomping the boy with their boots. He was arrested without charge and subsequently released. The original photo, which showed a profile shot of Khdeir's facial injuries, was then anonymously reconfigured so that his injured profile was juxtaposed next to the face of a young pig. Due to the significant swelling caused by his severe facial injuries, Khdeir's face was so disfigured that it appeared zoomorphologically to resemble a pig's face. Placed in symmetrical profile shots, the two subjects appeared to be mirror images. The manipulated image was circulated widely across social media. The meme of Khdeir as/with pig stands as a visual instantiation of what Suvendrini Perera sees as constitutive of the politico-cultural significance of trophy photographs: "Through the representational, aesthetic and technological processes of its framing, mediation and circulation, the practice of the trophy," she notes, "invests the spectacles of power it re-represents with new meaning."[108] My concern, in what follows, is to examine the complex vectors that Perera identifies as constitutive of the trophy image in the context of the meme of Khdeir as/ with pig and to materialize the dense "shadow archive" that informs the palimpsestic semiotics of this image.[109]

Tariq Abu Khdeir was the cousin of Mohammed Abu Khdeir, the sixteen-year-old Palestinian who, following the murder of three Israeli teenagers by a Palestinian, Hussam Qawasmeh (later charged and convicted by an Israeli military court),[110] was seized by Israeli settlers from a street in occupied East

Jerusalem, thrown into a car, and driven to the Jerusalem Forest. There, as Sarah Imhoud documents, his "attackers filled his lungs with gasoline and burned him alive."[111] In her analysis of the killing of Mohammed Abu Khdeir, Imhoud refuses to frame his murder as "a random act of 'revenge' by a few 'extremist' Jewish youth"; rather, she positions his killing within the larger historical frame of the settler state. Imhoud quotes the dead boy's parents, who describe how the site in the forest at Deir Yassin, where Mohammed was burned alive, was the infamous site of a 1948 Nakba massacre of Palestinians.[112] She writes:

> That the killers chose to murder Mohammed in a space so haunted by the phantom of the Palestinian Nakba—to ritualistically "return him to his proper place" as a form of historical citation of earlier colonial violence—is further evidence of the symbolic nature of their crime. . . . The Zionist attack on Mohammed's body is deeply intertwined with the attack on the collective body—a process of fragmentation and dismemberment of the Palestinian social body inherent in the settler colonial project's aim of native elimination.[113]

In his history of the 1948 Nakba, Pappé examines the massacre at Deir Yassin and the other massacres that attended the foundation of the state of Israel. What transpired in the Nakba, he contends, qualifies in terms of the standard definitions of ethnic cleansing: "When it created its nation-state, the Zionist movement did not wage a war that 'tragically but inevitably' led to the expulsion of 'parts of' the indigenous population, but the other way round: the main goal was the ethnic cleansing of all Palestine, which the movement coveted for its new state."[114] Pappé, by juxtaposing archival sources with standard definitions of ethnic cleansing, works at once to challenge the "silence," or what he terms the Israeli "memoricide" of this violence, and to demonstrate that the "general definition of what ethnic cleansing consists of applies almost verbatim to the case of Palestine."[115] Ihmoud, in her historical citation of Deir Yassin in the context of the killing of Mohammed Abu Khdeir, works to challenge acts of memoricide by tracing relational genealogies of violence that continue to inscribe contemporary Palestinian life.

In my reading of the meme of the brutally beaten and zoomorphically disfigured face of Khdeir, I want to elaborate, from a zoopolitical position, Ihmoud's argument that such instantiations of violence be understood as forms of citation of layered histories of violence. Reproduced in the spliced image of Khdeir and a pig is the morphing of the boy into a zoological creature that, through the conjoined acts of both physical and symbolic violence, is seen to become his pig counterpart. As the embodied counterpart of a nonhuman animal, he is relegated to the extrajudicial space of the vestibularity of nature, where he can be savagely beaten in a noncriminal manner. Inscribing the meme of Khdeir as/with pig is a logic of violent redoubling: it is not enough that the Israeli state discursively frames Palestinians as animals; to confirm this zoopolitical framing, acts of physical violence are needed to bring into ontological light the latent but naturally immanent animality of the Palestinian. Through acts of physical violence, the interior animality of the Palestinian is compelled to assume its true-to-type exterior form: the spliced zoomorphic image of the Palestinian boy-as-pig stands as the incontrovertible evidence of this natural truth. It is only through revelatory acts of violence that the process of Palestinian speciation can truly be exposed. Fouad Moughrabi, citing the work of Daniel Bar-Tal and his analysis of the anti-Palestinian stereotypes in Israeli culture, draws attention to the range of nonhuman animal stereotypes that has been variously deployed and then observes that, because Palestinians are framed as "violence prone," they are considered to "only understand the language of force."[116] A statement by the mayor of Jerusalem, Meir Turgeman, suggests as much: "We lived in false hope," he intones, "that if we would help them [Palestinians] they would change their animal behavior, but it turns out that nothing helps."[117] In the face of the unreconstructable Palestinian animals who recalcitrantly refuse any carrots he might throw their way to entice them to cease their stubborn practices of continuing to contest the occupation, the mayor of Jerusalem concludes: "I shelved all of the plans. They say carrots and sticks. There are no carrots left, only sticks."[118]

The framing of the Palestinian as nonhuman animal is inflected with zoopolitical metaphors of biologism, mobilized to ground this figure in a recalcitrant and unreconstructable animality. In this way the atavistic animality that is brought to light through the savage beating of Khdeir evidences that the Palestinian is congenitally predisposed to criminal-animal behavior. Palestinians are thus scripted as degenerate evolutionary "throwbacks." In Cesare Lombroso's criminal anthropology, "this atavistic 'degeneracy' was believed by many criminologists to cause the victims both to look more like an 'animal' and also to behave 'in more primitive and savage ways' than their civilized counterparts. These 'animal people' (called 'criminaloids') were also thought to be far more likely to become involved in criminal activities."[119] Also inscribing this meme is the history of Social Darwinism as deployed to advance colonial projects by scripting Indigenous people as located at the bottom of the evolutionary hierarchy. As Ryan Frazer and Bronwyn Carlson note in their analysis of neocolonial memes and their contemporary terra nullius effects, "According to this evolutionary logic, Indigenous people were grouped with animals. . . . Translated into law, this meant that Indigenous people were not permitted to own land because they were not considered people."[120] This history of criminal physiognomy and anthropology, of Social Darwinism, colonialism and criminal anthropocentrism, is what undergirds the discursive infrastructure of this meme of Khdeir as/with pig.[121]

The racio-speciesist tropes that the Israel state and its operatives deploy in their rendering of Palestinians as nonhuman animals are, in this meme, seen to achieve their inarguable literality; in other words, the figure of the Palestinian boy-pig works, retroactively, to literalize all the other animal tropes (cockroaches, grasshoppers, wild beasts, and so on) that configure the Palestinian as the animal other in the Israeli state's bestiary. The meme enunciates the visual fact that what you thought were mere animal tropes must now be understood as demonstrative biological indexes of literal fact—the Palestinian is the other: *the animal*. The visual charge of this meme's category fusion is incisively captured in the closing lines of George Orwell's *Animal Farm*: "The creatures outside [the farmhouse] looked from pig to man, and from man to pig, and from pig to man again; but already it was impossible to say which was which."[122] Operative here, in what Mel Chen identifies as "the literalized figures of such human-animal biopolitics," are "human-animals" that evidence "how the borders between genres cannot hold up so cleanly."[123] As I demonstrate below, the iconographic representation of Khdeir as a transhuman animal works, in other words, to self-deconstruct the very racio-speciesist biologizing forces at work in this act of zoopolitical transmutation.

In her expansive conceptualization of transgender studies as a field that is "most broadly conceived," Susan Stryker notes its larger deconstructive potentialities. Transgender studies, she underscores, "is concerned with anything that disrupts, denaturalizes, rearticulates, and makes visible the normative linkages we generally assume to exist between the biological specificity of the sexually differentiated human body . . . and the cultural mechanisms that work to sustain or thwart specific configurations of gendered personhood."[124] Stryker asks us to insert into this theorization of the disruptive power of the figure of the *trans* all the attendant categories that work in tandem with gender to delineate non/normative identities. In the visibly spliced meme of Khdeir as/with pig, it is precisely the transversal relation between boy and pig that creates the zoomorphic resonance between the two, even as the cut between the boy and the pig visibilizes, as Stryker would say, the differences between the two bodies. The splice, which simultaneously sutures and marks the line of division between the boy and the pig, works to bring into focus the very cultural apparatuses that must be mobilized to construct this zoopolitical image.

The zoopolitical figuration of Khdeir evidences, at the microlevel of the individual subject, the different and interlocking forces that are at work in the Israeli state's exercise of epistemic and physical violence against Palestinians. In what follows, I want to examine the macro-operations of these interlocking systems of violence in the specific context of Gaza by elaborating on the Israeli state's architectonic transpositions of the killing sectors of the abattoir to Gaza's civilian spaces in the context of Operation Protective Edge.

The Trap

If, as discussed above, the Israeli checkpoints accurately reproduce the animal forcing and holding pens, then the macrospace of Gaza can be viewed as instantiating the sector of the shambles known as the "trap." In her work on the development of the industrial-scale abattoir, Vialles has, with a number of other theorists, drawn attention to the "analogies expressed on a number of occasions, inside abattoirs themselves, between the mass slaughter of animals and the equally large-scale extermination of human beings."[125] Facilitating the process of slaughter is the use of the trap or restraining pen. Through the lethal use of the trap, the "animal does indeed now find itself in a cul-de-sac: it can neither turn around nor escape, being tightly contained."[126] Thus begins, Vialles explains, the process of the systematic slaughter of the trapped animals.

As numerous analysts and NGOs have commented in their discussions of Operation Protective Edge, "the level of destruction and killing in this war was unprecedented."[127] In wake of the killing of more than 2,200 Palestinians, "77 percent of which were civilians, including 521 children and 297 women," a number of Palestinian survivors described their conditions as equivalent to the slaughterhouse trap. They drew attention to the impossibility of escaping the bombardment of their neighborhoods, as all avenues had been either blocked or rendered impassable: Israel "closed all emergency exits, blocked all escape routes and sealed Gaza on land, at sea and the air."[128] The slaughterhouse trap must be seen, in zoopolitical terms, as inherently transportable and reproducible across diverse zones of armed conflict. It is precisely what was configured in the "landscapes of massacre" that Perera examines in her compelling analysis of the war in Sri Lanka and that, tellingly, went by the name of "the Cage," as a site of the mass killing of entrapped civilians by the Lankan army.[129]

This is not to say that Palestinians do not exercise what Laila El-Haddad calls "everyday resistance" in the face of Israeli state violence.[130] On the contrary, despite being imprisoned in their iron cage, Palestinians resist and contest this regime of subjugation. The broad array of apparatuses and technologies of biopolitical management, control, and subjugation that are deployed by the Israeli state attests to undiminished resistance and contestation of settler rule by Palestinians. The checkpoints, the Wall, the serial wars—all index what Patrick Wolfe terms as the "substantial incompleteness" of Israeli settler rule. "Settler colonialism," Wolfe emphasizes, "is a project, not a fait accompli."[131] In their analysis of the settler colonial construction of the Israeli state, Marcelo Svirsky and Ronnen Ben-Arie outline how "resistance, whatever its sources and operations, always plays a part in the shaping of the developing oppressive structure."[132] Palestinian acts of resistance encompass everything from stone throwing to their giving voice to an "aesthetic of resistance."[133]

Zoopolitics of the Laboratory

The forces that converge and intersect in the zoopolitical assemblage of Gaza-as-zoo and as slaughterhouse trap can be further amplified. Examining the development of the zoological dimensions of the zoo, Baratay and Hardouin-Fugier track how the very deployment of the term *zoo* shifts the focus on the animal "content of the space (zoology) rather than the space itself." This enables the space itself to be rendered, they conclude, "as a perfect laboratory" in which all sorts of experiments can be scientifically conducted on the animal-objects held captive in this zoopolitical space.[134] The zoopolitical dimensions of Gaza as experimental laboratory are clearly identified in what Amira Hass refers to as the Israeli state's "extended experiment called 'what happens when you imprison 1.3 million human beings in an enclosed cage like battery hens.'"[135] These zoopolitical transpositions must be seen as *dispositifs* that infrastructurally shape the lives of Gazans through such different modalities as the forcing and holding pens of the checkpoints, the slaughterhouse trap, and, as I analyze below, the animal-testing laboratory. The Israeli state and its armaments industry view Gaza and its captive population as their ideal weapons-testing laboratory. "A key selling point," writes Ismael Mohamad, a point "stressed repeatedly by Israeli arms companies and officials—is that Israel's weapons are 'field tested' in 'real time.'"[136] This means they are tested on a captive Palestinian population. In this field-testing schema, Palestinians emerge as live test targets on which Israel conducts ongoing experiments of its latest military technologies.

Situated at the nexus of Israeli settler occupation and the military-industrial-surveillance complex, Gaza emerges as a laboratory where "Israel tests and refines various techniques of management, continuously experimenting in search of an optimal balance between maximum control over the territory and minimum responsibility for its non-Jewish population."[137] Avner Benzaken, the head of the Israeli army's technology and logistics division, emphasizes the significance of Gaza as Israel's weapons-testing laboratory: "If I develop a product and want to test it in the field, I only have to go five or ten kilometres from my base and I can look and see what's happening with equipment. . . . I get feedback, so it makes the development process faster and much more efficient."[138] Conveniently located only a few kilometers from the bases of Israeli arms manufacturers, Gaza's captive Palestinian population offers instant feedback on the experimental deployment of Israel's latest weaponry. Drew Marks of ESC BAZ, an Israeli company that manufactures unmanned surveillance systems, boasts that, in its marketing campaigns, the company successfully capitalizes on the fact that its systems are "battlefield proven" and that, for him, there is "a lot of pride in that statement."[139] The IDF, for example, intensively deployed Elbit drones in hundreds of strikes during Operation Protective Edge. This drone assault on Gaza reaped significant financial rewards for the Israeli drone manufacturer Elbit: "In the month of July 2014 alone, during the peak of the assault on the Gaza Strip, Elbit's profits increased by 6.1%."[140] A number of IDF personnel and arms merchants argue that the "lessons learned in Gaza and the West Bank" are applicable across diverse geopolitical contexts; Benjamin Ben Eliezer, a former Israeli defense minister and industry minister, contends, "Israel's advantage is that 'people like to buy things that have been tested. If Israel sells weapons, they have been tested, tried out. We can say we've used this 10 years, 15 years.'"[141]

I want to underscore that I do not deploy the concept of the laboratory as a mere spatial trope. On the contrary, I am interested in fleshing out how the concept is underpinned by violent histories of zoopolitical violence that, simultaneously, suture it to scientifico-military regimes of experimentation. In the context of the laboratory, the biopolitical modality of zoopolitics operates as the switching center that interconnects anthropocentrism, racio-speciesism, and colonial violence. In the annals of the Western laboratory, born in the seventeenth century in the crucible of empire, the nonhuman animal took center stage in the biological and medical sciences as a key subject for experimentation. The transnational scientific trade in Indigenous people and African slaves, both living and dead, from such settler colonial sites as Australia or the Americas was predicated on the violent metaphysics of a racio-speciesism that transmuted Indigenous people and slaves into nonhuman animal life that could also be experimented on within the clinical space of the laboratory.[142]

I invoke these other histories of the laboratory as they problematize and complexify reductive notions of the term. They exemplify, indeed, Rhys Machold's call to theorize Palestine-as-laboratory in terms of a complex assemblage that cannot be reduced to an insular and self-contained space. Rather, drawing on actor-network theory (ANT), Machold argues that the "very 'inside' character of laboratories is a direct function of the relationship of scientists to the 'outside' world. ANT situates the laboratory as a physical site of experimentation as well as a relational construct, operating through interactions that bring disparate elements together."[143] The conceptualization of Gaza-as-laboratory brings into precise focus this relational interface of inside-outside and, as Machold explains, "the concept of the laboratory is employed in making sense of Israel's perceived centrality in global patterns of violence and militarism."[144] Eyal Weizman, in naming Gaza as a "laboratory of the extreme," examines how this inside/outside nexus enables "the exchange of technologies, mechanisms, doctrines, and spatial strategies between various militaries and the organizations that they confront, as well as between the civilian and the military domain."[145]

The violent interface of the laboratory's inside (Palestine) and outside (world) finds its material instantiation not only in the international selling of weapons and surveillance systems by Israeli arms manufacturers but also in their marketing of techniques of repression to US police departments, which "are far more likely to test these new skills and techniques on poor black populations than [on] so-called terrorists." In his analysis of the Israeli and US arms/techniques of repression nexus, Leroy notes how "such exchanges expose the intimate relationship between the projection of state power inward in response to domestic unrest, and its projection outward as warfare."[146] US funding enables Israel to invest in military "research and development in the United States and for military purchases from Israeli manufacturers."[147] The United States recently signed "a record $38bn deal to provide Israel with military assistance over a 10-year period—the largest such agreement ever by the U.S. with any country."[148] This fact, if nothing else, underscores the valency of Machold's contention that, in analyses of the laboratory, emphasis needs to be placed on the binding relation between the "inside" of the laboratory and the larger geopolitico-economic forces of the "outside" world.

The field-testing of military arms on Gaza's civilian populations in Israel's numerous wars is, as I discuss below, topologically bound to the scientific experimentation by the IDF on nonhuman animals in its various weapons-testing sites. This is not to collapse one site and one subject into another; rather, it is to make visible lines of zoopolitical relation that are, in turn, differentially marked and reoriented by site-specific subjects and conditions. The testing of ammunition on a civilian population is conducted under a different political and epistemological regime than the testing of military technologies on nonhuman animals—even as both regimes are, in the context of Palestine, underpinned by the infrastructural metaphysics of zoopolitics. "ANT scholars," Machold elaborates, "argue that scientific facts are not verified independently inside the space of the laboratory but rather validated through their 'extension' into other arenas of social reality, thereby consolidating truth effects."[149] Here the spatiality of the laboratory emerges as mobile, extensive, and crosshatched by diverse social forces and relations. The laboratory's truth claims are, in other words, cross-referenced and consolidated precisely by the inside/outside nexus. The IDF's field-testing of new military technologies on the civilian population in Gaza is, as I discuss below, inscribed by the cross-referencing to its experimentation on live pigs in its weapons-testing sites.

Forensic Ecologies of Military Livestock

If the figure of the wounded animal, as Theodor Adorno suggests, both incites and licenses the violence of the pogrom through the assertion that what is being killed is, after all, "only an animal,"[150] then this same figure, in the context of the military laboratory, of Gaza-as-laboratory, must also be seen as the expendable target of live experimentation for weapons testing. And I return here to the meme of Tariq Abu Khdeir as/with pig. Reading this zoomorphic image in the context of weapons experimentation brings into focus the violence and suffering that nonhuman animals, pigs in particular, are exposed to in militarized laboratory settings. Informing the image of Khdeir as/with pig is a shadow archive of zoopolitical militarized violence. In what follows, I draw on two other images that are sourced from two interlinked settler colonial states, Israel and the United States, and their militarized regimes of zoopolitical violence.

First image: IDF personnel describe "an experiment that the Israeli Defense Forces carried out to find out what would happen to creatures as a result of an explosion." The laboratory in question was constituted by an assemblage of trailers positioned in a weapons-testing site:

> We took seven pigs and put them inside one of the trailers. I detonated the explosives. What happened after that comes back to me in my nightmares. Even though we were far from the explosion, we could immediately hear the horrific screams coming from inside the trailer. When we opened the door . . . the pigs were lying crying and screaming. The blast obviously

blew them up from the inside and glass that had been blown down from the windows lacerated them from the outside. The walls were all full of the blood, urine and excrement of the pigs, which had been tied up. . . . The trailer was so filthy and smelly that it was decided to put the next batch of pigs in large plastic bags and to place them inside the trailers.[151]

The body of language that constitutes this testimony shifts from the phantasmagorical register of nightmares to the composed passive voice that will, in the wake of the horror, conduct the next experiment in a more clinical and sanitized manner by sealing the live pigs in plastic bags to contain the corporeal detritus of their explosive shredding and dissolution. Between these two registers, there opens an abyssal gap that designates the realm of the unspeakable: the cries and screams of the dying pigs. This is the trauma that cannot be curbed or contained by the clinical voice of the military scientist and will insinuate itself as the stuff of nightmares, inciting the confessional impulse to offer testimony and bear witness, even as the IDF's scientifico-military experimentation on live animals continues: "In 2015 alone, more than 600 animals, including rats, pigs and sheep were experimented on [by the IDF]," including "exposure to poisons, gases and extreme heat."[152]

The scientifico-military experiment described by this IDF official articulates a juncture where zoopolitical lines of force and violence intersect and bind the human and nonhuman animals of Gaza with the IDF's experimental use of "livestock." "Politics," Derrida remarks, "presupposes livestock."[153] Israeli zoopolitics presupposes both human and nonhuman livestock. As with the IDF's experimental pigs, the human and nonhuman animals trapped in the Gazan cage are instrumentalized into livestock that will serve the Israeli state's political and economic ends. As experimental live targets for the testing of new military weapons, both the human and the nonhuman livestock will supply Israel's arms manufacturers with the "key selling point" that their equipment is "field tested" in "real time."

What can be discerned in the context of the occupation is a dynamic of militarized experimentation that, topologically, conjoins the IDF's local experimental field stations to the larger laboratory designated by the sign "Gaza." In wake of the destruction unleashed by Operation Protective Edge, Raghad Qudeh, who managed to survive the IDF's destruction of Khuza'a, describes what she found on her return to what "used to be a small farm with goats, doves, chickens and dogs. All of the farm animals have been killed, their bodies scattered around what used to be a lovely garden amid the stench of dead meat. One can't tell if this comes from the animals or the human bodies next door.["154] In the aftermath of the IDF's military campaign, animal and human bodies are here assimilated into the zoopolitical category of "dead meat." The "stench of dead meat" signals a molecular binding in death of the diverse entities felled by the IDF. It also initiates the process of grieving over a loss that transcends the strictures of biopolitical categories. Abu Hadaeid, a survivor of another IDF attack during Operation Protective Edge, speaks to this consanguine sense of loss and grieving: "Abu Hadaeid walked to the other side of his farm to find more sheep flattened by bulldozers. 'You feel very sad to see an animal you raised and cared for, for years, slaughtered like this. Imagine how it feels to lose a brother,' he said while following the tracks of the bulldozer as it flattened his land and whatever animals stood in the way."[155]

Surveying the devastation of his land, the slaughter of his sheep, and the killing of his neighbors, Hadaeid articulates his grief and then "mention[s] animal rights groups. 'If the abuse of our human rights is not condemned by the world, then I hope at least animal rights groups will have something to say about this.'"[156] In raising the issue of human and animal rights, Hadaeid is not being flippant: he has just marked his grief over the bulldozing to death of his sheep. Hadaeid, indeed, reveals a clear understanding of the arbitrary and unstable assignations that govern biopolitical hierarchies of life positioned within rights frameworks. As mentioned above, rights frameworks—human or otherwise—because of their predication on hierarchical taxonomies and principles of ex/inclusion and recalibration, are inherently invertible, violable, and open to politically opportunistic suspension and appropriation.[157] The limits of rights frameworks become particularly evident once they are situated within forensic ecologies of militarized violence. In these volatile contexts, rights frameworks may fail on two counts: on the one hand, they may be suspended to gain a military advantage, so that the human rights of civilians in war are made redundant, regardless of the principles of international humanitarian law; on the other hand, they are inscribed by fraught logics that generate, as I flesh out below, a number of contingent contradictions—such as the adherence to animal rights in Israel and, by contrast, their complete dismissal by the IDF in their campaigns of destruction in Gaza.

My argument is not that one should promote one modality of rights (human) at the expense of the other (animal).[158] Rather, as Matthew Calarco argues in his trenchant critique of rights frameworks and their infrastructural ex/inclusion mechanism, "what needs to be reformed, or rather transformed, is the juridicism and exclusionary logic that underlies our dominant practices and ways of thinking and the legal and political institutions that encode and reinforce these practices."[159] I would juxtapose rights-based frameworks against the Indigenous ethics of "all our relations." Whereas rights-based frameworks are founded on proprietorial and essentialized categories, hierarchical taxonomies and disciplinary normativities that determine who may count as a rights-bearing subject, "all our relations" embodies both a horizontal universality (*all* our relations, not just the chosen few) and the particularity of every being situated in the lived positionality of ethical encounters and negotiations. Reflecting on the power of Euro-anthropocentric language to reduce more-than-human entities to object-things ("it"), Robin Wall Kimmerer, member of the Potawatomi Nation, outlines how, conversely, Potawatomi language is constituted by a "grammar of animacy" that "could lead us to whole new ways of living in the world, other species as sovereign people, a world with a democracy of species, not a tyranny of one; with moral responsibility to water and wolves, and with a legal system that recognizes the standing of other species."[160] By contrast, rights-based frameworks, with their Euro-anthropocentric determinations and limits, fail to account for the ethico-jural standing of the broad spectrum of more-than-human entities (rocks, trees, rivers, and so on) and their lifeworlds. My deployment of a forensic ecology approach is oriented precisely by a concern to bring into focus the heterogeneity of more-than-human entities that, from loci of militarized destruction and injury, fail to be encompassed by rights-based frameworks, with their inbuilt juridical exclusions, and that yet stand as forensic witnesses that call for the very justiciability that this same framework only delivers to the select few.

Furthermore, my concern with regard to rights frameworks hinges on the inbuilt points of irreflection that inscribe it and that are instrumental in producing their own forms of disavowed violence. In the Israeli context, for example, there is an increase in animal rights movements and the expansion of animal rights laws. In a ten-thousand-strong animal rights parade held in Tel Aviv, "participants chanted and held up signs protesting the consumption of meat and dairy products, as well as placards opposing animal experimentation. 'Justice, compassion, veganism' and 'Meat is murder' were chanted repeatedly."[161] The chant "Meat is murder" needs to be incorporated into the dead meat that is so systematically produced by Israel's wars on Palestine. Quarantined from the larger purview of these wars, the slogan "Meat is murder" fails to address the intercorporeal relations that bind one modality of dead meat to its elided other.

In another Israeli animal rights protest, "members of an animal rights group stood silently in the center of Tel Aviv. Each member held a dead chicken in his or her hands, wearing T-shirts that read 'Their lives are in your hands.'"[162] It is the very exclusionary and hierarchical structurality of rights frameworks that produces these sorts of greenwashing effacements, where the chickens massacred by the IDF in Khuza'a, for example, fail to signify in the hands of these same animal rights protesters holding up the bodies of chickens slaughtered in an Israeli abattoir. These structural contradictions and critical elisions perhaps find their most egregious manifestation in the pronouncement by Eyal Megged, Israeli animal rights activist, calling on "Prime Minister Benjamin Netanyahu to champion animal rights as a default option":

> "What's there to stop Netanyahu from being a real reformer in animal welfare? After all, peace with the Arabs isn't going to happen, so why don't Livni and Netanyahu harness their futile efforts on talks with the Palestinians to a goal that would truly make us a light unto the nations? Why not make ourselves the champions of progress on an issue that enlightened people around the world take seriously?" Netanyahu apparently likes the idea: This week he announced his support for the Meatless Monday project and noted that he and his family are very sensitive to the issue of cruelty to animals.[163]

How can one begin to reconcile the contradictions that inscribe this passage? On the one hand, Netanyahu, over his four terms as Israel's prime minister, has been responsible for violating a raft of humanitarian and international human rights laws by ordering a number of military assaults of collective punishment on Gaza and by passing increasingly draconian laws that have tightened Israel's biopolitical noose around Palestinians and their more-than-human relations. On the other hand, Netanyahu appears to be "very sensitive to the issue of cruelty to animals," modestly abstaining from the excessive consumption of meat through his observance of a meatless Monday. Furthermore, he is supportive of animal rights advocates' work to make Israel a "light unto the nations." In attempting to make sense of these contradictions, I would draw attention to the fact that there is not a simple and homogenized binary opposition between the human and the animal. Rather, "there are, between different organizational structures of the living being, many fractures, heterogeneities, differential structures."[164] Viewed in this light, context-determined differentials generate shifting configurations that position animals along contradictory axes, so that a sheep, for example, can either be protected as a "pet" in one context or, in another, be mechanically dispatched to the slaughterhouse. This seemingly incoherent picture of Netanyahu (known colloquially as the "Butcher of Gaza"),[165] who can proclaim his progressive commitment to animal rights while simultaneously violating the rights of the living entities of Palestine—this seemingly incoherent picture can be seen to be enabled by the very contradictions, elisions, and structural violences that are endemic to rights frameworks. The contradictions and incoherencies that inscribe

Netanyahu's position are all of a piece with what rights frameworks enable and reproduce: the hierarchical elevation of one selected group over another; the inclusion of one worthy group (the dead chickens of Tel Aviv) over the exclusion of another less-than-worthy group (the militarily slaughtered chickens of Gaza); and the ongoing oppression and killing with impunity of those deemed to be outside the purview of the contingently privileged category that organizes membership within a particular rights framework.

Second image: In a series of interviews with military personnel that he conducted for the writing of his book *Virtuous War*, James Der Derian speaks of his final interview with a military medic:

> I met Corporal Cleveland, whose job was to treat the wounded on the battlefield. To better the survival odds, the Marine Corps had developed a new two-week program in which an anesthetized pig is wounded with increasing severity, beginning with a knife, then a 9 mm handgun, followed by an AK-47, and finally subject to smoke and fire. The task of the Corpsman is to keep the pig alive as long as possible. Corpsman Cleveland was good: he kept his pig breathing for twelve hours. No one wanted to talk about the possibility of their own deaths on the battlefield, but it seemed like every Marine had a story about the pig. And every squad wanted a Corpsman who had gone to "pig school."[166]

Der Derian documents the existence of this "pig school" and leaves it unremarked. I want to discuss the zoopolitical significance of the US military's use of the pig for military experimentation in the context of what it terms "live tissue training." Every incision into the flesh of this pig is instrumentalized into a timekeeping notation that will graph the pig's trajectory toward death. The violent scoring of the body of the pig becomes the coefficient of a graduated death. The different wounds inflicted on their body become, in Cartesian terms, equivalent to the markings inscribed on a bio-machine that is clocking up the process of dying. The clinical findings of this experiment are abstracted from the violated body of the dying pig and, simultaneously, embedded in their flesh and enabled by it. The combined effects of smoke and fire will, finally, put an end to the life of this victim and to the ritualized torture they have been compelled to endure.

The conceptual ground that supplies the conditions of possibility of both these experiments on live pigs pivots on the zoopolitical deployment of the logic of the analogue and its contradictory structure of sameness and difference. In his analysis of the analogue, Anthony Wilden notes that it is constituted by a dialectical system of "binary relations or differences," which take the form of things such as "presence and absence."[167] In these live pig experiments, the analogic reading of the transanimal-human pigs is predicated on the understanding that both pig and human bodies are effectively interchangeable. Simultaneously, the pigs can be exposed to the lethal violence of these experiments only by invoking the biopolitical caesura that at once impounds and negates their sentience. Even as, for example, the IDF officer notes the screams and the writhing in pain and terror of the pigs overwhelmed by the blast, the facticity of their sentience needs to remain inconsequential. Transmuted into the property of the military, they are denied, as wholly instrumentalized biomedical assemblages of animal flesh, the capacity to feel pain. Simultaneously, their live flesh will be the surface that records the trauma consequent to the violence of the blast: the wounds, burns, and lacerations inscribed on the analogue of human flesh will enable the deductive transposition from one (the animal) to the other (the human).

In pursuing the Hegelian dimensions of the analogue, Wilden explains how he would "define analogue 'negation' as *Aufhebung* (which suppresses and conserves contradictions)": "The *Aufhebung* of a situation refers to the diachronic overcoming of contradictions in a referent system and the subsequent emergence of (what is in relation to it) a metasystem."[168] The *Aufhebung* that enables the live-animal experiments that I have analyzed at once suppresses the sentience of the pigs in question, even as it conserves this contradiction— as is made graphically manifest by the witness's attestation of the terror and pain experienced by the pigs. The metasystem that emerges as the biopolitical sovereign that governs the life and death of these pigs is anthropocentrism. As metasystem, anthropocentrism selectively determines the differential calibrations that will be at play in the governance of the animal, including where meaningful analogical similarities will be made (for example, the skin of a pig) and where unbridgeable differences will produce a cut that enables the legal fiction of nonsentience in a living being and that, in turn, licenses its exposure to noncriminal obliteration.

The two images I have described constitute a shadow archive of zoopolitical violence that links the montage of Khdeir as/with pig to a corpus of latent referents. The shadow archive I have invoked informs this particular image and supplies it with its signifying substrate and conditions of cultural intelligibility. The military experimentation on live pigs transmutes living animals into "live tissue" experiments ostensibly positioned as animal substitutes for humans. Yet what these pigs ultimately configure is neither animal nor human; rather, the immobilized pigs emblematize organic life instrumentalized into nothing more than a live assemblage of captive meat: the elision of the word *animal* and its replacement with *live tissue* ensures the symbolic effacement of the animal and its clinical transmutation into object-thing. As such, the pigs' value lies only in their ability to sustain increasing degrees of trauma up until the point where they cease to be "live" and hence cross the death threshold, which will turn them into useless carcass-things. And when they finally expire, they will not, in Heideggerian terms, die: "To die means to be capable of death as death. Only man dies. The animal perishes."[169] The unintended corollary of this anthropocentric dispatch of animals to an indefinite state of perishing is that, "because animals are unable to achieve the finitude of death, they are also destined to remain 'live,' like electrical wires, along the transferential tracks. Unable to die, they move constantly from one body to another, one system to another."[170]

Unable to die, the revenant pigs that are caught in the matrix of militarized violence cross from one body to another. Through this transferential process, as electrified flesh of the world, they leave indelible traces of the violence that has been inflicted on their bodies. These same forensic traces delineate lines of connection between the assemblage of subjects seized, violated, and killed by the exercise of zoopolitical power. Despite their empirical death, like electric wires, they all remain "live," animating a vast shadow archive of racio-speciesist images and zoopolitical practices. It is thus that I see in Tariq Abu Khdeir's zoomorphically mauled face the physiognomic articulation of a muted howl of anguish, of a physical contortion shaped by the trauma and pain endured by the victims of zoopolitical violence.

2———Biopolitical Modalities of the More-Than-Human and Their Forensic Ecologies

Settler Colonial Paradigms and Aporias

One of Patrick Wolfe's most salient encapsulations of the operations of the settler colonial state is his assertion that "invasion is a structure not an event."[1] In his transposition of Wolfe's settler colonial analytic to the context of the Israeli state's occupation of the Palestinian territories, Ron Smith resignifies Wolfe's formulation to "occupation is a process, not an event," and then analyzes the various phases of the occupation in the context of their historically specific contours and textures: "Throughout the many phases, the occupation continues and adapts itself to political and military concerns as it becomes increasingly entrenched, including the enactment by the Israeli government of policies of varying strictness regarding permits and entry of Palestinians into Israeli colonies. These changing policies correspond to the complex relationship of Israeli society within occupation strategies and shift based on Israel's need for unskilled labour or for resources, like water and land."[2] Having marked the different and shifting occupation strategies deployed by the Israeli state in order to respond dynamically to the demands and exigencies arising from site-specific contexts and historical forces, Smith then makes a particularly valuable observation: "While the occupation changes along dimensions of time based on the priorities of the occupier, it also varies from place to place, creating an array of microgeographies based on strategic concerns."[3] In terms of this chapter's key concerns, Smith's analysis of the occupation of Palestine resonates along three intersecting axes: it establishes the macroframe of settler colonialism as a key analytic informing the occupation; it names such resources as water and land as pivotal to the regime of settler occupation; and it delineates the significance of an "array of microgeographies" that evidences the differential and context-bound modalities through which strategies of occupation are grounded in practice. In this chapter I examine the forensic ecologies situated across a number of microgeographies in order to investigate the range of biopolitical modalities that impact both human and more-than-human life in the context of the occupation.

In asserting that the concept of settler colonialism supplies a key analytic to the concerns of this chapter, I want to pause for a moment to elucidate briefly the concept. Wolfe's critical work—which built on a preexisting body of Indigenous decolonizing scholarship[4]—fleshing out the theory/praxis nexus in the context of settler colonial states has been productively transposed to the study of the occupation of Palestine.[5] A significant corpus of scholarship has worked to demonstrate both the validity of analyzing the occupation through the settler colonial lens and the contradictions and misalignments that are generated in the process.[6] The settler colonial paradigm operative in occupied Palestine has also been located within the larger, transnational historical frame of European history. As Tariq Dana and Ali Jarbawi contend, "Any discussion of the nature and dynamic of the Zionist colonization of Palestine must be anchored in the triple dynamics that constituted the essence of nineteenth-century Europe: nationalism, colonialism, and anti-Semitism."[7] As I noted in the introduction, Aboriginal peoples, Native Americans, and representatives of First Nations in Canada have marked the transnational valency of the settler colonial paradigm in its application to the occupation and have articulated their solidarity with the Palestinian people. Simultaneously, Israeli settler colonialism has also been examined in terms of its particular historical inflections, religio-political attributes, and geopolitical alliances.[8]

Wolfe's thesis on the settler logic of elimination has been at once affirmed as having both "immense power as a means of mapping forms of injustice and indignity as well as strategies of resistance and refusal" and a number of built-in "operational weaknesses"—including the impossibility to realize projects of decolonization as, paradoxically, the settler state can "never . . . be fully extinguished until the native is."[9] Wolfe was attentive to the structural conditions of this process of incompletion, even as he also viewed the very grain and texture of settler practices of elimination as inscribed at every turn by the resistant Native: "The quest to replace Native society," he emphasizes, "only maintains the refractory imprint of the Native counter-claim."[10] Furthermore, in his analysis of Israeli settler dynamics oriented toward both the elimination of Palestinians and the ongoing expropriation of territory, he tracks a number contradictions that refuse either/or formulations and that bring into focus a number of aporias captured by the following assertions: "The Jewish state cannot live with Palestinians and it cannot live without them," and "Success [of the settler project of total elimination of Palestinians] would be failure."[11]

Rana Barakat observes how, in Wolfe's thesis, the binaries he tracks (and, I would add, the aporias and anxieties they generate) "signal 'incompleteness'" of the settler project in the face of the resistant Indigene.[12] Barakat suggests that this incompleteness illustrates how Wolfe's understanding of Israeli settler colonialism in Palestine is grounded in the "idea of a permanent frontier"[13]—as emblematic of the concept of incompleteness and as generative of the acts of violence and resistance that characterize the locus of the settler frontier. A number of studies that situate the frontier dynamics of the occupation within comparative transnational contexts demonstrate the significance of applying the frontier thesis to the Israeli occupation of Palestine. In his analysis of "frontier geography," Eyal Weizman, for example, opens with a comparative analysis of other settler states and their frontier wars and then examines how the "frontier space" of the Israeli occupation "is a military and political pattern of elastic and shifting geography" scored by the "perpetuation of violence."[14]

Biopolitical Interlacement of Settler Colonialism and Ecocide

The concept of a permanent frontier opens up fraught spaces inscribed by tensions and contradictions that produce what Omar Jabary Salamanca and colleagues term an "instability" that "plagues" the "settler colonial structure undergirding Israeli practice."[15] In response to this instability, they argue that the Israeli state deploys "a painful array" of practices, including "aerial and maritime bombardment, massacre and invasion, home demolitions, land theft, identity card confiscation, racist laws and loyalty tests, the wall, the siege of Gaza, cultural appropriation, [and] dependence on willing (unwilling) native collaboration." In this state of instability and, as noted above, in the context of the impossibility of bringing to a closure the process of settler state formation due to the realities of the permanent frontier and the ongoing resistance and survivance of Palestinians, Barakat explains how this compels the Israeli settler state to mobilize a "particularly wide range of settler-colonial modalities [that] co-exist simultaneously."[16]

In this chapter, my concern is to identify and name the specificity of a number of settler colonial modalities that are characterized by their biopolitical and necropolitical targeting of more-than-human entities in the context of the occupation, its permanent frontier, and across its microgeographies and forensic ecologies; these modalities constitute differential aspects of the "painful array" of practices for ensuring the ongoing violent dynamics of the occupation.[17] In the context of the forensic ecologies I examine, it is clear, as Jad Isaac and Abeer Safar underscore, that "the Palestinian environment has been the first victim of Israel's occupation and practices."[18] This is not to establish a hierarchy of victims. Rather, the significance of this statement resides in the fact that any form of life, human or otherwise, is foundationally based on the viability of the very ecologies that constitute life's conditions of possibility; concomitantly, the destruction of one impacts the other. Ecologies are at once biological *and* spatial: living entities cannot subsist outside the nutritive locus of a material territory. My approach, in other words, aims to address Samer Alatout's call for a "new focus on the double, territorial-and bio-effects of power"[19] that effectively combines settler colonial territorial practices with regimes biopolitically oriented by statist objectives "to *foster* life or *disallow* it to the point of death."[20]

Situated in this context, settler biopolitical practices of ecological destruction emerge as intersectionally linked with settler colonial ambitions of territorial expropriation and expansion. This settler-biopolitical nexus is implicit in Wolfe's assertion that "land is life—or, at least, is necessary for life. Thus contests for land can be—indeed, often are—contests for life."[21] And settler colonial practices of the clearing of Indigenous peoples from their land are critically interlinked with the deployment of ecocidal strategies.[22] Kyle Powys Whyte speaks to what is at stake for Indigenous peoples when contesting settler colonial ecocidal regimes: "Settlers can only make a homeland by creating social institutions that physically carve their origin, religious and cultural narratives, social ways of life and political and economic systems (e.g., property) into the waters, soils, air and other environmental dimensions of territory or landscape. That is, settler ecologies have to be inscribed into indigenous ecologies."[23] The correlative of this, he concludes, is that "settler colonialism can be interpreted as a form of *environmental injustice* that wrongfully interferes with and erases the sociological contexts required for indigenous populations to experience the world as a place infused with responsibilities to humans, nonhumans and ecosystems."[24] Glen Sean Coulthard elaborates on the intersectional nature of anticolonialism and relational ecological ethics: "Stated bluntly, the theory and practice of Indigenous anticolonialism, including Indigenous anticapitalism, is best understood as a struggle primarily inspired by and oriented around *the question of land*—a struggle not only *for* land in the material sense, but also deeply *informed* by what the land *as system of reciprocal relations and obligations* can teach us about our lives in relation to one another and the natural world in nondominating and nonexploitative terms."[25] Both Whyte and Coulthard here bring into acute focus the key intersectional categories that orient this chapter: the nonnegotiable nexus between decolonizing practices and relational ecological ethics, and the biopolitical links between settler colonialism, ecocidal practices, and the attendant destruction of ethical responsibilities to humans, more-than-humans, and ecosystems.

A number of studies have emerged that track the imbrication of settler colonialism with practices of ecocide and environmental degradation in the context of the occupied territories, such as the work of Damien Short and Haifa Rashed, who analyze the ecocidal impact of settler practices in Palestine, and Seif Da'Na, who discusses the destructive impact of Israel's water policies on Palestine's environment by examining how "the nature of Zionist colonial scheme (agriculture, industry, life style, etc.) is one of the underlying reasons for the interlacement of national and ecological factors."[26] In "Settler Colonialism and Ecocide," D. A. Jaber outlines the entangled nature of these two titular categories in the context of the occupied territories: "As settler colonial ideology, Zionism seeks to erase all traces of Palestinian indigenous life from Palestine (inclusive of present-day Israel and the o[ccupied] P[alestinian] T[erritories]). This erasure produces inevitable ecological destruction. As such, it is fundamental to re-write the formulation settler 'space' as inherently ecocidal, as it implicates not only the indigenous population but also the local and regional ecologies."[27] Jaber examines the consequences of this formulation in the specific context of Al-Khader in the occupied Palestinian territories: "The case of Al-Khader . . . provides a framework to understand how the environmental degradation resulting from the creation of settler space becomes ecocide, through the intersections of land expropriation, settler violence and devastation, acts of war . . . and discriminatory policies."[28]

In his historical account of the emergence of the term *ecocide*, David Zierler discusses how the term was first coined in 1970 by botanist Arthur W. Galston and a group of fellow scientists "to denounce the environmental destruction" and its potential impact on human health that resulted from the US military's use of herbicidal warfare in the Vietnam War.[29] U. C. Jha, in his analysis of ecocide, glosses the term as referring to "human activities and practices that cause widespread damage to habitats and environments."[30] In his analysis of ecocide and modern warfare, Franz Broswimmer writes that acts of "war associated with ecocide include . . . the military use of defoliants . . . the uses of explosives to impair soil quality or to enhance the prospect of disease; the bull-dozing of forests or croplands for military purposes . . . and, finally, the forcible and permanent removal of humans or animals from their habitual place of habitation on a large scale to expedite the pursuit of military or other objectives."[31] As I evidence in this chapter, all these ecocidal techniques have, in varying degrees, been deployed by the Israeli state in the occupied territories.

Interlocking Biopolitical Modalities of the More-Than-Human

In working to name the different and site-specific modalities that biopolitical formations of power assume in relation to the particularity of their intended targets and confronted by Israel's biopolitical destruction, expropriation, and control of Palestine's water resources and infrastructure, I coin the term *aquapolitics* to highlight the biopolitics of water. Similarly, in my examination of Israel's large-scale destruction in the occupied territories of vegetal life, including orchards and olive groves, I develop the term *phytopolitics* (from the Greek word, *phyton*, for plant). Drawing on the Greek word for soil, *pedon*, I deploy the term *pedonpolitics* to describe the poisoning by Israeli military forces of the soil on Palestinian land: directly through the injection of toxic herbicides and indirectly through the contamination of the soil by the leaching of toxic chemicals from spent ordnance. I add to this biopolitical ensemble of the more-than-human the modality of *aeropolitics* (from the Greek word, *aer*, for air)—as a biopolitical modality that affects the air and atmosphere. As I discuss below, the IDF's bombardment of Gaza effectively weaponized Gaza's air and atmosphere, both during the actual campaign and continuing long after its cessation, with pathogenic elements that continue to generate deleterious health effects on Gaza's population and its more-than-human entities.

In deploying the terms *zoopolitics*, *aquapolitics*, *phytopolitics*, *aeropolitics*, and *pedonpolitics*, my intention is to enlarge the biopolitical aperture to encompass qualitatively different targets—animals, water, vegetal life, air, and soil—that require the state to exercise different techniques of operation in order to realize its intended bio- or necropolitical goals. These different modalities of statist operation must be seen as operating within inextricable systems of relation that are nested in the superordinate matrix of the biopolitical. These different modalities of statist operation are tributaries that flow from the governing category of biopolitics. As tributaries, they affirm, consolidate, and extend biopolitical relations of power in a capillary manner through grounded, site-specific modalities. They are at once its adjuncts and its site-specific on-the-ground operatives designed to target specific ecological entities. Collectively, they delineate the contours of the forensic ecologies that, in the context of the occupied Palestinian territories, evidence Israel's differential and diffuse operations of biopolitical war by other means.[32] Moreover, as I discussed in the book's introduction, my analysis of the operations of biopolitics on both human and more-than-human entities is critically informed by a forensic concentration on ecologies that constitute their conditions of survival and that, in death, work to proffer, in terms of their forensic attestation, evidence of the violence that transpired in those sites of destruction.

Even as they emerge as differential categories, these configurations simultaneously evidence interlocking relations of site-specific modalities of biopower that work to intensify biopolitical outcomes in the conduct of war by other means: for example, Israel's aquapolitical expropriation of Palestinian water resources augments its phytopolitical campaign of the destruction of Palestinian vegetal life. Simultaneously, there are also operative relations of discontinuity between these different biopolitical modalities in that they work to produce their own unintended effects. For example, Israel's phytopolitical bulldozing of Palestinian olive groves generates insurgent Palestinian practices of resistant, clandestine replantings of olive trees. In sum, I deploy the named specificities of these different modalities of biopolitical power to (1) heterogenize the otherwise homogeneous category of biopolitics; (2) disrupt and overturn the anthropocentric presuppositions that are otherwise embedded in the superordinate category of biopolitics, presuppositions that lead to the effacement of the other-than-human entities that are also the targets of biopolitical power in the context of militarized zones; and (3) cast the operations of biopolitics in a distinctly ecological register by focusing specifically on its ecocidal effects.

In reflecting on how "the dynamic and spatially varied nature of the occupation has allowed the Israeli occupation of the West Bank and Gaza to continue for so many years,"[33] Smith proposes that the resilience and tenacity of the settler project is enabled by its dynamic capacity to respond and adapt to the different demands of site-specific microgeographies—precisely by deploying a variegated ensemble of techniques to secure the occupation. In this chapter, my attention to the Israeli state's deployment of different biopolitical modalities of the more-than-human across a diverse spectrum of ecologies works to illuminate another biopolitical dimension of the larger settler apparatus and its differential (yet often interlocking) strategies for the securitization and expansion of the settler project across Palestinian land. Furthermore, by intertwining a decolonizing critique of settler colonialism and a biopolitical analysis of the more-than-human, I intend to demonstrate, in line with the

Indigenous scholars discussed in my introduction, that the two approaches must operate at the same time to materialize decolonizing and deanthropocentrizing strategies that challenge the violent intersectional formation constituted by the settler colonial biopolitical state.[34] As I show throughout this chapter, Palestinian life is deeply entangled with what Winona LaDuke terms "all our relations":[35] trees, animals, air, water, and soil. The world of the more-than-human is coconstitutive of Palestinian identity—my discussion, in the latter part of this chapter, of Hala Al-Ghawi and her beloved lemon tree in occupied East Jerusalem exemplifies this point.

Facilitating Ecocide: "No Rules of Engagement"

In the context of Operation Protective Edge, as a number of IDF soldiers testified in the report *This Is How We Fought in Gaza*, "the IDF's modus operandi . . . was *shoot to kill anything that moves*," and its "mission [was] to leave the area razed." As I discuss in detail below, this often ensured the destruction of a range of more-than-human entities caught in the crosshairs of the military campaign.[36] After noting that "on the basis of an analysis of satellite imagery . . . some areas [of Gaza] were virtually razed," the UN's report on Operation Protective Edge continues: "The evidence gathered by the commission, including the assessment of the episodes above, video and photo materials, observations by UNITAR-UNOSAT [which provides satellite imagery to the UN system] and anecdotal testimonies by IDF soldiers, indicate that the vast scale of destruction may have been adopted as tactics of war."[37] These acts of what the laws of war term *wanton destruction* were often facilitated by the failure to adhere to rules of engagement.[38] As an IDF soldier located in the northern Gaza Strip notes, in the conduct of the IDF's Operation Protective Edge, "There were no rules of engagement." His company operated, he explains, under the principle of "just blasting things away."[39] Another IDF soldier states: "There was no such thing as requesting authorization. Just fire."[40] Rules of engagement are, according to the laws of war, the military directives that authorize and limit the exercise of military force in a combat situation. An IDF captain further evidences the soldier's admission: "Rules of engagement are part of the combat procedure, it's the first thing given to every company that goes in—and [during Operation Protective Edge] there were none."[41] "You shoot at bushes, trees," says another IDF soldier, "at all sorts of houses you suddenly run into, at more trees. You fire a blast and don't think twice about it."[42]

The lack of rules of engagement establishes a killing practice that is at once systematic (the mission is to raze everything) and governed by chance:

who gets killed is also based on the aleatory variables of contingency. Operative in the IDF's lack of rules of engagement and its resultant indiscriminate killing practices is the military concept of "obligatory contingency," in which, as Manuel DeLanda notes, the relations between the parts "are not logically necessary but only contingently obligatory."[43] There is no logical necessity, to draw on an example I discuss below, for IDF soldiers to kill a horse they may encounter; rather, as there are no rules of engagement, the chance encounter with anything the soldiers "suddenly run into" is the trigger that catalyzes the soldier's contingent obligation to kill. The lethality of the IDF's military mission is encapsulated by the complex admixture of overdetermined forces (including settler colonial, military, and religio-nationalist) that resulted in the razing of certain areas in Gaza (for example, Shujai'iya, Rafah, and Khuza'a)[44] and the random, nonlinear forces governed by the contingent obligation to shoot to kill any entity unfortunate enough to stray into the soldiers' path. In other words, even if there are no rules of engagement as such, this does not mean that there is only unregulated chaos in the military conduct of the IDF in their deployment in Operation Protective Edge. On the contrary, in keeping with the operational logic of chaos theory, the seemingly random acts of shooting, bombing, and bulldozing of any Palestinian entity must be seen as local self-organizing fractals of militarized violence that expose clear patterns of self-similarity even in what appears to be the chaos and fog of war. Analogous to the operations of fractal logic, the IDF's alleged practices of wanton military destruction evidence patterns of repetition that are reproduced at progressively smaller scales: for example, the bulldozing of an orchard, the shooting of a tree, a man, a sheep, a dog, and so on. As partly random practices that are yet inscribed by patterns of self-similarity, they constitute what DeLanda terms military forms of "organized chaos."[45]

A number of IDF soldiers evidence the seemingly random acts of shooting whatever Palestinian entity is unfortunate enough to stumble across their path. One IDF soldier describes the shooting of a horse: "It was night, and our night vision showed white and green—white indicates someone's body heat. This soldier turned around and looked at the screen and suddenly saw something white, so he fired a burst at it straight away, and suddenly I saw a horse collapse to the ground."[46] Terrorized by the barrage of machine-gun fire systematically disintegrating their orchard refuge, a white horse breaks into the field of vision of these soldiers. Caught in the crosshairs of machine-gun fire, the horse is reduced to little more than a bullet-ridden carcass. This phantom horse, specter of *Guernica*, embodies the terror of a machinic violence that kills whatever strays across its path. The lethality of this military practice is brought into sharp focus by the IDF's murder of an elderly and unarmed civilian. I cite from the testimony of another IDF soldier: the Palestinian civilian, "in his late 60s, early 70s," posing no threat, was first shot "beneath his left ribs. . . . The old man took the bullet, lay down on the ground, then a friend of that soldier [who fired the shot] came over and also shot the man, while he was already down. For the hell of it, he shot two more bullets at his legs." Following the shooting of this civilian, "a D9 (armoured bulldozer) came over and dropped a mound of rubble and that was the end of it."[47] With the dumping of a mound of rubble on his corpse, this Palestinian civilian was dispatched with a decisive finality: his "neutralization" was "verified." His unceremonious burial beneath a tumulary mound deposited by a bulldozer evokes a spectral archive of similar homicidal acts perpetrated by military forces that have violated Rule 89 of international humanitarian law, which unequivocally states, "Murder is prohibited."[48]

The IDF's repeated failure to apply rules of engagement in the context of Operation Protective Edge is also evidenced in the account of another IDF soldier who describes the destruction of chicken coops, with live chickens still inside, "flattened by the D9s [armoured bulldozers]. You saw all kinds of chickens . . . totally in pieces."[49] In this case, the IDF's bulldozers violently transmute these living birds into a crushed heap of avian waste. When this soldier's battalion finally left the area, all that remained was "a hill of ruins, pretty much—lots of concrete, and sadly also large swaths of agricultural land dug up by tanks."[50] Ali Alommor, a Palestinian farmer, describes the other-than-human victims of the IDF's military assault: "'We escaped almost-certain death, leaving dead camels, donkeys, cows and birds. The tank shells hit the trees, the stones and even the animals,' he said as he inspected the massive damage caused to his crops, surrounded by the stench of the decaying flesh of the dead animals around him."[51] In Alommor's testimony, the binding relations that inscribe forensic ecologies of military violence are clearly enunciated: "He acknowledged that animals that were lucky enough to avoid Israeli missiles or bulldozers on the farm eventually died from starvation. Food and water were unavailable when the family had to escape their home." "Israeli troops," says Alommor, "shoot at anything that moves, even when they can see it's only a camel, donkey or chicken, kept outdoors in summer."[52] An IDF soldier describes the "issue of the [military's] killing of animals": "It was during one of the operations in the Achzarit, even the first, I think. The company sergeant major was a commander of one of the APCs [armored personnel carrier], and there were horses and sheep there, maybe even donkeys, and he sprayed bullets with the MAG [machine gun] out of the window and maybe even over them. . . . He shot the animals."[53]

The affective dimensions that result from the IDF's killing of Palestinian more-than-human life are repeatedly marked by Palestinian survivors of Operation Protective Edge. On his return to his home, Ali Alommor found that

> all 30 sheep had been savagely killed. "I wish I knew that they hadn't suffered," he said. But his brother and neighbours doubt this. Some of the sheep were riddled with bullet holes. One had its head sliced off, and all were covered with flies and worms. Among more dead animals lying around, some were killed by tiny shrapnel wounds. Other dead animals had no visible physical wounds: they probably died from fear, hunger and thirst, with the land destroyed around them, the water polluted and Israeli bulldozers demolishing everything in sight.[54]

Alommor's testimony articulates the material evidence of a forensic "ecology of the aftermath."[55] Omer's description of animals dying "from fear, hunger and thirst, with the land destroyed around them" evinces the interlocking bio- and necropolitical effects of militarized violence as it unfolds across a devastated landscape. The zones of militarized violence that Omer describes in his war testimonies delineate a matrix of suffering that is multidimensional in terms of its spatiotemporal attributes and a/effects. In the wake of the IDF's military campaign of destruction, he documents how different modalities of violence interpenetrate and radiate from these ecologies of destruction. Suffering emerges as diffuse, multiple, enchained, and differentially experienced along the trauma continuum: a ruined and uninhabitable home, animals riddled with bullets, sheep dying the slow agony of thirst and hunger, the water polluted, and a cratered field saturated with toxic residues leaching from spent ordnance.

The prohibition of "wanton destruction" in the conduct of war is encoded in both the 1907 Hague Conventions and the 1949 Geneva Conventions.[56] The IDF's acts of military violence that I have documented here would also constitute war crimes as defined in the Rome Statute of the International Criminal Court, specifically, articles 8(2)(a)(iv) and 8(2)(b)(ii): "extensive destruction or appropriation of property, not justified by military necessity and carried out unlawfully and wantonly" and "intentionally directing attacks against civilian objects, that is, objects which are not military objectives."[57] Under these articles, animals and trees are afforded protection against military violence not in their own right but only as long as they remain under the protective aegis of "civilian objects" and "property" (for a detailed critique of the animal-property nexus in the context of war, see chapter 4). Israel, however, is not a signatory to the statute and thus sees itself as not obligated to comply with any of the articles. Moreover, after the Palestinian Authority joined the International

Criminal Court and prompted it to investigate the alleged war crimes committed by the IDF during Operation Protective Edge, Israel declared it "would seek to 'dismantle this court, a body that represents hypocrisy and gives terror a tailwind.'"[58]

In what follows, I analyze the specific biopolitical modalities of the more-than-human that have been deployed by Israel in the occupied territories and discuss their enduring impact across the broad spectrum of Palestinian life.

Aquapolitics

In the numerous accounts of the destruction of Gaza wreaked by Operation Protective Edge, the focus has been on how Israel targeted the destruction of Gaza's infrastructure: water, electricity, sewerage, hospitals, schools, civilian homes, farms, and so on. Stephen Graham, in his analysis of Israel's large-scale demolition of key infrastructure in the occupied territories, names this process "urbicide."[59] Mohammed Omer titled his meticulous day-to-day account of surviving the 2014 war on Gaza *Shell-Shocked: On the Ground under Israel's Gaza Assault*. Omer's naming of the fact that his observations are "on the ground" highlights the testimonial eyewitness status of his account, while drawing attention to the fact that his observations were conducted on the very harrowed soil of Gaza. In his introduction, Omer reflects on why Gaza's infrastructure was targeted for destruction in this latest IDF assault: "This occupation is not about religion, biblical history or any other excuse used to justify it. It is about water: headwaters, rivers and aquifers. It is about who controls and prospers from natural resources ranging from arable land to natural gas reservoirs under the West Bank and beneath Gaza's coastal waters."[60] Omer then draws attention to what has been termed "Israel's water warfare," in which the objective is to dry Palestine to the point that life is only barely sustainable:

> Amongst the casualties of Israel's latest assault on the Gaza Strip has been the coastal enclave's water infrastructure, which has not been spared deliberate targeting by Israeli missiles. This attack on water infrastructure is neither a new practice nor one that is specific to Gaza but is rather part and parcel of a sustained Israeli campaign to . . . make everyday life unbearable. . . . The policy of denying Palestinian communities access to water can be seen as a tool of warfare. . . . The ramifications of this policy are vast. They include long-term environmental degradation, both short- and long-term dangers to public health, and the effective denial of access to clean drinking water to a substantial civilian population.[61]

In the context of Israel's biopolitical water warfare, one can identify the specific operations of *aquapolitics*, as the control and management of an ecology's water supply so as to enable the flourishing of Israeli life and, conversely, to bring Palestinians to the point of virtual survival. The ecocidal effects of the Israeli state's aquapolitics encompass, in enchained relations, both vegetal and animal life. The illegal settlement of the municipality called Ariel, for example, produces wastewater overflows that impact the Palestinian area governed by the Salfit Council: the polluted water has destroyed seasonal crops and "has brought about the extinction of the deer, rabbits, and foxes once common in the area."[62] A report on the entangled ecological effects of settler aquapolitical strategies on Palestinian life documents how "sewerage water from Israeli settlements—industrial, agricultural, and domestic—flows untreated onto Palestinian land [of each of the governorates visited], impacting both people's health and livelihoods. . . . Some farmers have been forced to cease production, harvesting crops, and grazing livestock because of the impact of the unknown toxins in the wastewater."[63] As Jaber documents in the case of the town of Al-Khader and the dumping of settler sewerage onto Palestinian farmlands, "sewerage water is acidic[,] causing the crops to burn, poisoning fruit and creating a long-term toxicity threat."[64]

Israel's aquapolitics is being played out not only through the expropriation of Palestinian rivers and aquifers but also through Israel's targeted destruction of wells and sewer systems.[65] Operation Protective Edge saw the IDF destroy "about 778 underground wells."[66] This destruction of the water infrastructure has been worsened by the power Israel exerts on the rebuilding of water projects in the West Bank: "On the one hand, Palestinian water projects all over the West Bank need an approval by the Joint Water Committee (JWC), where Israel has de facto veto power. Only 56 percent of Palestinian projects regarding water and sanitation were granted permits by the JWC (against a near 100 percent approval rate for the Israeli projects), and only a third of those could actually be implemented."[67] Further, Palestinian water projects "also require a permit by the Israeli Civil Administration, which are notoriously difficult to obtain." Palestinians, desperate to secure their water and sanitation infrastructure, often build without official approval, thereby giving Israel license to destroy these same water projects.[68] Israel's aquapolitics operates along at least two identifiable axes: the literal drying up of Palestinian life because of the theft of water resources and the production of pathogenic ecologies that have destructive effects on the broad spectrum of Palestinian life. Erin McKenna outlines the discriminatory laws that underpin Israel's aquapolitics and facilitate settler expansion:

In violation of the UN Declaration on Permanent Sovereignty over Natural Resources (1962), Israel controls the water of the West Bank. At the same time that Israel diverts West Bank water for its own purposes, permission to drill new wells and construct new systems of irrigation is denied the Palestinians. This policy promotes the idea of a West Bank dependent on Israel, integrated into its water system, the two become one, not by annexation, but by the necessity of the situation.[69]

As Palestinian farmers can no longer cultivate land because of the lack of a reliable supply of water, Israel deems the land "dry, barren": "Once left uncultivated, the land is claimed as the state's property . . . or it is simply sold because it is useless to the Palestinian farmer who cannot water it."[70] Aquapolitics, in other words, enables the expansive project of settler expropriation of Palestinian land.[71] Stephen Gasteyer, Jad Isaac, Jane Hillal, and Sean Walsh demonstrate, in their mapping of the historical nexus of land/water in the context of the occupied territories, how "land grabbing has been linked to water grabbing" and has been crucially implicated in the Israeli state's "colonial schemes."[72] In her analysis of what she terms "Israel's systemic water war," Muna Dajani elaborates on how Israel's aquapolitics further facilitate settler practices of displacement: "Over the long term, Israel's targeting of water infrastructure also deeply influences the relationship that Palestinians have with their land. By depriving farmers of water, they drive them off their land."[73]

Israel's aquapolitics is instrumental in generating interlinked and amplified practices of expropriation: its theft of Palestinian water compels Gaza's municipality to buy "an extra 5 million cubic meters of water every year from Israel."[74] Palestinians' water resources are so rationed as to place them within a situation that generates an aquapolitical version of the restricted caloric regime:

> Palestinians are allotted a small fixed amount, resulting in constant water shortages. Strikingly, figures show that the average water consumption for domestic, commercial, and industrial water consumption in the West Bank is approximately 79 liters a day per person, less than the World Health Organization recommendation of 100 liters of water per person per day. At the same time, the average domestic, commercial, and industrial water consumption in Israel is more than four times that figure, or about 287 liters per person per day.[75]

Articulated in this metrical measurement and asymmetrical allocation of water resources is a biopolitical regime constituted, on the one hand, by a

Palestinian aquapolitics of water deprivation and bare subsistence and, conversely, an Israeli aquapolitics of abundance and flourishment.

The IDF's destruction of Gaza's sewer system in Operation Protective Edge and the resultant contamination of water supplies have resulted in widespread outbreaks of diverse illnesses and disease in Gaza, including gastric diseases, scabies, and lice.[76] Abu Rida, a Gazan whose son and brother were killed in Khan Younis by Israeli air strikes, articulates the epidemiological stakes of Israel's aquapolitics: "We escaped almost certain death from Israeli gunfire, but now it seems instead of sending missiles to kill us, Israel wants to kill us with disease."[77] The use of epidemiological warfare, a topic I discuss in more detail below, is another characteristic feature of how the settler state works to ensure the subjugation, displacement, and elimination of Indigenous populations.[78]

The biopolitical dimensions of Israel's aquapolitics are complexly enmeshed in terms of their toxic effects. For example, the destruction of Gaza's sewerage plants has caused millions of litres of raw sewage to pour into Gaza's coastal waters, creating a toxic marine ecology of "widespread algal blooms": "This then contaminates . . . the fish upon which many Gazans rely."[79] One report on the environmental impact of Operation Protective Edge on Gaza evidences the biopolitical effects of polluted seawater on Gazans: "Since the war more people have suffered from skin rashes and diseases after swimming in the sea as compared to before the war."[80]

Framed as pollutable spaces that can be rendered into ecological wastelands, the Palestinian territories become sites for Israel's dumping of toxic wastes:

> Solid wastes from Israeli settlements and military camps throughout the West Bank are dumped without restriction on Palestinian land, fields and side roads, and industry regularly moves from Israel to the West Bank, where labour is cheaper, environmental regulations are lenient and waste products, generated from the production of aluminium, leather tanning, textile dyeing, batteries, fiberglass, plastics and other chemicals, can flow freely down to Palestinian villages in surrounding valleys.[81]

Eleven Israeli chemical factories have been built on the "seam zone on confiscated Palestinian land"; in this zone they "can pollute with impunity," as "industrial settlements in the West Bank operate under the ambiguous legal frameworks controlled by the occupying Israeli military. . . . Even the Israeli State Comptroller described these conditions as 'bordering on lawlessness' which 'place the well-being, health and lives of the workers in the industrial zones in real danger.'"[82] An environmental report on the unregulated disposal of toxic chemicals in the West Bank from Israeli industries documents the "dumping of solid wastes transported from inside the Green Line, which contain a high content of lead. In the same village, they are investigating the deaths of 25 cows in 2014," suspected of having died due to the "high ammonium content in the water, specifically as connected to sewerage water discharges from settlements."[83] In her conceptualization of settler colonial "wastelanding," Traci Voyles identifies the wasteland as a "racial and spatial signifier that renders the environment and the bodies that inhabit it pollutable."[84] Operative in this process of wastelanding Palestinian lands and ecologies is what Ben Lorber terms "Israel's environmental colonialism and ecoapartheid."[85] Mazin Qumsiyeh describes the ecocidal effects of the occupation in Palestine in terms of an "environmental 'nakba,'" cataloging in detail its devastating effects across the diversity of Palestinian ecologies, even as he refuses to lapse into a nihilist posture: "As our current situation is unconscionable," he writes, "we overcome the innate human tendency to adapt. Instead, we resist."[86] In what follows, I analyze the wastelanding of Gaza's ecologies in the wake of Operation Protective Edge, focusing specifically on the ecocidal impact of the military campaign on Gaza's soils, air, and water and the resultant epidemiological effects on its diverse living entities.

Pedonpolitics and Aeropolitics

In the report 2014 War on Gaza: Participatory Environmental Impact Assessment, Ahmad Saleh Safi writes how, over the fifty-one-day military campaign, "Israel bombed thousands of tons of ammunition onto Gaza through airstrikes, naval and terrestrial artillery, and land invasions. Numerous types of bombs and missiles were used by the Israelis including arguably unlawful weapons such as Flechettes artillery or rocked rounds, white phosphorus, Dense Inert Metal Explosive (DIME), and Depleted Uranium (DU). These bombs may cause chemical or even radioactive material air pollution."[87] The IDF's use of white phosphorus targeted both Palestinian civilians, setting their bodies on fire and often burning them "to the bone," and Palestinian shrubs and trees, burning them so as to create smoke screens for its troop movements.[88] The "very high" concentrations of phosphorus found in Gaza's soil have been identified as causing a range of ecocidal effects, including the destruction of "the natural ecosystem of animals and plants and the contaminat[ion] of agricultural products through the food chain."[89]

The above-listed "nonconventional and experimental weapons usually contain a mixture of explosive material, cobalt, nickel, iron and tungsten which work together to create extremely dense microshrapnel, as well as its carcinogenic substances."[90] In the wake of the fast violence generated by the explosive material dropped on Gaza by the IDF, what unfolds in these ecologies of the aftermath is something that Rob Nixon terms "slow violence." This is "a violence that is dispersed across time and space, an attritional violence that is typically not viewed as violence at all. Violence is customarily conceived as an event or action that is immediate in time, explosive and spectacular in space, and as erupting into instant sensational visibility."[91] Slow violence is "incremental and accretive," so "its calamitous repercussions play out across a range of temporal scales."[92]

Slow violence names the delayed environmental impacts of war. After Operation Protective Edge, "In almost all the localities in the Gaza Strip, the participants in the focus group discussions [assessing the environmental impacts of the war] attested to significant impacts on soil fertility and quality . . . first, the removal and burning of the top soil as a result of heavy air-bombing; and second, damage to the physical characteristics of the soil due to the compaction caused by the use of heavy machinery including tanks and bulldozers."[93] Safi documents the combined pedonpolitical effects of fast and slow military violence in Gaza: "The lands which were hit by air bombs have sustained extensive soil damage due to the explosion of these rockets which created crater size holes in the ground, displacing all of the soil. . . . Such loss means losing all the biological, physical and biotic characteristics that made the soil suitable for agriculture."[94] The slow ecocidal violence that inscribes this bombed soil has meant a loss of soil fertility: "Even after being levelled and treated, these lands are either completely infertile or produce significantly lower crop yields than before as reported by focus group participants in 88% of the localities of the [Gaza] Strip."[95]

As biopolitical operations are always already situated within an ecology, the different biopolitical modalities that operate in a given ecology often have interlocking relations in terms of their ecocidal effects. Amal Sarsour, who works in the field of environmental health in Gaza, describes how the bombing of Gaza over fifty-one days "led to pollution with high levels of hazardous contaminants." The air pollution generated by explosive material, Sarsour writes, was further amplified by the IDF's "targeting of Gaza Power Plant (GPP) which provides about a third of the Gaza strip with electricity, causing a release of large amounts of black smoke clouds, resulting from the burning of 2 million litres of diesel, which was stored in the tanks before the aggression. These clouds were loaded with large quantities of toxic gases and fine particles of toxic and carcinogenic [sic] that spread into the air and inhaled by people around, which led to many serious respiratory diseases." She then outlines the slow violence effects of aeropolitics on Gazan life: "The real concern is that people can inhale uranium [emitted from spent ordnance], and this can lead to diseases and health problems, including congenital deformities in children." Sarsour points to the transgenerational trauma that exposure to radioactive waste can generate: "Bombarding the agricultural lands [of Gaza] with thousands of tons of explosive materials of different types may pollute the soil with heavy metals such as chromium, cobalt, cadmium, copper and lead. . . . Some of these pollutants might be radioactive in nature such as depleted uranium."[96] The biopolitical effects of pedonpolitics on Gazans may thus "result in the pollution of crops cultivated in the impacted lands, which may cause serious diseases and epidemics in the long run including but not limited to cancer."[97]

The issue of air pollution in Gaza generated by Operation Protective Edge has persisted beyond the cessation of the military campaign due to the existence of demolition waste resulting from the ongoing clearing of bombed civilian structures:

> Participants from 96% of the 25 localities of the Gaza Strip asserted that the air quality in the areas that host demolition waste removal sites, storage facilities, and crushers are still widely degraded. These areas suffer from dust, particulate matter, and sometimes lead air pollution . . . as confirmed by experts. Chemical tests of the air quality of sites that host demolition waste crushers, storage facilities and removal sites proved the existence of particulate matter and lead air pollution many times above the levels identified by WHO [World Health Organization] as acceptable.[98]

I have included the discussion of both pedonpolitics and aeropolitics under one subhead because the environmental impact of Operation Protective Edge on Gaza's air quality was indissociably linked to the military strategies deployed by the IDF on the very soil of the Gaza Strip.[99] The interlocking effects of biopolitical modalities of pedonpolitics, aquapolitics, phytopolitics, and aeropolitics are also illustrated by the practice of "the Israeli military . . . spraying Palestinian crops with chemicals that will cause the surrounding vegetation to wilt and prevent its growth."[100] An IDF spokesperson explains the rationale behind it: "The aerial spraying of herbicides and germination inhibitors was conducted in the area along the border fence last week in order to enable optimal and continuous security operations."[101] The so-called no-go zone that runs along the border fence of Gaza and "amounts to an estimated 17 per cent of the entire territory of the Gaza Strip and a third of its agricultural lands, erodes into the Strip's most vital and fertile soils."[102] As Palestinian officials remarked, "After maintaining an unofficial 'no-go zone' on the Palestinian side of the border with Gaza, the IDF is now seemingly implementing a 'no-grow zone.'"[103] The resultant no-grow zone emerges, to draw on an apposite settler colonial trope, as a type of terra nullius that has been biopolitically voided of life. Anwar Abu Assi, a manager at the Palestinian Ministry of Agriculture, describes the ecocidal effects thus: "Herbicides are sprayed in high concentrations. Thus, they remain embedded in the soil, and then find their way to the water basin."[104] Assi draws attention here to the combined effects of interlocking biopolitical modalities that operate, as I discuss below, at atomized levels and that have diffuse and complex results.

Atomized Biopolitics of Attritional Violence

In the introduction, I invoked Merleau-Ponty's concept of the "flesh of the world" as a way of conceptualizing an ecological understanding of life that overrides anthropocentrism's epistemological limitations and constraints. A biopolitical conceptualization of the flesh of the world entails, in the context of Gaza after Operation Protective Edge, the assumption of a multiperspectival vision on the deployment of ecocidal campaigns of statist violence—military or otherwise. In what follows, I return to the report by Ahamad Saleh Safi, *2014 War on Gaza Strip: Participatory Environmental Impact Assessment*, to put this multiperspectival vision into practice. The report mobilizes both participatory informants and professionals working in public health and the environment to identify the impact of Operation Protective Edge on the environment and its human and more-than-human entities. It names particular localities; it identifies, through the combined use of participatory accounts and expert medical knowledge, epidemiological phenomena; and it attempts to correlate them to the sources of the environmental pollution that resulted from the war.

In the context of the report, the macrogeography of the Gaza Strip is disaggregated into a series of microgeographies delineated by the neighborhoods that experienced the worst impact of the military campaign: for example, Shujai'iya, Rafah, and Khuza'a. Embedded within these microgeographies are multiple microecologies that, in fractal terms, are replicated in ever-descending order: housing estates, fields, beaches, human bodies, plants, soil biota, and so on. Situated in this multiperspectival vision, a biopolitics of the more-than-human attests to the way state violence directed toward a targeted population (here, Palestinians) addresses, in Foucauldian terms, a "multiplicity" and affects "a global mass"[105] that encompasses everything from human subjects to marine and soil biota.

In their analysis of Israel's policy of regularly "mowing the grass" in Gaza through the deployment of recursive military operations, Efraim Inbar and Eitan Shamir state, "Israel finds itself in protracted intractable conflict with extremely hostile non-state entities, which is qualitatively different from an inter-state conflict."[106] As discussed in chapter 1, Inbar and Shamir argue that "the use of force is therefore not intended to obtain impossible political goals, but rather to debilitate the capabilities of the enemy to harm Israel."[107] I view the Israeli state's deployment of different biopolitical modalities of the more-than-human as working toward this effect of debilitation—understood here precisely in Puar's biopolitical terms.[108] In the context of the postbellum ecologies of Gaza, the deployment of aquapolitical, pedonpolitical, phytopolitical, and aeropolitical modalities works to generate debilitating regimes of slow violence. This lingering, incremental, and attritional mode of violence is exercised through the assemblage of interlocking biopolitical modalities. My use of the term *attritional* is not rhetorical. I take it from Avi Kober's *Israel's Wars of Attrition*. Kober glosses attritional warfare thus: "What is unique to such wars is that the depletion is gradual in the true sense of erosion: i.e., progressing over a considerable period of time. Furthermore, characterizing a war as being one of attrition requires that the cumulative effect of erosion over a protracted period be determined one of the most prominent characteristics of the conflict."[109] Israel's wars of attrition in the occupied territories, once situated within a comparative frame, emerge as standard erosive strategies deployed by other settler colonial states.[110]

In what follows, I enlarge the scope of Israel's policy of attritional wars beyond the period of actual armed conflict. My focus is largely on Gaza's postbellum ecologies of the aftermath. In these war-ravaged contexts, a different type of war of attrition unfolds well after the cessation of military operations. As discussed above, this is an attritional war of slow violence that operates on the principle of "the cumulative effect of erosion over a protracted period." In the Palestinian context, this attritional war is spatially extensive, as it differentially encompasses Gaza's microgeographies and its microecologies. It is temporally lingering and diffuse: its effects are often deferred across time and transgenerational bodies. Viewing the living body (human or otherwise) as a microecology positioned within a matrix of different biopolitical modalities of attritional violence, its physiological processes of ingestion (of contaminated food and water), inhalation (of polluted air) and percutaneous absorption (of heavy metals such as lead) become inscribed with pathogenic and necropolitical effects. Couched in Foucauldian biopolitical terms, a war-induced pathology in Gaza is "something that slips into life, perpetually gnaws at it, diminishes it and weakens it."[111] When understood in the biopolitical sense, Foucault underscores, "kill-ing" also resides in the simple "fact of exposing someone to death"—in this case, through a range of different biopolitical modalities of the more-than-human and their cumulative effects of attritional, ecocidal violence.

One can, at this juncture, analyze what is operative here in terms of an *atomized biopolitics* that impacts targeted entities in the absence of a visibly identifiable agent of violence. In the aftermath of Operation Protective Edge, the IDF is no longer present in the microgeographies of Gaza. What remains is a legacy of ecological destruction and multimodal pollution—of water, soil, and air. In the context of the aftermath of the militarized violence that was inflicted on Gaza, an atomized biopolitics works so that Gazan subjects (in all their multiplicity) expose themselves to a spectrum of pathologies sim-ply through the standard physiological processes that are ineluctable to life: breathing, drinking, and eating within the medium of now-toxic ecologies. An atomized biopolitics of toxic ecologies generates the convergence of physiol-ogy with pathology to form *pathophysiologies* of slow violence. In the absence of a visible and directly identifiable agent of violence (for example, the explosion of a missile), biopolitics, in this toxic context, becomes so atomized and diffuse that it now operates, as Foucault would say, in a capillary-like fashion, gnaw-ing at the body in question and weakening it. This is biopolitics operating at a nucleic level—such as the ingestion of the invisible bacteria and heavy metals contaminating a drink of water or the inhalation of a breath of air laden with invisible carcinogenic particulates.

One significant aspect of the report under analysis pertains to the mapping of the differential impact of toxic biopolitical modalities along gender lines, with Palestinian women consistently identified as most at risk of contracting diseases induced by the military impact. This critical gender differentiation is explained, in the report, by gendered divisions of labor that put women more at risk of being exposed to pollutants: for example, in the context of polluted water, "women are the ones who use such water every day, multiple times to wash clothes and dishes, cook, clean children etc. Thus women's extended ex-posure makes them more vulnerable to any changes in water quality."[112] The report's findings on the differential gendered impact on Palestinians living under occupation align with other studies that demonstrate how women have been placed most at risk within this toxic regime. As Elise Young underscores in her analysis of Palestinian women's health in the context of the occupation, the "concept of health is historically specific, gendered and, in . . . Palestine, connected to the processes of colonization and the formation of the modern [Israeli] nation-state."[113]

In the report's sustained documentation and analysis of the environmental impact of Operation Protective Edge on Gaza, under the rubric of "Environmental Related Diseases," Safi writes:

> In almost all localities (100%) people complained of increases in the spread of many diseases that *may* stem from environmental pollution. As can be seen from the following table, the most repeatedly mentioned diseases are skin diseases including rash, cancer (72% of the localities)[,] . . . premature birth resulting in death (48% of all localities), and respiratory diseases (44% of all localities). . . . Air pollution *can* cause cancer, premature birth, lung and respiratory disease. . . . Exposure to organically polluted seawater *may* impose a set of health risks such as eye and ear infections, skin lesions, hepatitis, diarrhea and gastroenteritis, and respiratory illness. . . . Moreover, exposure to contamination by war remnants including the remnants of exploded shells, rockets, etc. *can* be the cause of an unknown number of diseases.[114]

The report then names the different Gazan microgeographies that were heavily impacted by the war and, over the next four pages, tabulates the various "war induced environmental pollution induced diseases" that were found to be prevalent in each locale: for example, "Locality: Al Nuseirat; Impacts: Skin disease, Cancer, Infant deaths, Congenital anomalies, Respiratory diseases; Gender: Women; Vulnerable Groups: Children."[115] The gridded structure of report's tables establishes a relational system among a microgeography, a pathology, the participants' "opinion regarding potential gender differentiation in terms of impact," and those most vulnerable to the named disease. The matching of the experiential dimensions of a disease with the clinical symptomatologies of an identifiable pathology enables the transition from the category of anecdotal account to the domain of medico-scientific evidence. Yet even as the report states that "these increases in incidences of disease are supported by the literature as a result of air pollution, seawater contamination, soil pollution, and use of unlawful weapons during war,"[116] I want to draw attention to the many qualifications in the above excerpt, as they underline the complex nature of biopolitical modalities that operate at atomized levels within the polluted ecologies left in the wake of a military operation.

An atomized biopolitics effectively works to embed itself within the body of a subject exposed to toxic pollutants. As emblematic of the operations of slow violence, it marks the "persistence of unofficial hostilities in the cellular domain, the untidy, attritional lethality that moves through the tissue, blood, and bones."[117] It evinces a biopolitical modality that blurs the outside/inside nexus of environment/body through molecular agents that become coextensive with the very physiological processes that are constitutive of life and that simultaneously convert these processes into phenomena of morbidity: from reactive diseases such as eye inflammation (resulting from exposure to demolition waste) to gene-altering diseases such as cancer (resulting from the effects of genotoxicity). A biopolitical chiasma signs the polluted sites of occupied Gaza and its flesh of the world, as the body of a living subject becomes interleaved with the toxic particulates of the microecologies through which it moves and which it inhabits. Inscribed at the nucleic level of the body, an atomized biopolitics generates a pathological double helix that braids toxic particulates with the very physiological processes that are essential to life—altering and damaging, in the process, the cellular fabric constitutive of life.

Transboundary Biopolitics of Autoimmunity

As *proxy* agents of the biopolitical state, toxic pollutants are, by definition, actors that vitiate univocal lines of cause and effect, premeditation and intentionality. Because of its very proxy status, the polluting agent opens a gap between itself and the originary agent that released it into a given site. In the quotation above from Safi's report, the distance between one and the other compels both the recognition of the correlation between symptoms and diagnosis *and* the need for iterative qualifications. Postbellum toxic ecologies and their proxy biopolitical operatives generate assemblages of pathological agents that unfold according to the rhythm and tempo of their own pathogenic trajectories as they become imbricated with the physiological process of an individual or collective body—thereby generating *autoimmune pathophysiologies* of the aftermath that may defy categorical medico-legal identification of *the* causal agent. Cast in Derridean biopolitical terms, there is operative here the signature trait of *autoimmunity* as predicated on a process of "self-destruction ruining the idea of self-protection (that of maintaining its self-integrity intact)."[118] In the absence of a visible and identifiable causal agent of violence, an atomized biopolitics attenuates and obfuscates clear-cut lines of cause and effect precisely because of its autoimmune operational logic. It reproduces, in other words, a torsive biopolitical logic that inverts and then implodes the asymmetrical binary of aggressor/victim. In this autoimmune biopolitical schema, the Palestinian body becomes an aggressor-victim.

The biopolitical impact of this autoimmune operational logic, however, has ramifications beyond Palestinians and their more-than-human relations in the context of both Gaza and the occupied West Bank. The helical structure of biopolitical autoimmunity means that, by definition, it encompasses the very subject who has deployed prophylactic measures against the other to secure and protect their own bodily health and integrity. In this case, civilian subjects of the state of Israel are now being exposed to the epidemiological effects ensuing from the destruction and collapse of sanitary infrastructure in Gaza and the toxic wastelanding of a number of locations in the West Bank. In biopolitical terms, an autoimmune logic of transboundary crossing is unfolding that is now having impacts on the health of Israeli citizens and the ecologies they inhabit. A report titled *Health Risks Assessment for the Israeli Population Following the Sanitary Crisis in Gaza* outlines how "the current sanitation, environmental and health conditions in Gaza have a multi-dimensional impact on the population of Israel."[119] It documents the transboundary ecological effects of aquapolitics ("pollution of sea water, rivers, beaches and drinking water reservoirs in Israel" and closure, for example, of the "Ashkelon desalination plant and of the Zikim bathing beach, as well as the Shikma facility for groundwater penetration"); aeropolitics ("severe air pollution" in Israeli airspace); and their epidemiological effects, including the "development of antibiotic resistant pathogens" in Gazan citizens and the resultant spread of these resistant pathogens by Gazans "who were hospitalized in Israel," "caus[ing] infections among dozens of Israeli patients" who were treated in the same facility.[120] In effect, the report documents a critical redistribution of biopolitical agency across a spread of more-than-human actors with the resultant generation of a series of unintended ecological and pathogenic consequences that are transboundary in nature.

In their analysis of the effects of Israeli "targeting of infrastructure and livelihoods in the West Bank and Gaza," Erika Weinthal and Jeannie Sowers document the impact of the occupation across all the key environmental sectors and then conclude that: "In both the West Bank and Gaza Strip, we have found that Israeli control over infrastructure, construction, land use and movement undermines civilian welfare even as the effects are 'walled off'—literally and in public discourse—from the Israeli public and, increasingly, from the international community. Our findings show how the systematic targeting of the water, energy and agricultural sectors is an important feature of the 'occupation regime' that directly undermines the ability of Palestinians to stay in place."[121] What remains implicit in the telling phrase "the ability of Palestinians to stay in place" is spelled out by Gideon Bromberg, the Israeli director of EcoPeace Middle East, who explains that if "something isn't done, the upshot could be the political horror in the form of hundreds of thousands of Gazans fleeing for their lives toward Israel—for fear of catching disease."[122]

The *Health Risks Assessment for the Israeli Population* report underlines that one of the "risks with the most dramatic impact that may occur due to the continuous deterioration of the sanitary, environmental and health conditions in the Gaza Strip is a scenario situation causing unwillingness to continue living in the environment, perceived as being dangerous. In current public health and environmental literature this situation is described as an 'environmental refugees' situation."[123] Gaza's prospective environmental refugees are here cast as a national security issue founded on the biopolitical health of Israel's citizens. The fear of Gaza's environmental refugees failing "to stay in place" resonates with that stratified zoopolitical history that I tracked in chapter 1, where I demonstrated that "their place" was, in fact, the confines of the vestibularity of Gaza-as-cage. The production of yet one more category of Palestinian refugeedom—"environmental refugees"—underscores both the multimodal strategies of ongoing displacement at work in the settler context of the occupation regime and the embodied inscription of Gazans into the unfolding disaster narrative of global (anthropocenic) ecological collapse. The autoimmune ensnarement of Israel's citizens into Gaza's unfolding ecological crisis testifies that, once situated in the larger frame of anthropocenic geopolitical ecology, "from now on there are no more spectators, because there is no shore that has not been mobilized in the [Anthropocene's] drama of geohistory." As Bruno Latour remarks, there are no more spectators because there is no longer an "outside" to the Anthropocene's *"generalized state of war."*[124] In the Palestinian/Israeli context, this generalized state of war is both locally situated in terms of its ecocidal inscriptions and globally distributed in terms of its transboundary ecospheric effects.

The biopolitical question concerning the health and epidemiology of a population is, a priori, an autoimmune question that pivots on the antinomies of life and death: "If autoimmunity," Derrida writes, "is *physio*logical, *biologi*cal, or *zoo*logical, it precedes and anticipates all these oppositions."[125] As I discussed in chapter 1, the physiological, biological, and zoological inscribe the biopolitical intelligibility of the category of "the Palestinian" in the context of its Israeli statist embodiments. Autoimmunity precedes this series of oppositions precisely because it operates as the condition of possibility for the very construction of the Palestinian/Israeli binary and its asymmetrical relations of power: the one is, in biopolitical terms, always already bound in an aporetic hold that enfolds the other. Within this aporetic fold, the biopolitical dimensions of autoimmunity are brought into sharp focus precisely because the question "concerning 'political' autoimmunity" is inextricably bound to "the relationship between the *politikon, physis,* and *bios* or *zōē,* life-death."[126] Political autoimmunity, once positioned in this conceptual series, is, by definition, *bio*political. Crystalized in this biopolitical formulation is the interlaced relationship between politics and bios, the a priori politicality of *zoē* and the life-death nexus in the context of the entangled couplet Palestine/Israel. Once the Israeli biopolitical governance of Palestinians is operationalized, rogue autoimmune effects, as instantiations of the future anterior, will have already been unleashed, breaching the prophylactic measures designed to protect the Israeli corpus—right down to the nucleic level of antibiotic-resistant pathogens infecting Israeli patients. Instantiated here is an indivisible articulation between interiority/exteriority that is, at the same time, inscribed by graphic asymmetries of power that pivot on the Palestinian/Israeli binary. Transboundary biopolitics of autoimmunity engender two interlinked movements: on the one hand, they mark the irreducible difference of the hierarchical binary Israeli/Palestinian by interpellating its differentially located subjects and the boundary apparatuses that secure distinct categorical identities; on the other hand, through the very movement of the *trans*, they transgress and override these same borders through ecocidal topologies of mutual entanglement that respect no categorical containment.

Evidenced across the above-cited reports is the autoimmune failure to "wall off" Palestinian "pathogens": as Bromberg puts it, "No fence or Iron Dome can thwart them."[127] The impasse of the Wall—in all of its boundary-marking embodiments—is here breached, and its regime of biopolitical policing and exclusion is rendered inoperative. Inserted within the torsive logic of biopolitical autoimmunity, the antimonial categories of inside/outside and Palestinian/Israeli are bound in a topological fold. The transboundary biopolitics of autoimmune regimes is, by definition, driven by the crossing of borders across increasingly fractalized dimensions that overturn such distinct entities as the state, its bordered and walled geographies, its ecologies, its citizens and noncitizens, their bodies, and their microecologies of pathogens. The virulent logic of biopolitical autoimmunity ruptures self-contained entities and their seemingly securitized borders. It converts the seemingly obdurate walls of "the border" (understood in all of its delimiting and preclusive functions) into permeable membranes through which ungovernable movements transpire. In the process, it lays bare the unspoken but nonnegotiable fact that the other, in all its differential incarnations, is always already inscribed in the very move to eliminate it and that its return will take place by circuitous routes that override the very defense mechanisms established to thwart it. The contestatory imprint of the other here signs the contours of an autoimmune logic that breaches the settler's biopolitical apparatuses for categorical containment.

Instantiated through the twinned modalities of an atomized and transboundary biopolitics is a critical interrogation of the very structurality of the structure of the settler state. These twinned biopolitical modalities bring into focus what I would term the coconstitutive *astructurality* of the structure of the settler state, in that the very reason of state, the coherent assemblage of its apparatuses of biopolitical governance and its deployment of carefully calculated strategies ostensibly aimed at securitizing and consolidating settler power, can be seen as inscribed by points of irreflection that generate unintended effects and unthought consequences that work to destructure the structure of the settler state and thwart its teleological momentum. Transboundary crossings of the toxic agents of an atomized biopolitics work to defy and erode the settler state's calculative strategies, self-preserving logics, and prophylactic mechanisms. Within this schema, unidirectional relations of settler power are interrupted and relayed back to their points of origin with unsettling autoimmune effects. The risk of totalization that Wolfe's concept of "structure" runs is thus fissured and unsettled by the *unknowledge of the unintended effects* that inscribes the apparatus and that, by definition, can neither be governed nor mastered. The structure's coconstitutive astructurality guarantees these limited but disruptive outcomes.

Phytopolitics

Another crucial biopolitical modality of the more-than-human that operates in the context of the intersectional nature of the Israeli state's settler practices, its militarized campaigns, and their ensuing ecocidal effects is *phytopolitics*, which is concerned with the biopolitics of plant life. Israel's phytopolitics operates along a number of related axes. On one front, its phytopolitical control of vegetal life is manifested by the juridico-militarization of trees and plants on Palestinian land:

> Military Orders 1015 and 1039 forbid the planting of fruit trees or vegetables without permission. Permits are required for building any structure, drilling wells, and for using water for agricultural purposes. Palestinians whose land is in an area closed for military purposes cannot get to it to plant or harvest it. It becomes uncultivated and therefore the state's. Land taken for public purposes, such as roads, is so carved up that it becomes difficult to work and almost impossible to water. If it is left to waste, this too is claimed by the state.[128]

The phytopolitical prohibition on the planting and nurturing of vegetal life on Palestinian land turns the targeted land into "wasteland"; in other words, it effectively transmutes Palestinian land that is juridico-militarily voided of vegetal life into terra nullius open to sovereign expropriation by the colonizing state. The legal fiction of terra nullius and of the "myth of a 'land without people' . . . is not," Nur Masalha underlines, "an infamous fragment of early Zionist propaganda: it is ubiquitous in much of the Israeli historiography of nation-building."[129] Construction of the Wall, also known as the security or separation barrier, has alienated large swaths of olive groves from Palestinian farmers. Because of the Wall and the juridico-military apparatus that underpins it, "the Palestinian relationship to trees, and especially the olive tree, is now mediated and controlled through Israel's detailed and often incomprehensible military regulations."[130] This is phytopolitics at work at the granular level of everyday Palestinian life.

The scale of the ecocidal violence inflicted on Palestine's vegetal life is brought to the fore by the UN Food and Agriculture Organization's assessment that, during Operation Protective Edge, "about 42,000 acres of croplands had sustained substantial direct damage."[131] The repeated wars against Palestine, combined with the construction of the Wall and everyday IDF incursions into Palestinian land, have resulted in the destruction of hundreds of thousands of olive, almond, citrus, and other fruit trees. On another militarized front, Israeli ecocidal practices entail the shooting, firebombing, and direct poisoning of Palestinian vegetal life. An IDF first sergeant describes his company's destruction of Juhar al-Dik: "When we entered [the Gaza Strip] it was a full-on orchard. I pointed the cannon at an orchard, toward an area that was half built up, half open, and every few minutes we blasted a barrage of MAG (machine gun) fire into it, nonstop. . . . I was shooting fan-shaped bursts into the orchard the whole time—the right side, left side. You sort of keep playing around with it."[132] What term other than *phytocide* can most accurately describe this relentless machine-gunning of a living orchard? The raking bursts of machine-gun fire tear into the body of the orchard, splintering the bark, perforating the trunks and shredding the leaves and fruit. The unremitting violence of machine-gun fire transmutes the arborescent morphology of a collection of trees into vermiculated tissue that, with one more blast, implodes on itself, reducing the life of the orchard to nothing more than vegetal pulp. "If you are at Juhar al-Dik today," says the soldier, "you'll see nothing but a sand dune" where once stood an orchard.[133]

Another IDF soldier who contributed to the indiscriminate destruction of Juhar al-Dik's orchards exclaims: "Fuck, check it out, there's nothing left of Juhar al-Dik, it's nothing but desert now."[134] This same soldier then describes the work of "D9s [armored bulldozers]. They just took down all the orchards. Not a single tree left. . . . When they didn't have a specific job like leading our way or opening up a specific route for us or some other mission, they just went and flattened things. I don't know what their specific order was, but they were

on a mission to leave the area razed, flattened."[135] Derek Gregory incisively captures what is operative in these militarized acts of ecocidal destruction: "It is
as though the very earth has been turned into an enemy."[136] Gregory's observation raises these foundational questions: From whence can justice come when
the earth itself is designated as the enemy? What space is left from which to
initiate the realization of justice when the ground beneath one's feet has been
rendered into wasteland that precludes the very possibility of life as such?

Settler Phytopolitics of National Parks and Reserves, and the War on Palestinian Trees

While the Israeli state has been conducting a systematic campaign of phytopolitics against Palestinian vegetal life, it has also been engaged, through the
work of the Jewish National Fund (JNF), in a countercampaign of mass tree
plantings and the consequent creation of national parks and nature reserves
on land that has been cleared of Palestinian villages.[137] Israel's destruction of
trees, however, cannot be simply and symmetrically counterbalanced by its
programs of afforestation on expropriated Palestinian land. Its mass plantings of pine, for example, have been mobilized to erase all signifiers of previously existing, now demolished Palestinian villages. "Following the war of
1948," writes Emily McKee, "the Israeli state planted forests over the sites of
destroyed Arab villages, like Deir Yassin, demonstrating starkly the combative
use of trees to claim land as Jewish."[138] McKee unpacks the complex dynamics
of injustice operative in this combative use of trees and the consequent instrumentalization of trees as nationalist proxies: "Given the widespread appeal
among Jewish Israelis of Zionist narratives of redemption through afforestation, [Palestinian] advocates sought to reinterpret the ethics of tree-planting.
They depicted the JNF's trees not as environmental improvement and proof
of rightful ownership, but as weapons of dispossession. Advocates spread the
message that valued environmental idioms, such as tree planting, can be used
to mask injustice."[139] The JNF, because of its role in legitimating possession of
expropriated Palestinian land through the ecological screen of afforestation,
has been termed "Israel's land-laundering body."[140] The JNF, in other words,
emerges as a key apparatus in Israel's greenwashing program, a program designed to celebrate the apparently progressive ecological values of the settler
state. I want to pause here and bring into view another form of political wash-
ing, pinkwashing, that is also critical in the construction of the image of the
Israeli state as a progressive and enlightened nation. In her detailed examination of the "homonationalism-as-assemblage" that inscribes the Israeli state,

Puar unpacks the biopolitical ramifications of presenting Israel as a bastion of LGBT rights. In theorizing homonationalism as "an analytic to apprehend state formation and a structure of modernity," Puar demonstrates how: "pink-washing has been redefined as the Israeli state's use of its admittedly stellar LGBT rights record to deflect attention from, and in some instances to justify or legitimate, its occupation of Palestine. Resonating within a receptive field of globalized Islamophobia significantly amplified since September 11, 2001, this messaging is reliant on a civilizational narrative about the modernity of the Israelis juxtaposed against the backward homophobia of the Palestinians."[141] Situated within this settler homonationalist assemblage, pinkwashing, Puar argues, "functions dually, as a form of discursive preemptive securitization that marshals neo-orientalist fears of Palestinians as backward, sexually re-pressed terrorists, and as an intense mode of subjugation of Palestinians under settler colonial rule."[142] These seemingly disconnected modalities of green- and pinkwashing function to construct progressive visions of the Israeli state that are underpinned by forms of both epistemic and physical violence. They emerge, in Puar's analysis, as biopolitical elements that are instrumental in Israeli state for-mation and the coterminous production of its national identity along the settler axis of progressive modernity. Greenwashing, once conjoined with pinkwashing in this schema, compels the coining of the quasi-tautological couplet "anthropo-homonationalism," where green-pinkwashing is based on the settler fiction of bringing enlightened rule to savage nature/Palestinians through modes of sub-jugation that entail settler ethnic cleansing of Palestinian lands to create wilder-ness reserves and national parks. National parks and Indigenous reserves emerge in the context of the modernist project of the anthropo-homonationalist assem-blage, with the attendant subjugation of the backward and sexually bestial Indi-gene and the simultaneous carving out of both Indigenous and nature reserves, as foundational acts that assert the progressive, civilizational, and autochtho-nous status of the settler state.[143] In what follows, I briefly want to situate the Israeli state's creation of national parks and reserves in the larger historical and transnational context of two settler states that were at the forefront of establishing these constructs of settler colonial modernity.

It is not coincidental that the world's first and second national parks were created by settler colonial states—specifically, the United States (Yellow-stone, 1872) and Australia (Royal National Park, 1879).[144] National parks were founded on the back of the settler colonial exercise of biopolitical power after the attempted genocide of the Indigenous owners of the lands in question and the securitization of the remnant population by corralling them within the confines of reserves.[145] Yellowstone established the settler template for the twin operations of Indigenous removal and the consequent expropriation of Indigenous land for "wilderness" reserves: "The now universal Yellowstone model of the national park," Marcia Langton underscores, "is a disguised and politically acceptable dispossession of indigenous people."[146]

The establishment of both Yellowstone and Royal National Park was enabled by practices of environmental colonialism undergirded by settler policies of the enforced displacement and exclusion of the people indigenous to the expropriated lands. That the world's first and second national parks were the product of two settler states must be seen as a system effect of the settler state and its infrastructural Euro-anthropocentric logic of partition, segregation, and paternal management of nature and its various "objects," including Indigenous people, wilderness, flora, fauna, and so on. Once operationalized, this violent logic of double subjugation forcibly brought into existence the various modalities of reserves. Both the reserve system and the national park system are spatialized enactments of settler colonial sovereignty along a continuum of absolute externality, encompassed by the rubric of "nature," punctuated by the specificities of the contingent differentials that accrue to the various categories of fauna and flora, which in turn need to be biopolitically governed and administered by the relevant colonial authorities. The authority to make the requisite biopolitical cuts into the diverse aspects of "nature" to be colonially administered was based on the legitimacy that accrued from the self-evident notion that the settler colonial state embodied civilizational culture. The proprietorial ownership of this category worked at once to legitimate settler acts of epistemic and physical violence and to obfuscate the immanent violence that inhered in the very logic of this binary system of conceptuality and lived practice.

The greenwashing of injustice through the promotion of politically driven ecological values that in fact work to advance and consolidate settler expansion and possession is exemplified by Israel's erasing of hundreds of Palestinian villages and the JNF's work in establishing nature reserves and national parks on these same sites. Carol Bardenstein recounts how the Palestinian villages of Imwas, Yalu, and Beit Nuba were all effectively bulldozed out of existence, and "an Israeli national park, camping ground, and picnic area" were established on the expropriated land of these three villages.[147] Here the settler ecology of a national park is founded on the forensic ecology of destroyed Palestinian villages. The flourishing of settler colonial constructions of wilderness, and the biopolitical fulfillment of Israeli practices of leisure and recreation to further the population's physical and psychic health, are enabled by the destruction and erasure of Palestinian life in all of its heterogeneity. "Nature," in this schema, is mobilized to biologize and nativize the settler's connection to the land through such acts as tree planting and through nomenclatural moves that erase Indigenous names and impose settler colonial ones that function to declare sovereign possession of the land. Hundreds of Palestinian villages have been destroyed by Israel in the process of its settler expansion, and the expropriated Palestinian ground has either been "taken over by Jewish settlers" or planted over by the JNF with forests designated as parks, nature reserves, or national parks, all bearing "newly coined Hebrew names."[148] As Uri Davis notes, these practices perform a type of ethnic cleansing through afforestation: "The first priority of JNF's afforestation is to hide its war crimes."[149]

In Memoriam: Phytopolitics of Forensic Trace Evidence

Yet perduring beneath these settler colonial acts of erasure are forensic traces that attest to the seemingly obliterated Palestinian presence. Walid Khalidi, in his monumental catalog of the hundreds of Palestinian villages destroyed by Israel since 1948, describes his work as "an attempt to breathe life into a name, to give a body to a statistic, to render those vanished villages a sense of their distinctiveness. It is, in sum, meant to be a kind of 'in memoriam.'"[150] Bardenstein recounts visiting one destroyed Palestinian village, Ghabsiyah in the Galilee, that has been forested over by the JNF. The forest, she writes, which had grown over four decades since the initial JNF planting, made "it seem as if perhaps that is all that was ever there."[151] Yet this settler act of afforestation, as an act designed to produce a collective forgetting of the village's Palestinian past, is problematized and contested by the forensic remainders that have survived the village's obliteration: "But subsequent visits to the site, accompanied by former villagers, now refugees, reveal another layer of memory. Among the trees, one can find bits of rubble from some of the destroyed homes, some remains of the village mosque, and the large round stone remaining at the site of the village olive press. But the primary way the former villager reconstructs his map and memory of the village for me is through his reading of the landscape and trees."[152] This site of forensic archaeology is layered by the shattered remainders of past Palestinian lives and practices, metonymically signified by the rubble from destroyed homes, the shards of the mosque and the olive-press stone. In the midst of this forensic debris, the Palestinian refugees focus on the cactuses and palm, lemon, pomegranate, and fig trees that have managed to survive the JNF's erasure of the Palestinian village. Ensconced in the midst of the forest of pines, they stand as landmarks. The enduring presence of these trees enables the refugees to read the dramatically altered landscape and to reconstruct it in terms of its original topography in order to find the position of their former homes. The surviving trees, in other words, operate as arboreal archives of Palestinian history. As vegetal archives, the trees inscribe their sedimented histories in their concentric rings, even as they externalize their lived history in situ through their morphology and their rooted hold on place. The surviving trees are, in the first instance, trees unto themselves, assiduously attempting to subsist in the midst of an overarching pine forest, but their vegetal life also embodies the memories and desires of their surviving Palestinian kin. As such, they retain and continue to signify the power of the forensic trace.

"If the trace," Derrida writes, "arche-phenomenon of 'memory,' which must be thought before the opposition of nature and culture, animality and humanity, etc., belongs to the very movement of signification, then signification is a priori written, whether inscribed or not, in one form or another, in a 'sensible' and 'spatial' element that is called 'exterior.'"[153] Standing their ground in the afforested space of a now-effaced village, the trees continue to signify as forensic traces of an otherwise erased Palestinian history; they are, as such, arche-phenomena of memory. They are at once vegetal forms of life that are inscribed in nature *and* cultural repositories of a relational history between the Palestinian refugees and the material specificity of the locus they continue to occupy. This biocultural history is intextuated in the postural extension of the trees' arborescent life and their concomitant marking of historically resonant space-as-place despite the dramatic changes to the landscape. The trees, in other words, embody what I would term a *phytosemiotics* of biocultural history. Phytosemiotics inscribes, through the resources available to vegetal life, a sensible and spatial history in the locus of this settler forest. This history is phytosemiotically written through a combinatory semantics of cellulose and lignin and a syntax of roots, trunks, bark, branches, and leaves.

The trees, once situated in the emergent field of plant cognition, can be said to embody an understanding both of place and of their relation to their surroundings.[154] They instantiate, moreover, in their interlocution of the Palestinian refugees, that arboreal modality of sentient relationality espoused by a number of Indigenous plant epistemologies: the Palestinian refugees are acutely attentive to what the trees "have to tell them."[155] In her marking of the critical differences between Western and Indigenous plant epistemologies, Robin Wall Kimmerer, member of the Potawatomi Nation, notes how the questions Western "scientists raised were not, 'Who are you?' but 'What is it?' No one asked plants, 'What can you tell us?'"[156] In the asking of the question "Who are you?" there is articulated a respectful stance toward another living being that does not perceive the entity as an object or thing. In asking the question "What can you tell us?" there is evidenced a recognition of the knowledge that another living being may possess. In the context of the destroyed Palestinian village of Ghabsiyah, now overlaid with a JNF pine forest, the returning Palestinian refugees ask the surviving pomegranate and lemon trees of the village: "What can you tell us about the location of our respective but now-demolished homes?" And the trees, drawing on their arboreal epistemologies, reply in kind, phytosemiotically articulating, through the indexicality of their rooted posture, the loci of the vanished homes. As such, these surviving trees effectively embody the category of forensic witnesses that continue to speak to an otherwise obliterated past.

In the process of acknowledging the alterity between the one and the other, an ethical exchange of experiential knowledge is magnetized between the surviving trees of the razed village and the returning Palestinians. Outlined here is an experiential domain that cannot be reduced to, or contained by, symbolics, tropology, allegory, or the "category error" of prosopopoeia or anthropomorphism. The facticity of survival in the face of iterative Israeli state violence establishes the exchange of one's life-logic with another: it traces a chiasmic relation that binds one, a tree, with the other, the Palestinian, in the practice of survivance. This instantiation of intertwined arboreal/Palestinian survivance is emblematically captured in reports by the villagers of the razed village of Mujaydial who, on their return to a space afforested with the JNF's pine trees, found "that some of the pine trees had literally split in two and how, in the middle of their broken trunks, olive trees had popped up in defiance of the alien flora planted over them fifty-six years ago."[157]

The trees' animating attributes of "voice," "witness," and "embodied subjecthood" can be reduced to mere anthropomorphic projections only after they are situated within circumscribed Euro-anthropocentric understandings of life. "English doesn't give us many tools," writes Kimmerer, "for incorporating respect for animacy. In English, you are either a human or a thing. Our grammar boxes us in by the choice of reducing a nonhuman being to an *it*. . . . Where are our words for the simple existence of another living being?"[158] In Potawatomi language, Kimmerer explains, other-than-human entities speak in the medium of their own language, and humans become "audience to conversations in a language not our own." In Potawatomi language, she adds, "of an apple, we must say, '*Who* is that being?' And reply *Mshimin yawe*. Apple that being is. The language reminds us, in every sentence, of our kinship with all the animate world."[159] Through their living presence, the remnant trees continue to memorialize the material reality of a Palestinian past that would otherwise be rendered inaccessible to the refugees due to the creation of what Masalha terms "landscapes of erasure and amnesia."[160] These landscapes thus embody a phytopolitics of enforced Israeli amnesia through homogeneous pine afforestation and of ineradicable Palestinian anamnesis through the phytosemiotics of surviving cactuses and palm, lemon, pomegranate, and fig trees.

The vegetal life of these surviving trees is inscribed, for the Palestinian refugees, by an interleaved ensemble of spatiotemporal relations that phytosemiotically brings to life seemingly vanished chronotopes. In Latourian terms, the trees *articulate propositions* about the otherwise obliterated history of the place. Phytosemiotically, they work to resituate and thus emplace the more-than-human entities (the houses, mosques, mill, and so on) violently razed by the JNF. Complexly, the surviving trees exemplify the operations of three topologically conjoined spatiotemporal dimensions: the diachronic, synchronic, and protentive. Diachronically, their steadfast rootedness to the ground in the face of violent historical upheavals marks the coordinates of a site-specific location that would otherwise be unreadable in the lie of the changed landscape. Synchronically, they continue to temporalize a seemingly erased Palestinian past into the immediacy of the living present. Protentively, as remainders (of an effaced past) that are firmly rooted in the living present, they contemporize Palestinian history and, through their ongoing survival against all the odds, project an otherwise denied Palestinian futurity. The surviving trees thus stand as living chronotopes: temporally, they animate a Palestinian past and present that, spatially, materialize the topography of an otherwise expropriated and altered landscape. Yet something more dynamic than topography is realized here. As the embodiment of living chronotopes, the trees signify beyond the spatial planes of topography by simultaneously magnetizing a temporal fold that topologically bridges the near and the far, the past and the present, in a powerful instantiation of more-than-human distributed memory and cognition.

Corpus Delicti of Phytopolitical Destruction

The crucial role that ecocide has played in the expansion and consolidation of Israel's settler project is perhaps best illustrated by the following fact: "Israeli authorities have uprooted over 800,000 Palestinian olive trees since 1967, the equivalent to razing all of the 24,000 trees in New York's Central Park 33 times."[161] On the one hand, this statistic highlights the scale of Israel's phytopolitical campaign in the relentless pursuit of its settler project. On the other hand, this statistic reproduces a mass homogenization that effaces the individual significance of every tree destroyed by the Israeli state as a being in its own right. As such, it instrumentalizes the olive trees in terms of their numerical value and economic worth. In his critique of anthropocentric accounts of vegetal life, Michael Marder outlines how such instrumentalist views "fail to take into account vegetal life *as* life, aside from the external ends it might be called to serve."[162] In other words, the exclusive focus on the economic value and benefits of the destroyed olive trees occludes the fact "that vegetal life is laden with meaning in all of its spatiality, materiality, and finitude."[163]

This affective relation to a tree's unique materiality and finitude, as what transcends the instrumentalized value of a tree, is succinctly expressed by Nabil, a Palestinian farmer, who says: "The olive trees are my life. My soul. My olives are like my children."[164] Salah Abu Ali, another Palestinian farmer, names his sense of embodied kinship with the olive trees: "This [olive tree] is life, like water, honestly I love this tree. I have a relationship with this tree. I know what it needs, what pains it. When I'm around it, I feel safe, I would give it my sweat."[165] In elaborating on the profoundly embodied relation to his olive tree, Abu Ali overturns and displaces the logic of the anthropocentric hierarchy: "I am honoured to be this tree's servant. The connection goes back to my father and grandfather. I feel so connected to this tree, it's as if it's part of my body and soul."[166] In both these impassioned attestations, the olive trees are ensouled. This "ensoulment,"[167] to draw on Gregory Cajete's term, of other-than-human entities such as the olive trees is also powerfully demonstrated by an act of collective mourning performed by Palestinian villagers following the uprooting by Israeli forces of more than 3,300 olive trees in the village of Midya: "Black banners were raised at the entrance to the village and on individual homes, as done in mourning the death of a human being."[168] This act of mourning commemorates the kinship ties between vegetal and human life. The funereal black banners enunciate a ceremonial in memoriam for the death of their arboreal kin.

Following the mass uprooting of the olive trees in the village of Midya, the Palestinian villagers deposited three "huge olive-tree trunks left behind by Israeli 'Green Patrol' bulldozers . . . in front of the Israeli prime minister's office, with the following slogans on their trunks: 'You've uprooted 3,300 olive trees like me in Midya!' and 'Look at my trunk! I'm more than 60 years old!'"[169] These performative speech acts attest to vegetal life as flesh of the world that is also victim to acts of ecocide. They also highlight, through the formidable presence of the dead trunks, the individuated singularity of every tree killed. The phytosemiotic speech acts of the dead tree trunks are both corporeal and textual. Forensically, through the *corpus delicti* of their lopped limbs and truncated lives, they impugn their violently ruptured existence and the violation of the reverence their age should elicit: "Look at my trunk! I'm more than 60 years old!"

Israel's phytopolitical acts of mass uprooting of trees on Palestinian soil must not be seen as mere "allegories" of Palestinian displacement. Rather, they must be understood as signifying in a double register: on the one hand, they are violent acts that perpetrate the collective destruction of individual beings rooted in their own nutritive locus and flourishing in their own place in the sun; on the other, they are violent acts that bind each destroyed tree and plant in *singularly embodied*, and thus *nonanalogical*, biopolitical relations across forensic ecologies of militarized destruction that pivot on Israeli settler expansionism.

Speaking with a Lemon Tree

Across an expansive body of work, Nadera Shalhoub-Kevorkian has documented the devastation unleashed in Palestinian communities by the Israeli occupation.[170] One story in particular, as told by Shalhoub-Kevorkian, has continued to captivate me. It is the story of a lemon tree and its relation to Hala Al-Ghawi, a Palestinian child. Through both her perception of and interaction with a lemon tree, Hala contests and experientially overturns dogmatic assumptions that "plants are passive, mute, and morally inconsiderable."[171] Hala was a five-year-old child who, together with her family, had "recently been evicted from the Sheikh-Jarrah home they had lived in for fifty-six years to make way for a family of Jewish settlers."[172] The eviction from their home was both violent and traumatic: "After receiving a final eviction notice, the door of the Al-Ghawi residence was detonated with a small explosive. Police rushed in and a familiar scene commenced. After the family members had been removed their possessions followed, although most belongings were destroyed during the eviction. Violently evicted from their home, they were reduced to literally living in the streets."[173] Hala's father, Fuad, describes the toll this eviction has exacted on his family: "The reaction of the children has been terrible. They are afraid and unable to forget that they once lived in that house."[174] As Shalhoub-Kevorkian personally evidenced for me as we walked the streets and alleys of occupied East Jerusalem, the Israeli state systematically evicts Palestinians and occupies their homes and quarters in a capillary-like movement that Masalha calls "creeping annexation, a process by which Israeli administration, jurisdiction and law gradually, incrementally and draconianly were imposed on the West Bank and the Gaza Strip, over ever-expanding areas, yet without a comprehensive act of legal annexation."[175] "Through such a uniquely complex and incremental form of colonialism," writes Rosemary Sayigh, "space within which Palestinians can subsist is reduced meter by meter, day by day."[176]

In her interview, Hala tells Shalhoub-Kevorkian that one of the things she misses most about her home is the lemon tree in their garden (figure 2.1):

Figure 2.1 The lemon tree in the front garden of Hala's house expropriated by Jewish settlers, in occupied East Jerusalem. Photo by the author.

Hala talks about the lemon tree, and her love of the fact that the lemon tree is still giving wonderful lemons, as Hala explained: "The lemon tree keeps on giving more and more lemon, to tell me and my mom that she misses us. It gives lemon, while she knows that the settlers won't touch, eat or use its juices. So, it is giving more lemon, to call us to come back. You see, my mom and I visit the lemon tree a lot, and even apologize that we are not close to her, and ask her to take care of our house. . . . We visit and talk to her [the lemon tree] a lot."[177]

In the interval between the knowledge of enforced separation through violent dispossession and the emotion of loss that colors this knowledge, something altogether signifies: we have here a mutual recognition between Hala and the lemon tree—one beckons to the other through a series of memory traces. And I want to preempt the possible misunderstanding that I am here only speaking metaphorically of memory traces or that I am lapsing into some unreflexive form of anthropomorphism. I situate this relation of memory traces between Hala and the lemon tree within the emergent science of plant neurobiology, which posits that plants "are communicative, relational beings"[178] that experience touch, intelligence, and memory: "They communicate with each other with chemicals, whether we want to call this taste, or smell, or pheromones. Plants 'know' when they are being touched . . . [and they] also manage to remember things without the benefit of neurons."[179] Plant neurobiologists are now identifying trees as "embodied agents" complexly interacting with their world: "In plants, cognition and bodily functions are not separate but are present in every cell: a real, living example of what artificial intelligence scientists call an 'embodied agent,' that is, an intelligent agent that interacts with the world with its own physical body."[180] Western science is finally coming to the realization that vegetal life, as a number of Indigenous cosmo-epistemologies clearly articulate, has its own purposive force to flourish, procreate, and maintain its own viable community; that vegetal life engages in both intra- and interspecies communications and relations; that it deploys feints, tricks, and ruses to confuse, entrap, or ward off its predators; and that plants "are sensitive to the soundscape that surrounds them and, most importantly, are capable of emitting their own clicking sounds as well as detecting acoustic signals from others."[181]

In the context of the relation between the lemon tree and the child, Merleau-Ponty's flesh of the world becomes embodied in a vegetal form invested with agency, cognition, and memory traces. For Hala, these memory traces manifest themselves in the recollection of the tree and its bounty of fruit. In the other direction, the tree itself is inscribed by a different series of traces: the very morphology of the tree has been shaped by the loving hands of Hala's mother, pruning its arboreal growth and nourishing its roots so that it will continue to flourish. Overlaying these material traces are the ephemeral traces of the child's touch and the tree's intextuation through the child's voice as she engages the tree with speech, thereby breaching what Hegel dogmatically termed "the sealed reticence of the plant"[182]—"it calls us to come back," Hala says, and she responds: "[We] apologize that we are not close to her."

In his essay "Speaking to Trees," Erazim Kohák asks: "What is the epistemological status of a world within which speaking to trees would appear as an appropriate behavior? It would be a world perceived as a community of autonomous beings worthy of respect."[183] Even as Kohák envisages in his ecophilosophy a community of autonomous beings worthy of respect, his use of the monologic preposition "to," "to speak *to* a tree," reproduces a structural hierarchy and asymmetry. By contrast, the use of the dialogic preposition "with" opens the possibility for dialogue between oneself and the other, as exemplified by the Nayaka people, who stress, in their relational phyto-epistemology, the importance of "talking *with* trees": "'Talking with' stands for attentiveness to variances and invariances in behavior and response to things in states of relatedness and for getting to know such things as they change through the vicissitudes over time of the engagement with them."[184] Echoing the Potawatomi people's dialogic relations to vegetal life, Hala asks the tree: "What can you tell us?" And the lemon tree replies in the distinctive register of its own vegetal voice: it phytosemiotically articulates—through an arboreal syntax of trunk, branches, and twigs and a semantics of leaves, buds, and flowers—an exuberant syntagm of lemons that bespeaks loss and beckons Hala to return: "The lemon tree keeps on giving more and more lemon, to tell me and my mom that she misses us. It gives lemon, while she knows that the settlers won't touch, eat or use its juices. So, it is giving more lemon, to call us to come back."

In a reflective essay on the power of trees in place and time, Owain Jones and Paul Cloke write, "Trees have the capacity to engender affective and emotional responses from the humans who dwell amongst them—to contribute to the haunting of place via exchanges between the visible present and the starkly absent in the multiple and incomplete becoming of agency."[185] Hala and the lemon tree materialize the multiple and incomplete becomings of agency. Hala's affective calls to her expropriated lemon tree instantiate an exercise of agency that can only come to fruition through the tree's agentic reply. Situated in the locus of enforced displacement and separation, both the tree and the child delineate a ground haunted by the stark reality of absence and loss. Hala's relationship with the lemon tree resonates with the relational epistemology of the Nayaka, which emphasizes "the being-together of oneself and the other and to learning mutualities within the *pluralities* that *are* in the world."[186] In Nayaka relational epistemology, the focus is on "joint selves and how each one affects and is affected by the other. . . . For example, a tree would be regarded as a being who is influenced and who influences others. Its behavior within mutual relations would be studied more than what it is made of."[187] Hala's lemon tree is an agentic actor in the lives of her family as it actively shapes and transforms their lives and their experience of suffering. Shalhoub-Kevorkian cites Hala's "mother's harkening back to the lemon tree: 'I wanted to pickle the olives, but couldn't bring myself to do it this year without a lemon from our lemon tree,' she tells me with a heavy sigh."[188] The mother's sigh corporeally marks her embodied sense of grief and loss in the absence of her lemon tree. "Our relationship to plants," writes Cajete, "is a part of our body memory."[189] As Hala and the lemon tree attest, this is a body memory that intertwines, through root and branch, one with the other.

The lemon tree emerges from Hala's testimony as a nucleus of suffering that inflects multiple relations and shapes different temporal dimensions: the past continues to inform and affect both the present and the future. The lemon tree stands as a central axis in Hala's lived drama of the settler dispossession that precipitated such a profound and multivalent sense of loss. The lemon tree constitutes the ground on which Hala's memories, desires, and emotions intersect. The ground that radiates outward from this lemon tree articulates the contours of a forensic ecology of displacement and separation—even as it marks the impossibility of affectively cleaving one from the other, the child from her lemon tree. As a key coordinate of violent dispossession and ongoing loss, the tree persists in orienting the lives of Hala and her family. Indissociably inscribed in their everyday lives, despite its material absence the tree is a protagonist that evidences the ongoing corrosive effects of the attritional violence of settler dispossession and displacement.

Meditating on the unseen complexities of interaction, Latour concludes that "no interaction is synchronic" but that, rather, an interaction is constituted by "different actors unfolding at different paces and through different materialities."[190] Latour's theorization of the distributed nature of interaction and of its inscription by different spatiotemporal vectors is borne out by Hala and the lemon tree. Two different actors, a tree and a child, enact an interactive choreography that plays out at different paces and through different materialities. The lemon tree's rooted emplacement is counterpointed by Hala's enforced displacement and her recursive visits to the tree. The fleeting temporality of Hala's vocalizations to the lemon tree is counterpointed by the slow coming to fruition of the lemons that give embodied vegetal voice to the tree. Hala's vocal enunciations, with their ephemeral acoustics that brush and resonate through the tree's embodied being, dissipate into the air once spoken; they are counterpointed, in turn, by the communicative materiality of the fruit that can be seen, touched, and incorporated, as fleshly gift, into the body of the other. The enactment of loss and memory that transpires between the lemon tree and Hala emerges, then, as a complex and embodied choreography constituted by different actors, diverse spatiotemporal materialities, and two microecologies that are indissociably intertwined: one of enforced displacement and loss and the other inscribed by unbroken lines of desire and affect. In Latour's terms, these lived performatives of engagement with the world and its different actors should "be felt as a node, a knot, and a conglomerate of many surprising sets of agencies."[191] Hala and the lemon tree are precisely a node within a network of different spatiotemporalities; they come together in a knot that is at once vegetal and affectively embodied and that endures despite being prized apart.

Figure 2.2   The aftermath of Operation Pillar of Defense, November 22, 2012. Screengrab from a video shot by Voice of America correspondent Scott Bobb.

Bodies of Forensic Evidence and Testimony of Forensic Remainders

In this chapter, I have traced the impact of the biopolitics of the more-than-human in the context of occupied Palestine and their relation to the imbricated practices of settler colonialism and ecological destruction. Having enlarged the biopolitical aperture to bring into view the differential and often interlocking modalities of a biopolitics of the more-than-human in the context of sites saturated by acts of military and settler violence, my concern has been to address the complex relations that transpire in such sites and the ecocidal and pathological effects that ensue from this violence. In the wake of the acts of destruction and displacement I have delineated, I have also highlighted the ensemble of surviving material entities, such as Hala's lemon tree, that, for Palestinians, become a "memory of the present."[192] This Derridean phrase captures the complex spatiotemporalities of displacement, loss, memory, and continued survivance in the face of ongoing trauma.

The thanatographical image of the ruins left in the wake of an IDF strike in Gaza (figure 2.2) evidences the complex dimensions of the forensic ecology of a postbellum aftermath that I have attempted to bring into focus in the last two chapters: blasted trees and their truncated limbs, broken doors and shattered windows, mangled domestic utensils and disabled satellite dishes, scattered bricks and twisted iron—all are entangled within an ecology that forensically testifies to the moment of catastrophic violence and its aftermath.

The ecological approach I have deployed in my analysis of human and more-than-human entities within contexts of armed conflict and occupation has been predicated on the relations of binding consanguinity between the different entities that, as flesh of the world, are the victims of militarized and/or settler violence. The expansive compass of the consanguinity that binds the remainders of a military attack is captured by Atef Abu Saif in his documentation of a site of military carnage perpetrated by the IDF in Gaza during Operation Protective Edge: "An expressionless corpse, lungs hanging out of a caved-in chest, a leg severed into three pieces, fingers lying on the ground like scattered sticks. . . . All these images build up, flesh becomes like the wreckage of a house: walls and ceilings, beams and staircases, windows and bits of roofs, all in the wrong places, scattered, amputated, lying on top of one another."[193] Flesh becomes the wreckage of a house and the wreckage of a house becomes flesh. And the question shifts from resemblance or analogy to an articulated coextensiveness through which there is an exchange of properties that collapse, like a caved-in chest, the parameters of an individuated entity and the borders between inside and outside, between the flesh of the body and the flesh of the world. The shattered fragments of this corpse-house delineate the contours of a forensic ecology. The violence of the military strike at once severs and conjoins heterogeneous attributes, including limbs and beams, lungs and windows. As remnants of the aftermath, they are entangled in an embrace of intimate finitude, even as they continue, as forms of geobiophysical evidence, to bear forensic witness to the IDF's act of militarized destruction.

3————Animal Excendence and Inanimal Torture

Toxic Militarism

Guantánamo's Camp Justice is steeped in toxins. According to a report compiled by the Navy and Marine Corps Public Health Center, Camp Justice is replete with a pharmacopedia of poisons: mercury concentrations have been found lodged in the crevices and seams of the camp's buildings; the camp's plywood, fiberboard, resins, and glue exhale formaldehyde; chloroform and bromodichloromethane contaminate the water supplied to the camp's showers; the soil oozes arsenic and benzene concentrates; and carcinogenic asbestos has been found in a number of the camp's buildings.[1] The material toxicity of Camp Justice emblematizes the role of the US military in contaminating and destroying many different ecologies that encompass both domestic sites (for example, Navajo lands, the Yucca Mountain project in Nevada, and Los Alamos in New Mexico)[2] and offshore territories (such as Afghanistan, as I discuss in chapter 4). Camp Justice, moreover, needs to be situated within the global matrix of US militarism, its inordinate consumption of resources, and its role as one of the world's largest polluters: "The United States military [is] the single largest landowner, equipment contractor and energy consumer in the world."[3] In her analysis of what she terms "toxic militarism," Déborah Berman Santana exposes the strategies through which the US state obfuscates this critical fact: "The [US] military, as the largest corporation and most egregious polluter, has been subject to less oversight, regulation, and sanction than any other toxic criminal has."[4] By mobilizing the biopolitical ruse of "state security" to ostensibly securitize and protect its citizens' freedoms, the US administration gives itself carte blanche to override both oversight and regulation of its toxic military activities. The freedom of some, in other words, is predicated on the unfreedom and even death of others—including Native Americans, Yemeni, Afghans, Somalis, and Pakistanis. Santana underscores what is at stake in the operations of US toxic militarism: "Among its many contradictions the purported military mission to protect society is violated by its activities, which endanger human and environmental health. Moreover, as befits a rigidly hierarchical institution charged with assuring global dominance by the U.S. elite, these activities disproportionately threaten communities where people of color live and work: urban ghettoes, tribal lands, and colonized countries."[5] Santana does not deploy theories of either bio- or necropolitics in her analysis of toxic militarism, but her conclusions resonate powerfully with this type of analytical framework. "If corporate criminals all too often get off with a mere slap on the wrist," she notes, "the military is literally getting away with murder."[6] Significantly, law is complicit in the legitimation of the US military's production of toxic ecologies: "If those who try to stop abuse of colonized and oppressed peoples and lands are punished, while the criminals go free, then the legal system is facilitating toxic capitalism in its most lethal form: militarism."[7] The poisonous ecology of Camp Justice stands, on one level, in a homologous relation to the toxic legal processes and practices that are supposed to administer and deliver justice to Guantánamo's inmates. Presently I will discuss the travesty of justice that transpired in the camp in the context of the singular life and death of one of its detainees, Adnan Farhan Abdul Latif, and the way a biopolitically driven legal process ensured that, for Latif, justice was not served.

"In order to cover Guantánamo," writes the journalist Janet Reitman, "you must agree to become a captive of the U.S. military."[8] Once journalists gain clearance to enter Guantánamo, what they actually get to see is largely controlled by their assigned military guides. Describing her heavily circumscribed journey through the military prison, Reitman concludes that the tour was "frustrating, and utterly pointless in many ways other than to serve what I [had] come to believe is its central purpose: to blight out the existence of the prisoners." "And yet," she adds, "they exist. For a brief 15 minutes, we are allowed to glimpse them, behind one-way glass, while touring Camp Six, a medium-security prison where 'highly compliant detainees' live in communal blocks." After watching the detainees behind the one-way glass, Reitman concludes that "the effect is like watching animals at a zoo."[9] Detainees, such as Lakhdar Boumediene and Mustafa Ait Idir, described their cells as similar to "cage[s] at the zoo": "They were meant for animals, not people."[10]

The last stop on Reitman's tour is Camp X-Ray, where the detainees were imprisoned soon after their 9/11 capture: "During that time, the prisoners lived in dog cages, and the dogs that helped guard them lived in air-conditioned kennels."[11] Evidenced here is the built-in capacity within zoopolitical regimes of power to invert hierarchies, subjects, and spaces in the quest to secure the governance and control of subjects designated as outliers within the racio-speciesist schema of "the human." Mark Fallon, a former Naval Criminal Investigative Service special agent who witnessed the torture practices deployed in Guantánamo, describes Camp X-Ray as a "high-security, low-rent zoo."[12] Here the zoopolitics of capture, encagement, securitization, and racio-anthropocentric torture intersect and work to delineate spaces of confinement and subjects nonnegotiably exposed to regimes of instrumentalized violence. As I discuss later in this chapter, the zoopolitical template for practices of human torture is founded and animated by the violence that can be, and has been, perpetrated on the nonhuman animal with a sense of clinical impunity.

Reitman's account of her visit to Guantánamo encapsulates a number of the concerns of this chapter. Synoptically, it brings into visibility intersecting levels of captivity with zoopolitical forces that invert certain categories, so that nonhuman animals (dogs) are contingently elevated in the biopolitical hierarchy, while human subjects are dispatched down this same hierarchy and are held captive in the vestibularity of a zoological cage. This chapter examines the Guantánamo Bay military prison through the biopolitical lens of forensic ecology to bring into focus the complex relations between the detainees and animals that inhabit that space. I begin the chapter with a discussion of Adnan Latif, one of the first detainees to be imprisoned in Camp X-Ray. Guantánamo's military commissions recommended Adnan for transfer at least three times, yet he continued to be indefinitely detained. On September 8, 2012, Latif was found dead in his cell. Drawing on the official forensic report into this death, I illuminate the way the report incidentally documents Latif's relationship with the animals that shared his cage and recreation yard. In the context of the official forensic report, the animals with whom Latif established interspecies relations are seen to offer a type of testimony that escapes the anthropocentric concerns of the report's legal authors. Guantánamo's flesh of the world, I suggest, is constituted by binding interspecies relations between the disparate actors that live and die within the forensic ecologies of this military prison.

Adnan Farhan Abdul Latif

Adnan Farhan Abdul Latif was one of the detainees captured in Afghanistan in the early roundups of "suspects" soon after the 9/11 attacks. Latif repeatedly stressed his innocence, to no avail. He described how he had gone to Afghanistan to seek charitable medical treatment for a head injury he had received in a car accident in Yemen. Regardless of the protestations of his innocence and medical evidence documenting his injury, he was dispatched to Guantánamo. Marc Falkoff, one of Latif's habeas lawyers since 2004, describes the nightmare situation that Latif was plunged into once he entered Guantánamo: "Adnan was brought to Guantánamo in January 2002 on suspicion of being associated in some manner with enemy forces in Afghanistan. It's hard to say exactly what the U.S. military thought Adnan had done. Over the years, the government made allegations and then abandoned them."[13] Falkoff unfolds a legal narrative inscribed with multiple unsubstantiated allegations against Latif, a narrative that appears to shift, change, collapse, and resurrect itself in the face of a clear lack of evidence against Latif:

> At one point, the government accused Adnan of "associating" with Al Qaeda. But the military never produced any credible evidence to sustain the charge, so the government dropped it. More recently, the government argued that it was lawful to detain Adnan for 10 years or more at Guantánamo because it believed he had served as a Taliban foot soldier for a few weeks before the U.S. began bombing Afghanistan. But even this diminished allegation could not be proved, as U.S. District Judge Henry H. Kennedy Jr. determined in 2010.[14]

Judge Kennedy ordered Latif's release. Yet he continued to be detained. Falkoff identifies what he regards as the "grimmest fact about Adnan's death": "that since his early detention, no one really thought he should be at Guantánamo at all. During the Bush administration, the military recommended Adnan for transfer at least three times—in 2004, 2006 and 2008. Then, when President Obama came into office, a task force reviewed all the evidence in Adnan's case and recommended him for repatriation to Yemen in 2009."[15] Despite this recommendation, "Obama chose to appeal the district court's order to release a prisoner whom his own task force had (privately) already designated for transfer home." "Why appeal?" asks Falkoff. "To all appearances," he writes, "the new administration, like the old one, was chiefly concerned with limiting the power of the courts in wartime." Falkoff describes the consequences of this appeal: "The result was that last year [2012] the appeals court, in a widely criticized 2–1 ruling, vacated Kennedy's order and remanded the case for a do-over. The dissenting judge criticized the majority for 'moving the goal posts' in the government's favor. This June, the Supreme Court refused to review that ruling. Eight years after we filed a habeas petition on Adnan's behalf, we were back to square one. And that may have been more than Adnan could bear."[16]

On September 8, 2012, Adnan Latif was found dead in his cell in Guantánamo. The letters that Latif wrote to his attorneys, David Remes and Marc Falkoff, document the torture he was compelled daily to endure. In one letter, Latif writes: "Here I am drowning in my blood and you are still looking for justice and seeking hearings. Meanwhile they are leading me to death."[17] The endlessly deferred realization of justice appears both remote and disconnected from the very real effects of the law of indefinite detention that he is forced to embody and endure. Latif continues: "Everything has a price here except human life. It became cheap. In their view, life became less than refuse to be thrown in a garbage can."[18] Latif identifies his subject position in terms of a carceral life that has been reduced to the category of biopolitical waste. Aware of his disposable status, Latif writes: "I am being pushed towards death every moment. The way they deal with me proves to me that they want to get rid of me but in a way that they cannot be accused of causing it."[19] He clearly names and identifies the biopolitical forces that are systematically driving him to that point of self-annihilation that will exempt the state from the charge of homicide. Latif is here writing in the register of the future anterior: in the future, he contends, they will have killed me already through the deployment of lethal practices that will exculpate them from the charge of murder, even as I, Adnan Latif, persist in naming it as such, that is, as homicide.

In the sentence that immediately follows, in his letter to his attorneys, Latif writes: "I have been isolated in Alpha block, camp five, in a cell that resembles a lion's cage."[20] Alpha block is the high-security isolation prison in Guantánamo. As Latif explains, Alpha block is a site saturated by physical and psychological violence: "I was hurt by the IRF [Immediate Reaction Force] teams. Imagine that one night, from sunset to sunrise until six in the morning, they entered my cell fifteen times. During those times, they tied me to a stretcher and carried me to the clinic in camp five then returned me back to my cell. They repeated that fifteen times until I lost my mind; they broke my bones and made me bleed."[21] The IRF teams are Guantánamo's infamous terror squads. Appareled in full riot gear, they burst into cells and unleash the full force of their violence on their unarmed inmates. The violence that Latif endured was repeated the very next day: "This also happened on the second day when they entered my cell ten times hitting my head against the wall and dragging me on the floor and leaving me there in the middle of the cell which was full of water, urine and feces. I was left in this dirty mixture all day with my hands tied firmly behind by back."[22] Shackled in his "lion's cage," Latif is left to stew in the cesspit of his cell. In this passage, he names the operation of the biopolitical caesura, as he physically and psychologically is compelled to embody the status of nonhuman animal. Latif experienced the violent cut of the biopolitical caesura on his entry into Guantánamo when he was dispatched to Camp X-Ray's wire cages: "Latif spent his first weeks at Camp X-Ray in an open-air cage, exposed to the tropical sun, without shade or shelter from the wind that buffeted him with sand and pebbles. His only amenities were a bucket for water and another for urine and feces."[23] The decisive cut of the biopolitical caesura is not negotiable within these loci of saturated violence and torture. Terry Holdbrooks, a former guard at Guantánamo, describes the doctrinal implementation of the biopolitical caesura: "Our interaction with the detainees was such that we were told not to talk to them, not to treat them as humans, to not engage in conversation whatsoever. . . . So the instructions I was given were simple—don't interact, don't talk, they are not humans."[24]

Guantánamo's Nonpersons

The biopolitical forces that traverse and constitute Guantánamo effectively preclude detainees from embodying the figure of "the human," specifically the legal category of "person"—and the attendant rights that accrue to this juridical figure. I can perhaps best illustrate this by turning to an attempt by the detainees' attorneys "to ensure that their religious freedoms are recognized."[25] In their submission to the US District Court in Washington, DC, the detainees' attorneys noted that the "Supreme Court ruled that [the corporation] Hobby Lobby was legally a 'person' entitled to religious freedom under the RFRA [Religious Freedom Restoration Act]" and argued that the detainees should be granted the same religious freedom to practice—specifically, the right "to pray communally during Ramadan."[26] The Guantánamo detainees were denied this right on the following grounds:

> The current binding Circuit precedent, which holds that Guantánamo detainees, as non-resident aliens outside the United States sovereign territory, are not protected "person[s]" within the meaning and scope of RFRA. In *Hobby Lobby*, the Supreme Court held RFRA rights extend to for-profit closely held corporations, reasoning in part that the Dictionary Act, 1

U.S.C. § 1 defines a "person" to include "corporations." 2014 WL 291709 at *14. That case did not involve or resolve any other question regarding the meaning of "person" under RFRA. As a result, that opinion cannot be read as extending RFRA rights to Petitioners: simply put, the Supreme Court never addressed whether unprivileged enemy belligerents detained overseas during a period of ongoing hostilities are "persons" to whom RFRA applies.[27]

Putting aside the fact that the majority of Guantánamo's detainees have been cleared for release after having been formally found not to be enemy belligerents, what is of interest here is the intersection of state and juridical power in the policing of the category of the human-rights-bearing subject. In this case, a disembodied for-profit corporation, Hobby Lobby, is juridically represented as qualifying to embody the rights-bearing category of a "person," whereas the detainees, precisely as embodied persons, are denied this right. Operative in this distinction is a series of disjunctions and displacements that positions the detainees as disembodied of their corporeal status as persons. Consequently, the juridical repositioning of a disembodied entity such as a corporation up the biopolitical hierarchy, so that it is seen to embody the locus of a human-rights-bearing subject, appears both rational and logical.

The violent asymmetries of power at work in this case become clearly manifest when the detainees' submission is fully contextualized: they are lodging their request for the right to pray communally during Ramadan because this very practice is being precluded by the violent practices of enforced feeding of those detainees participating in hunger strikes—as a form of protest against their indefinite detention. Agreeing with the brief filed on behalf of President Obama, the court, under the rubric of "facts," dismissed its request on the following grounds: "In both of their applications, they merely incorporate (1) the cites regarding the traditions of communal prayer during Ramadan taken from their initial applications for a preliminary injunction concerning various alleged aspects of enteral feeding, and (2) allegations by another detainee that detainees who were being enterally fed were not permitted to pray communally during Ramadan in 2013."[28] Here the force-feeding of the detainees is glossed by the neutralizing term *enteral feeding,* thereby effacing what is yet another practice of torture inflicted on the hunger strikers at Guantánamo. Under the rubric of "facts," the brutal flesh-and-blood facticity of the force-feeding of the hunger strikers is rendered in terms of a mere "allegation" of "aspects of enteral feeding."[29] This neutralizing legal logic is all of a piece with the discursive maneuvers that effectively disembody the detainees of their very flesh-and-blood status in order to void their juridical status as persons: "Petitioners argue that inclusion of the term 'individuals' within the Dictionary Act's definition of 'person' necessarily means that 'person' includes all 'flesh-and-blood human beings,' including noncitizens, regardless of circumstances or whether they are in or resident in the United States."[30] According to the brief filed on behalf of President Obama, this apparently cogent argument failed on a number of counts: "This Court cannot go so far as to conclude that 'person' under RFRA now includes any individual, even if a nonresident, noncitizen held in military detention outside the United States."[31] Furthermore, the brief observed that Congress "had legislated against a backdrop of decisions establishing that nonresident aliens were not among the 'person[s]' protected by the Fifth Amendment, and were not among 'the people' protected by the Fourth Amendment."[32] The position of the Obama administration, which was ultimately adopted by the court, is unequivocal: the detainees do not qualify as persons. As Roberto Esposito remarks in his incisive analysis of the biopolitics of the category of "personhood," "the personhood-deciding machine," here the US District Court, "marks the final difference between what must live and what can be legitimately cast to death."[33] The detainees thus become, in Jasbir Puar's terms, voided of "identitarian markers" and thus rendered "illegible as legal subjects."[34]

In his analysis of the juridical category of the "person," Esposito discloses how the repeated failures of human rights frameworks to provide universal protection for their named and intended subjects are due to infrastructural contradictions built into the actual framework. The category of "person" is foundationally dependent on its structural separation from whatever "thing" it stands in contradistinction to. Esposito unfolds the broad spectrum of figures and entities that encompass this constitutive process of separation and denegation through which the identity of the category of the "person" is maintained: "The general transition of humankind toward thingness, which has become the predominant tendency of our time, was opened up by this continuous transition from human to animal, from animal to vegetal, and from vegetal to mineral."[35] The cultural intelligibility of the category of "person" and its juridical saliency are predicated on an exclusionary process of negative differentiation that, no matter how much it is enlarged in terms of its inclusive capture of disparate subjects and entities, will always produce those very outlaw figures who will continue to supply, negatively, its conditions of intelligibility: "As long as the identity of the person is derived negatively from the thing—from its not-being a thing—the thing is destined to become the continually expanding space of everything the person distinguishes and distances itself from."[36] Shaker Aamer, another Guantánamo detainee, exemplifies this process in one of his accounts of life in the prison:

> They [the guards] referred to me as a "package" when they moved me from my cell. This is nothing new. I have been a package for 12 years now. I am a package when en route to Camp Echo, the solitary confinement wing. I am a package en route to a legal call. "The package has been picked up. . . . [T]he package has been delivered." It is not enough that we are called packages. At best, we are numbers. I worry that when I get home that my children will call for "Daddy," and I will sit unmoving. I am 239. I even refer to myself as 239 these days. I am not sure when I will ever be anything else. It is much easier to deny human rights to those who are not deemed to be "human."[37]

The rendering of the detainee as a mere package only individuated by the assignation of a number works to transmute the human subject into a fungible, serial commodity or thing. The biopolitical transmutation of the detainees into inanimate things is what, by definition, enables the continuing inapplicability of the category of "person" to Guantánamo's detainees and the ongoing derogation of their human rights. "Once assumed as an attribute or predicate of subjects rendered such by possessing specific social, political, and racial characteristics," Esposito notes, "a right ends up coinciding with the dividing line that separates and opposes them to those who are deprived of it."[38] The dividing line that separates and opposes the two categories, "person" and "non-person," effectively establishes a conceptual disjunction and an unbridgeable fault line ensuring that the one cannot align with the other. The US District Court's use of the negatives "nonresident" and "noncitizen" in its categorization of the detainees nullifies the detainees' claim to embody the status of flesh-and-blood human personhood. Guantánamo's detainees are thereby dispatched to the "locus of the 'non,'" to borrow a term from Anthony Wilden's work on paradoxical systems and structures.[39] Embodying the "locus of the 'non,'" the detainee is the figure inscribed in the rift of a "nonlocus in which an infinite number of negative sign-substitutions come into play":[40] "nonresident," "noncitizen," "nonlawful," and, signally, nonhuman "package" and "serial number" that can be tortured and liquidated without legal consequences. Law delineates the borders of this nonlocus at the same time as it authorizes the detainees' exile from the category of "person," instituting in the process the detainees' lived experience of a double externality: they are formally both before the law and yet extraneous to it—in the sense of being beyond the purview of any of the protective measures that law might extend or ensure under its aegis of rights. Crucially, in identifying how the category of "person" is founded "on an interaction between subjects characterized as being split between a site of legal imputation and a corporeal area subject to its control," Esposito reveals the contrivance at work in the transmutation, say, of a human subject into a "package." Consequent on Aamer's transition from human animal to inanimate commodity, a number of biopolitical effects are set in motion whereby "the body remains exposed to a mechanism of appropriation, disassemblage, and manipulation that ends up assimilating the body to a thing owned by others."[41] The violent operations of Guantánamo's carceral mechanism—which entailed the appropriation of Latif's body, the juridical disassemblage of his status as person, and a torturous regime of physical and psychological manipulation—powerfully evidence Esposito's thesis.

A dense history of zoopolitical metaphysics, founded on the hierarchized human/animal binary, underpins Guantánamo's onto-epistemological transmutation of its detainees into "things." In his analysis of the zoopolitical metaphysics that inform and enable the Kantian subject, Derrida discloses its axiomatic predication on the animal other: "The subject that is [hu]man is a person, 'one and the same person [die selbe Person],' therefore, who will be the subject of reason, morality, and the law. What exists in opposition to this person? Well, the thing. . . . The person is an entirely different thing (ganz verschiedenes Wesen), in rank and dignity (durch Rang und Würte), from these things (Sachen), which are irrational animals."[42] The power/knowledge effects that flow from this violent predication are visible in Guantánamo: "One has power and authority (walten) over these irrational animals because they are things. One can use them and lord over them as one pleases.'"[43] The testimonies of Guantánamo's detainees attest to the expansive capacity of the biopolitical state to lord it over them as one pleases and, as in the case of Adnan Latif, to wield this lethal modality of sovereign power and authority to the point of death.

The Animal in the Cage

Following Adnan Latif's death, an official AR 15-6 Investigation and Report was compiled by the Department of Defense. It was publicly released only due to a Freedom of Information request lodged by the investigative journalist Jeffrey Kaye. In his analysis of the report, Kaye notes: "The tenor of this report is captured in the fact that after the report's first page, Latif is never referred to by name but only as a number: ISN156. Additionally, the stressors of indefinite detention, 'forceful cell extractions' (beatings), isolation, and other forms of abuse and torture are practically never mentioned, while camp medical authorities are quick to label the young traumatic brain injury victim as someone who is personality disordered and antisocial."[44] As Kaye has already staged a detailed and trenchant critique of the report, exposing in the process the untenability of the report's key finding—specifically, that Latif managed to hoard a stash of medications and to overdose—I will not replicate his findings. Rather, the discussion that follows will center on certain incidents that are documented in the report but are relegated to a marginal status through the use of such textual apparatuses as the footnote.

Reading the military's AR 15-6 Investigation and Report on the death of Latif, I was struck, at point 42, by a perplexing instance of redaction. I reproduce here the fragmented syntax of this text:

> 42. (U/FOUO) At approximately 1740 25 July 2012, while in the BHU Recreation Yard 1, ISN156 ⟨(b)(7)(E),(b)(7)(F)⟩ ISN156 was able to ⟨(b)(7)(E),(b)(7)(F)⟩ .40.[45]

The nature of Latif's redacted activity in the recreation yard is, despite the redaction, clarified by footnote 40:

> 40 (U/FOUO) The issue of passing food at the recreation areas is linked to the issue of detainees feeding wildlife at GTMO, as detainees at Camp V, Camp VI, the BHU, and the DH encounter wildlife while in the recreation yards. The JDG Wildlife and Pest Control SOP [Standard Operating Procedures], and instances of the SOP not being enforced, are included later in the report ⟨(b)(7)(E),(b)(7)(F)⟩ .[46]

I cannot fathom the logic of staging this redaction in the first place, when the footnote explains what the redacted activity is: Latif is feeding the animals in the recreation yard. The situation regarding the relations between the detainees and Guantánamo's wildlife is addressed in full at point 153:

> 153. (U/FOUO) JDG Procedure #22 addresses Wildlife and Pest Control. . . . Commanders and subordinates shall ensure that camp leadership and guard force personnel are trained and "are aware of their responsibilities with respect to wildlife and pest control."[47]

The responsibilities with respect to wildlife extend to the nonhuman animals that inhabit the camp, even as these same responsibilities concerned with "pest control" can be read against the grain as what is captured in the standard operating procedures (SOPs) that govern the management of the camp's human detainees, who are effectively treated as nonhuman animals. Latif had firsthand experience of trying to survive his quartering in an animal cage. As discussed above, Latif was imprisoned in the camp's open-air cages soon after his arrival at Guantánamo. Murat Kurnaz, imprisoned for five years in Guantánamo only to be found innocent and eventually released, writes: "An animal has more space in its cage in a zoo and is given more to eat. I can hardly put into words what that actually means."[48] The zoopolitical inversions at work in Guantánamo ensure that while the detainees at Guantánamo are denied basic legal rights, the iguanas that inhabit the camp are protected by US law under the Endangered Species Act. As a technology of power founded on the hierarchization of life, the biopolitical caesura recalibrates and assigns its subjects along this hierarchy according to the exigencies of the regime that deploys it. In this case, the US government has deemed Guantánamo's detainees to be lower forms of life than the reptiles that inhabit the island and thus, as Mahvish Rukhsana Khan, a lawyer who volunteered to translate for the prisoners, remarks: "The prisoners at Guantánamo are entitled to fewer protections than the iguanas."[49]

Transcendence in the Animal

The human-animal relations framed by the JDG standard operating procedures regarding "wildlife and pest control" are inscribed by a series of prohibitions:

> 154. (U/FOUO) The SOP notes that iguanas "can and will become aggressive once they have been domesticated through feeding by humans." Accordingly, guards are instructed to not attempt to "feed, capture, or harm an iguana." "At no time will a detainee be allowed to feed an iguana." Similarly, noting that banana rats will bite if fed by guards or detainees, "at no time will a banana rat be fed." . . . Finally, because of the number of human diseases that pigeons carry, "[d]etainees that feed and give water to the birds should be discouraged from doing so. At no time should a detainee touch or pet these birds."[50]

Despite these prohibitions, a number of detainee testimonies illustrate how Guantánamo's SOPs have been repeatedly breached. The detainees' accounts describe how many animals intrepidly overcome the hypersecurity mechanisms of the prison, enter the detainees' recreation yard, and establish the possibility of the Open, a concept that I will presently discuss in some detail. The Open, to give a succinct definition at this juncture, is the space that the animals work to bring into being in concert with the detainees through acts of solicitation, promise, gifting, and intercorporeal communication. All these illicit activities override Guantánamo's SOPs, even as they trace the contours of another space within which, temporarily, other forms of being come into play. In the space of the Open in the cage, the animals and the detainees manage to engage in what Donna Haraway terms interspecies "responsive relationship[s]."[51] The responsive dimensions of these otherwise interdicted relations are evidenced in both points 155 and 156 of the report.

> 155. (U/FOUO) On numerous occasions, the Investigative Team observed stray cats, iguanas and pigeons lined up at the BHU/DH recreation yards.[52]

The lineup of this motley crew—stray cats, iguanas, and pigeons—cuts across the camp's series of blocks and interdictions designed to govern entry into the camp. This transgressive lineup of animals interpenetrates the layers of barriers that constitute Guantánamo's security regime, and agentically, the animals, in illicit relation with the detainees, establish fragile and transitory relations of interdependence and responsiveness. The animals, in fact, give the detainees the very intimate contact that is denied them at every level of their isolating and indefinite detention:

> 156. (U/FOUO) Several guards and medical personnel spoke of the detainees regularly feeding wildlife. A nurse at the BHU/DH ([(b)(3): 10 usc §130b, (b)(6).(b)(7)(C)]), for example, noted that one of the things that stuck out in her mind about ISN156 [Adnan Latif] was that he was allowed to leave food out for the iguanas at the BHU/DH recreation yards. She noted that stray cats, iguanas, and banana rats sometimes line up outside of the recreation yards, waiting for food. She also noted that one detainee, [(b)(6)(7)(C)], has pigeons regularly come and sit on his shoulder.[53]

In the soul-destroying context of Guantánamo's cage there emerges, in these instances of illicit human-animal contact, moments of intercorporeal communication and haptic exchange. The fragile materialization of the Open that the detainees and the animals bring into being, even though it is circumscribed by the bars of the cage, works momentarily to hollow out the rules and the very steel bars of the prison in order to establish a completely other locus. Rather than following either Heideggerian or Agambenian understandings of the Open[54]—as the space for the disclosure of being and so on—I want to draw on their term to resignify it. Indeed, my reading stands in contradistinction to Martin Heidegger's strictly anthropocentric understanding of the Open. In his theorization of the Open, Heidegger posits language, which he views dogmatically as an exclusively human attribute, as what is actually constitutive of the Open:

> But language is not only and not primarily an audible and written expression of what is to be communicated. It not only puts forth in words and statements what is overtly or covertly intended to be communicated; language alone brings what is, as something that is, into the Open for the first time. Where there is no language, as in the being of stone, plant, and animal, there is also no openness of what is, and consequently no openness of that which is not and of the empty.[55]

Predicating his thesis on the Open on the most reductive and ethologically untenable conceptualization of language, Heidegger precludes animals from accessing the Open. In my reading, animals work to bring the Open into being for Guantánamo's detainees. In the context of Guantánamo, the Open in the cage establishes a space that enables the intimate contact between one, the detainee, and the other, the animal. The Open must be seen as a paradoxical or heterotopic space precisely because it temporarily coexists within the very locus of the most violent and confining of prisons: Guantánamo. The cats, iguanas, and banana rats ferret their way through the bars and series of cages and emerge in the space of the detainees' recreation enclosure. In the context of this other cage, they construct the possibility of the Open: a creature of free movement enters the cage and beckons and solicits the prisoners for food. The animals initiate practices of haptic exchange and complex, indeterminate relations of affect that trace what Nicole Anderson terms both the "limits and possibilities of animal-human relations."[56] Rainer Maria Rilke, in one of his Duino Elegies, eloquently articulates the possibility of envisaging this other space and its possibilities for freedom. He writes:

> With all of its eyes the animal world
> Beholds the Open. Only ours
> are as if inverted and set all around it
> like traps at the doors to freedom.[57]

Even as it is couched in the language of *poiesis*, this is not an instance of mystic speech. Rather, Rilke's lines work toward the demystification of the epistemic occlusions so insistently reproduced by Euro-anthropocentric language-thought. Guantánamo's other animal residents—its banana rats, cats, and birds—see the Open precisely in the most impossible of loci: the cage. They stage their infractions of Guantánamo's rules and agentically navigate its fences, razor wire, and guard towers in order to enter the cage and assert the possibility of freedom in the face of its total denial by the forces of the military-security gulag. What is established in the space of the Open in the cage is a "difficult freedom" that is at once transitory and material.[58]

Through their transgressive movements and interactions, the animals carve out a new volumetric space that would otherwise remain unseen and unimaginable: the Open in the cage. The Open in the cage that Guantánamo's animals, in concert with its inmates, create defies the punitive geometry of the cage, the brutalizing logic of shackles, and the violent practices of enforced isolation and sensory deprivation. Guantánamo's animals temporarily unloose the shackles and release the traps set at the door of freedom. Their agentic acts, precisely as interlopers that evade and defy the circumscriptions of the cage, cause the bars, the shackles, and the razor wire to be held, for the briefest of moments, in suspensive animation—all these penal technologies of punishment and unfreedom become, on the entry of the animals, quasi-invisible as the detainees lose sight of their own harrowing conditions of imprisonment: for a moment, to draw on a memorable Levinasian phrase, "there is a transcendence in the animal!"[59] My invocation of the notion of transcendence in the animal is not hyperbolic. As I discuss in detail below, by drawing on the testimonies of a number of detainees, the experience of transcendence in the animal has been a lived and life-enhancing fact for the detainees in the context of this military prison. Furthermore, as previously discussed in the introduction, I note here the differential relations of power that inscribe the categories of "the human" and "the animal." Whereas "the human" is invariably individualized as always already a unique subject, the figure of "the animal" is, in Western discourses, invariably ensnared by the trap of the definite article and bound by the resultant strictures of homogenization, genericity, and fungibility.[60] This is a distinctly Western linguistic trait, in contrast to a number of Indigenous languages. "Most Native languages," Gregory Cajete writes, "do not have a specific word for 'animals.' Rather, when animals are referred to they are called by their specific name. The fact that there are no generic words for animals underlines the extent to which animals are considered to interpenetrate with human life." This exemplifies "an attitude of partnership and mutual participation."[61] It is precisely this attitude of partnership and mutual participation between the detainees and the animals in the context of the Open in the cage that I want to flesh out in some detail.

What the detainees describe in their testimonies is not, significantly, transcendence in the animal through theological acts of sacrifice or commodifying acts of possession or domestication. Rather, they attest to the experience of transcendence, in Merleau-Ponty's words, "as thought by divergence [pensée *d'écart*], not possession of the object."[62] The "absolute proximity" of an animal visitant in relation to a detainee is simultaneously inscribed by an "irremediable distance"—and it is this phenomenological relation that instantiates its ethical dimensions.[63] It is the encounter with animal alterity that establishes the conditions of possibility to be enveloped by the transient space of the Open and to be elevated, momentarily, beyond the binding shackles of the cage. This is transcendence, to couch it once again in Levinasian terms, through the *height* of the animal: the animals arrive and leave on their own terms, outside those assimilative frames that would ensnare them into the anthropocentric "imperialism of the same."[64] Through their volitional departures and returns, the animals produce discontinuous states of being for the detainees, between the violence of the cage and the life-enhancing space of the Open. Even as the animals establish relations of proximity with the detainees, they continue to maintain their own agency and alterity in the space of the Open. Guantánamo's animals cut across the Heideggerian grain: the very captivations and deficits Heidegger ascribes to them are, in Rilke's sense, precisely what they transgress, evade, and exceed.[65]

In the space of the Open in the cage, the roosting of a bird on a detainee's shoulder speaks otherwise to him of his plight: the bird establishes intercorporeal relations inflected by a lightness of touch and by the warmth of a body that is not there to inflict violence or to demand subjugation. As a material manifestation of the other, the bird comes from the outside and embodies everything that Guantánamo violently negates and prohibits. In the utter impossibility of experiencing that emblematic sign of freedom, the exterior horizon, the Open in the cage establishes the possibility to access the glancing reprieve of an interior horizon that offers the detainees some hope in the face of all the institutional forces mobilized to ensure its foreclosure. On the wing, the bird works to open the possibility of a horizon: in the wake of their flight, the bird traces the unseen and interdicted external horizon and, in a transversal arc and swoop, overrides the bars of the cage to bring this gift to the detainee. In the space of this encounter, the detainee, who is often literally riveted by shackles to the very ground of his being, momentarily experiences what Emmanuel Levinas would term an "excendence,"[66] or escape from that unrelenting subjection that constitutes his ontological reality within the prison. This excendence transpires precisely because of the detainee's relation to the animal. It is, indeed, the animal that establishes the conditions of possibility for the detainee to experience a rupture from the brutal rivetedness of his incarcerated being and, momentarily, to transcend his state of carceral subjection through the experience of the seeming paradox of "transcendence within immanence."[67]

Through practices of dialogic communication and exchange, relations of trust and, even more important, practices of acknowledgment between animal and human are established, and through these practices, Guantánamo's violent regime of prohibitions, negations, and arbitrary and retributive punishments is temporarily held in abeyance. The locus of the Open generates what is elsewhere interdicted in this prison: intimacy, communicative responsiveness, and mutual acknowledgment. And the positive effects of this on the detainees cannot be overestimated. Point 157 in the report on Latif's death underscores this:

> 157. (U/FOUO) The OIC for the BHU/DH and Camp Iguana (⎡ (b)(3): 10 USC §130b, ⎤
> ⎣ (b)(6).(b)(7)(C) ⎦) indicated he understood that although generally
> not allowed, certain detainees were allowed to interact with the wild-
> life. (⎡ (b)(3): 10 USC §130b, (b)(6).(b)(7)(C) ⎤ indicated that ⎡ (b)(6)(7)(C) ⎤ had
> ⎣ (b)(7)(E) ⎦ ⎣ (b)(7)(E) ⎦ . He also noted that ISN156 was "usually al-
> lowed to feed animals on doctor's orders because it helped keep him
> calm."[68]

Adnan Latif, only ever referred to by his identificatory and anonymizing number ISN156, reaches out to the animals in the space of the Open in the cage. In the context of Guantánamo, what unfolds in the space of the Open are provisional interspecies encounters that briefly punctuate the carceral continuum that constitutes virtually the entirety of his existence. These provisional interspecies encounters are, on the one hand, little more than transient rifts that disrupt the killing time of indefinite detention; on the other hand, they establish life-enhancing moments of reprieve in the face of the violence that bookends Latif's penal existence. As moments of excendence, they exemplify the "need to get out of oneself, that is, *to break that most radical and unalterably binding of chains, the fact that I [moi] is oneself [soi-même]*."[69] For the detainees, the binding of chains is at once symbolic and brutally literal in the context of a site where one's existence is defined entirely by an apparatus of wholesale subjection; yet the ephemeral creation of the Open in the cage enables the momentary loosening of the chains. The Open in the cage gifts to the detainees a passing experience of deriveting and excendence from the violent continuum of the gulag.

Entomology of Excendence

Of the five and a half years that Ahmed Errachidi was imprisoned in Guantánamo, he spent four in complete isolation in Camp Echo—described as the "worst facility" in the entire camp. "I was on my own," Errachidi writes. "In Echo there was only one cell, one guard. . . . That's where I broke down because I couldn't see the sky, couldn't see the sunlight, couldn't see the other prisoners, for many months. . . . I didn't know what I was doing."[70] In the context of his complete isolation, Errachidi discovers unexpected company:

> I became aware that I was not entirely alone when I was in punishment either. Visitors would come in their dozens, three times a day, after every meal. I'd eagerly await them and, after they pitched up, I'd sit with them and enjoy their company. I could spend long hours with them without becoming bored, for they offered me a hint that a normal life still existed. Their presence made me smile and comforted me. I'd watch them sneaking in so as not to alert the soldiers. I'm talking about ants.[71]

Errachidi describes the comfort, pleasure, and hope that a community of ants brought to him once they managed to infiltrate his cell: "These beautiful creatures would visit me in my metal prison carrying with them hope and life. I'd save food for them. I'd put it in a corner away from the prying eyes of the soldiers; if they saw my visitors they'd either spray them with insecticide or squash them with their boots. If I was caught feeding the ants I knew I'd be punished with either smaller rations or extra days in punishment, but, despite this, I continued to encourage them."[72]

In the blank space of his maximum-isolation cell and in the dead time of indefinite detention, this community of ants marks the passing of time, even as it enables Errachidi to emplace himself within a fragile agentic position that enables him to offer hospitality and to exercise a generosity of spirit toward the ants. What is instantiated by the presence of the ants is a covert, transitory, but real redistribution of power in which a prisoner reduced to a state of utter subjection is enabled to mobilize ethical agency toward the other:

> Sometimes I'd save a peanut, splitting the nut in half and putting each half on the floor, flat side down. The ants would come and eat the halves from the inside, leaving the skin. Such was their delicacy that, unless you turned over the nut, you wouldn't have been able to guess it was empty. . . . These ants were a rare sign of life, and when they appeared animation would creep into the deadness of my solitary cell and, for that moment, I'd feel optimism rather than despair.[73]

In the deadness of Errachidi's cell and in the killing solitude of maximum isolation, the entry of ants announces animation and life. In the midst of a cell devoid of all coordinates and stripped of all personal effects, a cell emptied of all living things except for the prisoner, the ants bring to Errachidi the gift of community through interspecies relations. This community of animals, focused on productive labor and nurturing solidarity, establishes for him the possibility to experience, for a moment, optimism rather than despair, peace rather than violence: "I loved to sit and study them and I learned a lot from them. When they came marching in their rows I saw how they helped each other to transport food. All their activity and organization was achieved with the finest discipline. Watching them would give me a sense of peace and tranquility."[74] This community of ants brings the external world into the detainee's cell, delineating in the process the configuration of the Open—precisely as that which allows Errachidi both to hope and to imagine an elsewhere not constituted by the existential nothingness and despair of his maximum-isolation cell. Through their delicate labors, the ants sculpt a downturned half-peanut into a hollowed shell that stays intact even though it has been emptied. Everything here pivots on the possibility of walking lightly on the earth: the soft fall of ants' feet is coextensive with their adroit ability to eat only what they need and to leave all else intact. This picture stands in stark contrast to the bludgeoning violence visited on the detainees by the Emergency Reaction Force (ERF), as described by Errachidi:

> When they were ready to attack a prisoner in his cell they'd form a human train, the soldier at the front wielding a large shield, the kind riot police use. . . . The cell door would be opened, another soldier would spray a hot gas know as OC (oleoresin capsicum) spray into the prisoner's face, causing excruciating pain to his eyes, skin and throat as well as choking the prisoner and making him collapse. Once the prisoner was on the ground, the other soldiers would rush in and beat him. . . . Some would lift our heads off the ground before smashing them down on the metal floor. Some would twist our fingers back hard enough to break them.[75]

In the face of this implacable violence, Errachidi reflects that it is "unimaginable to me how they [the guards] not only withstood our cries for compassion but also continued to live normal lives."[76] Acutely alert to the violence and destruction that shadows his every move within the prison, Errachidi extends to the community of ants the very thing denied to him: compassion. At the first sign of the guards, a well-aimed breath works to alert the ants to imminent danger, allowing them to flee back to their nests:

> But their presence also brought danger—when the soldiers inspected my cell, I was always frightened they'd find the ants. I developed a warning system: if I heard a guard on his way, I'd blow on the ants and they'd scatter back to

their homes while I got rid of the food. They soon became accustomed to this warning signal, and each time would run from it. Even so, after the soldiers had searched my cell, the first thing I'd look for were the remains of the ants. When they didn't find any I'd smile and know they'd escaped.[77]

Attentive to the ever-present threat of violence, Errachidi takes to heart the ants' exposedness and vulnerability and the possibility of their being crushed by a military boot or exterminated by pesticide. If they had been discovered, what would the guards have annulled—the lives of mere insects framed as little more than disposable vermin? On the contrary, within the micro-ethico-ecology of Errachidi's prison cell the ants establish the possibility for mutually constitutive relations:

And they were so intelligent. Whenever I put food in the corner, the first ant to find it would quickly show the others the food. Such a valuable lesson: one ant bringing prosperity to the whole nation. I used to think how beautiful the world would be if human beings behaved in the same way. The second lesson the ants taught me was that . . . the ants were so varied in their contributions; some carried small pieces while others carried pieces bigger than themselves. They were such a great example of the benefits of collective action.[78]

The ants enable Errachidi to offer his gift of hospitality, and in return the ants establish the Open in the cage, offering him the possibility to experience optimism and the consolations of philosophical reflection inspired by interspecies relations. This underground community supplies him with entomological lessons on the ecology of a mutually sustainable life. For Errachidi, the ants bring into visibility another world that occupies Guantánamo but that is otherwise entirely effaced from its official texts and practices. This other world inscribes the foundations of Guantánamo: ants' tunnels, trails, and nests that testify, for Errachidi, to the ongoing existence of an inspirational eusocial life of coexistence, cooperation, and productive labor. The ants impart, through their diverse practices, a number of entomological lessons configured by the specificity of their own formic epistemology. They compel Errachidi to reflect on the violent extinguishment of compassion for the other in his own carceral locus and on the absence of a communitarian sociality. He names, in a revelatory move, the *aesthetic* value of the ants that come into his cell: "These beautiful creatures would visit me in my metal prison carrying with them hope and life." Their formic beauty offers him a sense of hope that momentarily transcends the life-negating solitude of his prison-bound existence.

Shaker Aamer, imprisoned in Guantánamo for more than thirteen years without charge and, at one stage, isolated in Camp Echo for two years and ten months, further underscores this understanding of what animals could provide in the confines of his prison cell. During his time in an isolation cell, he describes how

> I ended up making friends with all kinds of creatures. One of them is the ants, because they were beautiful, the way they were doing things. . . . I start watching them. I start learning the different ants, the different colors, the different way of doing things. And it was beautiful and I learnt so much and they became so friendly with me that I believe, I do believe that animals, insects, all kind of things, that they do realize us, they do know us; but we don't know the difference between them because they are ants, but they know me, they knew me—as me—because I used to feed them three times a day, put them the food [sic].[79]

In the opening pages of his theorization of the different lifeworlds that are constituted by the diverse entities that inhabit the earth, Jakob von Uexküll asks the reader to imagine "a soap bubble around each creature to represent its own world, filled with the perceptions which it alone knows." It is only, he stresses, "when we ourselves then step into one of these bubbles" that a "new world comes into being."[80] Uexküll names the entity-specific world of a living being an *Umwelt*, which he glosses as "the *phenomenal world* or the *self-world* of the animal."[81] In his testimony, Aamer describes in detail the *Umwelt* of a detainee imprisoned indefinitely in the life-crushing isolation of a maximum-security cell. He also, however, testifies to the transformative agency of the ants that enter his cell. They experientially hail into existence an embodied identity that exceeds and momentarily transcends the limits of his prison confines and his carceral subjectivity: in Aamer's words, the ants "realize" him into a different type of existence. Moreover, in the life-negating anonymity that Aamer was forced to endure in his isolation cell at the camp—where, as I discussed above, he was only ever identified by his Internment Serial Number (239)—the ants individuate him as a unique subject: "They know me, they knew me—*as me*." "One should pay attention," says Black Elk, Lakota Indian elder, "to even the smallest of crawling creatures for these too have a valuable lesson to teach us, and even the smallest ant may wish to communicate to a man."[82] In his testimony, Aamer illuminates Black Elk's exhortation. He describes how, in the context of his isolation cell, the seemingly impermeable "bubbles" of his and the ants' *Umwelten* intersect and generate, in the process, intersubjective communications and intercorporeal relations and effects:

I used to sleep on the floor and they opened a small hole next to my head to cut the space, cut the journey short. I didn't like it because when they go through that hole they go over my face and all that and they wake me up. So, I went and touch my saliva and I put it on the hole . . . so they came and found the saliva and they got scared and they started running around. And then they cleaned it and then I saw them coming back again. And then I said, "Come on you guys, I'm feeding you and now you're bothering me. I'm waking up all night long" . . . so I put again the saliva. . . . The third day when I did, you know what they did? They sealed it. They sealed the hole, which is what I wanted. Brought little bits of rusted metals and things and they sealed it. . . . And that's one of the things that kept me going, that I had someone to talk to. I had some people to watch, some insect to watch, to give me time.[83]

In his account, Aamer evidences the zoosemiotics of interspecies language and communication, which in this case constitutes a lexico-syntax of saliva, gesture, speech, and bits of rusted metal. Remarking on how, for many Native Americans, "this phenomenon of interspecies communication has always been present,"[84] Vine Deloria Jr. invokes the words of Pretty Shield and her relationship with ants: "The ants help me. I listen to them always. They are my medicine, these busy, powerful little people, the ants."[85] Pretty Shield's words resonate with Aamer's. He identifies the ants as "people" that he could observe in the void of his isolation cell and that, therapeutically, "gave him time." As living entities sharing the space and food in his cell, they worked to disrupt the blank absence of time generated by both his term of indefinite detention and the total isolation from the markers that would allow him to perceive the passing of time. "It is precisely this help, from these, our other-than-human relatives," notes Deloria, "that indigenous thinkers are not embarrassed to call on."[86]

Across a number of Indigenous cosmo-epistemologies, animals are viewed as a priori *speaking subjects* that are in communicative relations with humans. In exhorting the assumption of one's "responsibilities for all living things," for example, Deloria asks: "Who will listen to the trees, the animals and birds, the voices of the places of the land?"[87] Unlike some Western animal rights groups that posit animals as "voiceless"—and thus only coming to voice via human mediation and translation and thereby reproducing, in turn, an anthropocentric parsimony of speech and language that unintentionally consolidates its own form of onto-epistemological violence—in Indigenous cosmo-epistemologies animals, rocks, plants, and the collectivity of the more-than-human world are seen as speaking subjects that one should attend to carefully as they speak in the specificity of their own languages. Deloria here offers a clear reply to Derrida's rhetorical question "And say the animal responded?"[88] Across a number of Indigenous worldviews, animals and other-than-human entities have always already responded. It is Westerners who have been inattentive to their voices.

Aamer's description of his relationship with the animals that would visit him includes accounts of the violence and subterfuges that also ensued, precisely because all contact between the detainees and the camp's animals was officially proscribed. He identifies a number of feral cats, including Amira and Susu, with whom he established close relationships, and then reveals that "they [the guards] keep hunting them, they keep trapping them and kill them because it brought so much joy to the brothers. We used to sacrifice so much because of them. The brothers, they used to hide the food, hide the meat, the tuna, and we used to get punished. If you feed them, you get punished. So the brothers used to go through a lot from the early days . . . to feed them."[89] Despite these interdictions, Aamer continued to maintain his relationship with the camp's animals. He describes the profound significance of this relationship:

> Specially for someone like me, who's been isolated all the time, I have to find something, someone to talk to, to play with, and I used to do that with the animals, with birds. . . . And it came . . . in the time, feeding them all the time, the time came when I was one with the world, with it, I didn't even care to be there forever, because they used to come and just sit with me . . . on my shoulder—the raven, which is a very smart bird, they would come and sit with me, *actually*, and just eat from my hand . . . and it makes you come out of Guantánamo *completed*.[90]

Aamer articulates here the power of the Open. He reflects on what Guantánamo's animals gifted to him in defiance of the gulag's regime of axiomatic violence and total isolation. His narrative becomes revelatory in tone and the repetition of the word *time* works to amplify the emotional import of what he has experienced: "And it came . . . in the *time*, feeding them all the *time*, the *time* came when I was one with the world." In an unexpected move, the reinscription of time in the timeless space of his indefinite detention is no sooner marked than Aamer dissolves it and makes it redundant: "I didn't even care to be there forever." His account bears witness to the transformative power of the Open in the cage and to his arresting experience of transcendence in the animal—to the point that he can contemplate the prospect of remaining in Guantánamo "forever": "The time came when I was one with the world," and this made him feel "completed." The power of this sense of completion becomes intelligible only when it is juxtaposed against the years of violent fragmentation, of the ravaging hunger strikes, isolation, and torture that Aamer endured and survived. For Aamer, the Open gives way to another space that heals the fractures, conjoins the fragments, and is imbued with the wonder that another living entity, the raven, would actually come and sit and feed from his hand and offer acknowledgment of his existence without violence. Everything that is magnetized in this utopic space—that transcends the prison, stanches his pain, and has the capacity to make Aamer whole again—is, I stress, transitory and wholly contingent on the fragile moment made possible by his experience of the Open. As Aamer's other testimonies document, these are rare rifts in time that punctuate the continuum of a carceral existence assailed by physical and psychological torture.

Mansoor Adayfi, imprisoned for fourteen years in Guantánamo, states: "Until I was 35 [the time of his release], the most significant relationship I'd had as an adult was with an iguana." "Even when we went outside for recreation," he writes, "we were not allowed to talk to the other detainees. But outside we did meet new friends: the cats, banana rats, tiny birds and iguanas that came through the fences, asking to share our meals."[91] Adayfi's most profound relationship was with an iguana:

> She used to come every day at the same time, and we would have lunch together. When I went on hunger strike, I had no food to give her, and I was ashamed to stand there without food as she came up to me. Sometimes the guards punished us for sharing our meals with the animals, but they couldn't stop me from talking to her.... As the years passed, our friendship grew into a strong bond. ... Thanks to my friend, the beautiful iguana, I learned how to take care of others. She reminded me how to connect with life while I was behind the fences of a prison.[92]

The daily visit of the iguana establishes a relationship of proximity, acknowledgment, and friendship. The art of friendship is practiced through rituals of loyalty and hospitality. When, due to his hunger strikes, Adayfi has no food to gift to the iguana, this rupture is marked by a sense of shame as she approaches and finds his hands empty. Regardless, the friendship survives these lapses and continues to grow. The friendship between the iguana and Adayfi suggests the possibility of experiencing interspecies relations that defy calculative economies of credits and debits. Their interspecies friendship worked to annul systems of hierarchical positionality grounded in the hubris of human exceptionalism: the iguana continues to teach Adayfi "how to take care of others." Reflecting on the many conceits of anthropocentrism that are punctured and overturned by Indigenous cosmo-epistemologies, Linda Hogan writes: "How greatly we have overvalued ourselves and ignored the other intelligences around us."[93] The ethics of care that the iguana taught Adayfi both defied and outlived the violent interdictions that governed his time in the prison: "My hope is still alive," writes Adayfi on his release from Guantánamo. "It helps me face the hardships of my daily life."[94] In this context, the Euro-anthropocentric slander that is the word *reptilious*—hideous, indifferent, and repulsive—is resignified into an affirmative adjective: Adayfi's reptilious friend connected him back to life, hope, and the nurturing compact of friendship.

The interspecies relations that transform Guantánamo, momentarily, into an entirely other space for the detainees can be further amplified by calling on the testimony of another detainee: Mohamed Bashmilah, a victim of the US practice of extraordinary rendition. As Bashmilah was held in a number of secret prisons for nineteen months before being released without charge, the Senate Intelligence Committee Report on CIA Torture identified him as "among 26 prisoners wrongfully detained" by the CIA.[95] During the time of his imprisonment, Bashmilah was forced to endure the gamut of torture practices. In an interview in which he documents his harrowing experiences in the CIA's black-site prisons, he interrupts his torture testimony with this story: "Whenever I saw a fly in my cell, I was filled with joy. Although I would wish for it to slip from under the door so it would not be imprisoned itself."[96] In the context of Bashmilah's prison cell and the traumatic regime of torture he was forced to endure, the interposition of the fly works to stall thoughts of death and to enable a moment of reprieve from the trauma of torture. There is, for Bashmilah, more than a temporary surcease of pain; there is, for him, the experience of a sense of joy that, however fragile, is affirming of his being in the midst of the otherwise torturous negation of the worth of his existence.

For the guards and jailers, the fly is both meaningless and invisible because of its quotidian status. As such, it is little more than what Maurice Blanchot terms a "platitude." But, Blanchot immediately adds, "this banality is also what is most important, if it brings us back to existence in its very spontaneity and as it is lived."[97] In the face of the trauma Bashmilah is compelled daily to endure, the fly enables Bashmilah to once again experience existence in its very spontaneity and as it is lived—with, crucially, the life-force of joy that he feels surge up within him as he sees the fly defy the imprisoning walls and bars of his cage and achieve an otherwise impossible freedom of movement. The dynamic, if fleeting, pathways that the fly traces through the air of the cell work to create the Open and to spatialize freedom in defiance of the prison's arsenal of constraints. The real freedom of the fly is generative, for Bashmilah, of the possibility of experiencing freedom as virtuality, as imagined flight on the wings of a fly. The anguished certitude of enchained captivity is momentarily replaced by joy in the free movement of the other and the promissory possibilities that this evokes for Bashmilah: he wishes the fly to escape under the prison door to a world of larger freedom.

In the stillness of his cell, the fly introduces new spatiotemporal dimensions to Bashmilah's solitary existence. The fly in Bashmilah's cell is at once their own being and also a charged emblem of freedom as they navigate the space of the prison. Through the vectors of their flight, the fly traces the very possibility of experiencing the Open in the cage and its promise of freedom. The fly is the essence of freedom emblematically condensed in entomological form. Ontologically, the fly enacts freedom as they succinctly sign the term through the facticity of their unencumbered flight. And, as with Aamer's ants, the fly disrupts the dead time of indefinite detention through their flight around the cell. The fly's flight liberates time through the changing articulations of their positional bearings across the space of the cell. The aleatory movements of the fly trace unexpected spatial configurations that resignify Bashmilah's place of confinement and enable him, despite his arrested existence, to experience joy. Emerging from the layered dimensions of this relation between a prisoner and a fly, Bashmilah's joy in the fly embodies his moment of excendence despite the chains that rivet him to a form of death-in-life. Through this transcendence in the animal, existence temporarily tears itself away from everything that grounds it in the immanence of captivity and pain. Within the carceral confines of his cell, through the flight of a fly Bashmilah experiences overflight: he accedes to a different order of existence that allows him, for the briefest of moments, to occupy a utopic plane not constituted by the otherwise inescapable reality of his unjust imprisonment and torture. Experienced as a moment of excendence, the buzz of the fly brings into Bashmilah's cell "the noise of the infinite in the small."[98]

Inanimal Violence: Zoopolitics of Torture Practices

In the context of Guantánamo, the affirmative relations that some of the detainees experienced with insects is counterpointed by an antithetical fact: insects were actually considered by the operatives of the Bush administration as prospective torture weapons that could be deployed against the detainees. In one of the Torture Memos, Assistant Attorney General Jay Bybee listed a series of what he deemed "legal" enhanced techniques for interrogating one of the detainees, Abu Zubaydah. These techniques constituted practices of torture that in fact contravened the US antitorture statute. One of the techniques he sanctioned for use against Zubaydah included the use of "insects placed in a confinement box" to capitalize on his assumed entomophobia.[99] Bybee's recommendation that insects be instrumentalized into weapons of torture can be situated within a long genealogy of the abuse of insects as weaponized instruments of war that stretches into the contemporary context. The US Defense Advanced Research Projects Agency (DARPA), for example, is working "to merge evolution and engineering, to take insects and 'turn them into war-fighting technologies.'"[100] In his history of the weaponization of insects for the conduct of war, Jeffrey Lockwood reveals, "Today, scientists are designing insect-machine hybrids—tiny cyborgs to infiltrate enemy positions, gather military intelligence, and assassinate key individuals."[101]

The histories of zoopolitical violence, with their instrumentalization of animals, that supply the onto-epistemic infrastructure of Guantánamo's torture practices are complex and layered, and I discuss them in detail elsewhere.[102] Suffice it here to identify and analyze one element of this history to disclose its zoopolitical continuities and violent operational logics. One of the torture techniques approved by the Torture Memos, and consequently deployed at Guantánamo, was that of "learned helplessness," which was intended to reduce a detainee to a compliant, docile, and confessional subject. This technique was developed by Martin Seligman, a psychologist at the University of Pennsylvania. Seligman tested and proved his original hypothesis on animals, specifically dogs:

> Various dogs were exposed to a series of shocks over the course of a week. One group of dogs came to understand that they could move to a different area to escape the shocks. Another group of dogs was conditioned to understand that there was no behavior that the dog could undertake to avoid the treatment. After days of confusing stimuli and persistent jolts of electricity, the dogs in the second group came to accept their fate as permanent. They would respond to pain lying down and whimpering "helplessly" rather than attempt an escape.[103]

Seligman's zoopolitical experiments on animals expose the otherwise invisibilized specter that haunts sites such as Guantánamo: the violent history of animal experimentation that has shaped and materially informed torture practices of behavior modification in the context of military and penal institutions. As I discussed in chapter 1, this zoopolitical specter cannot be relegated to the past, as animals continue to be the subjects of scientifico-military experimentation. The physical and psychological violence inflicted by Seligman on the dogs held as prisoners in his experiments establishes a type of baseline for what is acceptable in terms of the institutionalized practices of violence and torture deployed for the sake of behavior modification. The dogs in Seligman's experiment supplied the ontological ground that, through violence and trauma, was sublimated and reified into scientific knowledge. This abstracted scientific knowledge was exported to both US domestic and transnational military and penal sites, where it informed the torture practices inflicted on the targeted human prisoners. Under license from the Torture Memos, Seligman's technique was practically transposed to the torture chambers of Guantánamo, Bagram, Abu Ghraib, the Salt Pit, and so on. It would find its emblematic victim in José Padilla, who after three years of "learned helplessness" torture was transformed into an entity "so docile and inactive" that, in the words of his wardens, "he could be mistaken for 'a piece of furniture.'"[104] The torture practices that Padilla was compelled to endure trace an inexorable line of biopolitical descent from human to animal to, finally, a "piece of furniture."

The foundational status of this zoopolitical anthropocentrism is perhaps best evidenced by the fact that the UN Convention against Torture and Other Cruel, Inhuman or Degrading Treatment as Punishment tacitly codifies and enshrines the human/animal caesura in both the title and substance of its text. Tacitly animating the lexico-discursive logics of "inhuman" treatment, as outlined in the convention, is the speciesist knowledge of its nonhuman animal other—against whom unrestrained violence can be perpetrated with impunity. When, in article I, the convention declares that "it does not include pain or suffering arising only from, inherent in or incidental to lawful sanctions,"[105] it names by default the anthropocentric facticity of the "lawful" torture, degradation, and cruel abuse of animals that supplies the onto-epistemological substratum for human torture. The zoopolitical violence that underpins torture practices classified as "lawful sanctions" is graphically evidenced, for example, by the US Coast Guard's "trauma training drill in which live goats were shot, stabbed and dismembered." This exercise in "live tissue" training entailed "course instructors . . . repeatedly cutting off the limbs of live goats with tree trimmers, stabbing the animals with scalpels, and cutting into their abdomens to pull out their organs as they twitched, moaned, and kicked."[106] The torture of the live goats is here caught in a process of biopolitical transfiguration that converts the violence into the higher-order purpose of "homeland security," for the coast guard, as a branch of the US Armed Forces, operates under the aegis of the Department of Homeland Security.

Operative in this scene of violence is the reproduction and securitization of the settler state's biopolitical sovereignty, cast here in a distinctly zoopolitical register. As the US state's presumed inalienable sovereignty (alienated from the Native American nations it has colonized) is based on control over its borders, the border emerges as the site of physical and symbolic violence that dramatizes the nonnegotiable force of settler law.[107] On the border, the intersection of different modalities of zoopolitical violence is instantiated. On the border, the goats are compelled to embody all the descriptors that animate the enemies of the state. Caught in a matrix of zoopolitical vectors, the goats become other than themselves: they are transmuted into prospective terrorists, enemies, or illegal aliens who supply the live flesh for practices of systematic elimination through the performative violence of shooting, stabbing, and dismembering. The biopolitical securitization and flourishing of US citizens is purchased through the ritualized dismemberment of the animal transfixed in the lethal zone of the border. As the live flesh on which "trauma training drills" can be "lawfully" conducted, the goats cease to be anything other than convenient placeholders for the targeted human subject who, de jure, fails to qualify for the category of "the human." Here the literality of the border works to inscribe the hierarchized binaries of the biopolitical state that must be policed and violently securitized: citizen/alien, human/animal, and sovereign/beast. The system of equivalences that inscribes this interchangeable series is both enabled and guaranteed by the violent operations of zoopolitics. The category of "inhuman" torture merely serves as an obfuscatory ruse that deflects attention away from the baseline "lawful" torture of any entity classified as "animal." The a priori politicality of the animal is evidenced on the fault line of the border as the goats are inserted within circuits of zoopolitical violence that bind them topologically to the other (human) animals that can be tortured, killed, or left to die with impunity: asylum seekers, refugees, and "irregular migrants." Instantiated here is a zoopolitical relation animated by the serial logic of animal genericity and fungibility.

In this zoopolitical schema, the goats stand as "live tissue" that can be converted into dead meat to fulfill the coast guard's mission to protect the borders of the nation. The quartering of the goats' limbs with tree trimmers ensures the preservation of the state's polity—specifically, it ensures the safeguarding of the integrity of its borders and the protection of its indivisible sovereignty. The integrity of the one is secured through the dismemberment of the other. The symmetry of this proposition is predicated on the asymmetry of the biopolitical caesura. A secularized religious practice, *ars haruspicina* (art of entrails divination), informs this "trauma training drill" through which the sovereignty of the border is consecrated. The cutting into the goats' abdomens and the extraction of their organs places this scene of zoopolitical violence in the realm of ritual animal sacrifice. This enactment of ritual animal sacrifice, however, occludes the dimensions of its rituality and sacrificiality through the use of medico-military language: "trauma training drill." This deployment of terror and violence against animals is thus codified and neutralized as a form of scientific practice that will develop the coast guard's education skills ("trauma training"), precisely as it is routinized as nothing more than a mundane "drill." The clinical naming of live, sentient animals as nothing more than "live tissue" ensures their conversion into the instrumentalized assemblage of animal-object-thing that can be tortured and killed with impunity. Regardless of these occlusive moves, once situated at the violent intersection of zoopolitical violence, sovereignty, and the securitization of the border, the dismembering of the live goats stands as an instantiation of ritual animal sacrifice. What is left to do but to read the goats' entrails for signs that will disclose what the biopolitical gods augur with regard to the state of the border and all of the prospective enemies who stand to assail and dismember it?

The violent practices of treating a subject "like an animal"—with their attendant semantics of "dehumanization" and "inhumanity"—can only maintain their intelligibility and valency by being posited on the zoopolitics of an animal other that supplies the baseline telos for the trajectory of rendering the captive subject into an "animal," into a "beast." The system of conceptuality that enables the juridical identification of "inhuman" treatment is founded on the tacit knowledge of what can be executed on the body of its animal other as lawful practice. Inscribed in the Convention against Torture and Other Cruel, Inhuman or Degrading Treatment as Punishment, then, is an infrastructural Euro-anthropocentrism that achieves its "universal" status by simultaneously reproducing and denegating the Euro-anthropocentric values that at once found the category of the "inhuman" and that systemically exclude, for example, Indigenous cosmo-epistemologies that refuse, in their kincentric views, the posited biopolitical caesura.

Across the different loci of institutionalized torture I have examined, from the CIA's black sites to the gulags of Australia's offshore asylum seeker and refugee prisons, the carceral subjects of torture articulate the same desperate zoopolitical cry: "We are not animals," says Djamel Ameziane, imprisoned in Guantánamo for nearly twelve years: "The United States treated me like an animal, or worse than an animal, because the Iguanas that roam freely at Guantánamo were protected by laws. I lived in a cage and was protected by no laws."[108] Imran Mohammad Fazal Hoque, indefinitely detained in Australia's offshore refugee prison on Manus, says: "We no longer feel we are human beings—we are just human trash that is dumped here by Australia. . . . We are not animals, we are human beings like you."[109] These recursive cries achieve their politico-cultural intelligibility because the facticity of "inhuman" treatment is constituted through the baseline operations of zoopolitical violence. The practices of what can be lawfully categorized as "inhuman" treatment can be differentially defined only with reference to the nonhuman animal ground that constitutes the conditions of possibility for the "human" to cohere as a positivity. The category of "inhuman" is not the opposite of "human" or "humane"; rather, "in/human" must be seen as a conjoined couplet whose semantic intelligibility is predicated on its animal/beast other: the couplet operates as the obverse to the animal reverse—not as a categorical contrary but, rather, as a spectral modality that differentially constitutes the other's conditions of possibility and definitional intelligibility. At once inscribed but effaced in this spectral modality is the anterior fracture or categorical split that will have demarcated the irreducible difference between human and animal. The conjoined couplet "in/human" institutes the occultation of its foundational dependence on the denegated field of animality. The substructural figure of an unthought humanist anthropologism is what homologizes and unifies this seemingly bipolar couplet. It is what invests it with its jurisdictional power to continue to indict practices of torture through a convention that is in fact based on modalities of occluded, yet lawful, violence against animals. The very convention designed to outlaw torture reproduces, through a type of conceptual Möbius strip, the very thing it intends to preclude. This circular economy is what fuels the conceptual coherency of the techniques of torture against humans that can be mobilized and deployed by the torturer.

The first enactment—because of scientific, academic, military, and/or national security reasons—of what is seen as legitimate or lawful violence that can be executed on animals (for example, dogs or goats) is what enables and sanctions the institutional recalibrations and transpositions of this violence to human subjects (for example, José Padilla). The anthropocentric operations of zoopolitics inform and sign off on this modality of human-animal violence. The human sovereign, whose human status is predicated on disavowed animality, can "dehumanize" and thus "animalize" a captive subject only because the animal involuntarily supplies both the baseline ground toward which these torture practices are oriented and the embodied system of conceptuality that renders both the physical and epistemic violence intelligible as lawful and thus noncriminal—as legally codified, for example, by the Bybee Torture Memo.[110] "Inhuman" degradation is a process that can only unfold along a vertical axis of zoopolitical descent: for example, in Guantánamo, US torturers forced the detainee Mohammed al-Qahtani "to bark like a dog, wear a leash like a dog . . . and pick up piles of trash with his hands cuffed while being called a 'pig.'"[111] Here the spectral modality of animality that shadows acts of inhuman torture becomes embodied in practice in the context of its zoopolitical distributions and differentials: dog, pig, and so on. Its differential embodiments are simultaneously unified by the zoopolitical metacategory of "the animal"—as that which remains de jure degradable, torturable, and killable. Operative here is a double movement founded on the spectral virtuality of "the animal" (as sign and semiotic inscriptor) and the graphic enfleshing of this same virtuality to enact the violence of "dehumanization" in practice: the torture practice can realize its intelligibility *as torture* only by compelling the victim to vocalize and become "the animal" through kinesthesia. In the context of the antitorture convention, then, the very act of condemning torture through a process of juridical codification that is predicated on the human/inhuman couplet institutes, by unthought default, the reproduction of a founding violence that will continue to inscribe the anthropocentric baseline of what can be categorized as torture.

It is striking that European languages do not have the equivalent of *inhuman* for the torture that can be perpetrated against nonhuman animals. There is no term such as *inanimal* treatment, for instance, to describe torture or cruelty toward animals. *Inanimal* is a word that simply cannot be mobilized within the hegemonic field of Euro-anthropocentric intelligibility: it founders and dissolves due to an epistemic void. The lack of an ethico-epistemological infrastructure that would supply it with a modicum of intelligibility means that on the page, if not conceptually, it remains a nonsense word. Yet this crux must be, for ethical reasons, thought through. Inanimality is the zoopolitical phantom that beckons from the very limits of the Euro-anthropocentric discursive field, even as, from the outlaw locus of its bestial vestibularity, it is what is embodied in practice in the daily rituals of human culture and what inscribes the conjoined couplet "in/human" with its assumed self-identity. For the epistemic and physical violence that underpins the practices of inanimality to register as violence, Euro-anthropocentric language and thought would have to drop the dogma of human exceptionalism and its attendant reductionism, a reductionism insistently animated by a series of speciesist negatives: animals do not have language, emotion, subjecthood, society, law, play, altruism, and so on. In this zoopolitical schema, the stripping away of any of these attributes from captive human subjects sets in train the vertical descent, through torture practices, toward the state of a purely immanent animal biologism that stands as the baseline marker for the opposite of "the human." This locus on the anthropocentric hierarchy involves a set of double constraints: the physical apparatuses of enforced captivity and torture, including chains, leashes, and cages, and the epistemological infrastructure that ensures, through the strictures of anthropocentric denegation, the aporia of the nonsentient sentience of the tortured animal. This aporia underwrites the speciesist dogma of an irreducible animality that, in its mobile and contingent transpositions, can ensnare a range of targeted subjects: dogs, asylum seekers, pigs, detainees, goats, and so on.

Through a deconstructive move of tactical reversal and displacement enabled by Indigenous cosmo-epistemologies that refuse the biopolitical caesura, inanimal practices would signify the violent denial to animals of subjecthood, sentience, language, law, society, altruism, and so on. Through this move, the zoopolitical violence that founds and constitutes the conditions of possibility of what can be categorized as "inhuman" practices of torture would be exposed, rendering the category of the "inhuman" void and inapplicable as a legal descriptor for torture practices precisely because of its tacit complicity in its own denegated forms of lawful violence and its de facto legitimization of zoopolitical modalities of torture.

Adnan Latif's Last Flight

The small, seemingly insignificant moments of transcendence in the animal that I have traced in this chapter largely fail to register in traditional accounts of imprisonment and torture. Yet, for the prisoner, they produce life-affirming moments of joy in the face of the despair of indefinite detention. I have not dwelled on these animal-enabled moments of joy and excendence in such sites as Guantánamo to redeem the enormity of the violence unleashed and reproduced by the racio-speciesist assemblage of the biopolitical state and its attendant regimes of terror; rather, I mark these moments to make visible those very fragile and transient acts that reclaim the possibility of experiencing the affirmation of life through interspecies relations in these torture sites built on the obliteration of hope, pleasure, and life. In these most abject and life-negating of sites, the most tender of acts of compassion and the most fragile relations of interspecies acknowledgment, gifting, and hospitality trace hairline cracks that imperceptibly fissure Guantánamo's biopolitical apparatus.

As detailed in the footnotes in the forensic report on his death, for Adnan Latif, Guantánamo's animals bring into being the Open as that space that offers an interruption to an existence held fast, both physically and psychologically, by a regime of subjugation and suffering. Away from the Open and removed from his intercorporeal communication with the animals that visit Guantánamo's recreation yard, Latif again descends into a carceral morass of agitation and suffering:

45. (U/FOUO) On the night of 31 July 2012, ISN156 was agitated about recent events and was in his cell at the BHU. At one point, ISN156 began jumping around in the cell, from the bed to the sink to the table to the toilet. (xb3): 10 USC §130b, (b) (6) (bX7XC) the nurse at the duty desk at the BHU that night, observed ISN156 and asked him to stop what she explained was "very unsafe" behavior. ISN156 would stop once (xb3): 10 USC §130b, (b) (6) (bX7XC) spoke to him, but as soon as she left the tier, ISN156 would start jumping again.[112]

On the night of his death, he is described as "still jumping around, now with a towel tied around his neck that he was using as a cape and smearing honey on his face."[113] Smeared honey and makeshift wings will fail to save Latif. The inexorable weight and drag of Guantánamo's regime of torture and indefinite detention will ensure that, despite his broken attempts at flight, Latif will be brought to ground. The scenes documenting Latif's final moments disclose a man transmuted into hapless quarry, flapping across the circumscribed space of his cell in a desperate attempt to reach the Open beyond his cage.

The log that describes the events leading to the discovery of his death notes:

93. (U/FOUO) Sometime shortly before midnight, ISN156 finally appeared to go to sleep. Did not recall seeing ISN156 "lift his head or move all night" but did recall seeing ISN156 breathing. Noted that in his experience, it was "odd" that ISN156 would have slept that long, as he was usually a very active sleeper. * noted that he had "never seen [ISN156] sleep that much," pointing out that ISN156 usually slept for only a few hours at a time, and even then, continued to move all over his cell in his sleep.[114]

Latif had never "slept that long" before precisely because he was already dead.

Code Yellow: Dead after the Fact

The circumstances that surround the death of Adnan Latif remain murky, despite the official AR 15-6 Investigation report that was issued following his death. The report states:

2. (U/FOUO) the Armed Forces Medical Examiner (AFME) determined the cause of death of ISN156 to be suicide by overdose of paliperidone (Invega). ISN156 had 24 capsules of Invega, an anti-psychotic drug, in his stomach at the time of death. The toxicology examination revealed the presence of paliperidone (Invega), codeine (Tylenol #3), oxycodone (Percocet), quetiapine (Seroquel), mirtazpine [sic] (Remeron), and citalopram (Celexa), morphine (by-product of Tylenol #3), oxymorphone [sic] (active ingredient

in Percocet), and lorazepam (Ativan) were present in the system of ISN156 at the time of his death. ISN156 also had acute pneumonia.[115]

In addition to the physical restraints that were used to shackle Latif, the inventory of drugs that Latif was prescribed suggests that a regime of pharmacological restraints was also being applied. It is unclear how Latif managed to accumulate all the medications that were found in his system and to swallow all of them when, according to the camp's standard operating procedures, it would have been impossible for him to hide the medications or to ingest the bulk of them when he was supposed to be under constant observation. The investigative report suggests that the "JDG guard force failed to follow JDG Line of Sight SOP and the JDG Med Pass SOP, and failed to take remedial measures after ISN156 appeared to be sleeping an unusual length of time."[116] Reading the report, it is clear that SOPs were breached up and down the line. What is also clear is that Latif's death remains, in biopolitical terms, a type of manslaughter, as the necropolitical forces that were arraigned against him effectively ensured that he would be left to die. As Latif's attorney succinctly put it: perhaps Latif died because of suicide or because of the "cumulative effects of a decade's worth" of surviving the violent conditions at Guantánamo, but "either way, his death was caused by his detention."[117] Moreover, Latif and a number of other detainees repeatedly made "allegations of what they said were attempts [by the guards] to facilitate their suicide."[118] In what follows, I want to focus on the final moments of Latif's life.

In Guantánamo, a Code Yellow "is used to indicate a potentially life-threatening medical condition requiring immediate response."[119] A Code Yellow was only deployed when, in effect, Latif was already dead to the world:

106. (U/FOUO) Around 1400, [redacted] knocked on the glass of ISN156's cell, and when he did not receive a response, called a Code Yellow.

Once members of the guard team donned their protective gear, they stacked up against the cell door of ISN156 and waited for the other NCOs to arrive. [Redacted] called for the door to be opened, central control released the cell door lock, and [redacted] pushed the door open, with the guard team rushing in. [Redacted] indicated that when the guard team entered, ISN156 was lying on his right side with his head on a foam pillow, a blanket covering him, and his right arm extended.

108. (U/FOUO) As [redacted] secured ISN156's head, she saw "chunky vomit" and when she turned ISN156's head to the side, she stated that a large quantity of "yellowish bloody goo" drained out of ISN156's mouth. By

this time, [redacted] had secured ISN156's hands with restraints as a safety precaution. [Redacted] the corpsman, arrived, took ISN156's pulse, and indicated that there was no pulse. [Redacted] told the Watch Commander he thought ISN156 was dead to call the nurse.[120]

A guard team stacks up against Latif's cell door and then rushes in. Latif is lying on his side, his extended right arm gesturing toward the Open, to everything denied to him by his carceral confines, to everything out and beyond his cage. Latif is lying dead on the floor—he is described in the report as lying with his eyes "open, staring blankly at the cell door," and his "skin color looked gray"[121]—yet a guard secures him in a headlock. As the guard does this, Latif disgorges a corporeal statement to both the guards and Guantánamo: bloody vomit. This is Latif's last outpouring: visceral, pungent, final. In the muted anguish of his death, Latif can no longer speak or pen his impassioned letters calling for justice. His body, however, continues to communicate, even as it slides into an irreversible process of decomposition. Latif's vomit is the material evidence of this decomposition, of the complete dehiscence of his bodily hexis, and it is also the corporeal text of his poisoned innards. Latif presents his captors with a necrological discourse that issues from death and that overflows the limits of living speech. In death, Latif speaks a visceral speech that is oral but silent; its signifying conditions of enunciation are nonverbal: the semantics of bile and blood coagulated into the syntagm of vomit. "Yellowish bloody goo" must be read as Latif's final riposte to the violence that governed virtually every aspect of his penal existence. The vomit that issues from the mouth of the dead Latif articulates the burden that underscored so many of his verbal pronouncements on Guantánamo: that the prison works, insistently, to render its inmates into nothing more than biological waste. I am not, here, placing words in Latif's mouth. On the contrary, I am invoking one of the lines from Latif's letters that continues to resound for me. On his entry into Guantánamo, he wrote, "Life became less than refuse to be thrown in a garbage can."[122] As if all this physical evidence were not clear enough to signal that Latif no longer presented a threat, with his head still secured in a headlock, the hands of his corpse are tied with restraints. Even in death, the Muslim detainee represents a threat.

An obituary for Latif written by Emad Hassan, a fellow detainee, offers another glimpse of the personal anguish that Latif endured in Guantánamo. Hassan describes Latif as "a quiet man who yearned to be home. He thought continually of his son, pronouncing his son's name over and over again to himself, working slowly through all the syllables of his name as if thinking hard about the word would bring him closer. I think of the many occasions when I pretended to be asleep to give him the space to cry without worrying that he was being watched."[123] In the confines of Latif's cell, the only way to connect back to his absent son is through the articulation of his name. The incantatory practice of slowly speaking each syllable emerges as a desperate attempt to conjure his son's presence in this site of maximum isolation. It is as though the performative ritual of verbal repetition will work to reconnect the ruptured fil- iation. Through the affective labor of nomination, Latif attempts to institute what would otherwise remain absent. It is as though the material enunciation of each syllable will work to dispel absence, overcome distance, and deliver the figure of his beloved son in the space of the prison. Latif's purposive mode of address tenderly renders each syllable of his son's name as a way of re-creating his body from the letters that constitute his name. The slow, palpable pronun- ciation of each syllable of his son's name becomes an invocation to corporeal- ize his absent son through the embodied materiality of language: the physiol- ogy of respiration, tongue, and vocal cords work verbally to embody the figure of the absent son. The very articulation of the son's name sets in motion the chiasmic crossing of word and flesh; it enables Latif to project his son's pres- ence into his cell, precisely because it resonates within his own embodied locus of enunciation, fleshing out his son's absence through the modulated fusion of the father's words with his own corporeality. This moving ritual of conjuration fails, however, to bring his son into his cell. The quickening word is no sooner spoken than it dissipates—thus the need for the purposive repetition, "over and over again to himself." Latif's speech can only stand in lieu of his son. The structural logic of language is predicated on the very absence of the material referent. In this case, language's deficit is insurmountable: the marked inter- val between syllables emblematizes a distance that cannot be bridged and an absence that cannot be filled, even as Latif attempts to bind one syllable to the other in the process of deliberative recitation. The gap between a name and the corporeality of the invoked subject is abyssal, as anyone who has lost a loved one knows. The consolation of uttering an absent loved one's name is radically circumscribed by the ineluctable fact of this gap. The impossibility of bridging this divide expresses itself in Latif's tears. His fellow inmate, Emad Hassan, respectfully feigns sleep to give Latif the space to cry.

The necropolitical forces that were arraigned against Latif continued to work well past the moment of his solitary death in one of Guantánamo's cells. Following the postmortem, his body was left in yet another space of indefinite detention: Ramstein Air Base, Germany, where his corpse was "stored" for three months for political reasons.[124] Latif's body was eventually returned to his family in Yemen. Jason Leopold describes the scene that awaited Latif's brother, Muhammed Farhan Latif, once his body, encased in a plain aluminum box, was deposited at the police hospital in Sana'a, Yemen's capital: "At the hospital, Muhammed was led to a room by police investigators and a medical examiner to identify Adnan's remains. The box was opened. Adnan was wrapped in a shroud. 'I recognized the body of my brother. . . . But with great difficulty. His eyes were missing and his body was in an advanced stage of disintegration. Still, I could tell it was Adnan.'"[125] In the moment when he lifts the shroud from Adnan's corpse, Muhammed is compelled to bear witness to his brother's violated remains. Latif's gouged eyes stare back at his brother: cavernous sockets reflecting the horror he had seen and endured. Latif, who saw only too clearly the lies, corruption, and violence of the US state, had, with a violent finality, been rendered blind. What remains? Wounds for eyes that graphically embody a life harrowed by administrative torture to the point of disintegration and an abyssal stare transfixed by the *no exit* of indefinite detention. Latif's position as eyewitness to Guantánamo's regime of violence is literally voided, and in death his body becomes his corpus of evidence. In death, Latif's cadaver emerges as a site of locution that continues to signify in lieu of speech. In one of the letters he wrote to his attorneys, Latif explained that he was writing his personal "testimony against injustice . . . while in the throes of death."[126] The proleptical truth of this necromantic testimony now assumes a nonlinguistic register. Quartered in his mortuary box, in a final act of disclosure, Latif's body in ruins evidences his posthumous *testimony against injustice*. This final testimony needs to be quoted without quotation marks, as it is enunciated without speech. From the grave, it can be read only as testimony incarnate in the irreversible process of decomposition.

Forensic Ecology of Camp X-Ray

Camp X-Ray, with its chain-link fence cages in which Adnan Latif and hundreds of other detainees were first imprisoned on their arrival at Guantánamo, closed in April 2002. Over the years, the abandoned prison has been transformed. A number of visual essays that document the state of the camp more than a decade after its closure reveal a site that has been overtaken by the forces of nature.[127] The chain-link fence cages have now been tapestried by vines and creepers. The walls of the cages have been transformed into living trellises (figure 3.1).

The vines have now overwritten the original significance and purpose of those infamous chain-link fences. The transparent grid of the chain-link fence cages—in which the detainees were subjugated to a regime of relentless exposure

Figure 3.1   Camp X-Ray, Guantánamo, ca. 2007. Joint Task Force
Guantanamo.

and compulsory visibility—has now been infoliated and rendered virtually
opaque by the plants. The zoological spectacle of the caged detainee has been
occluded by vegetal screens. The concrete paths around the camp have been
fissured by the force of vegetal life and are now overgrown with plants and
fields of flowers. The life force of vegetal roots is undermining the solid foundations of the site and converting concrete slabs back into sediment and soil:
what was obdurate is compelled to yield to the probing and insertive fingers
of delicate root tips that pry at the concrete, opening hairline seams and fractures. The perimeter fences, topped with coils of razor wire, have also been
claimed by the vines as ideal supports. Rising from a ground inscribed by a
history of saturated violence, the vines reach up toward the sun, coiling themselves around spirals of barbed wire, creating green vortices that seem suspended in the air. A network of exuberant vegetal life is reclaiming the prison.
And the animals of Guantánamo, including the banana rats, wasps, ants, and
snakes, have made themselves at home once again in the derelict camp. In
one extraordinary image, a banana rat can be seen walking through the coiled
vortex of the razor wire, a virtuoso gymnast gingerly negotiating the barbs.[128]
A strange vortical topology is operative here. On both physical and symbolic
levels, the vortical partition of the razor wire is here breached by the banana
rat. The razor wire fence—the very material signifier of impassable exteriority,

a nonnegotiable border, and violently interdicted space—is here transformed by the banana rat into just another encoiled pathway for their purposive movement through the camp.

The camp in ruins is now the site for a new type of flourishing. The act of decommissioning is what liberates all the other forces that had otherwise been managed or suppressed. The act of abandonment is what releases a host of ontological potentialities. The site's dereliction is what enables a state of generative transition. It brings into being the shift from a penal grid of punitive power to a transitive modality of unmaking-making. The brutal architecture of torture and humiliation has been softened by the exuberance of vegetal life. Where once the razor-wired site announced the triumphant domination of nature, including its captive animal-detainees, Camp X-Ray has now been overcome by the very forces that had seemingly been vanquished. The site itself now appears as a strange garden that is slowly eclipsing the camp's dominant meaning. The military prison's phytopolitical and zoopolitical intentions are being inexorably displaced and resignified. On arriving at Guantánamo, the orange-garbed and hooded detainees were forced to kneel on the ground in a formation that the guards termed the "pumpkin patch."[129] Phytopolitically, they were dispatched to the locus of the vegetable on the biopolitical hierarchy. Hooded, muffled, and shackled, the detainees were meant to embody the Euro-anthropocentric understanding of plants—as dumb, insentient, and incapable of movement, literally rooted to the ground through shackles bolted to the floor of their cells. After their removal from the "pumpkin patch," the detainees were shifted up a notch along the biopolitical hierarchy to the locus of nonhuman animals and were thus penned in their zoological cages.

In the wake of the green, quasi-bucolic transformation of Camp X-Ray, I want to bring into focus two things that otherwise risk being effaced: the colonial genealogy that underpins the site and the forensic elements that must be preserved to enable the realization of justice for the victims who were compelled to endure the torture and trauma that was inflicted on the detainees of the camp. I want to situate the gridded architecture of Guantánamo's Camp X-Ray within the dense colonial genealogy that underpins it in order to begin to comprehend its complex range of significations. In her critical analysis of the camp as emblematic of colonial and biopolitical relations of power, Suvendrini Perera situates Camp X-Ray within its colonial genealogy and underscores its power as "a symbol of unfinished business of an older war"[130]—that is, of the United States' imperial annexation of this part of Cuba and of its past and ongoing use of the site as a place outside its jurisdiction: "Haitians were first interned in camps," she notes, "outside the reaches of U.S. law at

Guantánamo Bay, that recurring place of imprisonment for the denationalized internee, and then sent to Krome detention center on the U.S. mainland."[131] Once situated within this colonial genealogy, Guantánamo emerges as the quintessential zoopolitical vestibularity for housing the serially interchangeable racio-speciated subject—Haitian, Muslim, Arab—as captive and torturable nonhuman animal.

Inscribing Camp X-Ray, then, are two radically different ecologies that, palimpsestically, coexist within this singular space. On one level, there is the ecology of a resurgent nature reclaiming the site through its exuberant vegetal and animal returns. On the other, there is a forensic ecology that demarcates the site as a crime scene: "U.S. courts have forbidden the government from destroying portions of the facility [Camp X-Ray] where detainees where held at the request of defense lawyers who want it kept intact as a crime scene."[132] Following this court order, an FBI forensics team was dispatched to Camp X-Ray to record the trace evidence of the site before it fell into further ruin. Even as a resurgent ecology of plants and animals resignifies Camp X-Ray, the defunct prison remains as the site of the deceased and of those who survived the trauma of torture. The violent geopolitical economy of this past, indeed, must be seen to extend to the very destruction, suppression, and attempted exclusion of the site's original vegetal and animal ecology in the establishment of the military prison. Operative here is an assemblage of superposed and interlocking space-time configurations that defy my categorical frames and ordering methodologies. To outline, in writing, the multiple configurations that constitute this spatiotemporal assemblage necessarily constrains me to arrange them in a linear manner: the site prior to imperial possession; the decimation of Cuba's Indigenous people, the Aruacos, during the Spanish conquest of the island; the subsequent US annexation; the clearing of the site's original flora and fauna; the establishment of Camp X-Ray; the imprisonment, torture, and death of detainees in the camp; the incursions of a number of animals across the diverse spaces of Camp X-Ray while it was operating; the closing and abandoning of the camp; the insurgent reclaiming of the site by its previously banished flora and fauna. This process of linear articulation instigates phasal breaks and separations that are, in fact, untenable. The categorical cut of my taxonomies is challenged at every turn by the nature-culture blurring of the human and the more-than-human. What is operative in this site are spatiotemporal configurations and topological entanglements that are at once discontinuous and nested, disjointed and conjoined. The interlacing of the forces of entropy and self-organizing agents (plants, animals, biochemical interactions) with the extant structures of the prison manifest the recombinant workings of nature-culture in the generation of this prison-ruin-garden. This configuration is, in turn, overlaid by a juridical order that designates the place as a crime scene, even as this same directive has failed to thwart the heterogeneous entities and indeterminate forces that have asserted their claim to the place since its closure.

For me, this entangled topology, which resists unitary categories and either/or predications, is complexly materialized by the coiling of green tendrils around the vortices of razor wire that continue to surmount the fences of the decommissioned prison and the image of a banana rat cannily running the inner gauntlet of the barbed wire tunnel and purposively overriding its interdictory intentions. The metal mesh of life-crushing captivity is transmuted by the plants into a heliotropic trellis, and the razor wire, a material sign of absolute prohibition of movement, is transformed into a suspension bridge that facilitates the banana rat's mobility across their terrain. These topological intextuations of plant, animal, and metallurgical entities embody the fragile excendence of life in the face of Guantánamo's forces of violent foreclosure and negation: finitude-as-mutability is what enables transitive ontologies of becoming. The forensic remainders that inscribe this site also endure as trace evidence of a crime scene. As such, they constitute the physical evidence of the criminal acts that transpired in this carceral space of violence. As material remnants of the site's criminal past, they continue to call for the realization of justice.

4————Drone Sparagmos

Forensic Ecologies of Drone Death

In the forensic ecologies of Afghanistan, Pakistan, Somalia, and Yemen, the survivors of US drone strikes are compelled to gather the dispersed body parts of those killed by the drone's missiles. I open this chapter with the account of the aftermath of one of these drone strikes. I present my account as a telegraphic inventory, and I explicate the war crime in the context of its relevant forensic descriptors. In the latter part of the chapter, I will situate this forensic inventory within the layered matrix of its analytical coordinates.

Geolocation and macroscopic crime scene: Yemen.

Microscopic crime scene: The village of Mukalla. A group of villagers, members of a wedding party, were sitting under a canopy of date palms.

Taphonomic context, as "the immediate environment and surroundings where the body is found":[1] A community gathering into which a US drone fired four missiles.

Cause of death, as the "injury that initiated the lethal chain of events, however brief or prolonged, that led to death":[2] The explosive violence of Hellfire missiles.

Mechanism of death, as the "biochemical or physiologic abnormality produced by the cause of death that is incompatible with life":[3] Bodies were literally shredded into fragments due to the violent force of the explosion.

Necropsy, as the practice of "looking at the dead,"[4] and testimony: Abdullah Salim bin Ali Jaber, a cousin of two of the victims, describes the scene of the aftermath: "It was dark except for the burning car. We could make out many body parts scattered several meters apart—fingers, hands, internal organs. Most bodies had no legs and one was without a face. Another had no head. Until now they still have not found that head. . . . Imagine this horror."[5]

Forensic archaeology, as the practice of the "recovery of scattered remains":[6] The villagers were obliged to use "red and blue pails" in their desperate attempts to collect the dispersed fragments of body parts.[7]

Circumstantial evidence, as what "provides information about the events . . . after the commission of a crime":[8] The villagers identified shrapnel scattered throughout the target site. The missile blasts gouged the mortar of the walls of nearby homes and broke the branches of the date palms under which the villagers had sat—"trees that had been the pride of the village but no longer bear fruit."[9]

Information on the modus operandi, as "criminals' repeat behavior, . . . their signature or preferred method of operation":[10] Drone signature strikes are the United States' preferred mode of killing across the targeted nations of Afghanistan, Pakistan, Somalia, and Yemen. These strikes target groups of people whose identities are often not known but whom the US military categorizes as displaying patterns of behavior that render them suspicious and thus killable.

The practice of US drone killing of civilians that I have documented here is repeated across its targeted countries. In this chapter, my central concern is to begin to delineate the mechanisms that enable these serial drone deaths of civilians. I thus outline an itinerary that begins with the revelations of Edward Snowden and two former drone operators to trace the lines of convergence between the US Department of Defense (DoD) and the National Security Agency (NSA) in the conduct of the US drone-kill program. In the first part of the chapter, I focus on new tracking technologies developed by the NSA that have been incorporated into the DoD's drone targeting program, and I examine the increasing reliance on advanced mathematical formulas to identify drone targets on kill lists. My interest is in examining how the NSA's metadata interlocks with the DoD's algorithmic formulas to conduct drone kills in which often the identities of those killed are not known. The indiscriminate drone killing of human and more-than-human life, I contend, evidences the crucial role that automated technicity now plays in the lethal production of forensic ecologies. I examine what I term the *bioinformationalization of life*, which signals the reduction of living bodies to anonymous integers of data, within the drone-kill fields of Afghanistan, Pakistan, Somalia, and Yemen. The DoD's increasing reliance on death by metadata, I argue, is inscribed by a biopolitics that is predicated on anthropocentric hierarchies of life. Situated in the schema of anthropocentric hierarchies of life, I examine a judgment handed down by the Peshawar High Court. Even as the Peshawar High Court acknowledges the killing of animals through US drone strikes, it can only account for the animal dead in terms of anthropocentric understandings of property law; as such, these dead animals are represented not as deaths worthy of ethical consideration but merely as fungible objects whose loss only requires financial compensation. Accounted for solely in terms of the category of replaceable property, ecological justice cannot be served for the other-than-human dead. I conclude the chapter by arguing that what is instantiated in these sites of drone-enabled military violence is the practice of *sparagmos*, the Greek term naming the ritualized dismemberment and dispersal of bodies. Sparagmos names the militarized dismemberment of the targeted flesh of the lands of Afghanistan, Pakistan, Somalia, and Yemen and the attendant structural failure to hold accountable those culpable of the extrajudicial assassination of civilians and their more-than-human relations.

Death by Metadata

The US drone-kill program witnessed a significant escalation under the Obama administration. This escalation has been directly linked to Barack Obama's desire to shut down the damaging symbol that Guantánamo had become in the eyes of the international community. Rather than capture, detain, and interrogate targeted suspects, the administration shifted its focus to liquidating them on the extrajudicial assumption that they were guilty. The release of the much-anticipated Presidential Policy Guidance (PPG) titled *Procedures for Approving Direct Action against Terrorist Targets Located outside the United States and Areas of Active Hostilities* evidenced the causal connection between Obama's attempts to close Guantánamo and the expansion of the drone-kill program. The

PPG categorically states that "in no event will additional detainees be brought to the detention facilities at the Guantánamo Bay Naval Base."[11] The US drone program, with its "Kill, don't capture" dictate, means that those assassinated by US drones have no recourse to judicial review of their cases.

John Rizzo, former acting general counsel of the CIA and one of the CIA lawyers who played a key role in persuading the US Department of Justice to "legalize" torture through its infamous Torture Memos, explains this policy shift: "They [the Obama administration] never came out and said they would start killing people because they couldn't interrogate them, but the implication was unmistakable. . . . Once the interrogation was gone, all that was left was the killing."[12] Mark Mazzetti describes the changed role of the US military and the CIA in terms of a combined "military organization that could erase them [suspects]": "Killing by remote control was the antithesis of the dirty, intimate work of interrogation. It somehow seemed cleaner, less personal. Targeted killings were cheered by Republicans and Democrats alike, and using drones flown by pilots who were stationed thousands of miles away from the war made the whole strategy seem risk-free."[13]

In a debate at Johns Hopkins University on the topic of the NSA's surveillance programs, Michael Hayden, former CIA and NSA director, confirmed NSA general counsel Stewart Baker's observation that "metadata absolutely tells you everything about somebody's life. If you have enough metadata, you don't really need content."[14] I will presently discuss this notion of metadata as superseding the need for content, but first I want to examine Hayden's comments in some detail. After remarking that Baker's observation was "absolutely correct," Hayden asserted: "We kill people based on metadata."[15] Hayden's assertion did not come as a surprise to scholars working in the field of US drone strikes, as drone operators are crucially reliant on metadata to determine which targets on their kill lists to terminate. Furthermore, as was evidenced by documents released by Edward Snowden, "the agency analyzes metadata as well as mobile-tracking technology to determine targets, without employing human intelligence to confirm a suspect's identity."[16] An unnamed drone operator succinctly outlined this practice: "People get hung up that there's a targeted list of people. . . . It's really like we're targeting a cell phone. We're not going after people—we're going after their phones, in the hopes that the person on the other end of that missile is the bad guy."[17] These observations bring into focus two critical points: metadata will effectively supplant the need for "content," and human targets become so *somatechnically* instrumentalized that they become, in turn, entirely coextensive with the technology they use—in this case, their phones.[18] The indissociable coextensiveness of human targets with their mobile phone device is evidenced by a former drone operator who worked with Joint Special Operations Command (JSOC). This operator has disclosed the expansive dimensions of the NSA's surveillance and tracking sweep:

> The NSA doesn't just locate the cell phones of terror suspects by intercepting communications from cell phone towers and Internet service providers. The agency also equips drones and other aircraft with devices known as "virtual base-tower transceivers"—creating, in effect, a fake cell phone tower that can force a targeted person's device to lock onto the NSA's receiver without their knowledge. That, in turn, allows the military to track the cell phone to within 30 feet of its actual location, feeding the real-time data to teams of drone operators who conduct missile strikes or facilitate night raids.[19]

Known by the code name GILGAMESH, the program uses "advanced mathematics to develop a new geolocation algorithm intended for operational use on unmanned aerial vehicles (UAV) flights."[20] The former drone operator has also revealed crucial details about the NSA's use of the tracking program Geo Cell. Geo Cell identifies and geolocates a tracked mobile phone or SIM card without necessarily being able to determine who the person on the other end of the phone is:

> "Once the bomb lands or a night raid happens, you know that the phone is there," he says. "But we don't know who's behind it, who's holding it. It's of course assumed that the phone belongs to a human being who is nefarious and considered an 'unlawful enemy combatant.' . . . They might have been terrorists," he says. "Or they could have been family members who have nothing to do with the target's activities. . . . It's really like we're targeting a cell phone."[21]

Working in tandem with the GILGAMESH program is another NSA program called SKYNET, which "engages in mass surveillance of Pakistan's mobile phone network, and then uses a machine learning algorithm on the cellular network metadata of 56 million people to try and rate each person's likelihood of being a terrorist." Patrick Ball, a data scientist, has lambasted the program:

> On whether the use of SKYNET is a war crime, I defer to the lawyers. . . . It's bad science, that's for damn sure, because classification is inherently probabilistic. If you're going to condemn someone to death, usually we have a "beyond reasonable doubt" standard, which is not at all the case when

you're talking about people with "probable terrorist" scores anywhere near the threshold. And that's assuming that the classifier works in the first place, which I doubt because there simply aren't enough positive cases of known terrorists for the random forest to get a good model of them.[22]

Biopolitical Transduction Switch Points

At this juncture, I want to examine in some detail how the biopolitical state's categorization of suspects in terms of a set of preemptive indexes and biotypological categories is underpinned by algorithmic formulas. The multimodal, interoperative screening and security systems that the DoD is developing are designed to identify a cluster of disparate attributes, including "soft biometrics" information that captures such things as ethnicity, "skin color," gender, weight, height, and so on.[23] This bioinformation is, in turn, integrated into a system such as Adversary Behavior Acquisition Collection (ABACUS), with "data from informants' tips, drone footage, and captured phone calls. Then it would apply 'a human behavior modeling and simulation engine' that would spit out 'intent-based threat assessments of individuals and groups.'" Clear Heart, yet another hostile behavior and intent system that the DoD is funding, is, like ABACUS, founded on the use of "probabilistic algorithms th[at] determine the likelihood of adversarial intent."[24]

I want to situate the ongoing exchange of surveillance metadata between the NSA and the DoD within a Foucauldian frame in order to delineate its biopolitical dimensions. The metadata categories of "enemy combatants," "terrorists," and "suspects" can be seen, once they are situated within a biopolitical context, to fold over into the military's categories of anonymous, amorphous, and biotypologized suspect "patterns of life," that is, those human targets that, through the operations of racio-speciesism, can be exterminated with impunity by drones. The discursive crossover between the NSA's metadata and the DoD's "suspect" categories is facilitated by what Foucault terms a "switch point" (*échangeur*) that effectively enables a process of discursive exchange and categorical hybridization across different disciplines.[25] Significantly, Foucault locates these switch points, which work to establish a "continuum" across different disciplines and the resultant "institutional mixture," as "actually a response to danger."[26] In other words, he identifies the epistemic production of these discursive switch points, and their attendant biopolitical effects, as pivoting on the biopolitically charged freedom/security nexus.[27] The promise of protecting freedoms is predicated, in other words, on the securitization of the state in response to perceived threats and dangers posed by the targeted other.

What is operative in these metadata systems is a transduction of the phenotypical and biological into the algorithmic and, critically, the attendant production of what can only be termed bioinformational stereotyping. What is produced by these identificatory systems is bioinformational stereotyping precisely because the phenotypical bioinformation they process is always already predicated on a series of *infrastructural normativities* that are embedded in the operating software of these systems.[28] These infrastructural normativities supply the categorical parameters that enable the systems to make a series of stereotypical assumptions about a targeted subject's gender, ethnicity and so on. Dubious and unreliable descriptors such as ethnicity are built into the software as if they are neatly verifiable units of knowledge grounded in the empiricity of biology; for example, the untenable racialized descriptor of "Middle Eastern appearance" is presented as a transparent and self-evident category of knowledge that can be algorithmically formulated in order to ensure machinic and automated readings of race. The structural contradiction inscribed in such identificatory technologies hinges on the way in which the algorithmization of embodied difference must, by definition, produce a homogenization of difference through digital stereotyping in order to set viable working parameters for the program. An identificatory system such as ABACUS works to produce an abstraction of embodied singularities into mathematically manageable aggregates that are configured into digital biotypological stereotypes. Cast in Foucauldian biopolitical terms, the cultural intelligibility of "suspect" categories is underpinned and enabled by the tacit knowledges of essentialized biologism ("biological rootedness") which work to ensure the production of readily identifiable "regularities." As "techniques of power," these readily identifiable "regularities" (digital biotypological stereotypes) facilitate the operations of biopolitical governance.[29]

In thinking through the relation between biopolitical regimes of governmentality and population groups, Foucault writes:

> with the population we have something different from the collection of subjects of right, differentiated by their status, localization, goods, responsibilities, and offices: [We have] a set of elements that, on the one side, are immersed within the general regime of living beings and that, on the other side, offer a surface on which authoritarian, but reflected and calculated transformations can get a hold.[30]

The operations of bioinformational stereotyping that are reproduced by these identificatory technologies are based on the formulaic construction of a "set of elements" (of targeted phenotypical attributes) that designate "suspect" population groups and that, through the somatechnic apprehension of the embodied signs that function as indexes of hostile intent, offer a surface on which authoritarian relations of power can get a hold. "With the emergence of mankind as a species," Foucault concludes, "within a field of definition of all living species, we can say that man appears in the first form of his integration with biology."[31] Foucault's insight can here be elaborated in the context of the contemporary field of biopolitical technologies of social sorting and capture.[32] In effect, what is exemplified by such systems is not just the operation of the biopolitical sorting of population groups into identifiable and targetable subgroups but, more accurately, the somatechnic dividing and categorization of these subgroups into subspecies that, through the deployment of forms of racio-speciesism and attendant forms of biotypological stereotyping, may be terminated in acts of "anticipatory self-defense."

Bioinformationalization of Life

The practice of killing by metadata underscores the intensification of what I term the *bioinformationalization of life*, drawing on a Heideggerian critique of contemporary science. The bioinformationalization of life results from positivist science's demand "that nature reports itself in some way or other that is identifiable through calculation and that it remains orderable as a system of information."[33] The convergence of metadata networks and digitized identification technologies exemplifies the rendering of life into an orderable system of information through the application of algorithmic formulas. Through processes of bioinformationalization, life, in all its manifold forms, becomes transmuted into anonymous digital data that is trackable and that can be killed extrajudiciously. I say "anonymous" precisely because, as I have discussed elsewhere, through practices such as drone signature strikes, the United States often kills targets whose identities are not known.[34] Geolocation technology, the Department of Defense says, has "cued and compressed numerous 'kill chains' (i.e., all of the steps taken to find, track, target, and engage the enemy)."[35] The compression of the drone-kill chain has been enabled by the often lethal conflation of a mobile phone with the unknown identity of the user. Jeremy Scahill elaborates on how this compression of the kill chain escalates individuals up the targeting ladder: "Under programs run by the CIA and JSOC, individuals were given 'numbers and code names,' based on profiles defined by the changing locations of their mobile phone and its SIM card. . . . 'If that handset or that SIM card have been in a particular mosque and then in a certain restaurant, then they're in a gathering with three other SIM cards that they're monitoring, those people move up the list, even if their individual identity is not known.'"[36] Scahill explains what is at stake in this drone targeting program: "In some cases, the specific individuals are being targeted, even though the United States doesn't know their identities, and may not have any actual evidence that they're involved in terrorist activity."[37] In other words, the killing of subjects whose identities are not known must be seen as tantamount to extrajudicial executions precisely because "the identity of the targets was not established, their responsibility for criminal acts was not proven, no charges that could be considered a criminal offence were made against them, or finally, no attempt was made to arrest them and bring them before a judicial authority."[38]

Operating under the dubious rubric of exercising its right to self-defense in response to an imminent threat, the "U.S. believes determining if a terrorist is an imminent threat 'does not require the United States to have clear evidence that a specific attack on U.S. persons and interest will take place in the immediate future.'"[39] The category of "imminent threat" is built-in with an extraordinary latitude in terms of the subjects it enables the US military to target. It has resulted in the deaths of innumerable subjects whose names are unknown and who, when they are finally identified, are repeatedly found to have no connections at all to such groups as al-Qaeda. In fact, US drone strikes in Yemen "are believed to have killed more civilians in 2015 than Al Qaeda."[40] The United States, in other words, fully qualifies as a rogue state that is complicit in the extrajudicial assassination of innocent civilians. In his assessment of US drone kills, Björn Schiffler of the Institute for International Law at the University of Cologne concludes: "It is simply murder."[41] In its analysis of four hundred US drone strikes in Pakistan alone, the Bureau of Investigative Journalism found that "fewer than 4% of the people killed had been identified by available records as named members of al-Qaeda. A report by Reprieve has brought to light the fact that up to 874 'unknowns' have been killed by U.S. drone strikes in the hunt for 24 targeted individuals.' The report estimates that '96.5% of casualties from U.S. drone strikes are civilians.'"[42] Reprieve's Jennifer Gibson elaborates on the meaning of these statistics: "Drone strikes have been sold to the American public on the claim that they're 'precise.' But they are only as precise as the intelligence that feeds them. There is nothing precise about the intelligence that results in the deaths of 28 unknown people, including women and children, for every 'bad guy' the U.S. goes after."[43]

The Reprieve report documents that certain targeted individuals have been listed as having been killed up to six times, and consequently dozens of unknown civilians have actually been killed in the process of targeting a particular suspect. The report cites the following cases: "In targeting Ayman al Zawahiri, the CIA killed 76 children and 29 adults. They failed twice and Ayman al Zawahiri is reportedly still alive. In the six attempts it took the U.S. to kill Qari Hussain, a deputy commander of the Tehrik-e-Taliban Pakistan, 128 people were killed, including 13 children. Baitullah Mehsud was directly targeted as many as seven times, during which 164 people were killed, including 11 children."[44] One former US senior intelligence official has remarked on the US administration's "'deceptive' estimates of civilian casualties": "'It bothers me when they say there were seven guys, so that they must all be militants,' the official said. 'They count the corpses and they're not really sure who they are.'"[45] Another report into drone civilian deaths concludes: "In U.S. drone operations, reports suggest all 'military aged males' and potentially even women and children are considered 'enemies killed in action' unless they can 'posthumously' and 'conclusively' prove their innocence."[46] In the wake of a number of drone attacks in Somalia, the United States killed "at least 150 people." "As it virtually always does," Glenn Greenwald observes, "the Obama administration instantly claimed that the people killed were 'terrorists' and militants—members of the Somali group al Shabaab—but provided no evidence to support that assertion."[47] In what Louise Amoore has termed "algorithmic war," even when governments or their operatives do not know the identities of their targeted subjects, they "pretend that [they] do. Algorithmic logics appear to make it possible to translate probable associations between people and objects into actionable security decisions."[48] In their attempt to expose the US military's ongoing occlusion of civilian drone kills, three former drone operators have filed a legal brief in which they claim to have "witnessed widespread and deliberate misclassification of deaths as 'enemy kills.' In situations where targets were unknown, they were often classified as 'enemy kills.'"[49] The former drone operators have filed the brief in support of Faisal bin Ali Jaber, a Yemeni civilian who is seeking "an official apology and declaration of error—not money" for the US drone killing of his innocent relatives.[50]

In the release of a document that, for the first time, formally acknowledges the fact of civilian deaths by drones, the US administration, in its tabulated tally, refuses to use the term *civilian* for, tautologically, *civilian* deaths; it deploys instead the militarized euphemism "non-combatant deaths"[51]—a term, that, by definition, usurps the civilian status of the civilian dead, transmuting them, through a circumlocutionary and denegatory move, into combatants who are not combatants as such. This dubious lexical recoding of civilians stands in clear contradistinction to the language used in international humanitarian law, where, for example, Rule 1 of International Humanitarian Law unequivocally states that armed forces must observe the fundamental distinction "between civilians and combatants."[52] This is the necropolitical prerogative of empire: to categorize all members of a population as potential enemies, indiscriminately kill civilians through the extrajudicial principle of "guilt by association," and then posthumously bestow on the dead the now-redundant descriptor of "civilian" once their innocence has been proven after the fatal fact. The expansive latitude built into the United States' drone-kill program, as evidenced by the declassified Presidential Policy Guidelines, requires only "*near certainty* that non-combatants will not be injured or killed."[53] In addition, the document also provides an expansive loophole that allows for deviations from policy guidelines, stating that drone crews have the license to exploit a "fleeting opportunity" to take action, even though it may override other criterial guidelines.[54] In the wake of the release of the PPG for drone kills, "numerous international law experts said [that] the administration's overall terminology and justification for lethal strikes are novel and without precedent" and that the US government "has essentially invented its own set of standards . . . somewhere between international law covering war zones and outside areas. . . . This doesn't provide any more clarity about the substantive standards the government is using."[55] In the context of the election of Donald Trump, the Obama administration's PPGs have in fact "helped pave the way for President Donald Trump to kill more civilians," precisely through a number of moves designed to further loosen the PPG's already lax rulebook.[56] Trump has both facilitated and accelerated the US drone-kill program: "The first year of the Trump administration has resulted in more loss of life from drone strikes than all eight years of Obama's presidency. . . . This is now industrial-scale executions."[57] He has also issued an executive order revoking Obama's rule on the reporting of drone strike deaths, stating that the "rule was 'superfluous' and distracting."[58]

Having outlined the working practices of drone crews, their reliance on unreliable metadata for their targeting of "suspects," and the dubious policy guidelines that are meant to frame their extrajudicial killing practices within the domain of international law, I next theorize and analyze the lethal forces at work in this constellation of necropolitical factors.

The Approximative and Schematizing Logic of the Drone Kill

The combined factors of a drone kill's dependence on algorithmic formulas—that include the often-unknown identity of a mobile phone user's geolocation and algorithmic aggregations that purport to identify a suspect target—are predicated on a calculus of risk probability. In other words, the drone's algorithmic program works to transmute difference into serial sameness and bioinformational interchangeability. Knowledge, in this scientific schema, constitutes what Friedrich Nietzsche terms "the falsifying of the multifarious and incalculable into the identical, similar, and calculable."[59] Operative in the algorithmic formulation of drone targets is the serial conflation of a technological signature with the unknown identity of the user of the mobile phone. The knowledge of the one is rendered as interchangeable with the nonknowledge of the other. The contours of this convoluted scientific epistemology are clarified by Babette Babich in her critique of the field of contemporary science: "Today's science plays on the limits of knowledge, it exploits what it knows and uses it as a template for what it does not know."[60] In other words, once situated in the context of a geolocation drone cue and kill program, the knowledge of a mobile phone's electronic signature is superimposed as a schema onto the unknown identity of the phone's user to render the bioinformationalized subject "knowable."

Analyzing science's fraught truth/knowledge nexus, Babich concludes: "The claim to absolute truth made by contemporary science is prudently approximative, asymptomatic, a peripheral movement: one does not claim to have the truth, and this is one's claim to the truth."[61] One can productively transpose Babich's critical insight onto the field of drone death by metadata: in the practice of geolocation drone kills, the identities of human drone targets are inserted into a relation that approximates their cell phone; if it is revealed that the killing of a human target by a drone strike was based on a mistaken identity, this error is scripted as asymptomatic in the scheme of things and as peripheral to the larger concerns of winning the war on terrorists. "In this way science need not acknowledge its dissembling tactics. What is known and what is not known are thus continuously connected."[62] Nowhere, perhaps, is this more graphically evidenced than in the United States' geolocation drone-kill program, where what is known is inextricably and often fatally connected to what is unknown.

This lethal combination of algorithmic formulas, probability stakes, and gambles on people's lives in the world of US drone kills effectively enunciates the emergence of a new techno-military apparatus that I have elsewhere termed "drone casino mimesis."[63] Drone casino mimesis identifies the agentic role of casino and gaming practices in shaping the conduct of the United States' drone wars. In the words of Leon Panetta, former CIA director, "Very frankly, it's the only game in town."[64] Within the schema of drone casino mimesis, I contend, the mounting toll of civilian deaths due to drone strikes is not only a result of human failure or error—for example, as the misreading of drone video feed. Rather, civilian drone kills must be seen as a system effect of digital kill technologies that are underpinned precisely by both the mor-phology (gaming consoles, video screens, and joysticks) and the algorithmic infrastructure of gaming—with its foundational dependence on "good ap-proximation" ratios and probability computation. Drone-kill algorithms sort, classify, and select for screeners and pilots what they regard as a suspect "pat-tern of life." Generated by algorithms, drone-targeted suspect "patterns of life" emerge as networked and disembodied assemblages of flagged, bioinforma-tionalized data that are computationally presented as suspect in advance of the fact of either their named identities or affiliations actually being known. As algorithmic aggregations of anonymous data, they are underpinned by the extrajudicial principles of "guilty until proven innocent" or "guilt by associa-tion."[65] Guilt by association, in fact, perfectly captures the indiscriminate and lethal logic of US drone signature strikes: the assemblage of amorphous and anonymous data and its computational configuration into a targeted identity need only ever be approximate in terms of its suspect status and proximate in term of its guilt by association status: that is, as discussed above, the target need only use a "suspect" mobile phone to be terminated.

Networked and brought into video visibility through an array of algorith-mic formulas, drone kills executed under the imprimatur of "patterns of life" fulfill N. Katherine Hayles's summation of digitized life, which "in its most nefarious forms" is reduced to a mere "informational pattern that happens to be instantiated in a biological substrate."[66] Categorized as a suspect bioinfor-mational pattern of life, a drone death emerges as a mere biological substrate that has effectively been categorized and made killable by the operations of zoopolitics. Zoopolitically, what is a suspect pattern of life if not a lower form of life, such as a microbiological pathogen, that must be "sanitized" by what one senior US official terms the "antiseptic" use of "drone attacks"?[67] Crossing zoopolitical metaphors, after the deployment of an antiseptic drone attack, a virulent pattern of life will have been rendered into what drone operators term a "bugsplat" or a successful drone hit; in other words, the suspect pattern of life will have been neutralized into nothing more than entomological waste.

A Priori and A Posteriori Logics of the Drone Kill

Due to the preliminary computational work entailed in aggregating informa-tion into what will be subsequently flagged as a suspect bioinformational pat-tern of life, the military algorithms that are constitutive of drone operations must be seen as a priori *agents* in the lethal process of drone targeting and kills.

Prior to the moment of an actual drone kill, a constellation of computational processes governed by algorithmic formulas have already determined what can count as a killable, because suspect, drone target: this may include a *jirga* (a traditional gathering of male elders) or group of military-aged males, known in drone-speak as MAMs. Remarking on the US military's drone targeting of MAMs, a resident of one of the affected regions observes: "Anyone who grows a beard and has a gun and drives a car—people think he might be a Taliban fighter. . . . But over here [North Waziristan] every man carries a gun so you cannot tell who is Taliban and who is just a local in his village. . . . There's no difference in the dress; Taliban have long beard and we have beard as well."[68] Algorithms, by definition, organize information into identifiable patterns. As virtual entities, they effect the processual transmutation of a surveilled target into a bioinformational singularity of metadata inscribed with the lethal qualifier "suspect pattern of life."

Drone algorithms, in other words, constitute civilian subjects into virtualized aggregates of metadata (suspect patterns of life) that are then viewed by drone operators as killable targets (regardless of the unknown identities of these targets). The fatal drone strike, as I discuss below, ensures the literal decomposition of what were once human subjects and their more-than-human relations into undifferentiated necropolitical substance. Operative here are two distinct but ineluctably intertwined modalities of agency and power: one that is structurally overdetermined by the very typologizing dictates of the algorithmic formulas that process, screen, and select the data, and another that is aleatory because the algorithmic formulas aggregate and typologize random nonmilitary events or figures (for example, a wedding or funeral procession—all documented targets of fatal drone strikes) into suspect patterns of life. In effect, what unfolds here is a lethal combination of contradictory forces that are at once overdetermined and aleatory and that are inscribed by both a priori and a posteriori logics.

A priori, the drone algorithms detect their suspect target in advance of any intelligence that in fact proves its criminal status; the algorithms, furthermore, programmatically predetermine the digital phenomenality of what can be visible, precisely as they set the limits as to what can appear to the screeners as a semiotically intelligible suspect target: for example, a MAM or a suspect pattern of life. Inscribed in this a priori algorithmic process is a fatal act of prejudgment that violates legal procedure (innocent until proven guilty) and that structurally precludes the possibility of justice. An infrastructural illegality, an operating as outlaw, and a reiterative impugning of just law inform and enable the programmatic summary executions enabled by the semiautomatic technicity of drone kills. Unsurprisingly, leading researchers in the field are now talking of algorithms as the "'nervous system' of AI" and as built-in with their own biases.[69] Suresh Venkatasubramnian, who has exposed the infrastructural biases of algorithmic systems, notes that "many people believe an algorithm is just a code, but that view is no longer valid." "An algorithm," he concludes, "has experiences, just as a person comes into life and has experiences."[70] The a priori logics that animate algorithmically driven drone kills evidence the self-determining role of software in terms of Latour's theories of distributed cognition and actor-network theory.[71] A posteriori, after a fatal drone strike, the human operators "discover" their error and revise their findings—that is, that the identities of the victims were never actually positively identified as, in truth, legitimate targets and that they have in fact killed innocent civilians.

The troubling and lethal ramifications that accrue from the use of these schematizing surveillance and targeting programs can be further explicated in Nietzschean terms. In delineating the critical difference between "knowing" and "schematizing," Nietzsche brings into focus the relations of subjugating power that are enabled by the operations of schematizing calculability: "Not 'to know' but to schematize—to impose upon chaos as much regularity and form as our practical needs require."[72] Transposed to the drone metadata context, this Nietzschean insight resounds: the schematizing of a range of seemingly legitimate drone targets—including those captured under the dubious descriptors of MAMs, dismounts, irregular combatants, and so on—works to impose regularity and form on the heterogeneous subjects that populate the lands targeted by the US drone program. Reflecting on the constitutive power of schematization in science and philosophy, Nietzsche observes, "In the formation of reason, logic, the categories, it was *need* that was authoritative: the need, not 'to know,' but to subsume, to schematize, for the purpose of intelligibility and calculation."[73]

As the categories of drone targets make clear, the need to schematize is driven by the necessity to render intelligible and calculable the now-overwhelming volume of data being generated by the United States' global surveillance apparatus. In the words of one US intelligence analyst, this apparatus is producing "so much raw video imagery and such vast amounts of signals intercepts that they are literally drowning the intelligence in what is commonly referred to within the community as 'data crush.'"[74] In other words, the homogenizing and reductive power of schematization is what is being deployed by the US drone-kill apparatus to overcome data crush, even though its flagged targets might in fact be civilian subjects. Drone screeners and pilots need not know the actual identities of their targets; rather, the schematization of suspects into bioinformational patterns perfectly subtends the practical need to impose on the chaos of data crush an algorithmically guaranteed intelligibility and regularity that obviates the necessity actually to know the identities of drone-kill victims—for example, the syllogistic formula that targets MAMs and that effectively conflates all middle-age males into suspect targets. Couched in Nietzschean terms, the bioinformationalizing "apparatus of knowledge is an apparatus for abstraction and simplification—directed not at knowledge but for the taking possession of things";[75] it is, in other words, a techno-military apparatus directed at the domination of the subjects caught in its drone crosshairs. This lethal drone apparatus of partial knowledge and constitutive nonknowledge is instrumental in enabling the mastery over *other* lives, the lives of people of color and more-than-human entities, to the point of extrajudicial death. "The sign"—in this instance, a MAM—"is the violence of analogy, what masters and erases difference."[76] Specifically, it erases the difference between a MAM and a civilian. This erasure is facilitated, I underscore, by the asymmetrical relations of racialized power that inscribe these categories in the United States' drone-kill fields.

In the language of the military, a drone death by metadata is referred to as an "F3," or "Find, Fix, Finish." A former drone operator glosses this acronym: "Since there is almost zero HUMINT [human intelligence] operations in Yemen—at least involving JSOC [Joint Special Operations Command]—every one of their strikes relies on signals and imagery for confirmation: signals being the cell phone lock, which is the 'find' and imagery being the 'unblinking eye' which is the 'fix.'"[77] The "finish" is the actual drone-strike kill. "JSOC acknowledges," says one former drone operator, "that it would be completely helpless without the NSA conducting mass surveillance on an industrial scale. . . . That is what creates those baseball cards you hear about."[78] F3 emblematizes the reduction of life to a bioinformational calculus of risk probabilities. The gaming dimensions that inform these military gambles on human life are evinced by the naming of the drone-kill lists as so many "baseball cards" and successful strikes as "jackpots."

The calculus of risk probabilities that is produced by what the US military refers to as its "drone disposition matrix" must be seen as a structural effect of a biopolitical regime that instrumentalizes life in terms of an algebraic *formula* (a bioinformational pattern of life). Together with the objectifying effects of screen technologies, this formula works to render the material *abstract* (the human subject into a formulaic object such as a MAM), the individual *generic* (the figure in the landscape as mere index of risk factors), and the named *anonymous* (the individuating singularity of a proper name rendered superfluous in the face of a computational risk calculus predicated on an anonymous pattern of life). Suturing together the technology of the screen and the lethal practice of drone kills in the United States' dronescapes, Derek Gregory coins the term "screen territories" to materialize the enmeshment of targeted bodies and space: "The political technology that constitutes the territory of the screen thus not only invites but also requires those using it to transcribe their codes and conventions onto what then becomes a killable body enclosed by the terrible violence of the state."[79] These statist regimes of killing by metadata, in effectively abstracting its human targets and reducing them to a calculable bioinformational formula of "risk factors," is instrumental in enabling the administrative indifference to the obliteration of life that this type of semiautomated killing program enables and sanctions.

The numerous reports on the devastating toll on the everyday lives of those living under regimes of relentless drone surveillance and attendant kills present a picture of lives interpenetrated at every level by the fear of the ever-present threat of drone strikes. In Afghanistan, Pakistan, Somalia, and Yemen, the daily fear of living under drones has disrupted the conduct of everyday civilian practices such as communal gatherings in public spaces, school attendance, religious observances, and so on. In his acute analysis of the devastating impact of living under regimes of colonial and imperial power, Frantz Fanon deployed the term "atmospheric violence" to describe the insidious diffusion and interpenetration of violence into the everyday lives of colonized subjects. Fanon describes atmospheric violence as "this violence rippling under the skin."[80] I can think of no more apt way to identify the paralyzing effects of subjects living under regimes of 24/7 US drone surveillance and strikes. Sheikh Ibrahim al Shabwani, the brother of a victim killed by a US drone strike in Yemen, describes the toll of living under a drone-generated regime of atmospheric violence: "The drones are flying over Marib every twenty-four hours and there is not a day that passes that we don't see them. . . . The atmosphere has become weaponry [sic] because of the presence of U.S. drones and the fear that they could strike at any time."[81] Kareem Khan, whose son and brother were killed in a US drone strike in Pakistan, recounts how there is now "an 'atmosphere of fear' in the region [of North Waziristan], to the extent that children are frightened by the slamming of a door, for fear of a drone attack."[82] Fanon's atmospheric violence is attested to in these accounts. It is what ripples under the skin of those living under drones and also what can shred the flesh of its targeted subjects. This atmospheric violence, as I discuss in the latter part of the chapter, is what impacts the very biospheres of drone-targeted regions and what generates forensic ecologies of fast and slow violence.

Necropoiesis: The Art of the Drone Kill

In his discussion of the DoD's increasing use of metadata to conduct its drone-kill campaigns and the unreliable nature of this same metadata, a former JSOC drone operator explains how his GILGAMESH geolocation program instructors, at the end of training, stress that "'this isn't a science. This is an art.' It's kind of a way of saying that it's not perfect."[83] In a similar vein, the former director of Israel's Shin Bet secret service, Avi Dichter, has described Israel's drone-kill program as "the sexiest trend in counterterrorism," claiming that "the state of Israel has turned targeted killings into an art form."[84] There is something disingenuous in these comments that discount the scientific status of the death-by-metadata program deployed by both states. The whole program is undergirded by the discursive practices of science, including the use of advanced mathematics and an array of surveillance, imaging, and military technologies. The very viability of the program is based on the veridictional status of science and its promise to deliver empirical facts—in this case, the dead bodies of targets. There is, however, something that effectively troubles the seemingly pure scientificity of this death-by-metadata program: despite the drone program's claims to verifiable scientific facticity, the identity of a target killed by a drone so often remains *unknown*. In this context, one can see how the laws of science appear to give way to art on at least two counts: (1) science is here constitutively informed by the art of an esoteric hermeneutics that identifies a target from an algorithmic calculus of probabilities that constitutes a suspect pattern of life; and (2) science thus becomes art through the practice of *allopoiesis*, so that the system of positivist science ends up producing something that appears to stand in clear contrast to science as such: in other words, it becomes a hermeneutic art of conjuration and fabrication in which the facticity of the identity of drone targets is nothing more than the product of creative interpretation—with lethal effects. As Nietzsche remarks, "Against positivism, which halts at phenomena—'There are only facts'—I would say: No, facts is precisely what there is not, only interpretations. We cannot establish any fact 'in itself'" outside interpretation.[85]

I want to elaborate on what is at stake in the move whereby, through a tropological turn, the science of killing folds over into an art that appears to override the rigorous certitudes of science in the production of deaths of people whose identities remain unknown. Operative in this move from science to art is a double scene that can be illuminated by drawing on a profound Nietzschean meditation on the science/art nexus. In the interlacing of the science of drone kills with art is what Nietzsche identified as the "capacity to volatilize visual metaphors into schema, thus to dissolve an image into a concept."[86] The algorithmic formula that enables a drone to track and lock onto a mobile phone establishes its schematic conditions of cultural intelligibility precisely through its capacity to volatilize a visual metaphor ("geolocation") into a schema ("pattern of life"), thereby dissolving an image into a concept. The transmutation of visual metaphor into schema, and the conversion of image into concept, brings into focus what Nietzsche called science's "metaphysical illusion"—"which leads science again and again to its limits at which it must turn into *art*."[87] Through this turn, Nietzsche notes, the scientificity of science morphs into the "science of aesthetics."[88]

Drone-screen technologies supply the aesthetic conditions of possibility that ensure that science redoubles into art. The planarity of the screen operates as the digital canvas on which emerge the targeted "dismounts," as the figures that are juxtaposed against the ground before their actual obliteration. The parergonal or multiple framing dimensions of the screen are augmented by the superimposition of an inset tracking frame that provides the diagrammatic coordinates for the crosshaired target. It is within the circumscribed purview of this internal frame, with its focalizing crosshairs, that the drone screeners or imagery analysts, who provide the visual analysis of the video feed to the drone pilots manning their joysticks, deploy the "analytic of aesthetic judgment."[89] In other words, the screeners deploy a visual hermeneutics to interpret the visible signs and provide the necessary exegesis to their drone pilots in waiting. Theirs is an art of *divination*, or an art of second sight, of poring over the visual image to decode and clarify its semiotic status. It is a practice, moreover, that is at once avowedly secular (grounded in the positivist tenets of Western science) and disavowedly theocratic, if not theological (reproducing, through the totality of the global scopic-surveillance apparatus of the drone assemblage, a position of godlike omniscience and virtual omnipresence).

The screeners' art of tele-techno-mediated divination is invested with the very biopolitical question of who shall live or be killed. As a techno-theocratic practice, it requires, in the words of one drone pilot, "an even greater leap of faith—a leap that . . . often treats physical proximity as evidence" that the correct individual has actually been targeted and killed.[90] In the words of one imagery analyst, "I was the only line of defense between keeping someone alive and providing the intelligence for a strike using technology not accurate enough to determine life and death."[91] This divinatory self-representation by a screener succinctly encapsulates the contemporary secularization of the theocratic sovereign who, through the mediations of the drone tele-techno apparatus and the attendant "leap of faith," determines who shall live and who shall die. The bioinformational apparatus of drone targeting posits suspects whose identities are the result of a series of scientifico-aesthetic operations that schematize data-crush chaos into intelligible targets whose very continued existence hinges, in turn, on the divinatory skills of the screener. Art, in such instances, becomes "a necessary correlative and supplement for science."[92] This Nietzschean insight discloses how, in the art of the science of the drone kill, the subordinate supplement—art—works to override and substitute the superordinate figure of science, producing and determining lethal outcomes.

I deploy the term *divination* to describe the drone screeners' exegetical work because on occasion what they divine in their interpretation of the visual sign on the screen remains contentious in terms of its identity status. Brandon Bryant, a former US drone operator, discusses one case in which what he perceives to be a child killed by a drone strike is identified by screeners as a dog. After the drone kill, Bryant questions: "A dog on two legs?"[93] Evidenced here is the slippage between the perceptual and the conceptual and its constitutive reliance on interpretative schemas mediated by an array of visualizing technologies. In this case, the perceptual is mediated and made intelligible by the racio-speciesism of the zoopolitical: a child-dog on two legs that can be killed in an act of noncriminal putting to death of the animal. The scientific and algorithmic substrate of drone targets here wavers and dissolves into Nietzschean schemas of creative construal: "Inasmuch as we impose these fictions as *schemas*, in thinking the factual event we thereby simultaneously *filter* it through a simplifying apparatus. We thus relegate it to *symbolic expression* and to *communicability* and to the *remarkability* of logical procedure. . . . There is no logical thinking in reality and no axiom of either arithmetic or geometry can be deduced from it, just because it isn't there."[94] Transposing this Nietzschean insight to the field of drone targets, the axioms of arithmetic (here algorithmic formulas) and geometry (the geometric, pixelated grids of screen technologies) that constitute the "raw" drone data are filtered through a simplifying apparatus that sifts "noise" from meaningful "sound" to identify a suspect target. In turn, this data is interpretatively rendered by the screeners into symbolic expression and thence articulated through a linguistic system of communicability ("MAM" or "pattern of life"). In his trenchant critique of the nihilistic tendencies of contemporary science, Nietzsche repeatedly draws attention to its foundational predication on a life-negating will to abstraction, reductive simplification, and consequent domination. This Nietzschean perspective clearly resounds in the context of drone death by abstract metadata, as the entire apparatus of knowledge is directed not at proving the identity of the target but at taking fatal possession of it through the processes of schematic bioinformationalization and consequent targeting and execution.

In declaring that the GILGAMESH drone geolocation system is not a science but an art, the Department of Defense works to acknowledge that the mathematical certainty, clarity, and precision of science give way, in their drone-kill programs, to the conceptually ambiguous realm of art. Specifically, in the GILGAMESH geolocation drone targeting system, the precise operations of militarized science are ambiguated by a range of aestheticizing operations that include the spectral resonances of archaic poetry (*Gilgamesh*), the aleatory and ludic attributes of *first-person shooter* video games, the aestheticizing frames of imaging technologies, and the hermeneutic practices of drone screeners exercising their analytic of aesthetic judgment. The US military's decision to name the drone geolocation system after the epic poem *Gilgamesh* works intertextually to reference the translation of the Sumerian incipit *[S]a naq-ba i-mu-ru*:[95] "He who has seen the abyss,"[96] or, in another translation, "He who Sees the Unknown."[97] GILGAMESH sees into the unknown, only to identify a particular SIM card or mobile phone without necessarily being able to ascertain the actual identity of the human target. The omniscient optics and transcendental vision promised by GILGAMESH are in fact compromised by a syllogistic fallacy that insists on conflating a mobile phone's SIM signature with the (unknown) identity of its user.

The GILGAMESH geolocation system, in other words, emerges as an *art*, specifically, a deadly art of tropic fabrication through metonymic conflation. GILGAMESH evidences how the epistemic certainty of science is transmuted into the hermeneutic uncertainty of art, with its generative abyss of unknowns. In other words, the scientificity of advanced mathematics and military technologies is here shown to breach its own disciplinary boundaries and to merge into an occult art where the prosaic science of precision imaging is eclipsed by an art of occulting divination and lethal hermeneutics. Scientific *technê*, in such instances, returns to its originary ground in *poiesis*.[98] More precisely, the killing literality of this drone targeting system must be seen as a form of *necropoiesis*. Articulated at these junctures, Nietzsche notes, are those "boundary points on the periphery from which one gazes into what defies illumination." Science, he sardonically remarks, "coils up at these boundaries and finally bites its own tail."[99] With the GILGAMESH drone program, what defies illumination is the targeted pattern of life whose identity remains unknown. The "bite" that science-cum-art delivers in such cases is only ever experienced by the misidentified drone target at the receiving end of a Hellfire missile. As I discuss in some detail below, the transliteration of abstract metadata into flesh names the violent passage of drone victims through the instrumentalizing circuits of science and into the artifactual domain of the dead.

The art of the drone kill, however, cuts both ways. An artist collective known as #NotABugSplat has created its own antithanatological drone art in response to the United States' indiscriminate drone killing of civilians. On the surface of a field in the drone-bombed Khyber Pakhtunkhwa region of Pakistan, they have unfurled a large canvas patterned with an array of simulated pixels that, from an aerial height, fuse into the face of a Pakistani child whose parents and siblings were killed by a US drone strike. They have termed their giant art installation project *Not a Bugsplat*.[100] The large picture of the child has been designed to be seen and captured by both drone and satellite technologies, and it has thus been inscribed in the US military's metadata killing apparatus. The installation works to expose the fact that the drone's surveillance cameras are not merely visual recording devices but, rather, are themselves part of the lethal apparatus of the military kill. As such, the drone's cameras are prosthetic agents of the missiles: the one both instrumentally enables the other and is somatechnically coextensive with it. The digital pixels of drone screens are counterposed by the massive canvas's pixel simulacra that call into question the intersection of military technologies of weaponized visuality and the drone pilots' lethal practices of divination. The drone screeners' suspect pattern of life emerges, from the surface of this large canvas, as the face of a child who cannot own her civilian status and is therefore exposed to a number of tele-techno-metadata mediations that will render her, like her parents and siblings, nothing more than a prospective bugsplat on a drone screen somewhere in a ground control station in the United States. The *Not a Bugsplat* anti-drone art project triggers a series of exchanges between geopolitically different lines of sight that generate radically opposed relations of power: omniscient versus unseeing; the faceless, multispectral targeting sensor of drones, with its array of cameras and scopic technologies, is juxtaposed against the unblinking stare of the child; and the United States' unilateral and extrajudicial "right to kill" is counterposed to a targeted child who has no right to due process before being summarily terminated. *Not a Bugsplat*, thus, as a counter-aesthetic, graphically materializes across the drone-kill fields of Pakistan the necropolitical asymmetries of power that inscribe and enable the art of the drone kill.

Drone Kills and the Law of Animal Property

In a judgment handed down by the Peshawar High Court, Chief Justice Dost Muhammad Khan documents and condemns the violent toll exacted by US drone strikes on targeted Pakistani communities. In his judgment, the chief justice finds that the "majority of the victims of such attacks are women and small children including suckling babies, besides animals/cattle heads and wildlife."[101] Across a number of documented testimonies, the survivors of US drone attacks describe how, in the aftermath of a drone strike, they are left to disarticulate indeterminate pieces of flesh in which human and animal remains are commingled and fused. In his judgment condemning the ongoing US drone strikes in Pakistan and their toll on civilians and nonhuman animals, Chief Justice Khan draws on the constitution of Pakistan, human rights charters, and international humanitarian law to provide the legal reasoning underpinning his judgment:

> Under the Constitution of Pakistan, 1973, particularly Article 199 thereof put this Court under tremendous obligation to safeguard & protect the life and property of the citizen of Pakistan and any person for the time being in Pakistan, being fundamental rights, hence, this Court is constrained as follows:—
>
> *That the drone strikes, carried out in the tribal areas (FATA) particularly North and South Waziristan by the CIA and US Authorities, are blatant violation of Basic Human Rights and are against the UN Charter, the UN General Assembly Resolution, adopted unanimously, the provision of Geneva Convention thus, it is held to be a War Crime, cognizable by the International Court of Justice or Special Tribunal for War Crimes, constituted or to be constituted by the UNO for this purpose.*[102]

After underscoring that the violation of a raft of constitutional laws, international laws, and human rights conventions is "being carried out with impunity" by the US government, the chief justice catalogs the victims of US drone strikes: "*That the civilian casualties, as discussed above, including considerable damage to properties, livestock, wildlife and killing of infants/suckling babies, women and preteen children, is an uncondonable crime on the part of US authorities including CIA and it is held so.*"[103] Two critical issues stand out in this judgment: (1) the illegality of killing civilians by US drone strikes must be framed within a human rights discourse to gain legal traction; and (2) other-than-human entities killed or injured by these same drone strikes are all encompassed in one phrase that effectively enchains "properties, livestock, wildlife" as a lexico-legal subset of drone victims. It is significant that this subset is conjoined with "infants/suckling babies, women and preteen children" and that this second lexico-legal subset is hierarchically positioned as coming after the category of "properties." I draw attention to these points, as they succinctly emblematize the problematics generated by law's anthropocentric reliance on human rights discourses in addressing more-than-human victims of armed conflict.

As I discussed in chapters 1 and 3, the predication of a human rights discourse on the Eurocentrically inflected biopolitical caesura, with its categorical human/animal division, ensures that whoever is deemed not to qualify as a human-rights-bearing subject can effectively be killed or tortured with impunity. As I will presently examine in some detail, the deployment of raciospeciesism works, conceptually and materially, to enable the killing with impunity of those subjects dispatched beyond the categorical safeguards that attend the human-rights-bearing subject. The danger of continuing to rely on human rights discourses to afford protection to the more-than-human targets of armed conflict hinges not only on how the category of "the human" is predicated on its disavowed and outlawed other (the parenthetical animal) but also, as I have discussed across the preceding chapters, on the very instability of this category and the resultant hierarchical inversions to which it is subject. All of this is tersely evidenced by the structural hierarchy embedded in section 3 of Chief Justice Khan's judgment, which replicates a descending taxonomy of entities that positions property as taking legal precedence over livestock and wildlife. Furthermore, in this same lexico-legal sequence, the concept of property functions as the superordinate term, precisely because of its precedential position, which conceptually works to encompass both livestock and wildlife under its commodifying imprimatur. In other words, the animals killed by drone strikes have no juridical life outside the master category of "property." As Christopher Stone notes on the issue of the jural standing of other-than-human entities: "They have no standing in their own right; their unique damages do not count in determining outcome; and they are not the beneficiaries of awards [or reparations]."[104] This rendering of animals, here both livestock and wildlife, into property owned and governed by human subjects is part and parcel of the larger speciesism that controls and regulates human and animal relations across diverse jurisdictions and geopolitical zones. And as Pakistan's law has been largely based on the legal system of the British Raj,[105] it continues to reproduce Euro-anthropocentric values.

The centrality of animal life in ontologically underpinning and epistemologically animating the very concept of "property" is incisively illuminated by Dinesh Wadiwel: "Animals are not merely just one example of what might be considered property, but sit at the very centre of the property right itself, and underpin 'man's' earthly dominion and securitisation of self as a 'superior' being."[106] It is from this property-defined locus that human regimes of subjugation of the more-than-human, and the appurtenant biopolitical apparatuses crucial to consolidating, securitizing, and reproducing this violent anthropocentric order, find their proprietorial and instrumentalizing rationalities. Moreover, Wadiwel elaborates, this anthropocentrically propertied locus, with its violent and systematic conversion of animal life into disposable property, is what generates the larger conditions for the war on animals.[107] The classification of animals as forms of human property is explicitly addressed by Chief Justice Khan in his judgment. After cataloging the "many houses & vehicles of different category, make & model, worth millions of dollars," that "were destroyed during these [drone] attacks," the judge adds: "Besides, many cattle heads of different kinds were torn into pieces & charred, belonging to the local residents."[108] The suffering experienced by the cattle in this act of military violence is vitiated by their positioning within the serial order of property that is both fungible and serially replaceable: houses and cars. Inscribed in the category of property, as the only locus from which animals can realize a minimal jural standing, "the status of the animal is as *thing*."[109] As such, the animal is, as Gary Francione writes, a "chattel," which "is to say that it has no inherent value and that its value is exclusively instrumental."[110]

When Chief Justice Khan does raise the issue of pain in relation to animal kills, it is again attenuated by being situated in the commodified category of "portable property": "Beside damage [from US drone strikes] caused to the properties of the local population, their households and other moveable properties including cattle heads, in great number, is a painful phenomenon."[111] The anthropocentric order that organizes this judgment works to subordinate the suffering of the animal victims within a vertical schema predicated on monetary value: "The residential houses are burnt into ashes along with vehicles & cattle heads, the worst kind of cruelty to the animals."[112] Incinerated alive by drone missiles, the suffering of "cattle heads" remains subsumed under the categories of houses and vehicles that, in economic terms, take precedence over them and, through the signifying sequence of the property continuum, establish the cultural conditions of intelligibility that enable their destruction to be legally indexed. As "cattle heads," they are always already marked as appropriable "livestock" or "animal capital"[113] whose legal value can only be posited on the basis of their monetary exchange value as "moveable property." Enumerated as mere "cattle heads," they are thus rendered into fungible commodities branded by the substitutive logic of anthropocentrism and its law of undifferentiated animal genericity. The brutal fact that what the drone strikes enact on and exact from their animal victims is "the worst kind of cruelty to the animals" can only be acknowledged on the basis of this anthropocentrically circumscribed ground. As such, the physical violence enacted against the cattle is amplified by the epistemic violence of an anthropocentric legal discourse that, in effect, neuters the suffering of the animal victims, even as it attempts to acknowledge it.

In what follows, I want to analyze the complex entanglement of human and more-than-human victims in the context of drone strikes. The entangled forensic ecologies of drone strikes that I examine stand to defy the segregationalist ordering of the victims of war along the biopolitical hierarchy and its taxonomy of proprietorial categories. The proprietorial category of property, as individuating identifiably discreet entities, is, in fact, precisely what is rendered inoperative in the aftermath of a drone strike.

Geobiomorphologies of Drone Kills

In an interview on the lethal effects of a US missile strike in Al-Majalah, Yemen, Jeremy Scahill describes the survivors' account of the toll this strike exacted: "I talked to tribal leaders who went there within 24 hours of the strike, and they described a scene where livestock and humans—the flesh of livestock and humans was melted together, and they couldn't determine if it was goats or sheep or human flesh, and they were trying to figure out how even to bury their dead."[114] These accounts of human and animal flesh inextricably bound in the moment of violent death caused by US military strikes are to be found across the numerous investigative reports that document the toll of these attacks. In a statement to the US Senate Judiciary Committee, Subcommittee on the Constitution, Civil Rights and Human Rights on the US drone wars, Farea Al-Muslimi, a Yemeni farmer, describes the aftermath of a US missile strike on his village: "In the poor village that day, more than 40 civilians were killed, including four pregnant women. Bin Fareed was one of the first people to the scene. He and others tried to rescue civilians. He told me their bodies were so decimated that it was impossible to differentiate between the children, the women, and their animals. Some of these innocent people were buried in the same grave as animals."[115]

In another account, describing a drone strike in the Yemeni village of Khashamir, a similar scene of carnage is documented: "Animals died, and the bodies of all those who died were disintegrated and scattered over a large area. . . . They were all exploded, and we could not identify them, their limbs ripped apart."[116] In these survivor accounts, human and animal bodies are described as being fused into a composite residue of inextricable flesh. The one melts into the other. The one is buried with the other. Taking these accounts of war-torn and fused flesh as my point of departure, I want to trace the conceptual contours of a domain that would encompass both human and more-than-human subjects as entities worthy of ethical consideration in the wake of indiscriminate military violence. As I discussed in the introduction, scholars such as Vine Deloria Jr., Linda Hogan, and Maurice Merleau-Ponty have collectively established an invaluable conceptual framework by which to begin to do this. To recap, Deloria articulates the relations of interdependence between human and more-than-human entities and emphasizes the ethical imperative for humans to "take up their responsibilities to all living things."[117] Hogan underscores the need to assume this ethics of responsibility "for the relationships and relatives that constitute the complex web of life," and she enfleshes this ethics by drawing attention to what she calls the contemporary "destruction of this body of earth."[118] In conceptualizing our relation to the world, Merleau-Ponty posits the flesh as that which conjoins one to the other: "The presence of the world is precisely the presence of its flesh to my flesh."[119] His theorizing of flesh disrupts the circumscriptions of the anthropocentric frame. Flesh emerges, for him, as both a general and specific modality of being in the world. Understood phenomenologically, flesh signifies the condition of possibility of being in the world that effectively binds the human with the more-than-human.

In the melting of human and animal flesh after the violence of a missile strike, there emerges an indissociable interlinking of one to the other based on the material fact that, in Merleau-Ponty's affecting words, "there is this thickness of flesh between us."[120] The thickness of flesh is what conjoins one victim to the other and what, after a missile strike, cannot be categorically divided and taxonomically distributed up or down the biopolitical hierarchy. Through this thickness of flesh, human and animal, subject and object, figure and ground dissolve. The thickness of this flesh is also what evidences the materiality of the remainders of the dead: in its shredded and decomposing corporeity, this thickness of flesh is what forensically testifies to the act of fatal violence. It exposes to view what is virtually everywhere denied by the US administration: the fact that its missile strikes are never simply "surgical," that they kill much more than their designated suspect targets. If these strikes can be called "surgical" in any way, it is through their violent capacity to slice up living entities and reduce them to scattered fragments of undifferentiated flesh. In the wake of the violence unleashed by a missile blast, there is a denucleation of the identity of the one and the other.

Following a drone strike in the Yemeni village of Al-Shihr, Hassan Ibrahim Suleiman describes how the victims' "bodies were shredded. We collected the remains without knowing who they were."[121] The flesh of the one is so fused with the flesh of the other as to be reconstituted into an indeterminate and horizontal consanguinity. Articulated here, in this binding of different flesh, is "the relation of the human and animality . . . [as] not a hierarchical relation, but lateral, an overcoming that does not abolish kinship" but, on the contrary, works to materialize what Merleau-Ponty terms a "strange kinship."[122] Significantly, this kinship between the flesh of animals and humans is ethically envisaged by Merleau-Ponty as constituted at once by divergence (*écart*) or difference and a relational similarity: the qualifier *strange* in this kinship relation works to mark the unassimilable difference or alterity in the context of binding relations of consanguinity.[123] His concept of *intercorporeity* is what "founds transitivity from one body to another."[124]

In the harrowed ground of a lethal drone strike, the impossibility of unbinding this encrypted consanguinity calls for the burial of one with the other. In the aftermath of these drone massacres of civilians and animals, one can discern an otherwise effaced relation of correspondence between the metadata program and its resultant exsanguinated "outputs." In the first instance, death by metadata involves the killing of subjects whose identities are not known. The killing violence that is unleashed by the drone's missiles works, in turn, to render the very identity of the targets unknowable to the families and villagers who are left to collect their unidentifiable shredded remains.

Sheikh Saleh bin Fareed, in his testimony on US drone deaths, describes the poststrike scene he was compelled to witness: "Goats, sheep, cows, dogs, and people, you could see their bodies scattered everywhere, some many meters away. The clothes of the women and children were hanging from the treetops with the flesh on every tree, every rock. But you did not know if the flesh was of human beings or animals. Some bodies were intact but most, they melted."[125] In the context of this site of saturated violence, Merleau-Ponty's "flesh of the world" becomes critically resignified. Reading this scene of carnage, I am compelled to bear witness to "a flesh of things."[126] A flesh of things articulates the shredding of human and animal flesh by a missile and its transmutation into a corporeal materiality that literally *enfleshes* the world: hanging from treetops and rocks, human-animal flesh evidences, as dispersed fragments, the rendering of lives into the mere "tissue of things."[127] In such moments there are not indivisible beings; rather, there are intercorporeal assemblages of flesh where individual beings have been rendered into undifferentiated biological substance. Animals and humans are, in this site of explosive decomposition, situated beyond the taxonomic and hierarchical domains of species differentiation. Collectively, they embody not different species but "families of trajectories"[128] that, in the wake of the violence of the missile's explosion, meld into each other, even as they are compelled to assume the contours of the landscape. Citing Fritz London and Edmond Bauer's work on quantum physics, Merleau-Ponty describes how a "theory of species" can in effect dissolve into "an indiscernibility of particles of the same species."[129] One can indeed name this scene of violence as a site that graphically instantiates the indiscernibility of particles of different species through a process of fissile dissolution and recombination.

In such sites of saturated violence, the violent dissolution of life is articulated through the register of shredded flesh that becomes entirely coextensive with its *geocorpography*. In coining the term *geocorpography* some years ago, I wanted to underline the impossibility of disarticulating the body from its geopolitical locus and to materialize the multiple significations that accrue from this understanding of the geocorporeal nexus. In the massacre perpetrated by the US military in this Yemeni village, geocorpography enunciates the violent enmeshment of the flesh and blood of the body with the geopolitics of war and empire. This site of carnage, however, takes the concept of geocorpography to another level of signification. It compels the coining of a new composite term that acknowledges the specific modality of this violence as what dissolves a corpus into undifferentiated biological substance that is compelled to assume the morphology of a blast site: *geobiomorphology*. In such sites of saturated military violence, there is a complete dissolution of the body or corpus, and the dismembered and melted flesh becomes the tissue of things as it biomorphologically enfolds the contours of trees and rocks. What we witness in this scene of carnage is the material transliteration of abstract metadata to flesh. The abstracting and decorporealizing operations of metadata "without content" are, in these contexts of the militarized slaughter of humans and animals, geobiomorphologically grounded in the targeted lands of Afghanistan, Pakistan, Somalia, and Yemen.

I want to pause for a moment to elaborate on the significance of my choice of the term *transliteration*. Precisely as a term that is animated, to draw on Susan Stryker's words, by the power of the *trans*, this term establishes critical points of processual connection between metadata and flesh.[130] Transliteration figures forth the spatiotemporal process encompassed by the necropolitical assemblage of drone kills. The term draws attention, through its transitive semantics, to the shift from the space of a drone ground control station in some US metropolitan city to the targeted killing fields of Afghanistan, Pakistan, Somalia, or Yemen, as the so-called ungoverned lands that abut the extraterritorial edges of US empire and that are invariably positioned as posing "imminent threats" to its national interests. The term also materializes the tele-techno-mediated temporal shifts that establish fundamental contradistinctions between the insular time of execution from the safety and comfort of an ergonomically designed drone pilot's cubicle to the fatal time of unconditional exposure experienced in the site of a missile blast. Transliteration marks the process of converting an abstracted medium of numerals, algorithmic formulas, and bioinformational pixels to the earthly medium of flesh. It names the conversion of the metadata's algorithmic formula of a suspect pattern of life to the flesh of the world, and it identifies the conversion of what Gregory terms the apprehension of a drone target "as a screen image, a network trace and a sensor signature" into an "acutely and insistently material" entity.[131] I want to stress that what I am not positing here is the concept of flesh as some purely natural, biological substance. On the contrary, I understand flesh to be always already mediated by the very somatechnic processes that render it culturally intelligible precisely *as flesh*.

In other words, what I am drawing attention to is a different order of mediation predicated on a militarized series of instrumentalizing functions designed to render the flesh of US drone targets into little more than disposable biological substance ontologically abstracted from its targeted human-animal subjects. Networked through the abstracting schema of metadata, drone targets are configured as nothing more than generic, anomic, and wholly killable flesh. In elaborating on the "flesh of the visible," Merleau-Ponty writes that the "carnal being" concept refers to "a being of depths, of several leaves or several faces."[132] In the wake of the drone strike in the Yemeni village that I cited above, the flesh of the visible becomes something else altogether: the human and animal entities who are its victims become, through the force of explosive shredding, deprived of the depth of their being, precisely as they are transmuted into surface fragments, leaves of flesh without faces that sway from the treetops and that enfold the topography of the impact site. This, then, is the geobiomorphology of a drone kill, as the abstract algorithmic formulas that deliver to drone pilots suspect patterns of life "without content" are transliterated into the flesh of the world: the gaping contours of the cratered earth delineate the mouths of the dead; the flesh of the dead is the strange fruit that hangs from leaves and branches; the dispersed residue of hair, hide, and shards of bone traces the striation of the debris field; and the blood of the dead pools into scarlet soaks.

Drone Sparagmos

Reading Merleau-Ponty in the necropolitical context of this massacre, I am compelled to transpose his celebratory writings on the flesh of the world to the field of war, and consequently his writings signify a range of unintended meanings and affects. In theorizing the flesh of the world, he writes: "The space, the time of things are shreds of himself, of a multiplicity of individuals synchronically and diachronically distributed, but a relief of the simultaneous and of the successive, a spatial and temporal pulp."[133] The animals and humans who are the victims of the United States' drone kills are, after the strike, transmuted into the dead time of things in which the shreds of their flesh are synchronically and diachronically distributed. This flesh is synchronized in the killing instant of the strike and, in the wake of the force of the blast, a diachronic distribution of the shredded flesh unfolds. Caught in the violent simultaneity of the fatal moment, the victim's flesh is diachronically inscribed in the torsion that inscribes the consequent acts of dispersal and funereal gathering.

Instantiated in these sites of military violence is the practice of *sparagmos*, the Greek term for the ritualized dismemberment and dispersal of bodies. In ancient Greek culture, sparagmos identified the collective performative of ritualized murder in terms of an aesthetico-political art of the kill. I can think of no more effective way of describing, and accounting for, the deployment of the art of the drone kill in the context of the innumerable sites of US military carnage that I have thus far documented than through the practice of sparagmos. Sparagmos names the militarized dismemberment of the flesh of the targeted subjects of Afghanistan, Pakistan, Somalia, and Yemen as a ritualized practice codified by a set of tele-techno-mediated procedures and consecrated by a chain of command that includes the Principals Committee of the National Security Council, the Deputies Committee, and the US president, who signs off on the target, though not on individual strikes.

As drone kills are complexly inscribed by a priori logics of algorithmically driven processes of automated technicity that misidentify a killable target and an attendant a posteriori series of human interventions, including screener practices of divination, the agent of the kill can now never be categorically identified. Moreover, the US drone assemblage is geopolitically dispersed across a vast archipelago of military sites encompassing an array of international actors, including, for example, Africa (Cape Lemonnier), Australia (Pine Gap), Germany (Ramstein Air Base), Sicily (Sigonella Naval Air Station), and the UK (Menwith Hill Station). These international actors provide the NSA with satellite surveillance information, which in turn implicates them in US drone-kill operations; they further complicate the concept of a singular and identifiable locus of responsibility for drone kills. The drone assemblage of algorithmic, tele-techno, and human factors works to blur originary points of responsibility for a drone kill. This is perfectly in keeping with the intended effect of the traditional use of sparagmos: "The [sparagmatic] techniques of ritual murder," writes Eric Gans in his analysis of this ancient Greek practice, "reenact this irresponsibility by absolving any given individual of responsibility for inflicting death."[134] There is now no longer any individual responsibility for drone deaths, as the practice of killing has been effectively dispersed along an attenuated kill chain that absolves any one individual of the kill. In the process of sparagmatically absolving any individual agent of the actual act of killing, something else also takes place: the inversion of the victim into the killer and vice versa. "The violence of the sparagmos," Gans elaborates, "demonstrates that, in the minds of the participants, it is they rather than the central figure who are the original victim."[135] This inversion is exactly what has driven the United States' never-ending war on terror since 9/11. The United States has so arrogated the position of the victim of terror that all its declared wars (Iraq and Afghanistan) and shadow wars (Pakistan, Somalia, and Yemen) can be seen as "legitimate" only once they are situated in the open-ended process of revenging its righteous victim status. Perhaps this inverted killer-as-victim position is nowhere more accurately captured than in the United States' plaintive, geopolitically obtuse cry "But why do they hate us?"—a cry of victimhood that went up immediately after the 9/11 attacks and prompted this salutary riposte from one US commentator: "They hate us because we don't even know why they hate us."[136]

In "the sparagmos," Gans notes, "the figural nature of the victim, the object of original resentment, is precisely what is destroyed."[137] In the context of lethal drone strikes, the anomic genericity of suspect and targeted patterns of life is transliterated by the violence of a missile strike into fragments of flesh without bodies, names, or identities, with the consequent rendering of human and animal victims into deindividuated pulp. Evidenced in the aftermath of a drone-missile sparagmos, then, is the dissolution of the contours that differentiate figure from ground. This follows "the model of the sparagmos in its destruction of the worldly correlate of the scene of representation; it is the irreversible de-figuring of the figure."[138] Following the logic of sparagmos, a drone strike will indiscriminately obliterate the targeted scene of representation and all the figures that inhere in that scene through the deployment of the art of the drone kill. Evidenced here is art at its most nihilistic and technology at its most thanatological. The sparagmatic art of the drone kill is one predicated on ritualized desecration and dismemberment without the possibility for Dionysian redemption; it carves a void in the space of its targeted subjects, leaving a locus of complete destruction. In a blinding flash, the transparent window of the drone pilot's computer screen is rendered materially opaque through the turgid admixture of metal, dirt, and flesh. The nested frames of the drone pilot's screen hover over an unfolding scene of decomposition, continuing to contain the flare of the missile's explosion, the turbulent billows of smoke and dust and the atomized flesh of its victims.

I say "contain" because the tele-techno-mediations deployed by drone technologies and their attendant production of digital simulacra work to preclude the material indexes of militarized violence—the acrid smell of burned flesh and scorched earth—from piercing through and beyond the screen.[139] The material indexes of this violence are at once digitally encrypted within the containment screen and rendered as images ineluctably detached from the weight, stench, and bloody viscosity of macerated flesh. The mediative logic of the sign and the unbridgeable gap between a sign and its material referent work to neutralize the otherwise assaultive effects unleashed in this scene of sparagmatic violence. In the aftermath of a drone's pulverization of the scene of the living, one can no longer talk of the difference between figure and ground. The missile's blast renders the corpus of the animal-human into a shredded carnality that becomes geobiomorphologically coextensive with the flesh of the earth. Operative here is the dehiscence of the body through the explosive violence of a carno-centripetality that disseminates the flesh of the figure and renders it undifferentiated from its ground. This fusion of categories—of figure and ground—works to transmute ontology into thanatology.

In the wake of the sparagmatic dispersal of flesh, the survivors attempt to gather the remains for burial. Yet, through the practice of what drone operators term "double tap," the violence of the sparagmos is often redoubled as the very rescuers of drone victims are targeted by a follow-up drone strike. Mushtaq Yusufzai describes how the rescuers after one drone strike "were trying to pull out the bodies, to help clear the rubble, and take people to hospital" when "two missiles slammed into the rubble, killing many more. At least 29 people died in total."[140] The calculated redoubling of drone sparagmatic violence extends to the bombing of the funerals of the victims of previous drone strikes.[141] The double violence of drone double taps works to thwart centrifugal attempts by survivors to bring together the shattered residue of the dead and to offer them a burial. The torsive violence of drone sparagmos is here shown to be implacable and recursive in its production of sites of nonsaturatable trauma. In these fatal sites, the living who come to gather the dead are, in an abyssal manner, transmuted into the dead. Traced in these forensic sites of drone-enabled war crimes is the shredding of the flesh of the world and its violent molding and sedimentation into the necrosubstrate of the violated earth.

Forensic Insignia of Sovereign-Imperial Violence

Reflecting on how flesh must be seen "as 'element,' in the sense it was used to speak of water, air, earth, and fire, that is, in the sense of a *general thing,*" Merleau-

Ponty concludes that this conceptualization establishes "the inauguration of the *where* and the *when*, the possibility of exigency for the fact; in a word: facticity, what makes the fact be a fact. And at the same time, what makes the facts have meaning, makes the fragmentary facts dispose themselves about 'something.'"[142] In the postsparagmatic context of a drone-kill field, the flesh of the animal-human victims becomes an element in the forensic ecology of the place: it is inextricably bound to the soil, rocks, trees, and leaves of the site. As trace evidence of a US massacre, the fragmented flesh bears witness to the *where* and *when* of the killing. As trace evidence dispersed across the scene of the massacre, it signifies the very facticity of the war crime. These shards of lives, winnowed by the force of a missile blast guided by abstracting algorithms erroneously designating suspect patterns of life, emerge as the forensic traces of a criminal act that will evade any criminal prosecution.

Sheikh Saleh bin Fareed offers another perspective on a drone-strike massacre in al Majalah, Yemen:

> "When we went there, we could not believe our eyes. I mean, if somebody had a weak heart, I think he would collapse. You see goats and sheep all over, you see the heads of those who were killed here and there. You see their bodies, you see children." . . . Body parts were strewn around the village. "You could not tell if this meat belongs to animals or human beings," he remembered. They tried to gather what body parts they could to bury the dead. . . . As bin Fareed surveyed the carnage, most of the victims he saw were women and children. "They were all children, old women, all kinds of sheep and goats and cows. Unbelievable."[143]

In surveying the site of this massacre, bin Fareed talks not of flesh but of "meat" as that which remains after a missile blast. The use of the term *meat* brings into focus the way the US military's campaigns of zoopolitical violence work to transmute the living subjects of Yemen, Afghanistan, Pakistan, and Somalia into *carcasses*; in other words, they are divested of the juridical human-rights-bearing title of "corpses" and resignified as just so much meat, specifically, as mere animal carcasses that have no jural standing within the context of war crimes. Mohamed al-Qawli, a Yemeni civilian, articulates as much when he attempts to make sense of the carnage he was compelled to witness following another US drone strike: "All of us in the village heard a large explosion. . . . We picked up the burned body parts. They were all over. . . . My brother was completely charred. We identified him by his teeth. It's as if they killed animals."[144] A former drone pilot, indeed, describes his quarry in zoopolitical terms as little more than "vermin," specifically, "rats" and "mice" that he and his fellow drone operators hunt and kill.[145]

The biopolitical caesura, through its human/animal division, renders the civilians killed by the United States in its drone wars into so many animal carcasses that, in effect, do not die but merely perish. Inscribing this military production of human carcasses is the metaphysics of a virulent racio-speciesism that finds its clinical articulation in Heidegger. For Heidegger, "the animal," because it is defined by a fundamental series of privations and captivations, "cannot die in the sense in which dying is ascribed to human beings but can only come to an end."[146] "To die," Heidegger elaborates, "means to be capable of death as death. Only man dies. The animal perishes."[147] The violent operations of racio-speciesism turn the civilian targets of US drone strikes into nonhuman animals captivated in their lawlessness and savagery and deficient in everything that defines the human-rights-bearing subject. In contrast to the individuating singularity of the Western subject as named person, they embody the anonymous genericityof the animal and the seriality of the undifferentiated and fungible carcass. As subjects incapable of embodying the figure of "the human," they are animals who, when killed by drone attacks, do not die but only come to an end. In Western-mediated contexts, what remains is the carcass that is not worthy of mourning and that, as carcass that merely perishes, need not be taken into account as a human death. Situated in this zoopolitical drone context, the brazen denial by the US administration of the thousands of civilians it has killed assumes its own internal logic. No one dies in these US drone strikes. Only animals perish. And, precisely as animals, they are transmuted by the zoopolitical operations of the US state into "absent referents" that, to cite Carol Adams, cannot be accorded their own existence or death: "Animals in name and body are made absent as animals for meat to exist. Animals' lives precede and enable the existence of meat."[148]

The wholesale killing of the flesh of the world that the US state perpetrates in the militarized zones of Afghanistan, Pakistan, Somalia, and Yemen encompasses a heterogeneity of more-than-human entities. One report, *Our Condolences, Afghanistan*, documents the scale of the killing and destruction conducted by the US military in Afghanistan alone. The report offers a glimpse into the indiscriminate nature of the US military's devastation of Afghanistan's ecologies in its everyday military operations. On top of the documented human kills, the catalog includes the razing of grapevines, mulberry trees, and cherry trees; the incineration of crops; the obliteration of seeded fields by military convoys; and the killing of sheep, goats, and cows.[149] This necropolitical catalog evidences the operations of ecocide, in which the living ecologies of militarized zones are transmuted into forensic ecologies of death and ruination. There is, however, a critical difference that needs to be marked here in relation to the respective necropolitical campaigns waged by the Israeli and US militaries. Israel's military campaigns are largely driven by the settler state's imperative to destroy, clear, occupy, and secure Palestinian land. The United States' military campaigns, by contrast, are not about securing settler occupation—this objective has already been largely achieved on both the North American continent and the Hawaiian Islands. The US military, in fact, has historically been a key player in the expropriation of Indigenous lands and, drawing on Winona LaDuke's phrase, in the consequent "militarization of Indian country." "It is pervasive," she writes. "Native people have seen our communities, lands and life ways destroyed by the military. Since the first European colonizers arrived, the U.S. military has been a blunt instrument of genocide, carrying out policies of removal and extermination of Native Peoples."[150]

LaDuke maps in detail how Native American communities have also borne the brunt of environmental racism and ecocidal operations through the US military's siting of toxic waste dumps, nuclear test sites, uranium mines, and weapons testing sites on their lands. The United States' military campaigns interlock with the operations of racial capitalism and environmental racism to enable the exercise of imperial power across those territories which are seen as crucial to its geopolitical influence and from which it can continue to source its undiminished appetite for natural resources. Critically, the settler colonial expropriation and militarization of Indigenous lands is what enables the US state's transnational, imperial-military operations.

The United States' drone wars evidence the violent crossing of science into the field of militarized *technê* or art; they materialize the threshold where the analytic of scientifico-aesthetic judgment morphs, in turn, into techno-theocratic acts of lethal divination. The art of the drone kill generates screen scenographies of digital massacre and geobiomorphologies of the aftermath in which flesh of the world—trees, sheep, goats, humans—is transmuted into the necrosubstrate of the earth. This semiautomated killing practice signals the exercise of an extrajudicial violence that, in sparagmatic terms, arrogates the position of victim, occludes responsibility for the kill, techno-ritualistically dismembers its victims, and disperses their remains. It is through the transliteration of bioinformation into executed flesh that the US state asserts its claim, as victim, to victor's justice. The abstracting operations of an algorithmically driven technicity and of killing-at-a-distance practices find their teleological fulfillment and material instantiation in the cratered contours of a drone strike site. The devastated ecologies that are left in the wake of the US military's drone campaigns delineate the forensic remains of war crimes marked with the sovereign-imperial insignia of impunity.

The militarized production of geobiomorphologies of the dead flesh of the world needs, finally, to be contextualized within a larger frame that will necessarily bring into focus the global implications of these death zones. Once positioned within the contemporary global frame of the unfolding Anthropocene and its inextricable relation to the operations of the military-industrial-security complex, these localized sites of militarized geobiophysical destruction work to amplify and accelerate a number of the key anthropogenic factors—including ecosystem destruction, toxic pollution, massive carbon emissions, ongoing depletion of resources, and so on—that are contributing to macro anthropocenic changes. The geobiomorphologies of militarized destruction are, then, their own site-specific loci of the dead flesh of the world *and* transglobal sites that unleash multiscalar anthropogenic forces critical to altering the earth system. Situated within the theoretical framework of "geopolitical ecologies," these geobiomorphologies of militarized destruction index "the role of large geopolitical institutions, like the U.S. military, in environmental change" by bringing to the fore "the hydrocarbon logistical infrastructure that makes U.S. imperialism possible."[151] The geobiomorphologies that I have discussed in the context of the drone-kill fields of Afghanistan, Pakistan, Somalia, and Yemen emerge as interlocking with, and coconstituting, the geobiophysical deformations and death zones that are evidencing the lethal transition to the Anthropocene.

In his account of one of the serial wars unleashed by the Israeli state on the Palestinian territories, Ghassan Andoni, a resident of Beit Sahour in the occupied West Bank, describes the bombing of his village and the killing that ensued. On his return to the village, Sahour recalls one incident in particular: "I still remember an injured bird that had been trapped in my relatives' house after the bombing ended. I caught it and cared for it while waiting to go home. After a couple of weeks, the Red Cross arranged a bus ride for me and others back to Jordan. I tried to take the bird with me back home. I held it in my hands on the trip back, but it died on the way."[1] Sahour, in the midst of the large-scale destruction around him, rescues and cares for the bird. Cradled in Sahour's hands, the dying bird is also a refugee of war who, in this instance, embarks on a journey of no return. Articulated here is the overriding of the zoopolitical human/animal division through the practical exercise of care for the other in a zone of militarized violence. Sahour and the injured bird embody what has been a burden woven throughout the narratives of this book: the inextricable entanglement of heterogeneous lives riven by states of war and the defiant exercise of an ethics of care across species, including the detainees feeding ants in Guantánamo's maximum-isolation cells; the staging of a public ceremony of mourning by a group of Palestinian villagers for the venerable olive trees felled by the Israeli military; and the communal acknowledgment of the consanguinity of the animal-human victims of drone strikes through their collective burials. These dispersed practices establish, in their collectivity, grounds for hope. Across the testimonies of trauma and death that I have discussed in the book, what has emerged as a constant is the practical exercise of a relational ethics for the more-than-human that has been largely excluded from the bounded framework of Euro-anthropocentric law. This relational ethics is what is instantiated despite the failure of international law to safeguard from military assault and destruction a number of complex ecologies and their diverse entities. The relational ethics exercised by Sahour evidences the incommensurability of law to justice. Despite the failure of law to deliver justice for other-than-human entities in lethal zones of militarized violence, an ethics underpinned by the concept of ecological relationality is realized through a range of justice-oriented acts that defy law and, indeed, stand in contradistinction to it—specifically, to its anthropocentric gaps and its systemic failures.

Sahour's relational ethics materialize for me the quotidian sphere where the micropolitics of earth justice is realized in practice and where an ethics of biophilia, as the lived embodiment of our deep affinity with the more-than-human world, is practiced daily. In the midst of the overwhelming devastation unleashed on Gaza by Israel's Operation Protective Edge, Atif Abu Saif evidences in his war chronicles the ineradicable and unconditional biophilia that survives and defies military assaults and deprivations:

> My mother-in-law is watering her plants despite the shortage of water in the tanks. She keeps her plants in the living room in different pots arranged around the room. They make the house calmer, greener. . . . They make up her garden. Every morning she waters them and checks each leaf, remembers each one, and notices whenever a new leaf buds into life. She knows their length and their sheen. She knows when they're thirsty from the colors of their leaves. She always finds water for them.[2]

Despite the desperate water shortages, a Palestinian woman exercises a surplus affirmation of life that transcends the material limits so brutally and violently imposed by war. It is a surplus affirmation as it exceeds the calculative economies of instrumentalized reason with its bookkeeping notations of debits and credits: regardless of the desperate water restrictions, "she always finds water for them." In the fragile and intimate space of this interior garden, practices of nurturance and defiance trace the ethical contours of an ecology of entangled lives that projects life into the future despite the threat of imminent obliteration. "We must envision and enact," writes Daniel Wildcat, "a realization of beauty in the present for the future."[3] Both Sahour and Saif's mother-in-law realize, in the context of war, fragile acts of beauty. They enact affective practices that enable, in the fraught spaces of forensic ecologies, the affirmation of life in the context of intimate relations bound by the possibility of imminent death. These affective practices instantiate, in other words, a relational ethics of finitude. At the level of praxis and imbued with an embodied sense of poetic justice, they challenge instrumentalist law that is, in Richard Sherwin's words, "cut off from its figurative, poetic roots, [and] blinded by lack of a pragmatic ethical phenomenology." In this instrumentalist context, "justice recedes from view. In its place, legal forms endlessly proliferate: guidelines and principles, policies and regulations, rules and metrics—overwhelming in their disparate array."[4]

Sahour's enfolding of the injured and dying bird in the cup of his hands acknowledges the fact of a shared mortality and transmutes it into an act of compassion that defies the lethal violence of war, even as the bird succumbs to their fatal injuries. Saif's mother-in-law enacts a gesture of unconditional generosity that defies the conditional strictures of anthropocentric law, disbursing her family's limited supply of water to her more-than-human relations. In the context of the war-torn ruins that surround them and that materially index the facticity of finitude and the threat of obliteration through military violence, these practices both defy and overturn anthropocentric circumscriptions as to what constitutes a life worthy of ethical consideration. In the light of Wildcat's exhortation, collectively they work toward an ecological realization of the future. What other term is so indissociably tied to the very possibility of realizing the future as *ecology*? The one is unrealizable without the other. And from whence can justice issue if not from an ecology that generates the very conditions of possibility for life as such?

Indigenous cosmo-epistemologies of interrelated life, and their articulation of an ethos of ethical relation and negotiation, stand in contradistinction to some avowedly progressive animal studies positions that, for example, advocate that humans should leave "nonhuman animals alone by not interfering in their use for any reason."[5] This position is untenable on a number of levels.

First, it reenacts a neocolonial terra nullius understanding of nature-culture, reproducing, by default, yet another denegated form of Western anthropocentric exceptionalism: that is, it effaces, through a neocolonial turn, millennial histories of Indigenous interspecies relations founded on an ethic and law of shared existence and intertwined kinship relations. In advocating a zoopolitics of "hyperseparation" between (tacitly Western) humans and nonhuman animals, it relegates Indigenous cultures to the realm of "animal nature."[6] In the name of an avowedly progressive, because nonanthropocentric, call for the complete separation between humans and animals, it demarcates an inviolable line of division between the two, thereby reinstituting another form of anthropocentric exceptionalism cast in yet another variation of the imperial register: "not interfering in their use for any reason." The historical burden of this imperial register is entrenched in the operational logics of the settler colonial state and its lines of policed division between the tautological Westerner/human and the Indigenous/animal—as exemplified in the US and Australian settler states' twinned constitution of "wilderness" and Indigenous reserves (see chapter 2).

Second, this position of hyperseparation between humans and animals posits a prelapsarian space that, in the era of the Anthropocene, is nowhere available on this planet, with anthropogenic forces impacting on all dimensions of the biosphere and its ecologies—from the floating islands of plastic waste in the mid-Pacific, inexorably leaching toxic microparticulates into the oceans, to the melting ice sheets in Antarctica and the Artic. Operative in this anthropocenic geohistorical context is "an excessive dose of anthropo*mor*-*phism*" generating an "*anthropo*morphism of the critical zones." Bruno Latour's shuttling of emphases marks the topological redistribution of agency that now marks the massive impact of the "anthropos" (human) on the planet: "How could we avoid the traps of anthropomorphism," he exclaims, "if it is true that we are living from now on in the era of the Anthropocene!"[7]

Third, it disavows the fact that the nutritive exigencies of life can only be realized through the consumption of the other, whether animal, mineral, or plant, therefore reproducing yet another form of human supremacism that fails to acknowledge "what it means to be an animal, and in particular what it means to be involved in the stakes of life and death that characterize animality."[8] Val Plumwood articulates the cyclical dimensions of this ecological philosophy: "In the complex biological exchange which sustains all our lives, we must all gain sustenance at the expense of the other, 'the one living the other's death, and dying the other's life.'"[9] This crucial acknowledgment of the nonnegotiable fact that life is possible only through nutritive acts of incorporation of the other demands, consequently, that these same acts be grounded in an ethics of the incorporation of the other. This ethics of incorporation of the other needs, in turn, to take into account the ecological ensemble of life that is, in Indigenous terms, "ensouled." Reflecting on the ramifications of such an Indigenous ethico-ecology, Plumwood writes: "The American Indian view that considerability goes 'all the way down' requires a response considerably more sophisticated than those we have seen in the West, which consists in drawing lines of moral considerability in order to create an out-group, or in constructing hierarchies of considerability creating de facto out-groups in particular cases."

Finally, this exceptionalist view precludes the possibility of exercising ethical relations through the enactment of everyday practices founded on an "ecological compact." As Gregory Cajete underscores, many Indigenous worldviews are founded on the ethics of an ecological compact in which "humans are related to and interdependent with plants, animals, stones, water, clouds, and everything else."[10] This ecological compact between humans and all other entities does more, however, than acknowledge relations of interdependence; rather, these relations are seen to be foundationally underpinned by, in Vine Deloria Jr.'s words, the ethical imperative to "take up responsibilities for all living things."[11] And, as previously discussed, in a number of Indigenous cultures these ethical relations are embedded in law—a law, moreover, that issues from more-than-human communities and that guides and inflects human practices.

The failure of Western law, and its various international law incarnations, to embed this concept of an ecological compact within its frameworks provokes an interrogation of its ethical legitimacy in the face of its complicity in the production of widespread ecocide, as attested to globally by the unfolding anthropocenic crisis. Meditating on Western law's ecocidal complicity, Klaus Bosselmann asks: "What happens . . . if the life-destroying character of law remains unnoticed? Aside from individual resistance (of a few enlightened people) and possible survival of some self-contained elements of society, the collective will have to bear the consequences of its ignorance and may eventually perish. Such ecocide might be viewed as a tragedy, but again not as a failure of the rule of law."[12] Bosselmann here brings to light, without naming it as such, the autoimmune logic of obeying the rule of law when its observance actually leads to self-destruction, and implicitly he brings into focus the disjunction between the rule of law and justice, with the consequence that the tragedy of ecocide is seen neither as a failure of the rule of law nor as the legalized production of injustice. In such instances, he declares, we are right to mobilize practices of civil disobedience.

Yet the costs of such civil disobedience in challenging the entrenched anthropocentrism of Western law are nowhere more clearly staked out than in the United States' Animal Enterprise Terrorism Act. The act enables the prosecution of anyone who actively attempts to interfere "with the operations of an animal enterprise," and it carries terms of up to twenty years' imprisonment.[13] The act materializes the limits of law in terms of its capacity to deliver justice when it is circumscribed by the most virulent form of anthropocentrism predicated on the animal/property nexus: a person shall be charged who "intentionally damages or causes the loss of any real or personal property (including animals or records) used by an animal enterprise."[14] The onto-epistemology of animal life can only be legally captured and indexed by the proprietorial rubric of "personal property"—as mere chattels, animals are entirely fungible and disposable. In a striking example of the power of semantico-legal inversion, the act "provide[s] the Department of Justice the necessary authority to apprehend, prosecute, and convict individuals committing animal enterprise terror."[15] In other words, activists attempting to disrupt the institutionalized production of industrial-scale animal terror are branded as the agents of terror. Enabled and legitimated by no less august an authority than the Department of Justice, the Animal Enterprise Terrorism Act underscores the incommensurability between the rule of anthropocentric law and justice. The disjunction between law and ethics is also materialized in this act. That the production of animal terror that Western law legitimates is seen by animal rights activists and ecologists as unethical does not, as Bosselmann would say, mean that it is a failure of the rule of law. Rather, it emerges as a system effect of the machinic operations of the rule of anthropocentric law. In such cases, "law is the code of organized public violence"[16] that, crucially, cannot be read as violence as such; on the contrary, as the Animal Enterprise Terrorism Act evidences, it is those subjects who contest its codification of organized public violence, in the form of "animal enterprise terror," that are rendered the agents of terror.

In his essay, Bosselmann proposes that the rule of law be viewed not as absolute but, rather, as "context-bound and grounded in further requirements about its own validity."[17] Surely the minimum requirement with regard to the validity of the rule of law is that it must safeguard and protect the very ecological conditions that enable life, in all of its heterogeneous forms, to survive and flourish on this planet. Surveying the war-torn forensic ecologies I have delineated across the preceding chapters, it is clear that the laws of war and the environment, international humanitarian law, and international environmental law have failed to acknowledge in a substantive manner the significance of the ecological compact adhered to by a number of Indigenous nations. Within the domain of international law, of war or otherwise, more-than-human entities and their ecologies remain largely juridically unrecognizable—unless encompassed under the limited rubric of human property, and even then they can be obliterated with impunity. They are thus rendered as vulnerable to militarized obliteration as they are located beyond the purview of justiciability. By contrast, at the level of the practices of everyday life, the acknowledgment of, and ethical assumption of responsibility for, the more-than-human in the context of militarized zones and armed conflict is, as I discussed above, what is practiced regardless of the failure of law. Rather than seeing this as the end of the story, I want to conclude by taking this unrecognizability of the more-than-human in international law (of the environment, of armed conflict and the environment, and of war) as a point of departure inscribed by future possibilities.

Despite the failures of international law, the contingent acts of everyday life gesture toward what they materialize in practice: that, for example, the act of watering of plants in the face of severe, war-induced water restrictions, at once enjoins a respect for the more-than-human while confiding, through this same act, the nonnegotiable responsibility for the other as what in fact ensures the very possibility of a collective future. Kassem Eid, a Palestinian-Syrian caught in the unfolding violence of the Syrian civil war, documents in his memoir the torture, starvation, and killing of the civilians opposed to Bashar al-Assad's lethal regime. In the midst of his hunger strike, staged to protest the unrelenting violence he and his fellow civilians are compelled to endure, Eid stops to draw attention to the phytocide of his beloved olive and lemon trees:

> *Hunger strike day 23: Even the trees are their enemies*
> *Posted 18 December 2013*
> The trees help us. The olive orchards and lemon trees of Moadamiya are more than just a livelihood. They are friends and allies. More—they are the living legacy of my townsfolk. We love each tree. We know them from childhood, each knot. They put their arms around us. They shade our first love, our family picnics. Some are 400 years old. Think about that. What have these trees seen? What tyrants come and go while they stay, patient and wise? While they draw water from deep in the ground and put out their green and yellow fruit with generosity, year after year. So of course, of course, the Assad regime has been deliberately targeting our beautiful olive groves. . . . They are killing our friends, the trees we love. How can I describe to you the emotions we in Moadamiya feel when we see these trees killed? Bombed and shelled and broken. . . . My parents suffered the loss of their olive trees in a Palestinian village in 1948. . . . Whole groves of trees are shelled in Syria, and no one hears the sound they make. No one hears the branches crack and break but us. No one sees the roots shockingly torn above the exploded ground but us. Hear the trees. If you will not hear the human screams in Syria, hear the ancient screams of the trees.[18]

What is interlaced in this scene of phytocidal destruction? Love for the more-than-human inscribed in the lived singularity of each tree. Biocultural histories of intimacy bound in the embrace of bole, branch, leaf, and knot. Even in his state of literal starvation, Eid refuses to abandon his arboreal friends. Eid enfleshes here a colloquium charged with two registers: a linguistic one of words and a phytosemiotic one enunciated through the utterance of cracked branches and the splintering of upturned roots. Articulated from different embodied positions, these speech acts converge in their indictment of the regime's violence. His exhortation, "Hear the trees," refuses anthropocentric accounts of exceptionalist separation, effacement, and foreclosure. His recapitulated exhortation demands acts of listening that overturn the usual alibis mobilized to reduce the trees to nonsentient inarticulacy and vegetal obtuseness. Militarized practices of phytocide bind Palestine and Syria as their olive and lemon trees fall victim to the rage of tyrants. These theaters of war attest to the ecocidal intent to destroy the flesh of the world in all of its extensive modalities. Geographies of violated earth, severed roots, and truncated lives are inextricably entangled in these forensic ecologies of saturated violence. One stratum, Palestine, is interleaved with another, Syria. One life, Kassem Eid, intersects with another, that of the olive and lemon trees. Geopolitical spaces, in these instances, emerge as networked by the literality of soil, trees, and fruit and as enmeshed within campaigns of ecocidal violence that are transnational in their reach and effects.

In the larger scheme of things, these acts of, and urgent calls for, ecological justice might be dismissed as purely minoritarian practices that fail to address the infrastructural violence that is enshrined in anthropocentric law and that continues to shape and legitimize the broad array of disciplinary fields that are licensed by it, including the military, science, economy, and so on. Cast in this light, these intimate practices of interrelated lives emerge as nothing more than transient and fragile undercurrents that leave the hegemonic apparatus untouched. Yet, precisely as undercurrents governed by their own immanent rules of practice, they inscribe, through their insistent and dispersed iterations, microfissures in the anthropocentric hegemon: they open other experiential vistas that interrogate the legitimacy of the status quo and its self-authorizing claims to law and justice. Through their practical instantiations, collectively they work to materialize a substantive body of praxis that speaks and acts otherwise to the law of anthropocentric indifference, sovereign violence, and noncriminal killing. As practices inscribed by an ethics of the other, they gesture toward a lived politics animated by an ecological ethos. Collectively, they operate before the law, in the sense of being *avant la lettre*, and as such they prefigure in practice the destinal future of law if it is to fulfill its aspiration as just law. At once before the law and heteronomous to existing law, they yet articulate their own relation to law. As collective, if dispersed, practices of provisional ecological justice, they trace the contours of a lived praxis not yet legislatively acknowledged by state or suprastate authorities, but, precisely as praxis, they set the precedents for future juridical recognition.

At the same time, the Indigenous laws I have discussed, which situate the more-than-human as ethically preceding the human and, indeed, as giving law to human communities, at once predate and contemporize nascent international laws of ecological justice. In effect, from this critical position of a double temporality, they articulate an ecocentric law of the future that, in the context of international law, is still to eventuate, even as Indigenous laws continue to make transformative incursions at the level of domestic environmental law in countries such as Aotearoa–New Zealand. The successful Māori interventions on behalf of a place (Te Urewera), a river (Whanganui), and a mountain (Mount Taranaki) have enabled the recognition in Aotearoa–New Zealand law of these entities as having, in the words of Jacinta Rau, Māori legal scholar, "their own authority—they are recognised in law now as having their own presence, their own needs and their own wellbeing."[19] These laws signal a landmark challenge to Euro-anthropocentric jurisprudence, overturning questions of ownership, property, and more-than-human standing: "The laws completely flip the presumption of human sovereignty over the environment and embrace Māori relationship with land."[20]

Having articulated the importance of the collective significance of individual acts of ecological justice, I want to underline that individual acts of ecological justice risk remaining *provisional* realizations of justice as long as they remain at the level of individual performatives. Without apparatuses such as the law, individual acts of ecological justice will remain inherently provisional in terms of their larger transformative power. The urgency of inscribing, in a substantive and not token manner, the more-than-human within the field, for example, of international law of armed conflict and the environment is predicated on a pressing fact: maintaining the more-than-human outside law ensures the ongoing capacity to injure and/or obliterate the more-than-human in a noncriminal way, with little recourse to justice outside of the individualistic acts that I have tracked. Without the force of law, the militarized acts of ecocidal destruction that I have analyzed will remain only nominally "forensic" and thus will not be viewed as prosecutable crimes. Even if international law can be breached with impunity according to the geopolitical status of the transgressor state, what cannot be dismissed or effaced is the *unethicality* of the breach, and the grounds for accountability that this gives.

After reviewing the catalog of failures of the laws of war to protect civilians in times of armed conflict, Roger Normand and Chris af Jochnik conclude that, despite these failures, "the reality is that law *does* matter; that is both the problem and the promise."[21] The problem resides in how international law can be overwritten and violated by those states with geopolitical status; and the promise emerges in the potentiality that law has to effectively change global behavior, as evidenced by the Montreal Protocol on Substances That Deplete the Ozone Layer (1987). The Montreal Protocol "marked a major turning point in the consideration of the world's environmental problems" in that it compelled nation-states to confront the fact that environmental threats, such as ozone depletion, could effectively override insular understandings of state sovereignty.[22] Furthermore, I do not view the institution of law as *the* entity that, in a singular and magical manner, can dismantle the hegemonic Euro-anthropocentric apparatus and its entrenched imbrication with the lethal forces of empire, colonialism, extractive capitalism, armed conflict, and the military-industrial-security complex. Rather, I see it as one critical element in the complex assemblage that is instrumental in reproducing and consolidating the anthropocentric status quo and its institutionalized, and thus legitimated, practices of ecocidal violence. "Law is not everything," writes Joseph DiMento. But it is an "identifiable institution that influences behavior, even very complicated behavior that creates climate change, destroys the protective ozone shield, and threatens the existence of species."[23]

The state's monopoly on violence is, unsurprisingly, nowhere more graphically evidenced than in the fields of war and armed conflict. Under the all-encompassing ruse of "security," anything and everything can be obliterated. Nothing demonstrates this more clearly than the Israeli Defense Forces' conduct during Operation Protective Edge. If my chapters on Gaza have brought anything to light, it is that the dominant anthropocentric understanding of the biopolitical needs to be heterogenized to bring into critical focus the cluster of different modalities that constitute its operations—including zoopolitics, phytopolitics, aquapolitics, aeropolitics, and pedonpolitics—and that enable ecocidal effects that radiate beyond the locus of the state and that, critically, impact in a transboundary autoimmune manner on the larger biospheric level. The IDF's destruction of trees, its poisoning of aquifers and soil, its large-scale slaughter of animals, its obliteration of viable habitats, and so on—all show that the concerns of the human subject cannot be isolated from the larger relational context that constitutes that subject's very ecology of life. Furthermore, the ecological approach to justice that I have advocated in this book demands, once it is situated in the context of the unfolding global crises generated by anthropogenic forces, a supersession of state-centrism and a rethinking of the geopolitical so that it transcends statist self-interests. One would think that this is precisely the arena in which international law would best be positioned to stage an intervention. The reality is, of course, more complex, as the international law system is still foundationally underpinned by a state-centric orientation that is an ongoing legacy of international law's colonial and imperial origins.[24] Furthermore, the skewed geopolitical power relations that inscribe the observance and overwriting of international law continue to evidence this sober reflection: "*The international legal form assumes juridical equality and unequal violence.*"[25]

Situated in the unfolding era of the Anthropocene, Euro-anthropocentric conceptualizations of state-centric international law literally abut their potentially lethal autoimmune limits, with the unleashing of anthropogenic forces of ecological upheaval, such as climate change, that will not respect state borders or sovereignties. The concept of geopolitics, thus, has to be reconceptualized so that it can be thought outside state-centric frames: "Geopolitics can no longer be a matter of understanding relations of power over land and natural resources; it is a matter of thinking the Earth as a political subject."[26] Contextualized in this anthropocenic frame, even as the wars conducted by both Israel and the United States, as the focal states of this book, are chiefly concerned with the statist appropriation of land and resources and the extension and consolidation of geopolitical power and influence, their ecocidal effects impact, simultaneously, the larger scale of Earth as political subject. The ecocidal effects of armed conflict—including the unleashing of millions of tons of carbon emissions into the atmosphere through the operations of the military-industrial-security complex, deforestation and erosion through military campaigns, the toxic waste of spent ordnance, and so on—supersede statist boundaries; they are clearly biospherical in terms of their impact. The techno-geopolitical forces of armed conflict, then, must be seen as inextricably enmeshed within geophysical (forces of nature) and biospherical (earth ecosystems) domains. Human geopolitics are, in other words, entangled in the "polity of nature," with the result that, in the context of the Anthropocene, they are generating global ecocidal effects.[27]

In the space of the lacuna—the very space in which international law of armed conflict and the environment fails to recognize the more-than-human except in the most anthropocentrically circumscribed ways—is inscribed the very possibility for the emergence of ecological justice underpinned by an Earth jurisprudence: the suspensive space of the elliptical is marked, after all, by the haunting figure of the forensic trace and its generative logic of absence-presence. Yet the fact that a body such as the UN International Law Commission has put on indefinite hold the possibility of drafting new measures to protect the environment in times of armed conflict—and that both an Ecocide Convention and a Fifth Geneva Convention devoted to an environmental law-of-war treaty have been dispatched to the too-hard basket—gestures toward a bleak future in which an Earth jurisprudence remains marginal in the arenas of armed conflict and their related campaigns of war by other means. The placing of these proposed conventions on indefinite hold works to literalize, in an unintended manner, the Derridean conceptualization of justice as "an experience of the impossible, there where, even as it does not exist, if it is not *present*, not yet or never, *there is* justice [*il y a la justice*]."[28] This aporetic reflection on justice emerges in Derrida's text, uncoincidentally, in the context of his insistence that "one must [*il faut*] reconsider in its totality the metaphysico-anthropocentric axiomatic that dominates, in the West, the thought of the just and the unjust" and "the whole apparatus of limits within which a history and a culture have been able to confine their criteriology."[29]

Placed on indefinite hold in a parenthetical cage bounded and delimited by the criteriology of an entrenched Euro-anthropocentrism and inscribed by the aporia of not yet or never, (ecological) justice is what remains indefinitely to be determined. The violent axiomatics of war, and of anthropocentrism as a type of war by other means, continue to ensure the disarticulation and bracketing of the ecological from justice in the domain of international law. The enclosing of the ecological within parentheses typographically evidences its suspensive status in the context of the various relevant modalities of international law: it is merely an aside that can be indefinitely suspended because, as an entirely peripheral concern, it is still not viewed as central to international law's Euro-anthropocentric, and thus self-identical, universalizing mission. The imprimatur of the other, in its semantico-categorical formulation of the "other-than-human," ensures its relegation to some indefinite time to come. Yet Derrida's complex thinking on justice also opens onto the beckoning of a promissory possibility that solicits the space-time of indetermination. Claire Colebrook, in her address of the question "What is the Anthropocene-Political?," traces the glimmer of this promissory possibility: "From a strictly Derridean point of view, far from us therefore abandoning all promise of the future, the stakes of justice would be raised: because we cannot definitively erase the possibility of future justice, because no event can discount the potentiality of justice (including the direst predictions), the future seems to provoke us not to close down possibility."[30]

Ecological justice remains indefinitely to be determined even as the earth continues to lurch toward ecological crises that will override both existing Euro-anthropocentric inter/national law and the sovereignty of inter/national states. In reflecting on the contemporary violent struggle between science and politics in the charged environment of climate change, Latour refuses to lapse into euphemism: he declares outright, "The *state of war*, that is the defining trait of the Anthropocene."[31] Latour's phrase needs to be pluralized to *states of war*, precisely because, as I have demonstrated throughout this book, multiple states of war are being fought along diverse fronts and through the deployment of different ecocidal modalities: zoopolitical, phytopolitical, pedonpolitical, aeropolitical, aquapolitical, and geopolitical. And these states of war are leaving in their wake forensic ecologies of loss, trauma, and obliteration that articulate an inextricable relation between local militarized sites of ecocidal destruction and the global geobiophysical deformations and death zones of the unfolding Anthropocene. The anthropogenic impacts of the states of war that I have tracked—war against trees, water, humans, animals, and so on— necessarily bind the issue of ecological justice to expanded definitions of both the categories of intergenerational and global justice, in which the concept of the intergenerational must be seen to encompass more-than-human biota and the category of the global must be inscribed with an understanding of the earth as political subject.

The earth, it must be said, is not a passive witness to the collective anthropocentric violences that are impacting the planet. At play are those very agentic forces that emanate from the earth, precisely as envisaged in Aboriginal understandings of country: "Each part of country is not only alive, but has a life of its own—and is as capable as human beings of resistance and subversion."[32] If the Anthropocene is disclosing anything, it is the undiminished capacity for the earth to set in motion forces that at once challenge human exceptionalism and recalibrate the figure of human supremacism by exposing it to planetary forces over which it has little control. Operative here are forces that are at once the result of biopower and in excess of it, specifically in excess of its anthropocentric sovereignty.

The forces of the Anthropocene are, indeed, presciently envisioned in this acute Foucauldian observation: "This excess of biopower appears when it becomes technologically and politically possible" for humans to unleash forces "that cannot be controlled and that are universally destructive. This formidable power . . . will put it beyond all human sovereignty."[33] As anthropogenic climate change clearly evidences, this formidable power is already at work. In fact, this excess of biopower is not new. It is what has been repeatedly deployed by colonial states in the expropriated lands of Indigenous people across the globe—with devastating results. The Anthropocene was formed in the crucible of empire and violently seeded in the colonized lands of Indigenous people. The lands of the Western Shoshone (Nevada) and Aṉangu (Maralinga Tjarutja, South Australia), for example, sites of atomic and nuclear weapons testing and toxic waste dumping, stand as fragmented precursors that testify to the past and ongoing effects of an excess of biopower constituted by the lethal constellation of colonialism, militarism, extractive capitalism, and environmental racism.[34] Under the rubric of anthropogenic climate change, these scattered sites of ecocidal destruction become unified in a matrix of biopower that is in excess of itself in that its effects are no longer localized; rather, they are global. In an autoimmune manner, they breach the boundaries of their seeming geographical isolation and interpenetrate the very spaces that imagined themselves to be safely quarantined from their ecocidal effects. Chief Arvol Looking Horse, spiritual leader of the Lakota Nation, in his Elders Council Statement, articulates what is at stake: "We warned you that one day you would not be able to control what you have created. That day is here. Not heeding warnings from both Nature and the People of the Earth keeps us on the path of self-destruction."[35]

Challenging the dogma of human exceptionalism, the figure of the more-than-human, as flesh of the world, continues to interrogate the Euroanthropocentric hegemon, its narcissistic points of irreflection, its violent foreclosures, and its attendant ecocidal logic of autoimmunity. From this locus, the more-than-human persists in articulating the urgent need for an ethical awakening critical to the realization of ecological justice.

Introduction

1   Saif Atef Abu, "Eight Days in Gaza: A Wartime Diary," *New York Times*, July 27, 2014, http://www.nytimes.com/2014/08/05/opinion/atef-abu-saif-life-and-death-in-gaza-strip-jabaliya-refugee-camp.html?_r=0.

2   Atef Abu, "Eight Days in Gaza."

3   Atef Abu, "Eight Days in Gaza."

4   Foucault, *The History of Sexuality*, 138.

5   I deploy the terms *articulate* and *relational visibility* as conceptualized by a number of Indigenous cultural theorists. In his work on Indigenous ecologies of relationality, Daniel Wildcat, Euchee member of the Muscogee Nation, emphasizes how other-than-human entities are coconstitutive, precisely as coproducers and agents, of knowledge about the world: "Indigenous knowledge systems extend the notion of knowledge construction to a cooperative activity involving the other-than-human life that surrounds us" (*Red Alert*, 17). This relational epistemology, he adds, is predicated on "the fundamental connectedness and relatedness of human communities and societies to the natural environment and the other than human relatives they interact with daily" (*Red Alert*, 20). The refrain that spans a broad spectrum of Indigenous cosmo-epistemologies is to be attentive to, and ethically responsible for, "all my relations," including water, land, sky, plants, and animals; see Hogan, *Dwellings*, 41. To "know . . . reality requires respect for the relationships and relatives that constitute the complex web of life" and, Wildcat adds, to assume the "inalienable responsibilities" that attend this knowledge (*Red Alert*, 9).

6   Merleau-Ponty, *The Visible and the Invisible*, 248.

7   Foucault, *The History of Sexuality*, 138.

8   Dreyfus and Rabinow, *Michel Foucault*, 137.

9   Ahuja, *Bioinsecurities*, x.

10 See P. Wolfe, "Settler Colonialism and the Elimination of the Native"; Carlson, "'Disposable People' and Ongoing Colonial Violence."

11   Foucault, *"Society Must Be Defended,"* 242–43.
12   Foucault, *"Society Must Be Defended,"* 243.
13   Foucault, *"Society Must Be Defended,"* 61.
14   Derrida, "'Eating Well,'" 283.
15   Derrida, "Violence against Animals," 63.
16   See Derrida, *The Animal That Therefore I Am,* 40–41, and Cajete, *Native Science,* 152.
17   See Salaita, *Inter/Nationalism,* 1–70, for a discussion of these lines of solidarity.
18   Ali Abunimah, "Major Indigenous Studies Group Endorses Israeli Boycott,"
       Electronic Intifada, December 18, 2013, https://electronicintifada.net/blogs/ali
       -abunimah/major-indigenous-studies-group-endorses-israel-boycott. Uncle Ray
       Jackson, president of Australia's Indigenous Social Justice Association, writes:
       "It is far too long that the genocidal attacks against the civilian population
       of gaza must stop. and stop immediately. it now appears that the netanyahu
       government is in an all-out war of extermination of the palestinian people. . . .
       israel must stop this overkill. that is just a fact that must be done. . . . what
       must be possible, no, certain, is that the ethnocide of the palestinians in gaza
       must cease once and for all" (quoted in Perera and Pugliese, "Dgadi-Dugarang,"
       3; lowercase in the original). For a discussion of the long history of Aboriginal
       and Palestinian solidarity, see Foley, "Black Power Australia and Aboriginal-
       Palestinian Solidarity." For an eloquent comparative analysis of settler colonial-
       ism in the context of Palestine and the Americas, see Mikdashi, "What Is Settler
       Colonialism?," 30, where she writes: "We forget that American complicity in
       Israel's crimes is not only built on tactical, strategic, and politically engendered
       alliances, but also on the affective registers of a shared settlement project."
       See also the special issue, "Palestine Lives," of *Decolonization* 6 (2017) devoted
       entirely to examining settler colonialism in the interrelated context of Palestine
       and the Americas; Krebs and Olwan, "'From Jerusalem to the Grand River, Our
       Struggles Are One.'"
19   Quoted in Andrew Kadi, "Palestinians Back Standing Rock Sioux in 'Struggle for
       All Humanity,'" *Electronic Intifada,* September 10, 2016, https://electronicintifada.net
       /blogs/andrew-kadi/palestinians-back-standing-rock-sioux-struggle-all-humanity.
20   Kadi, "Palestinians Back Standing Rock Sioux."
21   Grindle and Johansen, *Ecocide of Native America,* 278.
22   Shadowing modern Western law is a largely effaced history in which more-
       than-human entities, such as insects, pigs, or horses, could be brought to
       criminal trial as defendants who were invested with some of the same legal
       rights as their human subjects. This other Western jurisprudential history
       once envisaged more-than-human entities as subjects with jural standing. The
       advent of Western modernity effectively dismissed this form of more-than-
       human jurisprudence as nothing more than a "superstition of the age": see, for
       example, Evans, *The Criminal Prosecution and Capital Punishment of Animals,* 12;
       Anderson, "A Proper Death." For a history of what he terms "dissenting" voices
       that challenged Western anthropocentrism, see Steiner, *Anthropocentrism and
       Its Discontents,* 38–52. I also mark here the role of Western thinkers such as

Henry Thoreau, heavily influenced by Native American cosmo-epistemologies; Aldo Leopold; John Muir; and others who sowed the seeds for Western environmental movements. See Sayre, *Thoreau and the American Indians*; Hanson, *Thoreau's Indian of the Mind*; Leopold, *A Sand County Almanac*; Muir, *My First Summer in the Sierra*.

23 Bodansky, Brunnée, and Hey, "International Environmental Law," 15.

24 *Convention Designed to Ensure the Conservation of Various Species of Wild Animals in Africa, Which Are Useful to Man or Inoffensive (1900),* International Environment Agreements (IEA) Database Project, accessed August 12, 2016, https://iea.uoregon .edu/treaty-text/1900-preservationwildanimalsbirdsfishafricaentxt.

25 DiMento, *The Global Environment and International Law*, 14.

26 Miéville, *Between Equal Rights*, 86.

27 Francione, *Animals, Property, and the Law*, 261.

28 Francione, *Animals, Property, and the Law*, 36–42.

29 Derrida, "Discussion with Jacques Derrida," 49.

30 Shukin, *Animal Capital*, 6–7.

31 Miéville, *Between Equal Rights*, 178.

32 Coyle and Morrow, *The Philosophical Foundations of Environmental Law*, 4.

33 Despret, *What Would Animals Say If We Asked the Right Questions?*, 7–8.

34 Anghie, *Imperialism, Sovereignty and the Making of International Law*, 3.

35 Bruch, "Introduction," 15.

36 Falk, "The Environmental Law of War," 86.

37 For an analysis of the afterlife of both Hiroshima and Nagasaki in the wake of their destruction, see Parlati, "Memory in T/Rubble."

38 See Zierler, *The Invention of Ecocide*, for a detailed discussion of how the US military's use of Agent Orange in the Vietnam War provoked an international movement to ban a new crime: ecocide.

39 International Committee of the Red Cross, "Protocol Additional to the Geneva Conventions of 12 August 1949, and relating to the Protection of Victims of International Armed Conflicts (Protocol I), June 8, 1997."

40 Dupuy and Viñuales, *International Environmental Law*, 344.

41 Hulme, "Armed Conflict," 60.

42 Falk, "Environmental Law of War," 93–94; Schmitt, "War and the Environment." Significantly, the two states that I examine in the book, the United States and Israel, have not ratified Additional Protocol I. The United States, in fact, termed the protocol a "'terrorist charter' for its provisions relaxing combatancy requirements" and dismissed as "revolutionary" a number of the articles "on protection of the environment" (Hulme, "Armed Conflict," 57).

43 Jha, *Armed Conflict and Environmental Damage*, 256.

44 UN International Law Commission, *Preliminary Report on the Protection of the Environment in Relation to Armed Conflict.*

45 UN International Law Commission, *Preliminary Report on the Protection of the Environment in Relation to Armed Conflict*, 15; emphasis added.

46 Bruch, "Introduction," 45; Drumbl, "Waging War against the World," 636–46.

47 McNeely, "War and Biodiversity," 362. For a detailed discussion of ecocide as "the fifth crime against peace," see Higgins, *Eradicating Ecocide*, 61–71.

48 Hulme, "Armed Conflict," 71.

49 Miéville, *Between Equal Rights*, 142.

50 Hutchins, *Cognition in the Wild*, xii.

51 S. Bell, *Crime and Circumstance*, 2.

52 On the constitutive role of affect in our understanding of the world and its entities, and for a problematization of the distinction between affect and emotion, see Ahmed, *The Cultural Politics of Emotion*.

53 See Gross, *The Rhetoric of Science*, 15.

54 Cajete, *Native Science*, 2, 14. On Native science, see also Muecke, "Wolfe Creek Meteorite Crater."

55 Houck and Siegel, *Fundamentals of Forensic Science*, 46.

56 Houck and Siegel, *Fundamentals of Forensic Science*, 46.

57 S. Bell, *Crime and Circumstance*, xi.

58 Weizman, *Forensic Architecture*, 53.

59 Weizman, *Forensic Architecture*, 64.

60 Quoted in Stauffer, "Haeckel, Darwin, and Ecology," 140.

61 Quoted in Stauffer, "Haeckel, Darwin, and Ecology," 141.

62 Grindle and Johansen, *Ecocide of Native America*, 107.

63 Kwaymullina and Kwaymullina, "Learning to Read the Signs," 196.

64 Langton, "European Construction of Wilderness," 16.

65 For a detailed discussion of the heterogeneity of Indigenous positions on these issues see, for example, Birch, "'On What Terms Can We Speak?'"; Vincent and Timothy, *Unstable Relations*.

66 Wildcat, *Red Alert*, 15, 9.

67 Hogan, *Dwellings*, 49. Here Hogan is citing the work of Evelyn Fox Keller.

68 Hogan, *Dwellings*, 26.

69 Quoted in Kurland, *Irrefutable Evidence*, 148–49.

70 Latour, *Pandora's Hope*, 303.

71 Latour, *Pandora's Hope*, 142.

72 Latour, *Pandora's Hope*, 143.

73 Latour, *Reassembling the Social*, 255n356.

74 Pugliese, "Identity in Question."

75 Cajete, *Native Science*, 27.

76 Viveiros de Castro, *Cannibal Metaphysics*, 56.

77 See Reynolds, *With the White People*, 41.

78 Mowaljarlai and Malnic, *Yorro Yorro*, 53.

79 Mowaljarlai and Malnic, *Yorro Yorro*, 54.

80 Quoted in Reynolds, *With the White People*, 24.

81 *Pathfinders: The History of NSW Aboriginal Trackers*, accessed August 12, 2016, http://pathfindersnsw.org.au/police-stations/.

82 Creative Spirits, "Aboriginal History Timeline (1900–1969)," https://www.creative spirits.info/aboriginalculture/history/aboriginal-history-timeline-1900-1969.

83 "Such terms," write Kwaymullina and Kwaymullina, "are inevitably burdened by historical constructions of Indigenous societies as inferior and lacking in 'real' law" ("Learning to Read the Signs," 198).

84 See Pugliese, *Biometrics*, 17.

85 See Pugliese, "'Demonstrative Evidence.'"

86 James, Nordby, and Bell, "Justice and Science," 10.

87 Netzel, Kiely, and Bell, "Evidence," 31.

88 Cajete, *Native Science*, 23.

89 Merleau-Ponty, *Phenomenology of Perception*, 334.

90 Merleau-Ponty, *The Visible and the Invisible*, 127.

91 Quoted in Cajete, *Native Science*, 64.

92 See, for example, Márquez-Grant and Roberts, *Forensic Ecology Handbook*.

93 Cajete, *Native Science*, 55; Merleau-Ponty, *The Visible and the Invisible*, 248.

94 Hogan, "We Call It *Tradition*," 25.

95 I use *actors* here in Latour's extended sense: "Things might authorize, allow, afford, encourage, permit, suggest, influence, block, render possible, forbid and so on, in addition to 'determining' and serving as a backdrop to human action." Complicating and attenuating reductive conceptualizations of cause and effect, Latour advocates for agency across the broad spectrum of other-than-human entities: "Anything that modifies a state of affairs by making a difference is an actor" ("Nonhumans," 226). Actors are not, he underscores in his actor-network theory, "the hapless bearers of symbolic projection"; neither is the role of the theoretician to "teach actors what they are, or to add some reflexivity to their blind practice" (*Reassembling the Social*, 10, 12). Latour, in these reflections, productively works to materialize horizontal relations of distributed cognition and affect, relations that, critically, refuse the paternalism of ventriloquizing on behalf of other-than-human actors that are otherwise anthropocentrically positioned as speechless and insentient.

96 See Plumwood, *Environmental Culture*, 56–71.

97 Martinez, Salmón, and Nelson, "Restoring Indigenous History and Culture to Nature," 89.

98 Bennett, "The Force of Things," 359.

99 Hogan, *Dwellings*, 26, 28.

100 Bennett, *Vibrant Matter*, 117; Little Bear, "Foreword," x.

101 Cajete, *Native Science*, 95.

102 Adamson, "First Nations Survival and the Future of the Earth," 34.

103 Adamson, "First Nations Survival and the Future of the Earth," 34.

104 See, for example, Bennett, *Vibrant Matter*; MacCormack, *The Animal Catalyst*; Dolphin and van der Tuin, *New Materialisms*; Coole and Frost, *New Materialisms*.

105 Bennett, *Vibrant Matter*, viii.

106 Bennett, *Vibrant Matter*, xiii.

107 Todd, "An Indigenous Feminist's Take on the Ontological Turn," 8, 14.

108 Todd, "An Indigenous Feminist's Take on the Ontological Turn," 16.

109 Adams, *The Sexual Politics of Meat*, 20–21.

110 Patrick Wolfe's formulation is that settler colonialism "is a structure not an event" (*Settler Colonialism*, 2).

111 Todd, "An Indigenous Feminist's Take on the Ontological Turn," 9. I discuss Vanessa Watt's work below. In the context of what he identifies as the "unfinished business of colonial history and its contemporary manifestations," Tony Birch ("'On What Terms Can We Speak?,'" 10) suggests that "if there is cause for optimism, it may be located in the spirit of generosity offered by Indigenous people inviting others to join with them in valuing and caring for country through cultural practice and exchange."

112 Bennett, *Vibrant Matter*, 122.

113 Cajete, *Native Science*, 21.

114 Deloria, *The World We Used to Live In*, 197.

115 Hogan, "We Call It *Tradition*," 22.

116 Latour, *We Have Never Been Modern*.

117 Konishi, "First Nations Scholars, Settler Colonial Studies, and Indigenous History," 300.

118 Deloria, *The World We Used to Live In*, 195.

119 Deloria, *God Is Red*, 296.

120 Derrida, "'Eating Well,'" 278.

121 Bigger and Neimark, "Weaponizing Nature," 14. See also Belcher et al., "Hidden Carbon Costs of the 'Everywhere War,'" 2.

122 Belcher et al., "Hidden Carbon Costs of the 'Everywhere War,'" 12.

123 Belcher et al., "Hidden Carbon Costs of the 'Everywhere War,'" 12; Crawford, "Pentagon Fuel Use, Climate Change, and the Costs of War," 1–2; LaDuke with Cruz, *The Militarization of Indian Country*, 31. See also Nuttall, Samaras, and Bazilian, "Energy and the Military," 3.

124 Jha, *Armed Conflict and Environmental Damage*, 161.

125 Lewis and Maslin, "Defining the Anthropocene," 174–75.

126 Fressoz, "Losing the Earth Knowingly," 70–71.

127 Birch, "The Lifting of the Sky," 197. See also Birch, "Afterword," 361, where he writes: "The relationship between colonialism, capitalism and environmental degradation and a consequent link to climate change is unambiguous."

128 See, for example, H. A. Smith, "Disrupting the Global Discourse of Climate Change," 206–12; Wilson et al., "Climate Change, Environmental Justice and Vulnerability"; Powys Whyte, "Is It Colonial Déjà Vu?"

129 White, *Crimes against Nature*, 20.

130 White, *Crimes against Nature*, 19.

131 Cullinan, *Wild Law*, 17.

132 Cullinan, *Wild Law*, 55.

133 See, for example, LaDuke, *All Our Relations*.

134 Campbell, *Justice*, 14.

135 Bosselmann, "Rule of Law in the Anthropocene," 44.

136 See Cullinan, *Wild Law*, 189; Melo, "How the Recognition of the Rights of Nature Became a Part of the Ecuadorian Constitution"; Kathleen Calderwood, "Why

New Zealand Is Granting a River the Same Rights as a Citizen," *ABC Radio National*, September 6, 2016, http://www.abc.net.au/radionational/programs/sundayextra/new-zealand-granting-rivers-and-forests-same-rights-as-citizens/7816456.

137 Jacinta Rau quoted in Calderwood, "Why New Zealand Is Granting a River."

138 Colón-Ríos, "On the Theory and Practice of the Rights of Nature," 120.

139 Steiner, *Animals and the Limits of Postmodernism*, 99.

140 Stone, *Should Trees Have Standing?*, 2. For a parallel critique on the issue of justiciability in the context of Indigenous sovereignty and colonial law, see Giannacopoulos, "Mabo, Tampa and the Non-justiciability of Sovereignty," 59.

141 Cullinan, *Wild Law*, 64.

142 Deloria, *God Is Red*, 300.

143 Derrida, *The Beast and the Sovereign*, 110.

144 LaDuke, *All Our Relations*, 137–43. In reflecting on interlinked acts of settler genocide, Adrian Stimson, Siksika (Blackfoot) Nation, explains: "For me, the fate of the buffalo is analogous to the fate of my people, the Blackfoot. When I look at the slaughter of the bison, I see how it affected my people and our way of life. . . . The Indigenous peoples of the Plains and the buffalo have endured their own holocaust. The destruction we have faced was caused by the same thinking as any genocide or holocaust." Quoted in L. Bell, *Adrian Stimson*, 6.

145 Milroy and Milroy, "Different Ways of Knowing," 38.

146 Rose, *Dingo Makes Us Human*, 57.

147 Watson, "Buried Alive," 269. Watson elaborates on what she terms Aboriginal "Raw Law," in which "there is a 'respect law' for all things—not just humanity, but the whole environment: plants, birds and animals, the earth and the natural world in its entirety" (*Aboriginal Peoples, Colonialism and International Law*, 31).

148 Kwaymullina and Kwaymullina, "Learning to Read the Signs," 203; emphasis added.

149 Watts, "Indigenous Place," 23.

150 Black, *The Land Is the Source of the Law*, 15.

151 Lena Odgaard, "Gaza Farmers Struggle in War Aftermath," *Al Jazeera*, October 7, 2014, http://www.aljazeera.com/news/middleeast/2014/10/gaza-farmers-struggle-war-aftermath-20141075578186995.html. See also Omer, *Shell-Shocked*, 209; Harriet Sherwood, "Gaza Counts Cost of War as More Than 360 Factories Destroyed or Damaged," *Guardian*, August 22, 2014, https://www.theguardian.com/world/2014/aug/22/gaza-economic-cost-war-factories-destroyed; Dan Cohen, "In the Last Days of 'Operation Protective Edge' Israel Focused on Its Final Goal—the Destruction of Gaza's Professional Class," *Mondoweiss*, October 13, 2014, http://mondoweiss.net/2014/10/protective-destruction-professional/.

Chapter 1: Zoopolitics of the Cage

1 For an account of these serial wars on Gaza, see Filiu, "The Twelve Wars on Gaza." For a detailed analysis of Operation Protective Edge, see Finkelstein, *Gaza*, 200–356; Erakat and Radi, "Gaza in Context" and the rest of that special issue of *JADMAG* (2016); Hasian, *Israel's Military Operations in Gaza*, 120–43.

2   Shkolnik, "'Mowing the Grass' and Operation Protective Edge," 188.

3   Shamir, "Rethinking Operation Protective Edge."

4   Atef Abu Saif, "Life under Fire in Gaza: The Diary of a Palestinian," *Guardian*, July 29, 2014, https://www.theguardian.com/world/2014/jul/28/four-days-under -siege-gaza-diary-palestinian.

5   Hogan, *Dwellings*, 26.

6   See, for example, Michael San Filippo, "Winning the Battle over Canine Post-traumatic Stress Disorder," *AVMA*, August 6, 2016, https://www.avma.org/news /pressroom/pages/Canine-Post-Traumatic-Stress-Disorder.aspx.

7   For a detailed discussion of Israel as a settler colonial state, see the introductory discussion in chapter 2.

8   Blumenthal, *The 51 Day War*, 57.

9   Miller and Jones, "Crime Scene Investigation," 44.

10   Haglund and Sorg, "Forensic Anthropology," 155.

11   Hearne, *Adam's Task*, 80.

12   Despret, *What Would Animals Say If We Asked the Right Questions?*, 5.

13   Robert Tait, "Gaza's Corpse-Ridden Farms Reveal Destruction of Palestinian Livelihoods," *Daily Telegraph*, July 31, 2014, http://www.telegraph.co.uk/news /worldnews/middleeast/gaza/11002480/Gazas-corpse-ridden-farms-reveal -destruction-of-Palestinian-livelihoods.html.

14   Bentham, *An Introduction to the Principles of Morals and Legislation*, 283.

15   Glenn Greenwald, "On the One-Year Anniversary of Israel's Attack on Gaza: An Interview with Max Blumenthal," *Intercept*, July 8, 2015, https://theintercept.com /2015/07/08/israel-gaza-anniversary-interview-max-blumenthal/.

16   Atef Abu Saif, "Eight Days in Gaza: Wartime Diary," *New York Times*, August 4, 2014, http://www.nytimes.com/2014/08/05/opinion/atef-abu-saif-life-and-death -in-gaza-strip-jabaliya-refugee-camp.html?_r=0.

17   Saif, "Eight Days in Gaza."

18   Saif, *The Drone Eats with Me*, 116–17.

19   Saif, *The Drone Eats with Me*, 118.

20   Quoted in Deleuze, *Francis Bacon*, 22.

21   Deleuze, *Francis Bacon*, 22.

22   Saif, "Life under Fire."

23   Ghanim, "Thanatopolitics," 68. For an analysis of the operations of thanatopoli-tics in the specific context of Operation Protective Edge, see Joronen, "'Death Comes Knocking on the Roof.'"

24   Saif, *The Drone Eats with Me*, 26.

25   Shalhoub-Kevorkian, "Criminality and Spaces of Death," 38, 42.

26   Shalhoub-Kevorkian, "Criminality and Spaces of Death," 39.

27   Shalhoub-Kevorkian, "Criminality and Spaces of Death," 43.

28   Shalhoub-Kevorkian, "Criminality and Spaces of Death," 45.

29   Breaking the Silence, *Our Harsh Logic*, 53.

30   Breaking the Silence, *Our Harsh Logic*, 53.

31   Breaking the Silence, *Our Harsh Logic*, 79.

32 Saif, "Eight Days in Gaza."

33 Saif, "Eight Days in Gaza."

34 Tom Little, "Zoo Animals Killed and Traumatized by War," *Daily Star*, August 19, 2014, http://www.dailystar.com.lb/News/Middle-East/2014/Aug-19/267631-zoo -animals-killed-and-traumatized-by-war.ashx.

35 Braverman, "Captive: Zoometric Operations in Gaza," 195. See also Salih, "The Animal You See," 321, and her articulation of the critical question that looking at the dead animals in Gaza's zoo prompts with regard to ethical hierarchies and the often elided question "about the moral significance of *this* animal rather than *that* one."

36 Saif, *The Drone Eats with Me*, 124.

37 R. I. Khalidi, *The Iron Cage*, 207.

38 Palestinian Center for Human Rights, "PCHR Publishes New Report in May 2016 as Part of the Closure Reports Series," *PCHR*, accessed August 7, 2016, http:// pchrgaza.org/en/?p=8205.

39 Deema El Ghoul, "Penned in Gaza and Dreaming of the World Outside," *Huffington Post*, March 30, 2016, http://www.huffingtonpost.com/deema-el-ghoul/penned -in-gaza-and-dreami_b_9573550.html.

40 Hammami, "On (Not) Suffering at Checkpoints," 5.

41 R. J. Smith, "Graduated Incarceration," 327.

42 Puar, "The 'Right' to Maim," 5.

43 Breaking the Silence, *Our Harsh Logic*, 252.

44 Latour, *Pandora's Hope*, 187.

45 Latour, *Pandora's Hope*, 188.

46 Latour, *Pandora's Hope*, 188.

47 Vialles, *Animal to Edible*, 35.

48 Fanon, *The Wretched of the Earth*, 7.

49 Breaking the Silence, *Our Harsh Logic*, 234. For a discussion of the historical dimensions of the framing of Palestinians as biological threats, see Pappé, "Shtetl Colonialism," 53–54.

50 Derrida, *The Animal That Therefore I Am*, 29.

51 Lentin, *Traces of Racial Exception*, 139.

52 Quoted in Kotef and Amir, "(En)Gendering Checkpoints," 977.

53 Spillers, "Mama's Baby, Papa's Maybe," 67.

54 Amira Hass quoted in Zureik, *Israel's Colonial Project in Palestine*, 128.

55 See Kotef and Amir, "(En)Gendering Checkpoints," 980, 975, for a detailed discussion of both the "excess" and "surplus" violence exercised in the context of the gendered relations of power operative at the checkpoints; Kotef and Amir, "Between Imaginary Lines," 55–80; Kotef, *Movement and the Ordering of Freedom*, 27–51, 52–60. See also Griffiths and Repo, "Biopolitics and Checkpoints," 24, for a discussion of how the checkpoints "support the settler colonial project of the Israeli state through the production and management of a docile yet physically able male Palestinian labour force."

56 Breaking the Silence, *Our Harsh Logic*, 40, 51.

57 Breaking the Silence, *Our Harsh Logic*, 51.

58   Braverman, "Captive: Zoometric Operations in Gaza," 197.

59   Deleuze, *The Fold*, 30.

60   Foucault, *The History of Sexuality*, 141.

61   Spillers, "Mama's Baby, Papa's Maybe," 67.

62   See, for example, Israeli lawmaker Ayelet Shaked's Facebook call for "the liquida-
     tion of all Palestinians." In her post, Shaked declares that "the entire Palestinian
     people is the enemy . . . including its elderly and its women, its cities and villages,
     its property and infrastructure." She calls for the killing of Palestinian mothers
     "who give birth to 'little snakes.'" Ali Abunimah, "Israeli Lawmaker's Call for
     Genocide of Palestinians Gets Thousands of Facebook Likes," *Electronic Intifada*,
     July 7, 2014, https://electronicintifada.net/blogs/ali-abunimah/israeli-lawmakers
     -call-genocide-palestinians-gets-thousands-facebook-likes.

63   Shaloub-Kevorkian, Ihmoud, and Dahir-Nashif, "Sexual Violence, Women's Bod-
     ies, and Israeli Settler Colonialism," 40. Pappé, *The Ethnic Cleansing of Palestine*,
     208–11, documents the IDF's historical use of sexual violence against Palestinian
     women in the 1948–49 campaign; Lentin, *Traces of Racial Exception*, 121–24, ana-
     lyzes sexual violence as evidencing the "intersection of race and gender in Israel's
     permanent war against Palestinians" (122); Sharoni, "Homefront as Battlefield,"
     examines gender, military occupation, and violence against women.

64   Muhammad Ali Khalidi, "Israeli Discourse Still Reflects Hatred," *New York Times*,
     May 24, 1996, https://www.nytimes.com/1996/05/24/opinion/1-israeli-discourse
     -still-reflects-hatred-068179.html?searchResultPosition=4.

65   Steven Erlanger, "Rafael Eitan, 75, Ex-General and Chief of Staff in Israel,
     Dies," *New York Times*, November 24, 2004, https://www.nytimes.com/2004/11
     /24/obituaries/rafael-eitan-75-exgeneral-and-chief-of-staff-in-israel-dies.html
     ?searchResultPosition=1.

66   Tamar Pileggi, "New Deputy Defense Minister Called Palestinians 'Animals,'"
     Times of Israel, May 11, 2015, https://www.timesofisrael.com/new-deputy-defense
     -minister-called-palestinians-animals/.

67   Zureik, *Israel's Colonial Project in Palestine*, 78. See also Lentin, *Traces of Racial
     Exception*, 1–48, for an analysis of the centrality of race in the operations of Israeli
     state.

68   Baratay and Hardouin-Fugier, *Zoo*, 13.

69   Quoted in Gregory, *The Colonial Present*, 121.

70   Spillers, "Mama's Baby, Papa's Maybe," 67, 78. Spillers is here quoting William
     Goodell.

71   Pappé, *The Biggest Prison on Earth*, 168. See also Hever, "Exploitation of Palestinian
     Labour in Contemporary Zionist Colonialism."

72   Leroy, "Black History in Occupied Territory," 10.

73   Leroy, "Black History in Occupied Territory," 11. On anti-Black racism in Israel,
     see also Lentin, *Traces of Racial Exception*, 86, 95, 129–30.

74   Leroy, "Black History in Occupied Territory," 12.

75   Quoted in Philip Weiss, "Bromwich: NYT Authority Morris Sees Palestinians as
     'Animals Not Yet Inducted into Full Humanity,'" *Mondoweiss*, December 31, 2008,

http://mondoweiss.net/2008/12/bromwich-nyt-authority-morris-sees-palestinians
-as-animals-not-yet-inducted-into-full-humanity/.

76   Quoted in Ari Shavit, "An Interview with Benny Morris," *Counterpunch*, January 16–18, 2014, http://www.counterpunch.org/2004/01/16/an-interview-with
-benny-morris/.

77   Fanon, *The Wretched of the Earth*, 5.

78   Fanon, *The Wretched of the Earth*, 5.

79   Dan Williams and Nidal al-Mughrabi, "Gaza Rockets, Israeli Air Strikes Persist Despite Truce Call," *Reuters*, March 14, 2014, https://www.reuters.com/article/us
-palestinian-israel-gaza/gaza-rockets-israeli-air-strikes-persist-despite-truce-call
-idUSBREA2CoJ92014313.

80   Mbembe, "Necropolitics," 27.

81   Derrida, *The Beast and the Sovereign*, 283.

82   Derrida, *The Beast and the Sovereign*, 283.

83   Derrida, *The Beast and the Sovereign*, 29.

84   See Puar, *The Right to Maim*, 150; Strand, "'Meeting with the Dietician,'" 3.

85   Puar, *The Right to Maim*, 109, 150, 144.

86   Puar, *The Right to Maim*, 144.

87   Puar, *The Right to Maim*, 145.

88   Quoted in Kapitan, "Historical Introduction to the Philosophical Issues," 6–7.

89   For a detailed discussion of the Wall, see Weizman, *Hollow Land*, 161–82.

90   Quoted in Barak Ravid, "Netanyahu: We'll Surround Israel with Fences 'to Defend Ourselves against Wild Beasts,'" *Haaretz*, February 9, 2016, http://www
.haaretz.com/israel-news/.premium-1.702318. For a detailed discussion of the Wall as instantiating a border "between a 'civilized us' and 'uncivilized them'" while, simultaneously, generating a number of significant political contradictions and effects, see Busbridge, "Performing Colonial Sovereignty."

91   Derrida, *The Beast and the Sovereign*, 309.

92   Fanon, *The Wretched of the Earth*, 7.

93   Foucault, *About the Hermeneutics of the Self*, 75.

94   Latour, *Pandora's Hope*, 291.

95   Derrida, *The Beast and the Sovereign*, 339.

96   Derrida, *The Beast and the Sovereign*, 17.

97   Derrida, *The Beast and the Sovereign*, 14.

98   Derrida, *The Beast and the Sovereign*, 14–15.

99   Viveiros de Castro, *Cannibal Metaphysics*, 56–57.

100 Agamben, *Homo Sacer*, 8–9.

101 Viveiros de Castro, *Cannibal Metaphysics*, 316.

102 Avelar, "Amerindian Perspectivism and Non-human Rights," 4.

103 Avelar, "Amerindian Perspectivism and Non-human Rights," 4.

104 Stauffer, "Haeckel, Darwin, and Ecology," 140.

105 Ahuja, *Bioinsecurities*, x.

106 Cajete, *Native Science*, 151.

107 Rose, *Dingo Makes Us Human*, 105.

108 Perera, "Dead Exposures," 4.

109 Sekula, "The Body in the Archive," 10.

110 "Palestinian Jailed for Murder of Israeli Teenagers," *BBC News*, January 6, 2015, http://www.bbc.com/news/world-middle-east-30697521.

111 Ihmoud, "Mohammed Abu-Khdeir and the Politics of Racial Terror," 3.

112 For a detailed account of the Deir Yassin massacre, see Pappé, *The Ethnic Cleansing of Palestine*, 90–91.

113 Ihmoud, "Mohammed Abu-Khdeir and the Politics of Racial Terror," 20.

114 Pappé, *The Ethnic Cleansing of Palestine*, xvi. On the topic of the ethnic cleansing of Palestine, see, for example, W. Khalidi, *All That Remains*. See also several works by Masalha—"Remembering the Palestinian Nakba"; *Expulsion of the Palestinians*; *A Land without People*; *The Politics of Denial*; and *The Palestine Nakba*, 19–87—for a detailed discussion of the historical ethnic cleansing of Palestine and its contemporary embodiments in "Jerusalem and other parts of the West Bank" (*The Palestine Nakba*, 14). See also Tofakji, "Settlements and Ethnic Cleansing in the Jordan Valley"; Green and Smith, "Evicting Palestine"; Hanafi, "Explaining Spacio-cide in the Palestinian Territory"; Falah, "The Geopolitics of 'Enclavisation'"; Gordon and Ram, "Ethnic Cleansing and the Formation of Settler-Geographies," 20–29.

115 Pappé, *The Ethnic Cleansing of Palestine*, xvii, 225. For a critique of Pappé's ethnic cleansing argument, see Lentin, *Traces of Racial Exception*, 10–12. Lentin, in her critical prioritization of race over ethnicity and her examination of the centrality of race in Israeli settler practices of elimination, writes: "The discourse of genocide is increasingly being applied to the elimination and continuing targeting of the Palestinian Natives by the State of Israel" (104–5). See also Ramzy Baroud, "Incremental Genocide: A Brief History of Israel's Violence Against Palestine," *Toward Freedom*, January 17, 2018, https://towardfreedom.org/story/archives/middle-east/incremental-genocide-a-brief-history-of-israels-violence-against-palestine/; Shaw, "Palestine in an International Historical Perspective"; Lendman, "Israel's Slow-Motion Genocide in Occupied Palestine"; Barghouti, "European Collusion in Israel's Slow Genocide"; Shaw and Bartov, "The Question of Genocide in Palestine, 1948"; Short, *Redefining Genocide*; W. Cook, *The Plight of the Palestinians*.

116 Moughrabi, "Israeli Control and Palestinian Resistance," 48.

117 Nir Hasson, "Calling Palestinians 'Animals,' Deputy Jerusalem Mayor Vows Retribution after Shooting Attack," *Haaretz*, October 10, 2016, http://www.haaretz.com/israel-news/.premium-1.746987.

118 Hasson, "Calling Palestinians 'Animals.'"

119 Bergman, "Darwinian Criminality Theory," 51.

120 Frazer and Carlson, "Indigenous Memes and the Invention of a People," 7. I'm grateful to Bronwyn Carlson for bringing the neocolonial dimension of this meme to my attention.

121 I note here that the figure of Khdeir as/with pig also generates subtextual references to the Muslim and Jewish prohibition of pork, as a signifier of dirt, impurity, and disease.

122 Orwell, *Animal Farm*, 120.

123 Chen, *Animacies*, 134; for a detailed analysis of the figure of the trans and its imbrication in vectors of speciesism, race, sexuality, and gender, see 127–55.

124 Stryker, "(De)Subjugated Knowledges," 3.

125 Vialles, *Animal to Edible*, 31. See also Patterson, *Eternal Treblinka*.

126 Vialles, *Animal to Edible*, 43.

127 Shehadeh, "The 2014 War on Gaza," 279. See also United Nations Office for the Coordination of Humanitarian Affairs occupied Palestinian Territories, "Gaza Emergency Situation Report," September 4, 2014, https://www.ochaopt.org /reports/situation-reports; United Nations, "Gaza Initial Rapid Assessment— OCHA Report," August 27, 2014, https://www.un.org/unispal/document/auto -insert-204696/. In Operation Protective Edge, the IDF destroyed crucial infrastructure such as water, electricity, and sewerage plants and "at least 10,000 houses and the damage of 30,000 more. . . . Many farming areas and industrial zones, filled with the small manufacturing plants and factories that anchored Gaza's economy, are now wastelands." Sudarsan Raghavan, "Month-Long War in Gaza Has Left a Humanitarian and Environmental Crisis," *Washington Post*, August 6, 2014, https://www.washingtonpost.com/world/middle_east/month -long-war-in-gaza-has-left-a-humanitarian-and-environmental-crisis/2014/08/06 /85772138-cad7-4812-90d9-6bdb21be1c63_story.html. This destruction of crucial infrastructure exemplifies what Stephen Graham, "Bulldozers and Bombs," 643, has termed Israel's "infrastructural warfare" against Palestinians.

128 Gilbert, *Night in Gaza*, 64.

129 Perera, *Survival Media*, 76–77.

130 El-Hadad, "After the Smoke Clears."

131 P. Wolfe, "Introduction," 10.

132 Svirsky and Ben-Arie, *From Shared Life to Co-resistance in Historic Palestine*, 25.

133 Junka, "Camping in the Third Space," 357. Palestinian practices of aesthetic resistance include Ayman Qwaider and Mohammed Alrozzi's Gaza Children Cinema, that facilitates cinema gatherings for vulnerable Palestinian children "at convenient community locations across the Gaza Strip," accessed June 23, 2018, https:// gazachildrencinema.org/. On the critical resignification by Palestinian artists of the images of bombed and war-torn Gaza, see D. Wyatt, "Palestinian Artists Transform Smoke-Filled Gaza into Symbols of Resistance," *Independent*, July 31, 2014, https://www.independent.co.uk/arts-entertainment/art/features/palestinian-artists -transform-smoke-filled-gaza-into-symbol-of-resistance-9639738.html. Magid Shihade, "Settler Colonialism and Conflict," maps the diverse tactics of creative resistance deployed by Palestinians during the occupation. These acts of creative resistance exemplify what Perera terms, in her analysis of acts of "improvised transmutations and forced improvisations" in the context of war, "survival media," which include "forms of cultural politics, corporeal poetics and their material effects" (*Survival Media*, 23). Thus, in the context of the militarized bombardment of Gaza during Operation Protective Edge, the act of baking cakes to celebrate the Eid holiday becomes a defiant performance of cultural politics and a celebratory gesture of corporeal poetics mobilized to carve out joy in the midst of war. Elham

Elzanin, a refugee fleeing the bombardment and sheltering with her children in a school in Gaza, explains: "I said to myself, 'We ought to make children feel the atmosphere of Eid, even if warplanes are bombing. . . . The Israelis should know they will not stop us [from] finding some joy in making Eid cake,' she said. The cake, she added, represents 'resilience and resistance'" (quoted in Omer, *Shell-Shocked*, 149). Through the practice of baking celebratory cakes, flour, and sugar become agents of political defiance and embodied resistance.

134 Baratay and Hardouin-Fugier, *Zoo*, 80.

135 Amira Hass, "Not an Internal Palestinian Matter," *Haaretz*, October 4, 2014, http://www.haaretz.com/not-an-internal-palestinian-matter-1.200451.

136 I. Mohamad, "New UK Drones 'Field Tested' on Captive Palestinians," *Electronic Intifada*, November 13, 2013, http://electronicintifada.net/blogs/ali-abunimah/new-uk-dronesfield-tested-captive-palestinians.

137 Li, "The Gaza Strip as Laboratory," 38–39. On Palestine as laboratory, see also J. Cook, "'The Lab'"; Dene, "From Tanks to Wheelchairs"; M. A. Khalidi, "Five Lessons Learned from the Israeli Attack on Gaza"; Graham, "Laboratories of War"; Yotam Feldman, "The Lab: A Unique Insight into the World of Israeli Arms Dealers Selling Weapons and Experience around the World," *Al Jazeera*, May 8, 2014, https://www.aljazeera.com/programmes/witness/2014/05/lab-20145475423526313.html.

138 Quoted in Rania Khalek, "Israeli Drone Conference Features Weapons Used to Kill Gaza's Children," *Electronic Intifada*, September 18, 2014, http://electronicintifada.net/blogs/raniakhalek/israeli-drone-conference-features-weapons-used-kill-gazaschildren.

139 Quoted in D. Cohen, "'Suicide Drones' and the Spoils of War," *Mondoweiss*, December 11, 2014, http://mondoweiss.net/2014/12/suicide-israeli-manufacturers.

140 Who Profits, "'Elbit Systems' Complicity in the Assault on Gaza 2014," *Who Profits: The Israeli Occupation Industry*, accessed December 1, 2014, http://www.whoprofits.org/content/elbit-systemscomplicity-assault-gaza-2014.

141 Quoted in J. Cook, "'The Lab.'"

142 See, for example, Pugliese, "'Demonstrative Evidence.'"

143 Machold, "Reconsidering the Laboratory Thesis," 94. I'm grateful to Derek Gregory for bringing this article to my attention.

144 Machold, "Reconsidering the Laboratory Thesis," 89.

145 Weizman, *Hollow Land*, 9–10.

146 Leroy, "Black History in Occupied Territory," 13.

147 Jeremy M. Sharpe, "U.S. Foreign Aid to Israel," *Congressional Research Service*, June 10, 2015, https://www.fas.org/sgp/crs/mideast/RL33222.pdf.

148 "US and Israel Sign Record $38bn Military Aid Deal," *Al Jazeera*, September 15, 2016, http://www.aljazeera.com/news/2016/09/israel-sign-record-38bn-military-aid-deal-160914135203821.html.

149 Machold, "Reconsidering the Laboratory Thesis," 94.

150 Adorno, *Minima Moralia*, 105.

151 Orna Rinat, "What the Israeli Military Is Doing to Animals," *Haaretz*, June 19, 2016, http://www.haaretz.com/opinion/.premium-1.725840.

152 Rinat, "What the Israeli Military Is Doing to Animals." The lines of connection that bind this experiment to Gaza and its human population are succinctly elucidated by what Hass terms "the good old Israeli experiment called 'put them [Gazans] into a pressure cooker and see what happens'" ("Not an Internal Palestinian Matter").

153 Derrida, *The Animal That Therefore I Am*, 96.

154 Quoted in Omer, *Shell-Shocked*, 198.

155 Omer, *Shell-Shocked*, 218.

156 Omer, *Shell-Shocked*, 219.

157 On the structural invertibility of human rights frameworks, see Perugini and Gordon, *The Human Right to Dominate*, 10: "Human rights discourses have the power to invert and subvert the definition of the relationship of power within which they are mobilized." Derrida, in *The Beast and the Sovereign*, brings into focus what he calls "a major failure of logic" in the regime of animal rights by disclosing the unthought specter of anthropocentric epistemic violence that continues to inscribe this regime: "As for the declaration of the rights of animals called for by some people . . . they most often follow, very naively, an existing right, the rights of man adapted by analogy to animals. Now these rights of man are in a relation of solidarity and indissociably, systematically dependent on a philosophy of the subject of a Cartesian or Kantian type, which is the very philosophy in the name of which the animal is reduced to the status of a machine without reason or personhood" (*The Beast and the Sovereign*, 111).

158 For relevant critiques of animal rights, see C. Wolfe, *Animal Rites*, 32–43; Benton, "Rights and Justice on a Shared Planet."

159 Calarco, *Zoographies*, 132.

160 Kimmerer, "Learning the Grammar of Animacy," 133. See also Chen, *Animacies*, 10, and the book's taking into consideration not only "the broadening field of nonhuman life as a proper object, but even more sensitively, the animateness or inanimateness of entities that are considered either 'live' or 'dead.'"

161 Ilan Lior, "10,000 March in Largest-Ever Animal Rights Parade in Israel," *Haaretz*, October 5, 2015, http://www.haaretz.com/israel-news/.premium-1.678801.

162 Haggai Matar, "The Rise of Israel's Animal Rights Movement," +972, November 9, 2013, http://972mag.com/the-rise-of-israels-animal-rights-movement/81605/.

163 Quoted in Ayel Gross, "Vegans for (and against) the Occupation," *Haaretz*, November 14, 2013, http://www.haaretz.com/opinion/.premium-1.557912.

164 Derrida, "Violence against Animals," 66.

165 Amayreh Khalid, "The Paris March of Imperialist Hypocrisy, Led by Netanyahu, the Butcher of Gaza Children," *Al Jazeera: Cross-Cultural Understanding*, January 5, 2015, http://www.aljazeerah.info/Opinion%20Editorials/2015/January/14%200 /The%20Paris%20March%20of%20Imperialist%20Hypocrisy,%20Led%20 by%20Netanyahu,%20the%20Butcher%20of%20Gaza%20Children%20By%20 Khalid%20Amayreh.htm.

166 Der Derian, *Virtuous War*, 293.

167 Wilden, *System and Structure*, 169.

168 Wilden, *System and Structure*, 182.

169 Heidegger, *Poetry, Language, Thought*, 178.

170 Lippit, *Electric Animal*, 192.

Chapter 2: Biopolitical Modalities of the More-Than-Human and Their Forensic Ecologies

1   P. Wolfe, *Settler Colonialism*, 2.

2   R. J. Smith, "Graduated Incarceration," 318.

3   R. J. Smith, "Graduated Incarceration," 318.

4   See, for example, Konishi, "First Nations Scholars, Settler Colonial Studies, and Indigenous History," where she stages a critical discussion of settler colonial studies in relation to "Indigenous-authored extra-colonial histories."

5   See, for example, P. Wolfe's *Settler Colonialism, The Settler Complex*, and *Traces of History*.

6   Fayez Sayegh, in *Zionist Colonialism in Palestine* (1965), traces the key components operative in the settler colonial occupation of Palestine, including the "forcible dispossession of the indigenous population, their expulsion from their own country, the implantation of an alien sovereignty on their own country" and the ongoing replacement of the Indigenous population on "land emptied of its rightful inhabitants" (v). Furthermore, he situates the settler colonization of Palestine within a transnational colonial frame and marks the various international points of solidarity with key decolonizing events, including the landmark First Asian-African Conference, held at Bandung, Indonesia, in 1955 (57). For a representative sampling on the growing body of scholarship on settler colonialism in the context of the Israeli occupation of Palestine, see the three special issues "Past Is Present: Settler Colonialism in Palestine," *Settler Colonial Studies* 2, no. 1 (2012); "Settler Colonial Studies and Israel-Palestine," *Settler Colonial Studies* 5, no. 3 (2015); "Settlers and Citizens: A Critical View of Israeli Society," *Settler Colonial Studies* 9, no. 1 (2019). See also Ram, "The Colonization Perspective in Israeli Sociology"; Masalha, *The Palestine Nakba*, 19–87, where he states: "Zionist settler-colonialism is particular but it is not unique. In line with common colonial practices the Israeli state was founded on ruin, ethnic cleansing, displacement and replacement of the indigenous people of Palestine" (56); Said, *The Question of Palestine*, 68–69; Kimmerling, *Politicide*, 214–15; Abdo and Yuval-Davis, "Palestine, Israel and the Zionist Settler Project"; Veracini, "The Other Shift"; Veracini, "What Can Settler Colonial Studies Offer to an Interpretation of the Conflict in Israel-Palestine?"; Veracini, *Israel and Settler Society*, which offers a comparative analysis of Israeli settler colonialism; Lloyd, "Settler Colonialism and the State of Exception"; Krebs and Olwan, "'From Jerusalem to the Grand River, Our Struggles Are One'"; Pappé, "Zionism as Colonialism" and "Revisiting 1967"; Salamanca et al., "Past Is Present"; Dana and Jarbawi, "A Century of Settler Colonialism in Palestine"; Svirsky and Ben-Arie, *From Shared Life to Co-resistance in Historic Palestine*, offer a detailed exposition of Patrick Wolfe's thesis in the context of Israeli settler colonialism; Busbridge, "Israel-Palestine and the Settler-Colonial 'Turn'"; Zreik, "When Does a Settler Become a Native?," who puts forward, among other things, the argument on the uniqueness of the Israeli settler colonial project and, in the process, unreflexively often reproduces

the colonial discourse of "development" and all its problematic racial inflections; Bhandar, *Colonial Lives of Property*, 116–48, for an analysis of Israeli settler law and racial regimes of ownership in the context of occupied Palestine; and Lentin, *Traces of Racial Exception*, who examines the centrality of race in Israeli settler colonialism. Maya Mikdashi, "What Is Settler Colonialism?," offers a comparative analysis of settler colonialism in Palestine and the Americas that refuses the traditionally anodyne academic register, investing her discourse with an affective charge that draws on complex lived histories of settler violence, displacement, and binary categories that fail to hold in the face of enmeshed racial histories.

7   Dana and Jarbawi, "A Century of Settler Colonialism in Palestine," 198. See Salaita, *Inter/Nationalism*, for a decolonizing critique that interlinks Native America and Palestine.

8   For a succinct account of the unique attributes of Israeli settler colonialism, see Dana and Jarbawi, "A Century of Settler Colonialism in Palestine." For a discussion of the productive applicability and shortfalls of using settler colonial theory in the analysis of the Israeli state, see Pappé, "Shtetl Colonialism."

9   Busbridge, "Israel-Palestine and the Settler-Colonial 'Turn,'" 101.

10   P. Wolfe, *Traces of History*, 267.

11   P. Wolfe, *Traces of History*, 267. As David Lloyd remarks in his analysis of the concrete workings of Israeli settler colonialism in the occupied territories: "The settler colonial model has, indeed, a peculiar explanatory force in accounting both for the phenomena and for the apparent contradictions of Palestine/Israel" ("Settler Colonialism and the State of Exception," 66).

12   In the context of the occupation, Lorenzo Veracini has argued for the complication of the settler thesis by asserting that what is operative is a "coexistence of successful and failed settler colonialisms: we are confronted by *one* Zionist settler colonial project and *two* outcomes: one largely successful [Israel proper], the other largely unsuccessful [the West Bank]" ("The Other Shift," 38). Barakat challenges this assertion by noting that "because of the way he casts settler colonial projects in terms of 'triumph,' some of Veracini's rhetorical divisions end up mirroring Zionist settler conquest and come eerily close to the Zionist narratives that treat 1948 and 1967 lands as two distinct areas rather than part of the whole of Palestine, albeit fragmented by the violence of the state of Israel. In fact, in this division, he seems to be neglecting a key element in understanding the settler colonial context, which is the demographics of elimination—still very much at play in all fragmented parts of Palestine" ("Writing/Righting Palestine Studies," 350).

13   Barakat, "Writing/Righting Palestine Studies," 356.

14   Weizman, "The Geometry of Occupation," 1, 2. See also Moughrabi, "Israeli Control and Palestinian Resistance."

15   Salamanca et al., "Past Is Present," 1.

16   Quoted in Barakat, "Writing/Righting Palestine Studies," 356.

17   For a detailed analysis of the intersection of Israeli settler colonialism and biopolitical and necropolitical techniques in the context of occupied Palestine, see Zureik, *Israel's Colonial Project in Palestine*, 135–60, 161–78.

18   Isaac and Safar, "The Impact of Israel's Unilateral Actions on the Palestinian Environment," 1. On the impact of the occupation on Palestine's ecologies, see also Isaac and Gasteyer, "The Issue of Biodiversity in Palestine," 5–6; Jon Pattee, "Ecocide: War Lays Waste to Palestine," *Albawaba*, June 11, 2001, https://www.albawaba.com/news/ecocide-war-lays-waste-palestine.

19   Alatout, "Narratives of Power," 311.

20   Foucault, *The History of Sexuality*, 138.

21   P. Wolfe, "Settler Colonialism and the Elimination of the Native," 387.

22   See Grindle and Johansen, *Ecocide of Native America*, for an extensive study of the interlinking of settler colonialism with ecocidal strategies.

23   Whyte, "Indigenous Experience, Environmental Justice and Settler Colonialism," 171.

24   Whyte, "Indigenous Experience, Environmental Justice and Settler Colonialism," 159. See also Gilio-Whitaker, *As Long as Grass Grows*, 12: "Settler colonialism itself is for Indigenous peoples a structure of environmental injustice."

25   Coulthard, *Red Skin, White Masks*, 13.

26   Short and Rashed, "Palestine," 81–85; Da'Na, "Israel's Settler-Colonial Water Regime," 50.

27   Jaber, "Settler Colonialism and Ecocide," 140. I wish to make clear that I do not view Zionism as purely coextensive and interchangeable with the Israeli state. The Israeli state is a heterogeneous entity inscribed by differential elements that cannot be simply homogenized under the Zionist imprimatur. For a history of anti-Zionist and anticolonial dissent within the context of the Israeli state, see Greenstein, *Zionism and Its Discontents*, particularly 145–94; Svirsky and Ben-Arie, *From Shared Life to Co-resistance in Historic Palestine*.

28   Jaber, "Settler Colonialism and Ecocide," 142.

29   Zierler, *The Invention of Ecocide*, 14–15.

30   Jha, *Armed Conflict and Environmental Damage*, 18. For a detailed discussion of ecocide in the context of armed conflict, see Broswimmer, *Ecocide*. Jaber offers a definition of ecocide and then tracks its (largely failed) itinerary through various examples of international law ("Settler Colonialism and Ecocide," 140–42), as do Short, *Redefining Genocide*, 38–49; and Higgins, *Eradicating Ecocide*, 61–71.

31   Broswimmer, *Ecocide*, 75.

32   For an overview of the ecological impact that Operation Protective Edge had on Gaza, see Amal Sarsour, "Impact of the Last Israeli Military Operation on the Vital Environment in Gaza Governates, 2014," *Tlaxcala*, November 11, 2014, http://www.tlaxcala-int.org/article.asp?reference=13881. For a detailed analysis of Operation Protective Edge, see Finkelstein, *Gaza*, 200–356.

33   R. J. Smith, "Graduated Incarceration," 318.

34   On the need to intertwine settler colonial regimes with their impact on Indigenous ecologies, see Whyte, "Indigenous Experience, Environmental Justice and Settler Colonialism."

35   LaDuke, *All Our Relations*.

36   Finkelstein, *Gaza*, 218.

NOTES TO CHAPTER 2

37 See, for example, UN Human Rights Council, "Report of the Detailed Findings of the Independent Commission of Inquiry," 110.

38 UN Human Rights Council, "Report of the Detailed Findings of the Independent Commission of Inquiry," 111.

39 Breaking the Silence, *This Is How We Fought in Gaza*, 106, 105.

40 Breaking the Silence, *This Is How We Fought in Gaza*, 110.

41 Breaking the Silence, *This Is How We Fought in Gaza*, 167.

42 Breaking the Silence, *This Is How We Fought in Gaza*, 64.

43 DeLanda, *A New Philosophy of Society*, 12.

44 See UN Human Rights Council, "Report of the Detailed Findings of the Independent Commission of Inquiry," 110.

45 DeLanda, *War in the Age of Intelligent Machines*, 79.

46 Breaking the Silence, *This Is How We Fought in Gaza*, 35.

47 Breaking the Silence, *This Is How We Fought in Gaza*, 191–92.

48 Henckaerts and Doswald-Beck, *Customary International Humanitarian Law*, 311.

49 Breaking the Silence, *This Is How We Fought in Gaza*, 40–41.

50 Breaking the Silence, *This Is How We Fought in Gaza*, 40.

51 Mohammed Omer, "Not Even Animals Are Safe in Gaza," *Middle East Eye*, February 12, 2015, https://www.middleeasteye.net/news/not-even-animals-are-safe-gaza.

52 Omer, "Not Even Animals Are Safe in Gaza."

53 Breaking the Silence, *Our Harsh Logic*, 41.

54 Omer, *Shell-Shocked*, 218.

55 Nixon, *Slow Violence*, 200.

56 Roberts, "Environmental Issues in International Armed Conflict," 260.

57 Rome Statute of the International Criminal Court, July 1, 2002, https://www.icc-cpi.int/nr/rdonlyres/ea9aeff7-5752-4f84-be94-0a655eb30e16/0/rome_statute_english.pdf, 5–6. See also R. I. Khalidi, "The Dahiya Doctrine, Proportionality, and War Crimes"; Weill and Azarova, "The 2014 Gaza War."

58 Mark Kersten, "Israel's Challenge to the International Criminal Court," *Washington Post*, January 20, 2015, https://www.washingtonpost.com/blogs/monkey-cage/wp/2015/01/20/israels-challenge-to-the-international-criminal-court/. In her analysis of Israel and its relationship to various bodies of international law, Lentin notes: "Even when it does ratify international conventions, Israel makes reservations, rendering itself immune from almost any action against it" (*Traces of Racial Exception*, 40–41).

59 Graham, "Bulldozers and Bombs." Pappé, in *The Ethnic Cleansing of Palestine*, 91–114, documents the historical precedents to these acts of urbicide.

60 Omer, *Shell-Shocked*, 11.

61 Dajani, "Drying Palestine."

62 Judith Deutsch, "JNF Greenwash," *Jewish National Fund—Colonizing Palestine since 1901* (JNF eBook, vol. 4, May 15, 2001), 31.

63 Joint APN-PANAP Mission in Palestine, "Human Rights and Toxic Chemicals in the Occupied West Bank," 8.

64 Jaber, "Settler Colonialism and Ecocide," 148.

65 For a detailed discussion of water and sewage "as a crucial battleground of the Israeli-Palestinian conflict," see Weizman, *Hollow Land*, 18–22.

66 Isra Saleh El-Namey, "Water Pollution Reaches Catastrophic Levels in Gaza," *Electronic Intifada*, May 10, 2016, https://electronicintifada.net/content/water -pollution-reaches-catastrophic-levels-gaza/16616.

67 Camilla Corradin, "Israel: Water as a Tool to Dominate Palestinians," *Al Jazeera*, June 23, 2016, http://www.aljazeera.com/news/2016/06/israel-water-tool -dominate-palestinians-160619062531348.html.

68 Corradin, "Israel: Water as a Tool to Dominate Palestinians." See also Haddad, "Palestinian Water Rights."

69 McKenna, "Land, Property, and Occupation," 193.

70 McKenna, "Land, Property, and Occupation," 193.

71 In their analysis of what they term "Israeli hydro-hegemony," al-Shalalfeh, Napier, and Scandrett view "Israel's systemic dehydration of Palestinian people" as a key tool in the growth and consolidation of the settler colonial state ("Water Nakba in Palestine," 122). Da'Na examines "the history of Israel's water regime as an integral part of the larger Zionist colonial system," and he concludes that "existing conditions of inequality and environmental degradation" must be "viewed as products of colonial Zionism" ("Israel's Settler-Colonial Water Regime,"45).

72 Gasteyer et al., "Water Grabbing in Colonial Perspective," 457. See also Isaac and Safar, "The Impact of Israel's Unilateral Actions on the Palestinian Environment," for a discussion of Israel's water grabbing of Palestinian water resources.

73 Dajani, "Drying Palestine," 5.

74 El-Namey, "Water Pollution Reaches Catastrophic Levels." The biopolitical dimensions of the Israeli state's deployment of aquapolitical strategies are encapsulated in the words of Abdul Kareem Muhammad, mayor of Azzun Atme: "In the end of the 1950s, before occupation, there were four to five artesian wells that were built for free use without any limitations. In 1975 the Israelis assembled water level counters on these wells. They began limiting water use so that they could control Palestinian farming. This left many people deciding whether to use the water for their lands or their families. The remainder of the water is used for settlements and their parks and fields. . . . There are no limitations on the water used in the settlements" (quoted in R. J. Smith, "Graduated Incarceration," 324).

75 Dana and Jarbawi, "A Century of Settler Colonialism in Palestine," 210. See also B'Tselem, "Thirsty for a Solution."

76 Omer, *Shell-Shocked*, 207.

77 Quoted in Omer, *Shell-Shocked*, 208. See also Shomar, "Water Scenarios in the Gaza Strip."

78 Epidemiological warfare has been historically documented as critical in enabling the consolidation of both the Australian and US settler states through the poisoning of the wells of Aboriginal people and Native Americans. See Pugliese, *State Violence*, 135–37.

79 Safi, *2014 War on Gaza Strip*, 60; AbuZayyad, "How the Occupation Affects Palestinian Natural Resources," 141.

80 Safi, *2014 War on Gaza Strip*, 60.

81 Ben Lorber, "Israel's Environmental Colonialism and Ecoapartheid," *The Bullet*, June 15, 2018, http://links.org.au/node/2956.

82 Friends of the Earth, "Environmental Nakba," 12. See also Qato and Nagra, "Environmental and Public Health Effects of Polluting Industries in Tulkarm, West Bank," S29.

83 Joint APN-PANAP Mission in Palestine, "Human Rights and Toxic Chemicals in the Occupied West Bank," 8. See also Qumsiyeh, "Environmental Justice and Sustainability in Palestine," 84–85; Isaac and Hilal, "Palestinian Landscape and the Israeli-Palestinian Conflict," 426–27; Ramahi, "The Environmental Impact of Israeli Settlements on the Occupied Palestinian Territories," 10–14; and Isaac, "Israeli Violations against the Palestinian Environment": "With respect to solid waste, around 80% of the solid waste generated by settlers living in the West Bank is dumped in sites throughout the Occupied West Bank" (2). See UN Environment Program, *Desk Study on the Environment in the Occupied Palestinian Territories*, 20–107, for a detailed overview of the impact of the occupation on the environment in Palestine.

84 Voyles, *Wastelanding*, 9.

85 Lorber, "Israel's Environmental Colonialism and Ecoapartheid." Lorber cites the words of Coya White Hat-Artichoker, member of the Rosebud Sioux Tribe in South Dakota and founding member of the LGBQT Two Spirit First Nations Collective, in order to underscore the transnational links that bind settler environmental colonialism with ecoapartheid: "I see what is happening in Palestine as an indigenous struggle for sovereignty, at times, even the right to exist. . . . I see Israel's systemic and intentional destruction and removal of Palestinian lives, homes, and communities as very similar to the destruction of communities, lives, and removal of Native people from their traditional lands. I no longer see terrorists there anymore; I see people resisting and fighting extinction. . . . I believe that as people in the U.S. who make these connections, it's important to be thoughtful about what is happening, in our names and with the U.S. government's money."

86 Qumsiyeh, "Nature and Resistance in Palestine."

87 Safi, *2014 War on Gaza Strip*, 8.

88 Human Rights Watch, *Rain of Fire*, 52, 4.

89 Hamada, Aish, and Shahwan, "Potential Phosphorus Pollution in the Soil of the Northern Gaza Strip," 297.

90 Sarsour, "Impact of the Last Israeli Military Operation," 4. See also New Weapons Research Group, "Gaza Strip Soil Has Been Contaminated Due to Bombings." On the IDF's use of white phosphorus during Operation Cast Lead, see Human Rights Watch, *Rain of Fire*, 1–71.

91 Nixon, *Slow Violence*, 2.

92 Nixon, *Slow Violence*, 2.

93 Safi, *2014 War on Gaza Strip*, 38.

94 Safi, *2014 War on Gaza Strip*, 63.

95 Safi, *2014 War on Gaza Strip*, 9.

96 Safi, *2014 War on Gaza Strip*, 29.

97 Safi, *2014 War on Gaza Strip*, 29.

98 Safi, *2014 War on Gaza Strip*, 9.

99 "The heavy bombing sparked many fires, which caused air pollution with soot, chemicals, and particulate matter" (Safi, *2014 War on Gaza Strip*, 17).

100 "Exposing Explosive Devices? Israel 'Destroys Palestinian Crops' along Security Fence," *RT*, December 31, 2015, https://www.rt.com/news/327571-israel-gaza-crops-herbicide/.

101 "Exposing Explosive Devices?"

102 Belal Aldabbour, "Israel Spraying Toxins over Palestinian Crops in Gaza," *Al Jazeera*, January 19, 2016, http://www.aljazeera.com/news/2016/01/israel-spraying-toxins-palestinian-crops-gaza-160114063046813.html.

103 "Exposing Explosive Devices?"

104 Quoted in Aldabbour, "Israel Spraying Toxins over Palestinian Crops."

105 Foucault, *"Society Must Be Defended"*, 242.

106 Inbar and Shamir, "'Mowing the Grass,'" 72–73.

107 Inbar and Shamir, "'Mowing the Grass,'" 72–73.

108 Puar, *The Right to Maim*, 109.

109 Kober, *Israel's Wars of Attrition*, 5. See also Inbar and Shamir, "'Mowing the Grass,'" 73.

110 In the Australian context, for example, both the unfinished business of the frontier wars and their ongoing effects on contemporary Indigenous lives are viewed, in Michael Anderson's words, in terms of "an ongoing war of attrition against Aboriginal Peoples to this day" ("Lest We Forget the Frontier Wars—Anzac Day 25th April 2012," *Sovereign Union—First Nations Asserting Sovereignty*, April 5, 2012, http://nationalunitygovernment.org/node/66). See also Clements, "Frontier Conflict in Van Diemen's Land," 331; Shea, "Virginia at War, 1644–1646," 144; Hoefle, "Bitter Harvest," 283; Moughrabi, "Israeli Control and Palestinian Resistance," 57.

111 Foucault, *"Society Must Be Defended"*, 244.

112 Safi, *2014 War on Gaza Strip*, 45.

113 Young, "The Case of Palestinian Women under Israeli Occupation," 159; see also Assaf, "Environmental Problems Affecting Palestinian Women under Occupation."

114 Safi, *2014 War on Gaza Strip*, 51; emphasis added.

115 Safi, *2014 War on Gaza Strip*, 53.

116 Safi, *2014 War on Gaza Strip*, 70.

117 Nixon, *Slow Violence*, 200.

118 Derrida, "Faith and Knowledge," 51.

119 Hermesh, Maya, and Davidovitch, *Health Risks Assessment for the Israeli Population*, 6, 7.

120 Hermesh, Maya, and Davidovitch, *Health Risks Assessment for the Israeli Population*, 20.

121 Weinthal and Sowers, "Targeting Infrastructure and Livelihoods in the West Bank and Gaza," 340.

122 Zafrir Rinat, "Collapsing Environmental State of Gaza Poses Threat to Israel's National Security, Report Warns," *Haaretz*, June 3, 2019, https://www.haaretz .com/israel-news/.premium-environmental-state-of-gaza-poses-threat-to-israel-s -national-security-report-warns-1.7328966.

123 Hermesh, Maya, and Davidovitch, *Health Risks Assessment for the Israeli Population*, 21.

124 Latour, *Facing Gaia*, 40, 73.

125 Derrida, *Rogues*, 109.

126 Derrida, *Rogues*, 109.

127 Quoted in Rinat, "Collapsing Environmental State of Gaza Poses Threat to Israel's National Security."

128 McKenna, "Land, Property, and Occupation," 196–97.

129 Masalha, *The Bible and Zionism*, 40.

130 Braverman, *Planted Flags*, 38.

131 Harriet Sherwood, "Gaza Counts Cost of War as More Than 360 Factories Destroyed or Damaged," *Guardian*, August 22, 2014, https://www.theguardian.com /world/2014/aug/22/gaza-economic-cost-war-factories-destroyed.

132 Breaking the Silence, *This Is How We Fought in Gaza*, 35.

133 Breaking the Silence, *This Is How We Fought in Gaza*, 35.

134 Breaking the Silence, *This Is How We Fought in Gaza*, 56.

135 Voyles, *Wastelanding*, 57.

136 Gregory, *The Colonial Present*, 131.

137 Pappé, *The Ethnic Cleansing of Palestine*, has termed the JFN "the principal Zionist tool for the colonization of Palestine" (16) and has documented its role in facilitating dubious land acquisitions, the eviction of Palestinians from their lands, the razing of entire Palestinians villages, and their consequent erasure through pine afforestation programs and the creation of national parks and reserves (227–34). See also Masalha, *The Palestinian Nakba*, 120–34, for a detailed account of the JFN's role in the practices of afforestation as a form of greenwashing.

138 McKee, "Performing Rootedness in the Negev/Naqab," 1179.

139 McKee, "Performing Rootedness in the Negev/Naqab," 1182.

140 Braverman, *Planted Flags*, 49.

141 Puar, *The Right to Maim*, 123, 96.

142 Puar, *The Right to Maim*, 123.

143 On the Israeli state's deployment of colonial rhetoric of modernity and progress to justify Palestinian displacement, land grabs, and nature reserves, see Gasteyer et al., "Water Grabbing in Colonial Perspective."

144 In the US context, Yellowstone National Park (1872) was created in the wake of the establishment of the Indian reservation system (beginning in 1851 with the Indian Appropriations Act, which set the precedent for the creation of Indian reservations) and its attendant forced removal of Native Americans from their traditional lands. See Limerick, *The Legacy of Conquest*. In the process of the US government's creation of Yellowstone National Park, the Shoshone Sheepeaters of the area were forcibly removed from their lands, many were hunted down

and killed by the cavalry, and a military fort was built in order to prevent their reentry onto their traditional lands—a literal enactment of the practice that has come to be known as "fortress conservation" (Merchant, *American Environmental History*, 165–66). In the Australian settler context, the state of New South Wales enacted the contemporaneous subjugation and quarantining of both Aboriginal people and nature through legislation that enabled (1) the segregation of Aboriginal people to reserves (beginning in New South Wales in 1850—see Goodall, *From Invasion to Embassy*, 61–65), and (2) the establishment of the Royal National Park (1879) south of Sydney, following the violent removal of the Dharawal people from their traditional lands (see Bursitt et al., *Dharawal*, 45) and the placing of the bounded "wilderness" under another form of paternal white protection. In the US and Australian contexts, the impetus to establish national parks emerged in the wake of the receding Frontier Wars and settler revalorizations of "wilderness" were critically predicated on this double movement of enclosure and quarantining through the establishment of Indigenous and nature reserves (see Cronon, "The Trouble with Wilderness," 15).

145 For a detailed discussion of what he terms the "dual 'island' system of nature preserves and Indian reserves" deployed by the US settler state in its management and control of both Native Americans and "wilderness," see Spence, *Dispossessing the Wilderness*, 3.

146 Langton, "Art, Wilderness and Terra Nullius," 18. See also Langton, "The European Construction of Wilderness"; Perera and Pugliese, "Parks, Mines and Tidy Towns."

147 Bardenstein, "Trees, Forests, and the Shaping of Palestinian and Israeli Collective Memory," 156–57.

148 See Masalha, *The Bible and Zionism*, 67.

149 Quoted in Braverman, *Planted Flags*, 100.

150 W. Khalidi, *All That Remains*, xvii.

151 Bardenstein, "Threads of Memory and Discourses of Rootedness," 9.

152 Bardenstein, "Threads of Memory and Discourses of Rootedness," 9.

153 Derrida, *Of Grammatology*, 70.

154 Gagliano, "In a Green Frame of Mind."

155 Kimmerer, *Braiding Sweetgrass*, 44.

156 Kimmerer, *Braiding Sweetgrass*, 42.

157 Pappé, *The Ethnic Cleansing of Palestine*, 227–28.

158 Kimmerer, *Braiding Sweetgrass*, 56.

159 Kimmerer, *Braiding Sweetgrass*, 56.

160 Masalha, *The Palestine Nakba*, 120.

161 "Since 1967 Israel Has Razed over 800,000 Palestinian Olive Trees, the Equivalent to Destroying Central Park 33 Times Over," *Mondoweiss*, October 10, 2013, http://mondoweiss.net/2013/10/palestinian-equivalent-destroying/.

162 Marder, *Plant-Thinking*, 25.

163 Marder, *Plant-Thinking*, 76.

164 Quoted in Braverman, *Planted Flags*, 124.

165 Quoted in Jeremy Bowen, "Israel and the Palestinians: A Conflict Viewed through Olives," *BBC News*, December 7, 2014, http://www.bbc.com/news/world-middle-east-30290052.

166 Quoted in Bowen, "Israel and the Palestinians."

167 Cajete, *Native Science*, 186.

168 Bardenstein, "Trees, Forests, and the Shaping of Palestinian and Israeli Collective Memory," 156.

169 Bardenstein, "Trees, Forests, and the Shaping of Palestinian and Israeli Collective Memory," 156.

170 See, for example, Shalhoub-Kevorkian, "Human Suffering in Colonial Contexts" and "Trapped."

171 Hall, *Plants as Persons*, 37. Hall also offers counter-understandings of plants in European thought that contest this dogma (*Plants as Persons*, 28–35, 120–35).

172 Shalhoub-Kevorkian, "Palestinian Children."

173 Civic Coalition for Defending Palestinians' Rights in Jerusalem, *Dispossession and Eviction in Jerusalem: The Cases and Stories of Sheik Jarrah*, accessed March 23, 2014, http://adalah.org/newsletter/eng/feb10/docs/Sheikh_Jarrah_Report-Final.pdf, 23.

174 Civic Coalition for Defending Palestinians' Rights in Jerusalem, *Dispossession and Eviction in Jerusalem*, 23.

175 Masalha, *The Bible and Zionism*, 218.

176 Sayigh, "Silenced Suffering," 8.

177 Shalhoub-Kevorkian, "Palestinian Children," 15.

178 Hall, *Plants as Persons*, 158.

179 Daniel Chamovitz quoted in A. Anathaswamy, "Roots of Consciousness," *New Scientist*, no. 2998 (2014): 6.

180 Mancuso and Viola, *Brilliant Green*, 137.

181 Gagliano, "In a Green Frame of Mind," 5.

182 Hegel quoted in Marder, *Plant-Thinking*, 32.

183 Kohák, "Speaking to Trees," 371.

184 Bird-David, "'Animism' Revisited," 96; emphasis added.

185 Jones and Cloke, "Non-human Agencies," 81.

186 Naveh and Bird-David, "Animism, Conservation and Immediacy," 28–29.

187 Naveh and Bird-David, "Animism, Conservation and Immediacy," 29.

188 Shalhoub-Kevorkian, "Palestinian Children."

189 Cajete, *Native Science*, 108.

190 Latour, *Reassembling the Social*, 200, 202.

191 Latour, *Reassembling the Social*, 44.

192 Derrida, *Memoires for Paul de Man*, 60.

193 Saif, *The Drone Eats with Me*, 35.

Chapter 3: Animal Excendence and Inanimal Torture

1 Navy and Marine Corps Public Health Center, *Public Health Report for Camp Justice*, i–iii.

2 See Voyles, *Wastelanding*; Kuletz, *The Tainted Desert*; Masco, *The Nuclear Borderlands*.

3   Bélanger and Arroyo, *Ecologies of Power*, 16.

4   Santana, "Resisting Toxic Militarism," 37.

5   Santana, "Resisting Toxic Militarism," 38.

6   Santana, "Resisting Toxic Militarism," 38.

7   Santana, "Resisting Toxic Militarism," 38.

8   Janet Reitman, "Inside Gitmo: America's Shame," *Rolling Stone*, December 30, 2015, http://www.rollingstone.com/politics/news/inside-gitmo-americas-shame -20151230.

9   Reitman, "Inside Gitmo."

10   Boumediene and Ait Idir, *Witnesses of the Unseen*, 78, 85.

11   Reitman, "Inside Gitmo."

12   Fallon, *Unjustifiable Means*, 48.

13   Marc Falkoff, "A Death in Gitmo," *Los Angeles Times*, September 20, 2012, http://articles.latimes.com/print/2012/sep/20/opinion/la-oe-falkoff-gitmo-death -20120920.

14   Falkoff, "A Death in Gitmo."

15   Falkoff, "A Death in Gitmo."

16   Falkoff, "A Death in Gitmo."

17   Letter from Adnan Latif to Attorneys David Remes and Marc Falkoff, May 28, 2010, https://www.documentcloud.org/536275-adnan-latif-may-28-2010-letter-to -attorneys.html.

18   Letter from Adnan Latif to Attorneys.

19   Letter from Adnan Latif to Attorneys.

20   Letter from Adnan Latif to Attorneys.

21   Letter from Adnan Latif to Attorneys.

22   Letter from Adnan Latif to Attorneys.

23   Marc Falkoff, "Poems from Guantánamo," *Amnesty International Magazine*, December 12, 2007, http://www.amnestyusa.org/news/news-item/poems-from -guantanamo.

24   "'Don't Interact, Don't Talk, They Are Not Humans'—Gitmo Guard's Basic Orders," *RT*, May 22, 2013, https://www.rt.com/news/guantanamo-guard-islam -torture-608/.

25   Cori Crider, "Obama Lawyers: Guantánamo Detainees 'Not Persons' Like Hobby Lobby," *Reprieve*, July 8, 2014, https://reprieve.org/2014/07/08/obama-lawyers -guantanamo-detainees-not-persons-like-hobby-lobby/.

26   Respondents' Opposition to Petitioners' Emergency Application for TRO Prohibiting Respondents from Depriving Petitioners of the Right to Pray Communally during the Month of Ramadan, *Hassan v. Obama*, 2914 US District 04-CV-01194-UNA 1–2 (2014), 4, 47.

27   Respondents' Opposition to Petitioners' Emergency Application, 2–3.

28   Respondents' Opposition to Petitioners' Emergency Application, 4.

29   For a detailed discussion of the practice of force-feeding and the detainees hunger strikes at Guantánamo, see Pugliese, "Reflective Indocility."

30   Respondents' Opposition to Petitioners' Emergency Application, 28.

31   Respondents' Opposition to Petitioners' Emergency Application, 29.
32   Respondents' Opposition to Petitioners' Emergency Application, 30.
33   Esposito, *Third Person*, 13.
34   Puar, *Terrorist Assemblages*, 158.
35   Puar, *Terrorist Assemblages*, 96.
36   Puar, *Terrorist Assemblages*, 96.
37   Shaker Aamer quoted in "In Guantánamo, 'National Security' Rides Roughshod over Human Rights," *Guardian*, January 6, 2014, http://www.theguardian.com /commentisfree/2014/jan/05/guantanamo-national-security-human-rights-us -military-constitution.
38   Esposito, *Third Person*, 101.
39   Wilden, *System and Structure*, 185.
40   Derrida, *Writing and Difference*, 280.
41   Esposito, *Third Person*, 147.
42   Derrida, *The Animal That Therefore I Am*, 92–93.
43   Derrida, *The Animal That Therefore I Am*, 93.
44   Jeffrey Kaye, "New DoD Report Details Nightmare Leading to Gitmo Detainee's Death," *Firedoglake*, June 29, 2013, http://dissenter.firedoglake.com/2013/06/29 /new-dod-report-details-nightmare-leading-to-gitmo-detainees-death/.
45   (U) AR 15-6 Investigation, *(U) Report on the Facts and Circumstances Surrounding (U) the 8 September 2012 Death of Detainee (U) Adnan Farhan Abd Latif (U) (ISN US9YM-000156DP) (U) at Joint Task Force-Guantanamo (JTF-GTMO)*, 8 November 2012, https:// www.southcom.mil/Portals/7/FOIA%20Docs/FOIA_RELEASE_AR2015-6_Mr _Adnan_Farhan_Latif_Investigation.pdf?ver=2017-08-15-095254-857.
46   (U) AR 15-6 Investigation, *(U) Report on the Facts and Circumstances*, 11.
47   (U) AR 15-6 Investigation, *(U) Report on the Facts and Circumstances*, 43.
48   Kurnaz, *Five Years of My Life*, 99.
49   Khan, *My Guantánamo Diary*, 40.
50   (U) AR 15-6 Investigation, *(U) Report on the Facts and Circumstances*, 43–44.
51   Haraway, *When Species Meet*, 25.
52   (U) AR 15-6 Investigation, *(U) Report on the Facts and Circumstances*, 44.
53   (U) AR 15-6 Investigation, *(U) Report on the Facts and Circumstances*, 44.
54   Heidegger, *The Fundamental Concepts of Metaphysics*, 249–61; Agamben, *The Open*, 57–62.
55   Heidegger, *Poetry, Language, Thought*, 73.
56   Anderson, "Pre- and Posthuman Animals."
57   Rilke, *The Poetry of Rilke*, 327.
58   I borrow this titular term from Levinas, *Difficult Freedom*.
59   Levinas, *Difficult Freedom*, 152.
60   See Derrida, *The Animal That Therefore I Am*, 40–41.
61   Cajete, *Native Science*, 152.
62   Merleau-Ponty, *The Visible and the Invisible*, 198.
63   Merleau-Ponty, *The Visible and the Invisible*, 8.
64   Levinas, *Totality and Infinity*, 39.

65   Heidegger, *The Fundamental Concepts of Metaphysics*, 236–39. For a discussion of
      the key differences between Heidegger's conceptualization of the Open and
      Rilke's, see Steiner, *Animals and the Limits of Postmodernism*, 104–5.

66   Levinas, *On Escape*, 54.

67   Blanchot, *Political Writings, 1953–1993*, 150.

68   (U) AR 15-6 Investigation, *(U) Report on the Facts and Circumstances*, 44.

69   Levinas, *On Escape*, 55.

70   Errachidi with Slovo, *The General*, 126.

71   Errachidi with Slovo, *The General*, 126.

72   Errachidi with Slovo, *The General*, 126.

73   Errachidi with Slovo, *The General*, 126–27.

74   Errachidi with Slovo, *The General*, 126.

75   Errachidi with Slovo, *The General*, 94.

76   Errachidi with Slovo, *The General*, 116.

77   Errachidi with Slovo, *The General*, 127.

78   Errachidi with Slovo, *The General*, 127.

79   "Guantánamo Bay: Shaker Aamer (Full Interview)," *BBC News*, December 14, 2015,
      https://www.youtube.com/watch?v=Ekgd9cEouFM. Interview transcribed by the
      author.

80   Von Uexküll, "A Stroll through the Worlds of Animals and Men," 5.

81   Von Uexküll, "A Stroll through the Worlds of Animals and Men," 5.

82   Quoted in Cajete, *Native Science*, 154.

83   "Guantánamo Bay: Shaker Aamer."

84   Deloria, *The World We Used to Live In*, 108.

85   Deloria, *The World We Used to Live In*, 35.

86   Deloria, *God Is Red*, 136.

87   Deloria, *God Is Red*, 296.

88   Derrida, *The Animal That Therefore I Am*, 119.

89   "Guantánamo Bay: Shaker Aamer."

90   "Guantánamo Bay: Shaker Aamer."

91   Mansour Adayfi, "Taking Marriage Class at Guantánamo," *New York Times*,
      July 27, 2018, https://www.nytimes.com/2018/07/27/style/modern-love-marriage
      -class-at-guantanamo.html.

92   Adayfi, "Taking Marriage Class at Guantánamo."

93   Hogan, "We Call It *Tradition*," 19.

94   Hogan, "We Call It *Tradition*," 19.

95   Senate Select Committee on Intelligence, *Committee Study of the Central Intel-
      ligence Agency's Detention and Interrogation Program, 3 December 2014*, https://www
      .amnestyusa.org/pdfs/sscistudy1.pdf, 16.

96   Shane Scott, "Amid Details on Torture, Data on 26 Who Were Held in Error,"
      New York Times, December 12, 2014, http://www.nytimes.com/2014/12/13/us
      /politics/amid-details-on-torture-data-on-26-held-in-error-.html?_r=o.

97   Blanchot, "Everyday Speech," 13.

98   Cajete, *Native Science*, 134.

99 Assistant Attorney General Jay Bybee, "Memorandum for John Rizzo, Acting General Counsel of the Central Intelligence Agency, Interrogation of al Qaeda Operative, August 1, 2002," 2, *Homeland Security Digital Library*, https://www.hsdl.org/?abstract&did=37518.

100 Lockwood, *Six-Legged Soldiers*, 287.

101 Lockwood, *Six-Legged Soldiers*, 5.

102 Pugliese, *State Violence*, 92–94, 111.

103 Patrick Tucker, "This Is Your Brain on Torture," *Defense One*, December 10, 2014, http://www.defenseone.com/news/2014/12/your-brain-torture/101001/print/.

104 George Monbiot, "Routine and Systematic Torture Is at the Heart of America's War on Terror," *Guardian*, December 12, 2006, http://www.guardian.co.uk/commentisfree/2006/dec/12/comment.usa.

105 UN Human Rights, Office of the High Commission, *Convention against Torture and Other Cruel, Inhuman or Degrading Treatment or Punishment*, http://www.ohchr.org/Documents/ProfessionalInterest/cat.pdf, 1.

106 Lindsey Bever, "Coast Guard Suspends Practice of Shooting, Stabbing and Dismembering Animals in Trauma Training," *Washington Post*, April 28, 2017, https://www.washingtonpost.com/news/animalia/wp/2017/04/28/coast-guard-suspends-practice-of-shooting-stabbing-and-dismembering-animals-in-trauma-training/?noredirect=on&utm_term=.c14973d3dc06).

107 For a detailed discussion and analysis of settler sovereignty and the politics of the border, see Bui et al., "Extraterritorial Killings."

108 Djamel Ameziane, "In Landmark Hearing Today, Djamel Ameziane, Formerly Detained in Guantánamo, Calls for Reparations, an Apology, and Action," *Center for Constitutional Rights*, September 7, 2017, https://ccrjustice.org/home/blog/2017/09/07/landmark-hearing-today-djamel-ameziane-formerly-detained-guant-namo-calls.

109 Imran Mohammad Fazal Hoque, "'I Have Never Experienced Safety since I Was Born': Life in the Manus 'Death Centre,'" *Sydney Morning Herald*, April 17, 2017, https://www.smh.com.au/politics/federal/i-have-never-experienced-safety-since-i-was-born-life-in-the-manus-death-centre-20170417-gvmi68.html.

110 Bybee, "Memorandum for Alberto Gonzales Counsel to the President, RE: Standards of Conduct for Interrogation under 18 U.S.C. §§2340–2340A, August 1, 2002." 172.

111 Center for Constitutional Rights, *Faces of Guantánamo: Torture*, http://ccrjustice.org/files/FoG_torture.pdf, 13, 12.

112 (U) AR 15-6 Investigation, *(U) Report on the Facts and Circumstances*, 11.

113 (U) AR 15-6 Investigation, *(U) Report on the Facts and Circumstances*, 22.

114 (U) AR 15-6 Investigation, *(U) Report on the Facts and Circumstances*, 22.

115 (U) AR 15-6 Investigation, *(U) Report on the Facts and Circumstances*, i.

116 (U) AR 15-6 Investigation, *(U) Report on the Facts and Circumstances*, 1.

117 Falkoff, "A Death in Gitmo."

118 Jason Leopold and Jeffrey Kaye, "Latif Letter about Guantánamo Speaks from the Grave," *Truthout*, December 10, 2012, http://www.truth-out.org/news/item

/13234-latif-letter-about-guantanamo-speaks-from-the-grave-i-am-being-pushed
-toward-death-every-moment.

119   (U) AR 15-6 Investigation, *(U) Report on the Facts and Circumstances*, 25.

120   (U) AR 15-6 Investigation, *(U) Report on the Facts and Circumstances*, 25.

121   (U) AR 15-6 Investigation, *(U) Report on the Facts and Circumstances*, 65.

122   Letter from Adnan Latif to Attorneys.

123   Emad Hassan, "An Obituary for My Friend, Adnan Abdul Latif," *Vice*, November 10, 2014, http://www.vice.com/read/adnan-abdul-latif-obit-emad-hassan
-gtmo-056.

124   Jason Leopold, "Widespread Breakdown of Safeguards at Gitmo: Military Inquiry Finds Systemic Failure Contributed to Guantanamo Prisoner's Tragic End," *Al Jazeera*, July 4, 2013, https://www.aljazeera.com/humanrights/2013/07
/20137324426228887.html.

125   Jason Leopold, "A Guantánamo Prisoner Is Buried as New Details about His Death Begin to Surface," *Truthout*, January 11, 2013, http://truth-out.org/news
/item/13818-guantanamo-prisoner-buried-new-details-death-surface.

126   Quoted in Andy Worthington, "'Guantánamo Is a Piece of Hell That Kills Everything': A Bleak New Year Message from Yemeni Prisoner Adnan Farhan Abdul Latif," *Andy Worthington*, January 1, 2011, http://www.andyworthington.co.uk
/2011/01/01/guantanamo-is-a-piece-of-hell-that-kills-everything-a-bleak-new-year
-message-from-yemeni-prisoner-adnan-farhan-abdul-latif/.

127   See, for example, Damon Winter and Charlie Savage, "Camp X-Ray: A Ghost Prison," *New York Times*, September 1, 2014, http://www.nytimes.com/interactive
/2014/09/01/us/guantanamo-camp-x-ray-ghost-prison-photographs.html?_r=0.

128   "Banana Rat at Gitmo," blogs.reuters.com, March 7, 2013, https://au.pinterest
.com/pin/316237205055842098/.

129   See Pugliese, *State Violence*, 95.

130   Perera, "What Is a Camp . . . ?," 3.

131   Perera, "What Is a Camp . . . ?," 6.

132   Carol Rosenberg, "Missed Deadline? Military Takes Step to Close Guantánamo," *McClatchy DC*, November 15, 2009, http://www.mcclatchydc.com/news/politics
-government/article24563869.html.

Chapter 4: Drone Sparagmos

1   Haglund and Sorg, "Forensic Anthropology," 147.

2   Wright, "Death Investigation," 116.

3   Wright, "Death Investigation," 116.

4   Wright, "Death Investigation," 119.

5   Quoted in Human Rights Watch, *"Between a Drone and Al-Qaeda"*, 64.

6   Haglund and Sorg, "Forensic Anthropology," 147.

7   Human Rights Watch, *"Between a Drone and Al-Qaeda"*, 64.

8   Netzel, Kiely, and Bell, "Evidence," 25.

9   Human Rights Watch, *"Between a Drone and Al-Qaeda"*, 65.

10   Miller and Jones, "Crime Scene Investigation," 44.

11   Presidential Policy Guidance, *Procedures for Approving Actions against Terrorist Targets Located outside the United States and Areas of Active Hostilities*, May 22, 2013, https://www.whitehouse.gov/sites/default/files/uploads/2013.05.23_fact_sheet_on_ppg.pdf, 10.

12   Quoted in Mazzetti, *The Way of the Knife*, 219.

13   Mazzetti, *The Way of the Knife*, 121.

14   David Cole, "'We Kill People Based on Metadata,'" *New York Review of Books*, May 10, 2014, http://www.nybooks.com/blogs/nyrblog/2014/may/10/we-kill-people-based-metadata/.

15   Cole, "'We Kill People Based on Metadata.'"

16   "Former CIA Director: 'We Kill People Based on Metadata,'" *RT*, May 12, 2014, http://rt.com/usa/158460-cia-director-metadata-kill-people/.

17   Quoted in "Former CIA Director: 'We Kill People Based on Metadata.'"

18   The term *somatechnics* refers to a theoretical understanding of the body as indissociably enmeshed within a spectrum of mediating technologies that work to render it culturally intelligible; see Pugliese and Stryker, "Introduction: The Somatechnics of Race and Whiteness."

19   Jeremy Scahill and Glenn Greenwald, "The NSA's Secret Role in the U.S. Assassination Program," *The Intercept*, February 10, 2014, http://firstlook.org/theintercept/2014/02/10/the-nsa-secret-role/.

20   Scahill and Greenwald, "The NSA's Secret Role."

21   Quoted in Scahill and Greenwald, "The NSA's Secret Role."

22   Quoted in Christian Grothoff and J. M. Porup, "The NSA's SKYNET Program May Be Killing Thousands of Innocent People," *Ars Technica UK*, February 16, 2016, http://arstechnica.co.uk/security/2016/02/the-nsas-skynet-program-may-be-killing-thousands-of-innocent-people/.

23   For a detailed critique of the concept of "soft biometrics," see Pugliese, *Biometrics*, 124–28.

24   Noah Shachtman, "Army Tracking Plan: Drones that Never Forget a Face," *Wired—Danger Room*, September 28, 2011, http://www.wired.com/2011/09/drones-never-forget-a-face/.

25   Foucault, *Abnormal*, 33.

26   Foucault, *Abnormal*, 34.

27   Foucault, *The Birth of Biopolitics*, 66.

28   Pugliese, *Biometrics*, 5–7, 128.

29   Foucault, *Security, Territory, Population*, 75.

30   Foucault, *Security, Territory, Population*, 75.

31   Foucault, *Security, Territory, Population*, 75.

32   See, for example, Lyon, *Surveillance Studies*, and Lyon, ed., *Surveillance as Social Sorting*.

33   Heidegger, *Basic Writings*, 304.

34   Pugliese, "Prosthetics of Law and the Anomic Violence of Drones."

35   Scahill and Greenwald, "The NSA's Secret Role."

36   Quoted in "What Is ABI?—And Will It Make Drones Even Deadlier?," *Channel 4 News*, February 22, 2014, http://www.channel4.com/news/drones-abi-activity-based-intelligence-yemen-strike-attack.

37 Quoted in "What Is ABI?—and Will It Make Drones Even Deadlier?"

38 Alkarama Foundation, *The United States' War on Yemen: Drone Attacks. Report Submitted to the Special Rapporteur on the Promotion and Protection of Human Rights and Fundamental Freedoms while Countering Terror*, June 3, 2013, http://en .alkarama.org/documents/ALK_USAYemen_Drones_SRCTwHR_4June2013 _Final_EN.pdf, 6.

39 Jack Searle, "Only 4% of Drone Victims in Pakistan Named as al-Qaeda Members," *Bureau of Investigative Journalism*, October 16, 2014, https://www .thebureauinvestigates.com/namingthedead/only-4-of-drone-victims-in-pakistan -named-as-al-qaeda-members/?lang=en.

40 Emran Feroz, "The Taxi Driver's Last Ride," *New York Times*, September 28, 2016, http://mobile.nytimes.com/2016/09/29/opinion/the-taxi-drivers-last-ride.html?_r =0&referer=http://dronecenter.bard.edu/weekly-roundup-10316/.

41 Quoted in Scahill et al., *The Assassination Complex*, 71.

42 Tova Dvorin, "96.5% of Casualties from US Drone Strikes Civilians," *Israel National News*, November 25, 2014, http://www.israelnationalnews.com/News /News.aspx/187922. The Reprieve report Dvorin cites is Reprieve, *You Never Die Twice: Multiple Kills in the US Drone Program*, November 24, 2014, http://www .reprieve.org/wp-content/uploads/2014_11_24_PUB-You-Never-Die-Twice -Multiple-Kills-in-the-US-Drone-Program-1.pdf, 6.

43 Quoted in Hassan Khan, "'Precise' Drone Strikes in Pakistan: 874 'Unknowns' Killed in US Hunt for 24 Terrorists," *Express Tribune*, November 25, 2014, http:// tribune.com.pk/story/797295/precise-drone-strikes-in-pakistan-874-unknowns -killed-in-us-hunt-for-24-terrorists/.

44 Reprieve, *You Never Die Twice*, 2.

45 Quoted in Jo Becker and Scott Shane, "Secret 'Kill List' Proves a Test of Obama's Principles and Will," *New York Times*, May 29, 2012, http://www.nytimes.com/2012 /05/29/world/obamas-leadership-in-war-on-al-qaeda.html?_r=0.

46 Reprieve, *Opaque Transparency: The Obama Administration and Its Opaque Transparency on Civilians Killed in Drone Strikes*, June 30, 2016, http://www.reprieve.org.uk /wp-content/uploads/2016/06/Obama-Drones-transparency-FINAL.pdf, 3.

47 Glenn Greenwald, "Nobody Knows the Identity of the 150 People Killed by U.S. in Somalia, but Most Are Certain They Deserve It," *The Intercept*, March 9, 2016, https://theintercept.com/2016/03/08/nobody-knows-the-identity-of-the-150 -people-killed-by-u-s-in-somalia-but-most-are-certain-they-deserved-it/.

48 Amoore, "Algorithmic War," 65.

49 *Jaber v. Obama*, 2016 US Dist. No. 16-5093, Brief of Amicus Curiae Brandon Bryant, Lisa Ling, and Cian Westmoreland in Support of Appellants, 7.

50 "US Ex-Drone Operators Join Yemeni Drone Victim in Court Challenge," Reprieve, September 8, 2016, http://www.reprieve.org/us-ex-drone-operators-join -yemeni-drone-victim-in-us-court-challenge/.

51 Office of the Director of National Intelligence, *Summary of Information Regarding US Counterterrorism Strikes Outside Areas of Active Hostilities*, July 1, 2016, https://www.dni.gov/index.php/newsroom/reports-and-publications/214-reports

-publications-2016/1392-summary-of-information-regarding-u-s-counterterrorism
-strikes-outside-areas-of-active-hostilities, 1.

52 Henckaerts and Doswald-Beck, *Customary International Humanitarian Law*, 3.

53 Presidential Policy Guidance, *Procedures for Approving Actions against Terrorist
    Targets*, 3.

54 Presidential Policy Guidance, *Procedures for Approving Actions against Terrorist
    Targets*, 16.

55 Karen De Young, "Newly Declassified Document Sheds Light on How
    President Approves Drone Kills," *Washington Post*, June 6, 2016, https://www
    .washingtonpost.com/world/national-security/newly-declassified-document
    -sheds-light-on-how-president-approves-drone-strikes/2016/08/06/f424fe50-5be0
    -11e6-831d-0324760ca856_story.html.

56 Tayler Letta, "How Obama's Drones Rulebook Enabled Trump," *Human Rights
    Watch*, September 26, 2017, https://www.hrw.org/news/2017/09/26/how-obamas
    -drones-rulebook-enabled-trump.

57 Maya Foa, "Trump's Secret Assassinations Programme," Reprieve, n.d., accessed
    February 5, 2018, https://reprieve.org.uk/update/game-changer-trumps-new
    -attacks-on-human-rights/.

58 President Donald J. Trump, "Executive Order on Revocation of Reporting
    Requirement," White House, March 6, 2019, https://www.whitehouse.gov
    /presidential-actions/executive-order-revocation-reporting-requirement/; BBC,
    "Trump Revokes Obama Rule on Reporting Drone Strike Deaths," *BBC News*,
    March 7, 2019, https://www.bbc.com/news/world-us-canada-47480207.

59 Quoted in Babich, *Nietzsche's Philosophy of Science*, 102.

60 Babich, *Nietzsche's Philosophy of Science*, 199.

61 Babich, *Nietzsche's Philosophy of Science*, 199.

62 Babich, *Nietzsche's Philosophy of Science*, 199.

63 Pugliese, "Drone Casino Mimesis."

64 Noah Shachtam, "CIA Chief: 'Only Game in Town' for Stopping Al Qaeda,"
    Wired, May 19, 2009, https://www.wired.com/2009/05/cia-chief-drones-only
    -game-in-town-for-stopping-al-qaeda/.

65 Becker and Shane, "Secret 'Kill List.'"

66 Hayles, "Unfinished Work," 160.

67 Rizzo, *Company Man*, 300.

68 Quoted in Amnesty International, "'Will I Be Next?,'" 28.

69 Jonathan Albright, "Algorithms Might Be Everywhere, but Like Us, They're
    Deeply Flawed," *The Conversation*, October 20, 2016, theconversation.com
    /algorithms-might-be-everywhere-but-like-us-theyre-deeply-flawed-66838.

70 Lauren J. Young, "Computer Scientists Find Bias in Algorithms," *IEE Spec-
    trum*, August 21, 2015, http://spectrum.ieee.org/tech-talk/computing/software
    /computer-scientists-find-bias-in-algorithms.

71 See, for example, Latour, *Reassembling the Social*, 1–87.

72 Nietzsche, *The Will to Power*, 278.

73 Nietzsche, *The Will to Power*, 278.

74 Aid, *Intel Wars*, 215.

75 Nietzsche, *The Will to Power*, 274.

76 Foucault, *Lectures on the Will to Know*, 212.

77 Quoted in Scahill and Greenwald, "The NSA's Secret Role."

78 Quoted in Scahill and Greenwald, "The NSA's Secret Role."

79 Gregory, "The Territory of the Screen," 146. See also Gregory's extensive body of work on drones available at his *Geographical Imagination: War, Spaces and Bodies* website, accessed August 30, 2018, https://geographicalimaginations.com/.

80 Fanon, *The Wretched of the Earth*, 31.

81 Quoted in Scahill, *Dirty Wars*, 358.

82 Quoted in "US Drone War Must Be 'Brought into the Light,'" *Channel 4 News*, February 25, 2014, http://www.channel4.com/news/drones-pakistan-kareem-khan -warfare-usa-cia-justice-video.

83 Quoted in Scahill and Greenwald, "The NSA's Secret Role."

84 Charlotte Silver, "Why Has Israel Censored Reporting on Drones?," *Electronic Intifada*, April 18, 2016, https://electronicintifada.net/blogs/charlotte-silver/why -has-israel-censored-reporting-drones.

85 Nietzsche, *The Will to Power*, 267.

86 Quoted in Babich, *Nietzsche's Philosophy of Science*, 97.

87 Nietzsche, *The Birth of Tragedy*, 95–99.

88 Nietzsche, *The Birth of Tragedy*, 33.

89 Derrida, *The Truth in Painting*, 69.

90 Quoted in Scahill et al., *The Assassination Complex*, 157.

91 AFSIR Predator, "Confessions of a Drone Veteran: Why Using Them Is More Dangerous Than the Government Is Telling You," *Salon*, September 16, 2014, http://www.salon.com/2014/09/16/confessions_of_a_drone_veteran_why_using _them_is_more_dangerous_than_the_government_is_telling_you/.

92 Nietzsche, *The Birth of Tragedy*, 93.

93 Nicole Abé, "The Woes of an American Drone Operator," *Spiegel Online*, December 14, 2014, http://www.spiegel.de/international/world/pain-continues-after-war-for -american-drone-pilot-a-872726-druck.html.

94 Quoted in Babich, *Nietzsche's Philosophy of Science*, 110.

95 George, *The Babylonian Gilgamesh Epic*, 238.

96 Castillo, "Nagbu," 220.

97 "The Epic of Gilgamesh," *cyclopedia.net*, accessed October 21, 2016, http://ko .cyclopedia.asia/wiki/The_Epic_of_Gilgamesh.

98 See Heidegger, *Basic Writings*, 315.

99 Nietzsche, *The Birth of Tragedy*, 98.

100 #NotaBugSplat, "A Giant Art Installation Targets Predator Drone Operators," accessed December 6, 2016, https://notabugsplat.com/.

101 Chief Justice Dost Muhammad Khan, Judgment Sheet in the Peshawar High Court, Peshawar Judicial Department, Writ Petition No. 1551-P/2012, April 11, 2013, http://www.peshawarhighcourt.gov.pk/image_bank/Mr_Justice_Dost _Muhammad_Khan/wp1551-12.pdf, 15.

102 Khan, Judgment Sheet in the Peshawar High Court, 17.

103 Khan, Judgment Sheet in the Peshawar High Court, 18.

104 Stone, *Should Trees Have Standing?*, 7.

105 Majid, *Effect of British Colonization on Pakistan's Legal System*, 35.

106 Wadiwel, *The War against Animals*, 147.

107 Wadiwel, *The War against Animals*, 147.

108 Khan, Judgment Sheet in the Peshawar High Court, 4.

109 Francione, *Animals, Property, and the Law*, 166,

110 Francione, *Animals, Property, and the Law*, 102.

111 Khan, Judgment Sheet in the Peshawar High Court, 5.

112 Khan, Judgment Sheet in the Peshawar High Court, 13.

113 Shukin, *Animal Capital*, 6–7.

114 Jeremy Scahill, "Yemeni Reporter Who Exposed U.S. Drone Strike Freed from Prison after Jailing at Obama's Request," *Democracy Now!*, July 25, 2013, http://www.democracynow.org/2013/7/25/yemeni_reporter_who_exposed_us_drone_strike_freed_from_prison_after_jailing_at_obamas_request.

115 Farea Al-Muslimi, "United States Senate Judiciary Committee, Subcommittee on the Constitution, Civil Rights and Human Rights, Drone Wars: The Constitutional and Counterterrorism Implications of Targeted Killing. Statement of Farea Al-Muslimi," April 23, 2013, http://www.emptywheel.net/wp-content/uploads/2013/04/04-23-13Al-MuslimiTestimony.pdf.

116 Alkarama Foundation, *The United States' War on Yemen*, 16.

117 Deloria, *God Is Red*, 296.

118 Hogan, "We Call It *Tradition*," 25.

119 Merleau-Ponty, *The Visible and the Invisible*, 127.

120 Merleau-Ponty, *The Visible and the Invisible*, 127.

121 Quoted in Alkarama Foundation, *The United States' War on Yemen*, 20.

122 Merleau-Ponty, *Nature*, 268, 271.

123 Merleau-Ponty, *The Visible and the Invisible*, 272.

124 Merleau-Ponty, *The Visible and the Invisible*, 141, 143.

125 Quoted in Human Rights Watch, *"Between a Drone and Al-Qaeda"*, 77.

126 Merleau-Ponty, *The Visible and the Invisible*, 248, 133.

127 Merleau-Ponty, *The Visible and the Invisible*, 135.

128 Merleau-Ponty, *Nature*, 93.

129 Merleau-Ponty, *Nature*, 92.

130 I am indebted here to Susan Stryker for her compelling work on the power of *trans* and for her exhortation to transpose its interrogative and creative effects across heterogeneous spaces, bodies, and entities. See, for example, Stryker, "(De)Subjugated Knowledges," and "My Words to Victor Frankenstein above the Village of Chamounix," 237–54.

131 Gregory, "Moving Targets and Violent Geographies," 276, 281.

132 Merleau-Ponty, *The Visible and the Invisible*, 136.

133 Merleau-Ponty, *The Visible and the Invisible*, 114.

134 Gans, *Signs of Paradox*, 145.

135 Gans, *Signs of Paradox*, 177.

136 David Wallenchinsky, "Why Do They Hate Us?," *Huffington Post*, November 12, 2011, http://www.huffingtonpost.com/david-wallechinsky/why-do-they-hate-us_2 _b_957277.html. As Derek Gregory demonstrates in "Little Boys and Blue Skies," this US practice of usurping victim status has a long history that includes projecting itself as the victim of a future nuclear war in the wake of its destruction of both Hiroshima and Nagasaki.

137 Gans, *Signs of Paradox*, 134.

138 Gans, *Signs of Paradox*, 163.

139 This is not to discount the posttraumatic stress that some drone operators experience, see, for example, Pugliese, "Drone Casino Mimesis," 504–5.

140 Quoted in Chris Wood and Christina Lamb, "CIA Tactics in Pakistan Include Targeting Rescuers and Funerals," *Bureau of Investigative Journalism*, February 4, 2012, https://www.thebureauinvestigates.com/2012/02/04/obama-terror-drones -cia-tactics-in-pakistan-include-targeting-rescuers-and-funerals/.

141 Wood and Lamb, "CIA Tactics in Pakistan Include Targeting Rescuers and Funerals."

142 Merleau-Ponty, *The Visible and the Invisible*, 139–40.

143 Quoted in Scahill, *Dirty Wars*, 305.

144 Quoted in Yara Bayoumy, "Al Qaeda Gains Sympathy in Yemen as US Drone Strikes Wedding Party," *Business Insider*, December 10, 2013, http://www .businessinsider.com.au/al-qaeda-gains-sympathy-in-yemen-as-us-drone-strikes-a -wedding-party-2013-12.

145 Martin with Sasser, *Predator*, 14, 43, 49, 51, 129, 141, 228, 252, 255, 277, 304.

146 Heidegger, *The Fundamental Concepts of Metaphysics*, 267.

147 Heidegger, *Poetry, Language, Thought*, 178.

148 Adams, *The Sexual Politics of Meat*, 20–21.

149 Cora Currier, Josh Begley, and Margot Williams, "Our Condolences, Afghanistan," *Intercept*, February 27, 2015, https://theintercept.co/condolences/.

150 LaDuke with Cruz, *The Militarization of Indian Country*, xvi.

151 Bigger and Neimark, "Weaponizing Nature," 14; Belcher et al., "Hidden Carbon Costs of the 'Everywhere War,'" 12.

Afterword

1   Andoni, "Interviewed in Beit Sahour, West Bank," 152.

2   Saif, *The Drone Eats with Me*, 128.

3   Wildcat, *Red Alert!*, 14.

4   Sherwin, *Visualizing Law in the Age of the Digital Baroque*, 5.

5   MacCormack, "Art, Nature, Ethics," 129.

6   See Plumwood, *The Eye of the Crocodile*, 84.

7   Latour, *Facing Gaia*, 109, 115, 110.

8   Lestel, "The Carnivore's Ethics," 165.

9   Plumwood, *The Eye of the Crocodile*, 60–61.

10 Cajete, *Native Science*, 52–53.

11 Deloria, *God Is Red*, 296.

12 Bosselmann, "Grounding the Rule of Law," 75.

13 S. 3880 (109th): Animal Enterprise Terrorism Act, Govtrack, https://www
.govtrack.us/congress/bills/109/s3880/text.

14 S. 3880 (109th): Animal Enterprise Terrorism Act.

15 S. 3880 (109th): Animal Enterprise Terrorism Act.

16 Poulantzas, *State, Power, Socialism*, 46.

17 Bosselmann, "Grounding the Rule of Law," 75.

18 Eid, *My Country*, 148. I'm grateful to Derek Gregory for bringing this book to my
attention.

19 Quoted in Kathleen Calderwood, "Why New Zealand Is Granting a River the
Same Rights as a Citizen," *ABC RN*, September 6, 2016, http://www.abc.net.au
/radionational/programs/sundayextra/new-zealand-granting-rivers-and-forests
-same-rights-as-citizens/7816456; see also Eleanor Ainge Roy, "New Zealand
Gives Mount Taranaki Same Legal Rights as Person," *Guardian*, December 22,
2017, https://www.theguardian.com/world/2017/dec/22/new-zealand-gives-mount
-taranaki-same-legal-rights-as-a-person.

20 Quoted in Calderwood, "Why New Zealand Is Granting a River the Same Rights
as a Citizen."

21 Normand and af Jochnik, "The Legitimation of Violence," 412.

22 DiMento, *The Global Environment and International Law*, 23.

23 DiMento, *The Global Environment and International Law*, 156.

24 Anghie, *Imperialism, Sovereignty and the Making of International Law*, 33.

25 Miéville, *Between Equal Rights*, 292.

26 Hamilton, Bonneuil, and Gemmene, "Thinking the Anthropocene," 10.

27 I borrow this term from Stauffer, "Haeckel, Darwin, and Ecology," 140.

28 Derrida, *Acts of Religion*, 243.

29 Derrida, *Acts of Religion*, 247.

30 Colebrook, "What Is the Anthropo-Political?," 105.

31 Latour, "Telling Friends from Foe in the Time of the Anthropocene," 146.

32 Kwaymullina and Kwaymullina, "Learning to Read the Signs," 201.

33 Foucault, *"Society Must Be Defended"*, 254.

34 See, for example, Kuletz, *The Tainted Desert*; Masco, *The Nuclear Borderlands*; Voyles,
Wastelanding; Yalat and Oak Valley Communities with Mattingley, *Maralinga*.

35 Chief Arvol Looking Horse, "Original Caretakers of Mother Earth—Elders
Council Statement," *Unsettling America: Decolonization in Theory and Practice*,
November 12, 2013, https://unsettlingamerica.wordpress.com/2013/11/12/original
-caretakers-of-mother-earth-elders-council-statement/.

Abdo, Nahla, and Nira Yuval-Davis. "Palestine, Israel and the Zionist Settler Project." In *Unsettling Settler Societies: Articulations of Gender, Ethnicity and Class*, edited by Daiva Stasiulis and Nira Yuval-Davis, 291–322. London: Sage, 1995.

AbuZayyad, Ziad. "How the Occupation Affects Palestinian Natural Resources: Interview with Dr Yousef Abu Safieh." *Palestine-Israel Journal* 19, no. 3 (2014): 140–50.

Adams, Carol J. *The Sexual Politics of Meat*. New York: Bloomsbury, 2015.

Adamson, Rebecca. "First Nations Survival and the Future of the Earth." In *Original Instructions: Indigenous Teachings for a Sustainable Future*, edited by Melissa K. Nelson, 27–35. Rochester, VT: Bear and Company, 2008.

Adorno, Theodor. *Minima Moralia: Reflections from Damaged Life*. Translated by E. F. N. Jephcott. London: Verso, 2005.

af Jochnick, Chris, and Roger Normand. "The Legitimation of Violence: A Critical History of the Laws of War." *Harvard International Law Journal* 35 (1994): 49-95.

Agamben, Giorgio. *Homo Sacer: Sovereign Power and Bare Life*. Translated by Daniel Heller-Roazen. Stanford, CA: Stanford University Press, 1998.

Agamben, Giorgio. *The Open: Man and Animal*. Translated by Kevin Attell. Stanford, CA: Stanford University Press, 2004.

Ahmed, Sara. *The Cultural Politics of Emotion*. Edinburgh: Edinburgh University Press, 2014.

Ahuja, Neel. *Bioinsecurities: Disease Interventions, Empire, and the Government of Species*. Durham, NC: Duke University Press, 2016.

Aid, Matthew M. *Intel Wars: The Secret History of the Fight against Terror*. London: Bloomsbury, 2012.

Alatout, Samer. "Narratives of Power: Territory, Population, and Environmental Politics in Palestine and Israel." In *Palestinian and Israeli Environmental Narratives: Proceedings of a Conference Held in Association with the Middle East Environmental Futures Project*, edited by Stuart Schoenfield, 299–312. Toronto: York University, 2005.

Amnesty International. *"Will I Be Next?" US Drone Strikes in Pakistan.* London: Amnesty International Publications, 2012.

Amoore, Louise. "Algorithmic War: Everyday Geographies of the War on Terror." *Antipode* 41, no. 1 (2009): 49–69.

Anderson, Nicole. "Pre- and Posthuman Animals: The Limits and Possibilities of Animal-Human Relations." In *Posthumous Life: Theorizing beyond the Posthuman,* edited by J. Weinstein and Clare Colebrook, 17–42. New York: Columbia University Press, 2017.

Anderson, Nicole. "A Proper Death: Penalties, Animals, and the Law." In *Deconstructing the Death Penalty: Derrida's Seminars and the New Abolitionism,* edited by K. Oliver and S. Straub, 159–74. New York: Fordham University Press, 2018.

Andoni, Ghassan. "Interviewed in Beit Sahour, West Bank." In *Palestine Speaks: Narratives of Life under Occupation,* edited by Cate Malek and Mateo Hoke, 148–73. San Francisco: Voice of Witness, 2014.

Anghie, Antony. *Imperialism, Sovereignty and the Making of International Law.* Cambridge: Cambridge University Press, 2007.

Assaf, Karen. "Environmental Problems Affecting Palestinian Women under Occupation." In *Women and the Israeli Occupation: The Politics of Change,* edited by Tamar Mayer, 164–78. London: Routledge, 1994.

Avelar, Idelber. "Amerindian Perspectivism and Non-human Rights." *alter/nativas* 1 (2013): 1–21.

Babich, Babette E. *Nietzsche's Philosophy of Science.* Albany: State University of New York Press, 1994.

Barakat, Rana. "Writing/Righting Palestine Studies: Settler Colonialism, Indigenous Sovereignty and Resisting the Ghost(s) of History." *Settler Colonial Studies* 8, no. 3 (2018): 349–63.

Baratay, Eric, and Elizabeth Hardouin-Fugier. *Zoo: A History of Zoological Gardens in the West.* London: Reaktion, 2004.

Bardenstein, Carol B. "Threads of Memory and Discourses of Rootedness: Of Trees, Oranges and the Prickly-Pear Cactus in Israel/Palestine." *Edibiyat* 8 (1998): 1–36.

Bardenstein, Carol B. "Trees, Forests, and the Shaping of Palestinian and Israeli Collective Memory." In *Acts of Memory: Cultural Recall in the Present,* edited by Mieke Bal, Jonathan Crewe, and Leo Spitzer, 148–70. Hanover, NH: University Press of New England, 1999.

Barghouti, Omar. "European Collusion in Israel's Slow Genocide." In *The Plight of Palestinians: A Long History of Destruction,* edited by William A. Cook, 181–84. New York: Palgrave Macmillan, 2010.

Bélanger, Pierre, and Alexander Arroyo. *Ecologies of Power: Countermapping the Logistical Landscapes and Military Geographies of the US Department of Defense.* Cambridge, MA: MIT Press, 2016.

Belcher, Oliver, Patrick Bigger, Ben Neimark, and Cara Kennelly. "Hidden Carbon Costs of the 'Everywhere War': Logistics, Geopolitical Ecology, and the Carbon Boot-Print of the U.S. Military." *Transactions of the British Institute of Geographers* 44, no. 2 (2019): 1–16.

Bell, Lynne. *Adrian Stimson: Beyond Redemption*. Saskatoon, SK: Mendel Art Gallery, 2010.

Bell, Suzanne. *Crime and Circumstance: Investigating the History of Forensic Science*. West-port, CT: Praeger, 2008.

Bennett, Jane. "The Force of Things: Steps toward an Ecology of Matter." *Political Theory* 32, no. 3 (2004): 347–72.

Bennett, Jane. *Vibrant Matter: A Political Ecology of Things*. Durham, NC: Duke University Press, 2010.

Bentham, Jeremy. *An Introduction to the Principles of Morals and Legislation*. Oxford: Clarendon, 2005.

Benton, Ted. "Rights and Justice on a Shared Planet: More Rights or New Relations?" *Theoretical Criminology* 2, no. 2 (1998): 149–75.

Bergman, Gerald. "Darwinian Criminality Theory: A Tragic Chapter in History." *Rivista di Biologia/Biology Forum* 98, no. 1 (2005): 47–70.

Bhandar, Brenna. *Colonial Lives of Property: Law, Land, and Racial Regimes of Ownership*. Durham, NC: Duke University Press, 2018.

Bigger, Patrick, and Benjamin D. Neimark. "Weaponizing Nature: The Geopolitical Ecology of the U.S. Navy's Biofuel Program." *Political Geography* 60 (2017): 13–22.

Birch, Tony. "Afterword." In *Unstable Relations: Indigenous People and Environmental-ism in Contemporary Australia*, edited by Eve Vincent and Timothy Neale, 356–79. Crawley, WA: UWA, 2016.

Birch, Tony. "'The Lifting of the Sky': Outside the Anthropocene." In *Humanities for the Environment: Integrating Knowledge, Forging New Constellations of Practice*, edited by Joni Adamson and Michael Davis, 195–209. London: Routledge, 2017.

Birch, Tony. "'On What Terms Can We Speak?': Refusal, Resurgence and Climate Justice." *Coolabah*, nos. 24–25 (2018): 2–16.

Bird-David, Nurit. "'Animism' Revisited: Personhood, Environment, and Relational Epistemology." In *Readings in Indigenous Religions*, edited by Graham Harvey, 72–105. London: Continuum, 2002.

Black, C. F. *The Land Is the Source of the Law: A Dialogic Encounter with Indigenous Jurispru-dence*. London: Routledge, 2011.

Blanchot, Maurice. "Everyday Speech." *Yale French Studies*, no. 73 (1987): 12–20.

Blanchot, Maurice. *Political Writings, 1953–1993*. Translated by Zakir Paul. New York: Fordham University Press, 2010.

Blumenthal, Max. *The 51 Day War: Ruin and Resistance in Gaza*. New York: Nation Books, 2015.

Bodansky, Daniel, Jutta Brunnée, and Elle Hey. "International Environmental Law: Mapping the Field." In *The Oxford Handbook of International Environmental Law*, edited by Daniel Bodansky, Jutta Brunnée, and Elle Hey, 1–28. Oxford: Oxford University Press, 2010.

Bosselmann, Klaus. "Grounding the Rule of Law." In *Rule of Law for Nature: New Dimen-sions and Ideas in Environmental Law*, edited by Christina Voigt, 75–93. Cambridge: Cambridge University Press, 2013.

Bosselmann, Klaus. "The Rule of Law in the Anthropocene." In *The Search for Environ-mental Justice*, edited by Paul Martin, Sadeq Z. Bigdell, Trevor Daya-Winterbottom,

Willemien du Plessis, and Amanda Kennedy, 44–61. Cheltenham, UK: Edward Elgar, 2015.

Boumediene, Lakhdar, and Mustafa Ait Idir. *Witnesses of the Unseen: Seven Years in Guantánamo*. Stanford, CA: Redwood Press, 2017.

Bouris, Dimitris. "The Vicious Cycle of Building and Destroying: The 2014 War on Gaza." *Mediterranean Politics* 20, no. 1 (2015): 1–7.

Braverman, Irus. "Captive: Zoometric Operations in Gaza." *Public Culture* 29, no. 1 (2016): 191–215.

Braverman, Irus. *Planted Flags: Trees, Land, and Law in Israel/Palestine*. New York: Cambridge University Press, 2014.

Breaking the Silence. *Our Harsh Logic: Israeli Soldiers' Testimonies from the Occupied Territories, 2000–2010*. New York: Picador, 2013.

Breaking the Silence. *This Is How We Thought in Gaza: Soldier's Testimonies and Photographs from Operation "Protective Edge" (2014)*. Accessed May 16, 2017. https://www.breakingthesilence.org.il/pdf/ProtectiveEdge.pdf.

Broswimmer, Franz J. *Ecocide: A Short History of Mass Extinction of Species*. London: Pluto, 2002.

Bruch, Carl E. "Introduction." In *The Environmental Consequences of War*, edited by Jay E. Austin and Carl E. Bruch, 13–15. Cambridge: Cambridge University Press, 2007.

B'Tselem. "Thirsty for a Solution: The Water Crisis in the Occupied Territories and Its Resolution in the Final-Status Agreement." *B'Tselem: The Israeli Information Center for Human Rights in the Occupied Territories*, July 2000. Accessed May 16, 2019. https://www.btselem.org/publications/summaries/200007_thirsty_for_a_solution.

Bui, Michelle, Dean Chan, Suvendrini Perera, Joseph Pugliese, Ayman Qwaider, and Charandev Singh. "Extraterritorial Killings: The Weaponisation of Bodies (Australia)." *Deathscapes: Mapping Race and Violence in Settler States*, 2018. Accessed November 12, 2018. https://www.deathscapes.org/case-studies/case-study-4-extraterritorial-killings-the-weaponisation-of-bodies/#parallaxcategory0.

Bursitt, Les, Mary Jacobs, Deborah Lennis, Aunty Beryl Timbery-Beller, and Merv Ryan. *Dharawal: The Story of the Dharawal Speaking People of Southern Sydney*. Accessed July 21, 2016. https://lha.uow.edu.au/content/groups/public/@web/@lha/documents/doc/uow162226.pdf.

Busbridge, Rachel. "Israel-Palestine and the Settler Colonial 'Turn': From Interpretation to Decolonization." *Theory, Culture and Society* 35, no. 1 (2018): 91–115.

Busbridge, Rachel. "Performing Colonial Sovereignty and the Israeli 'Separation' Wall." *Social Identities* 19, no. 5 (2018): 653–69.

Bybee, Jay S. "Memorandum for Alberto Gonzales Counsel to the President, RE: Standards of Conduct for Interrogation under 18 U.S.C. §§2340–2340A, August 1, 2002." In *The Torture Papers: The Road to Abu Ghraib*, edited by Karen J. Greenberg and Joshua L. Dratel, 172–217. Cambridge and New York: Cambridge University Press, 2005.

Cajete, Gregory. *Native Science: Natural Laws of Interdependence*. Santa Fe: Clear Light Books, 2000.

Calarco, Matthew. *Zoographies: The Question of the Animal from Heidegger to Derrida*. New York: Columbia University Press, 2008.

Campbell, Tom. *Justice*. Basingstoke, UK: Palgrave Macmillan, 2010.

Carlson, Bronwyn. "'Disposable People' and Ongoing Colonial Violence." Paper delivered at Slow Violence, Global Traumas symposium, Macquarie University, Sydney, Australia, November 29, 2017.

Castillo, Jorge Silva. "Nagbu: Totality or Abyss in the First Verse of Gilgamesh." *Iraq* 60 (1998): 219–221.

Chen, Mel Y. *Animacies: Biopolitics, Racial Mattering, and Queer Effect*. Durham, NC: Duke University Press, 2012.

Clements, Nicholas Patrick. "Frontier Conflict in Van Diemen's Land." Honors thesis, University of Tasmania, 2013.

Cohen, Shaul Ephraim. *The Politics of Planting: Israel-Palestinian Competition for Control of Land in the Jerusalem Periphery*. Chicago: University of Chicago Press, 1993.

Colebrook, Claire. "What Is the Anthropo-Political?" In *Twilight of the Anthropocene Idols*, edited by Tom Cohen, Claire Colebrook, and J. Hillis Miller, 81–125. London: Open Humanities, 2016.

Colón-Ríos, Joel I. "On the Theory and Practice of the Rights of Nature." In *The Search for Environmental Justice*, edited by Paul Martin, Sadeq Z. Bigdell, Trevor Daya-Winterbottom, Willemien du Plessis, and Amanda Kennedy, 120–34. Cheltenham, UK: Edward Elgar, 2015.

Cook, Jonathan. "'The Lab': Israel Tests Weapons, Tactics on Captive Palestinian Population." *Washington Report on Middle East Affairs*, September 2013. https://www.wrmea.org/2013-september/the-lab-israel-tests-weapons-on-captive-palestinian-population.html.

Cook, William A., ed. *The Plight of the Palestinians: A Long History of Destruction*. New York: Palgrave Macmillan, 2010.

Coole, Diana, and Samantha Frost, eds. *New Materialisms: Ontology, Agency, and Politics*. Durham, NC: Duke University Press, 2010.

Coulthard, Glen Sean. *Red Skin, White Masks: Rejecting the Colonial Politics of Recognition*. Minneapolis: University of Minnesota Press, 2014.

Coyle, Sean, and Karen Morrow. *The Philosophical Foundations of Environmental Law: Property, Rights and Nature*. Oxford: Hart, 2004.

Crawford, Neta C. "Pentagon Fuel Use, Climate Change, and the Costs of War." *Costs of War*, Watson Institute of International and Public Affairs, June 12, 2019. https://watson.brown.edu/costsofwar/files/cow/imce/papers/2019/Pentagon%20Fuel%20Use%2C%20Climate%20Change%20and%20the%20Costs%20of%20War%20Final.pdf.

Cronon, William. "The Trouble with Wilderness; or, Getting Back to the Wrong Nature." *Environmental History* 1, no. 1 (1996): 7–28.

Cullinan, Cormac. *Wild Law: A Manifesto for Earth Justice*. Totnes, UK: Green Books, 2011.

Dajani, Muna. "Drying Palestine: Israel's Systemic Water War." *Al-Shabaka: The Palestinian Policy Network*, September 4, 2014. https://al-shabaka.org/briefs/drying-palestine-israels-systemic-water-war/.

Da'Na, Seif. "Israel's Settler-Colonial Water Regime: The Second Contradiction of Zionism." *Holy Land Studies* 12, no. 1 (2013): 43–70.

Dana, Tariq, and Ali Jarbawi. "A Century of Settler Colonialism in Palestine: Zionism's Entangled Project." *Brown Journal of World Affairs* 24, no. 1 (2017): 197–219.

"Decolonization Is a Global Project: From Palestine to the Americas." Special issue, *Decolonization: Indigeneity, Education and Society* 6, no. 1 (2017).

Defense for Children International Palestine. *Operation Protective Edge: A War Waged on Gaza's Children*. Ramallah: Defense for Children International Palestine, 2015.

DeLanda, Manuel. *A New Philosophy of Society: Assemblage Theory and Social Complexity*. London: Continuum, 2007.

DeLanda, Manuel. *War in the Age of Intelligent Machines*. New York: Swerve, 1991.

Deleuze, Gilles. *The Fold*. Translated by Tom Conley. Minneapolis: University of Minnesota Press, 1993.

Deleuze, Gilles. *Francis Bacon: The Logic of Sensation*. Translated by Daniel W. Smith. Minneapolis: University of Minnesota Press, 2004.

Deloria, Vine, Jr. *God Is Red: A Native View of Religion*. Golden, CO: Fulcrum, 2003.

Deloria, Vine, Jr. *The World We Used to Live In*. Golden, CO: Fulcrum, 2006.

Denes, Nick. "From Tanks to Wheelchairs: Unmanned Aerial Vehicles, Zionist Battlefield Experiments, and the Transparent Civilian." In *Surveillance and Control in Israel/Palestine: Population, Territory and Power*, edited by Elia Zureik, David Lyon, and Yasmeen Abu-Laban, 171–96. London: Routledge, 2011.

Der Derian, James. *Virtuous War*. New York: Routledge, 2009.

Derrida, Jacques. *Acts of Religion*. Edited and translated by Gil Anidjar. New York: Routledge, 2002.

Derrida, Jacques. *The Animal That Therefore I Am*. Translated by David Wills. New York: Fordham University Press, 2008.

Derrida, Jacques. *The Beast and the Sovereign*. Vol. 1. Translated by Geoffrey Bennington. Chicago: University of Chicago Press, 2009.

Derrida, Jacques. "A Discussion with Jacques Derrida." *Theory and Event* 5, no. 1 (2001): 1–24.

Derrida, Jacques. "'Eating Well,' or the Calculation of the Subject." In *Points . . . Interviews, 1974–1994*, edited by Elizabeth Weber and translated by Peggy Kamuf et al., 255–87. Stanford, CA: Stanford University Press, 1995.

Derrida, Jacques. "Faith and Knowledge: The Two Sources of 'Religion' at the Limits of Reason Alone." In *Religion*, edited by Jacques Derrida and Gianni Vattimo, 1–78. Cambridge: Polity, 1998.

Derrida, Jacques. *Memoires for Paul de Man*. Translated by Cecile Lindsay, Jonathan Culler, Eduardo Cadava, and Peggy Kamuf. New York: Columbia University Press, 1989.

Derrida, Jacques. *Of Grammatology*. Translated by Gayatri Chakravorty Spivak. Baltimore: Johns Hopkins University Press, 1976.

Derrida, Jacques. *Rogues: Two Essays on Reason*. Translated by Pascale-Anne Brault and Michael Naas. Stanford, CA: Stanford University Press, 2005.

Derrida, Jacques. *The Truth in Painting*. Translated by Geoff Bennington and Ian McLeod. Chicago: University of Chicago Press, 1987.

Derrida, Jacques. "Violence against Animals." In *For What Tomorrow . . . : A Dialogue, Jacques Derrida and Elisabeth Roudinesco*, translated by Jeff Fort, 62–76. Stanford, CA: Stanford University Press, 2004.

Derrida, Jacques. *Writing and Difference*. Translated by Alan Bass. London: Routledge and Kegan Paul, 1981.

Despret, Vinciane. *What Would Animals Say If We Asked the Right Questions?* Translated by Brett Buchanan. Minneapolis: University of Minnesota Press, 2016.

DiMento, Joseph F. C. *The Global Environment and International Law*. Austin: University of Texas Press, 2003.

Dolphin, Rick, and Iris van der Tuin. *New Materialisms: Interviews and Cartographies*. Ann Arbor: Open Humanities Press, 2012.

Dowie, Mark. *Conservation Refugees: The Hundred-Year Conflict between Global Conservation and Native Peoples*. Cambridge, MA: MIT Press, 2011.

Dreyfus, Hubert L., and Paul Rabinow. *Michel Foucault: Beyond Structuralism and Hermeneutics*. London: Harvester Wheatsheaf, 1982.

Drumbl, Mark A. "Waging War against the World: The Need to Move from War Crimes to Environmental Crimes." In *The Environmental Consequences of War*, edited by Jay E. Austin and Carl E. Bruch, 620–46. Cambridge: Cambridge University Press, 2007.

Dupuy, Pierre-Marie, and Jorge E. Viñuales. *International Environmental Law*. Cambridge: Cambridge University Press, 2015.

Eid, Kassem. *My Country: A Syrian Memoir*. London: Bloomsbury, 2018.

El-Haddad, Laila. "After the Smoke Clears: Gaza's Everyday Resistance." *Journal of Palestinian Studies* 44, no. 1 (2014): 120–25.

Erakat, Noura, and Tareq Radi, eds. "Gaza in Context: War and Settler Colonialism." *JADMAG* 4, no. 1 (2016): 1–56.

Errachidi, Ahmed, with Gillian Slovo. *The General: The Ordinary Man Who Challenged Guantánamo*. London: Chatto and Windus, 2013.

Esposito, Roberto. *Third Person: Politics of Life and Philosophy of the Impersonal*. Translated by Zakiya Hanafi. Cambridge: Polity, 2012.

Evans, E. P. *The Criminal Prosecution and Capital Punishment of Animals*. 1906. Reprint, Clark, NJ: Lawbook Exchange, 2009.

Falah, Ghazi-Walid. "The Geopolitics of 'Enclavisation' and the Demise of a Two-State Solution to the Israeli-Palestinian Conflict." *Third World Quarterly* 26, no. 8 (2005): 1341–72.

Falk, Richard. "The Environmental Law of War: An Introduction." In *Environmental Protection and the Law of War: A "Fifth Geneva" Convention on the Protection of the Environment in Time of Armed Conflict?*, edited by Glen Plant, 78–95. London: Belhaven Press, 1992.

Fallon, Mark. *Unjustifiable Means: The Inside Story of How the CIA, Pentagon, and US Government Conspired to Torture*. New York: Regan Arts, 2017.

Fanon, Frantz. *The Wretched of the Earth*. Translated by Richard Philcox. New York: Grove Press, 2004.

Filiu, Jean-Pierre. "The Twelve Wars on Gaza." *Journal of Palestine Studies* 44, no. 1 (2014): 52–60.

Finkelstein, Norman G. *Gaza: An Inquest into Its Martyrdom*. Oakland, CA: University of California Press, 2018.

Foley, Gary. "Black Power Australia and Aboriginal-Palestinian Solidarity: An Interview with Dr. Gary Foley." Interview by Noura Erakat. *Status Hour*, July 17, 2019. http://www.statushour.com/en/Interview/2397.

Foucault, Michel. *Abnormal: Lectures at the Collège de France, 1974-1975*. Translated by Graham Burchell. New York: Picador, 2003.

Foucault, Michel. *About the Hermeneutics of the Self: Lectures at Dartmouth College, 1980*. Translated by Graham Burchell. Chicago: University of Chicago Press, 2016.

Foucault, Michel. *The Birth of Biopolitics: Lectures at the Collège de France, 1978-1979*. Translated by Graham Burchell. Basingstoke, UK: Palgrave Macmillan, 2008.

Foucault, Michel. *The History of Sexuality*. Vol. 1, *An Introduction*. Translated by Robert Hurley. London: Penguin, 1990.

Foucault, Michel. *Lectures on the Will to Know: Lectures at the Collège de France, 1970-1971*. Translated by Graham Burchell. Basingstoke, UK: Palgrave Macmillan, 2013.

Foucault, Michel. *Security, Territory, Population: Lectures at the Collège de France, 1977-1978*. Translated by Graham Burchell. Basingstoke, UK: Palgrave Macmillan, 2007.

Foucault, Michel. *"Society Must Be Defended": Lectures at the Collège de France, 1975-1976*. Translated by David Macey. New York: Picador, 2003.

Francione, Gary. *Animals, Property, and the Law*. Philadelphia: Temple University Press, 2007.

Frazer, Ryan, and Bronwyn Carlson. "Indigenous Memes and the Invention of a People." *Social Media + Society* 3, no. 4 (2017): 1-12.

Fressoz, Jean-Baptiste. "Losing the Earth Knowingly." In *The Anthropocene and the Global Environmental Crisis*, edited by C. Hamilton, C. Bonneuil, and F. Gemenne, 70-83. New York: Routledge, 2015.

Friends of the Earth. *Environmental Nakba: Environmental Injustice and Violations of the Israeli Occupation of Palestine: A Report of the Friends of the Earth International Observer Mission to the West Bank*. Amsterdam: Friends of the Earth International, 2013.

Gagliano, Monica. "In a Green Frame of Mind: Perspectives on the Behavioural Ecology and Cognitive Nature of Plants." *AoB Plants* 7 (2015): n.p. Accessed February 22, 2016. doi:10.1093/aobpla/plu075.

Gans, Eric. *Signs of Paradox: Irony, Resentment, and Other Mimetic Structures*. Stanford, CA: Stanford University Press, 1997.

Gasteyer, Stephen, Jad Isaac, Jane Hillal, and Sean Walsh. "Water Grabbing in Colonial Perspective: Land and Water in Israel/Palestine." *Water Alternatives* 5, no. 2 (2012): 450-68.

George, A. R., ed. *The Babylonian Gilgamesh Epic, Introduction, Critical Edition and Cuneiform Texts*. Vol. 1. Oxford: Oxford University Press, 2003.

Ghanim, Honaida. "Thanatopolitics: The Case of the Colonial Occupation of Palestine." In *Thinking Palestine*, edited by Ronit Lentin, 65-81. London: Zed, 2008.

Giannacopoulos, Maria. "Mabo, Tampa and the Non-justiciability of Sovereignty." In *Our Patch: Enacting Australian Sovereignty Post-2001*, edited by Suvendrini Perera, 45-60. Perth: Network, 2007.

Gilbert, Mads. *Night in Gaza*. London: Skyscraper, 2015.

Gilio-Whitaker, Dina. *As Long as Grass Grows: The Indigenous Fight for Environmental Justice, from Colonization to Standing Rock*. Boston: Beacon, 2019.

Goodall, Heather. *From Invasion to Embassy: Land and Aboriginal Politics in New South Wales, 1770-1972*. Sydney: Sydney University Press, 2008.

Gordon, Neve, and Moriel Ram. "Ethnic Cleansing and the Formation of Settler Colonial Geographies." *Political Geography* 53 (2016): 20–29.

Graham, Stephen. "Bulldozers and Bombs: The Latest Palestinian-Israeli Conflict as Asymmetrical Urbicide." *Antipode* 34, no. 4 (2002): 642–49.

Graham, Stephen. "Laboratories of War: United States-Israeli Collaboration in Urban Warfare and Securitization." *Brown Journal of World Affairs* 17, no. 1 (2010): 35–51.

Green, Penny, and Amelia Smith. "Evicting Palestine." *State Crime* 5, no. 1 (2016): 81–108.

Greenstein, Ran. *Zionism and Its Discontents: A Century of Radical Dissent in Israel/Palestine*. London: Pluto, 2014.

Gregory, Derek. *The Colonial Present: Afghanistan, Palestine, Iraq*. Malden, MA: Blackwell, 2004.

Gregory, Derek. "Little Boys and Blue Skies." *Geographical Imaginations: War, Spaces and Bodies*. Accessed September 17, 2018. https://geographicalimaginations.com/.

Gregory, Derek. "Moving Targets and Violent Geographies." In *Spaces of Danger: Culture and Memory in the Everyday*, edited by Heather Merrill and Lisa M. Hoffman, 256–98. Athens: University of Georgia Press, 2015.

Gregory, Derek. "The Territory of the Screen." *Media Tropes eJournal* 6, no. 2 (2016): 126–47.

Griffith, Mark, and Jemima Repo. "Biopolitics and Checkpoint 300 in Occupied Palestine: Bodies, Affect, Discipline." *Political Geography* 65 (2018): 17–25.

Grindle, Donald A., and Bruce E. Johansen. *Ecocide of Native America: Environmental Destruction of Indian Lands and Peoples*. Santa Fe: Clear Light, 1995.

Gross, Alan G. *The Rhetoric of Science*. Cambridge, MA: Harvard University Press, 1990.

Haddad, M. "Palestinian Water Rights: Past, Present and Future." In *Water: Values and Rights*, edited by C. Messerschmid, 41–52. Ramallah: Palestine Academy Press, 2009.

Haglund, William D., and Marcella H. Sorg. "Forensic Anthropology." In *Forensic Science*, edited by Stuart H. James, Jon J. Nordby, and Suzanne Bell, 145–69. Boca Raton, FL: CRC Press, 2014.

Hall, Matthew. *Plants as Persons: A Philosophical Botany*. Albany: State University of New York Press, 2011.

Hamada, Mazen, Adnan Aish, and Mai Shahwan. "Potential Phosphorus Pollution in the Soil of the Northern Gaza Strip." *AGRIVITA* 33, no. 3 (2011): 291–99.

Hamilton, Clive, Christophe Bonneuil, and François Gemmene. "Thinking the Anthropocene." In *The Anthropocene and the Global Environmental Crisis*, edited by Clive Hamilton, Christophe Bonneuil, and François Gemmene, 1–13. London: Routledge, 2015.

Hammami, Rema. "On (Not) Suffering at Checkpoints: Palestinian Narrative Strategies of Surviving Israel's Carceral Geography." *Borderlands e-journal* 14, no. 1 (2015): 1–15.

Hanafi, Sari. "Explaining Spacio-cide in the Palestinian Territory: Colonization, Separation and State of Exception." *Current Sociology* 6, no. 2 (2012): 190–205.

Hanson, Elizabeth I. *Thoreau's Indian of the Mind*. Lewiston, NY: Edwin Mellen, 1992.

Haraway, Donna J. *When Species Meet*. Minneapolis: University of Minnesota Press, 2008.

Harvey, Graham. *Animism: Respecting the Living World*. London: Hurst & Company, 2005.

Hasian, Marouf, Jr. *Israel's Military Operations in Gaza: Telegenic Lawfare and Warfare*. London: Routledge, 2016.

Hayles, N. Katherine. "Unfinished Work: From Cyborg to Cognisphere." *Theory, Culture and Society* 23, nos. 7–8 (2006): 159–66.

Hearne, Vicki. *Adam's Task*. New York: Skyhorse, 2007.

Heidegger, Martin. *Basic Writings*. Edited and translated by David Farrell Krell. London: Routledge and Kegan Paul, 1978.

Heidegger, Martin. *The Fundamental Concepts of Metaphysics: World, Finitude, Solitude*. Translated by William McNeill and Nicholas Walker. Bloomington: Indiana University Press, 1995.

Heidegger, Martin. *Poetry, Language, Thought*. Translated by Albert Hofstadter. New York: Harper and Row, 1975.

Henckaerts, Jean-Marie, and Louise Doswald-Beck. *Customary International Law*. Vol. 1, *Rules*. Cambridge: Cambridge University Press, 2005.

Hermesh, Barak, Ma'ayan Maya, and Nadav Davidovitch. *Health Risks Assessment for the Israeli Population Following the Sanitary Crisis in Gaza*. EcoPeace Middle East, March 2019. http://ecopeaceme.org/wp-content/uploads/2019/05/Gaza-Health-Report_ENG.pdf.

Hever, Shir. "Exploitation of Palestinian Labour in Contemporary Zionist Colonialism." *Settler Colonial Studies* 2, no. 1 (2012): 124–32.

Higgins, Polly. *Eradicating Ecocide: Laws and Governance to Prevent the Destruction of Our Planet*. London: Shepherd-Walwyn, 2015.

Hoefle, Scott William. "Bitter Harvest: The Frontier Legacy of U.S. Internal Violence and Belligerent Imperialism." *Critique of Anthropology* 24, no. 3 (2004): 277–300.

Hogan, Linda. *Dwellings*. New York: W. W. Norton, 1995.

Hogan, Linda. "We Call It *Tradition*." In *The Handbook of Contemporary Animism*, edited by Graham Harvey, 17–26. New York: Routledge, 2015.

Houck, Max M., and Jay A. Siegel. *Fundamentals of Forensic Science*. Amsterdam: Elsevier, 2015.

Hulme, Karen. "Armed Conflict, Wanton Ecological Devastation and Scorched Earth Policies: How the 1990–91 Gulf Conflict Revealed the Inadequacies of the Current Laws to Ensure the Effective Protection and Preservation of the Natural Environment." *Journal of Armed Conflict Law* 2, no. 1 (1997): 45–81.

Human Rights Watch. *"Between a Drone and Al-Qaeda": The Civilian Cost of US Targeted Killings in Yemen*. New York: Human Rights Watch, 2013.

Human Rights Watch. *Rain of Fire: Israel's Unlawful Use of White Phosphorus in Gaza*. New York: Human Rights Watch, 2009.

Hutchins, Edwin. *Cognition in the Wild*. Cambridge, MA: MIT Press, 1995.

Ihmoud, Sarah. "Mohammed Abu-Khdeir and the Politics of Racial Terror in Occupied Jerusalem." *Borderlands e-journal* 14, no. 1 (2015): 1-23.

Inbar, Efraim, and Eitan Shamir. "'Mowing the Grass': Israel's Strategy for Protracted Intractable Conflict." *Journal of Strategic Studies* 37, no. 1 (2014): 65-90.

International Committee of the Red Cross. "Protocol Additional to the Geneva Conventions of 12 August 1949, and relating to the Protection of Victims of International Armed Conflicts (Protocol I), 8 June 1977." *International Committee of the Red Cross*. Accessed August 23, 2016. https://ihl-databases.icrc.org/ihl/INTRO/470.

Isaac, Jad. "Israeli Violations against the Palestinian Environment." *Applied Research Institute—Jerusalem*. Accessed May 17, 2019. http://www.arij.org/files/admin/2007/Israeli%20Violations%20against%20the%20Palestinian%20Environment.pdf.

Isaac, Jad, and Stephen Gasteyer. "The Issue of Biodiversity in Palestine." *Applied Research Institute—Jerusalem*. Accessed May 19, 2019. https://www.arij.org/files/admin/1995_the_issue_of_biodiversity_in_Palestine.pdf.

Isaac, Jad, and Jane Hilal. "Palestinian Landscape and the Israeli-Palestinian Conflict." *International Journal of Environmental Studies* 68, no. 4 (2011): 413-29.

Isaac, Jad, Khaldoun Rishmawi and Abeer Safar. "The Impact of Israel's Unilateral Actions on the Palestinian Environment." In *Palestinian and Israeli Environmental Narratives: Proceedings of a Conference Held in Association with the Middle East Environmental Futures Project*, edited by Stuart Schoefield, 229-45. Toronto: York University Press, 2005.

Jabary Salamanca, Omar, Mezna Qato, Kareem Rabie, and Sobhi Samour. "Past Is Present: Settler Colonialism in Palestine." *Settler Colonial Studies* 2, no. 1 (2012): 1-8.

Jaber, D. A. "Settler Colonialism and Ecocide: Case Study of Al-Khader, Palestine." *Settler Colonial Studies* 9, no. 1 (2019): 135-54.

James, Stuart H, Jon J. Nordby, and Suzanne Bell. "Justice and Science." In *Forensic Science*, edited by Stuart H. James, Jon J. Nordby, and Suzanne Bell, 3-21. Boca Raton, FL: CRC Press, 2014.

Jha, U. C. *Armed Conflict and Environmental Damage*. New Delhi: Vij Books, 2015.

Joint APN-PANAP Mission in Palestine. "Human Rights and Toxic Chemicals in the Occupied West Bank (Palestine)." May 2016. http://files.panap.net/resources/OccupiedWB-Palestine-Human-Rights-Toxic-Chemicals.pdf.

Jones, Owain, and Paul Cloke. "Non-human Agencies: Trees in Place and Time." In *Material Agency: Towards a Non-Anthropocentric Approach*, edited by Carl Knappett and Lambros Malafouris, 79-96. New York: Springer, 2008.

Joronen, Mikko. "'Death Comes Knocking on the Roof': Thanatopolitics of Ethical Killing during Operation Protective Edge in Gaza." *Antipode* 48, no. 2 (2016): 336-54.

Junka, Laura. "Camping in the Third Space: Agency, Representation, and the Politics of Gaza Beach." *Public Culture*, 18, no. 2 (2006): 348-59.

Kadi, Andrew. "Palestinians Back Standing Rock Sioux in 'Struggle for All Humanity.'" *Electronic Intifada*, September 10, 2016. https://electronicintifada.net/blogs/andrew-kadi/palestinians-back-standing-rock-sioux-struggle-all-humanity.

Kapitan, Tomis. "Historical Introduction to the Philosophical Issues." In *Philosophical Perspectives on the Israeli-Palestinian Conflict*, edited by Tomis Kapitan, 3–45. Armonk, NY: M. E. Sharpe, 1997.

Khalidi, Muhammad Ali. "Five Lessons Learned from the Israeli Attack on Gaza." *Theory and Event* 18, no. 1 (2015): 1–4.

Khalidi, Rashid I. "The Dahiya Doctrine, Proportionality, and War Crimes." *Journal of Palestine Studies* 44, no. 1 (2014): 5–13.

Khalidi, Rashid I. *The Iron Cage: The Story of the Palestinian Struggle for Statehood*. Boston: Beacon, 2007.

Khalidi, Walid, ed. *All That Remains: The Palestinian Villages Occupied and Depopulated by Israel in 1948*. Washington, DC: Institute for Palestine Studies, 2015.

Khan, Mahvish Rukhsana. *My Guantánamo Diary*. Melbourne: Scribe, 2008.

Kimmerer, Robin Wall. *Braiding Sweetgrass: Indigenous Wisdom, Scientific Knowledges, and the Teachings of Plants*. Minneapolis: Milkweed Editions, 2013.

Kimmerer, Robin Wall. "Learning the Grammar of Animacy." *Anthropology of Consciousness* 28, no. 2 (2017): 128–34.

Kimmerling, Baruch. *Politicide: Ariel Sharon's War against the Palestinians*. London: Verso, 2003.

Kober, Avi. *Israel's Wars of Attrition: Attrition Challenges to Democratic States*. New York: Routledge, 2009.

Kohák, Erazim. "Speaking to Trees." *Critical Review* 6, nos. 2–3 (1992): 371–88.

Konishi, Shino. "First Nations Scholars, Settler Colonial Studies, and Indigenous History." *Australian Historical Studies* 50, no. 3 (2019): 285–304.

Kotef, Hagar. *Movement and the Ordering of Freedom: On Liberal Governances of Mobility*. Durham, NC: Duke University Press, 2015.

Kotef, Hagar, and Merav Amir. "Between Imaginary Lines: Violence and its Justification at the Military Checkpoints in Occupied Palestine." *Theory, Culture and Society* 28 (2011): 55–80.

Kotef, Hagar, and Merav Amir. "(En)Gendering Checkpoints: Checkpoint Watch and the Representation of Intervention." *Signs* 32, no. 4 (2007): 973–96.

Krebs, Mike, and Dana M. Olwan. "'From Jerusalem to the Grand River, Our Struggles Are One': Challenging Canadian and Israeli Settler Colonialism." *Settler Colonial Studies* 2, no. 2 (2012): 138–64.

Kuletz, Valerie L. *The Tainted Desert: Environmental and Social Ruin in the American West*. New York: Routledge, 1998.

Kurland, Michael. *Irrefutable Evidence: Adventures in the History of Forensic Science*. Chicago: Ivan R. Dee, 2009.

Kurnaz, Murat. *Five Years of My Life: An Innocent Man in Guantánamo*. New York: Palgrave Macmillan, 2008.

Kwaymullina, Ambelin, and Blaze Kwaymullina. "Learning to Read the Signs: Law in an Indigenous Reality." *Journal of Australian Studies* 34, no. 2 (2010): 195–208.

LaDuke, Winona. *All Our Relations: Native Struggles for Land and Life*. Cambridge, MA: South End Press and Honor the Earth, 1999.

LaDuke, Winona, with Sean Cruz. *The Militarization of Indian Country*. Minneapolis: Honor the Earth, 2011.

Langton, Marcia. "Art, Wilderness and Terra Nullius." In *Ecopolitics IX: Perspectives on Indigenous Peoples Management of Environment Resources,* edited by R. Sultan, P. Josif, C. Mackinolty, and J. Mackinolty, 11–24. Casuarina, Australia: Northern Land Council, 1996.

Langton, Marcia. "The European Construction of Wilderness." *Wilderness News,* no. 143 (1995): 16–17.

Latour, Bruno. *Facing Gaia: Eight Lectures on the New Climatic Regime.* Translated by Catherine Porter. Cambridge: Polity, 2017.

Latour, Bruno. "Nonhumans." In *Patterned Ground: Entanglements of Nature and Culture,* edited by Stephen Harrison, Steve Pile, and Nigel Thrift, 224–27. London: Reaktion Books, 2004.

Latour, Bruno. *Pandora's Hope: Essays on the Reality of Science Studies.* Cambridge, MA: Harvard University Press, 1999.

Latour, Bruno. *Reassembling the Social: An Introduction to Actor-Network-Theory.* Oxford: Oxford University Press, 2007.

Latour, Bruno. "Telling Friends from Foe in the Time of the Anthropocene." In *Anthropocene and the Global Environmental Crisis,* edited by Clive Hamilton, Christophe Bonneuil, and François Gemmene, 145–55. London: Routledge, 2015.

Latour, Bruno. *We Have Never Been Modern.* Cambridge, MA: Harvard University Press, 1993.

Lendman, Steve. "Israel's Slow-Motion Genocide in Occupied Palestine." In *The Plight of Palestinians: A Long History of Destruction,* edited by William A. Cook, 29–38. New York: Palgrave Macmillan, 2010.

Lentin, Ronit. *Traces of Racial Exception: Racializing Israeli Settler Colonialism.* London: Bloomsbury, 2018.

Leopold, Aldo. *A Sand County Almanac: And Sketches Here and There.* 1949. Reprint, London: Oxford University Press, 1968.

Leroy, Justin. "Black History in Occupied Territory: On the Engagements of Slavery and Settler Colonialism." *Theory and Event* 19, no. 4 (2016): 1–17.

Lestel, Dominique. "The Carnivore's Ethics." *Angelaki* 19, no. 3 (2014): 161–67.

Levinas, Emmanuel. *Difficult Freedom: Essays on Judaism.* Translated by Seán Hand. Baltimore: Johns Hopkins University Press, 1990.

Levinas, Emmanuel. *On Escape.* Translated by Bettina Bergo. Stanford, CA: Stanford University Press, 2003.

Levinas, Emmanuel. *Totality and Infinity.* Translated by Alphonso Lingis. Pittsburgh: Duquesne University Press, 1969.

Lewis, Simon L., and Mark A. Maslin. "Defining the Anthropocene." *Nature* 519 (March 12, 2015): 171–80.

Li, Darryl. "The Gaza Strip as Laboratory: Notes in the Wake of Disengagement." *Journal of Palestinian Studies* 35, no. 2 (2006): 38–55.

Limerick, Patricia Nelson. *The Legacy of Conquest: The Unbroken Past of the American West.* New York: W. W. Norton, 1988.

Lippit, Mizuta Akira. *Electric Animal: Toward a Rhetoric of Wildlife*. Minneapolis: University of Minnesota Press, 2000.

Little Bear, Leroy. "Foreword." In *Native Science: Natural Laws of Interdependence*, by Gregory Cajete, ix–xii. Santa Fe: Clear Light Books, 2000.

Lloyd, David. "Settler Colonialism and the State of Exception: The Example of Palestine/Israel." *Settler Colonial Studies* 2, no. 1 (2012): 59–80.

Lockwood, Jeffrey. *Six-Legged Soldiers: Using Insects as Weapons of War*. Oxford: Oxford University Press, 2009.

Lyon, David. *Surveillance Studies: An Overview*. Cambridge: Polity, 2007.

Lyon, David, ed. *Surveillance as Social Sorting*. Abingdon, UK: Routledge, 2005.

MacCormack, Patricia, ed. *The Animal Catalyst*. London: Bloomsbury, 2014.

MacCormack, Patricia. "Art, Nature, Ethics: Nonhuman Queerings." *Somatechnics* 5, no. 2 (2015): 120–34.

Machold, Rhys. "Reconsidering the Laboratory Thesis: Palestine/Israel and the Geopolitics of Representation." *Political Geography* 65 (2018): 88–97.

Majid, Ayesha. *Effect of British Colonization on Pakistan's Legal System: An Under-looked Aspect*. Humanities Commons, 2017. Accessed December 3, 2017. https://hcommons.org/deposits/item/hc:23889/.

Mancuso, Stefano, and Alessandra Viola. *Brilliant Green: The Surprising History and Science of Plant Intelligence*. Washington, DC: Island Press, 2015.

Marder, Michael. *Plant-Thinking: A Philosophy of Vegetal Life*. New York: Columbia University Press, 2013.

Márquez-Grant, Nicholas, and Julie Roberts, eds. *Forensic Ecology Handbook: From Crime Scene to Court*. Chichester, UK: Wiley-Blackwell, 2012.

Martin, Matt J., with Charles W. Sasser. *Predator: The Remote-Control Air War over Iraq and Afghanistan: A Pilot's Story*. Minneapolis: Zenith Press, 2010.

Martinez, Dennis, Enrique Salmón, and Melissa K. Nelson. "Restoring Indigenous History and Culture to Nature." In *Original Instructions: Indigenous Teachings for a Sustainable Future*, edited by Melissa K. Nelson, 88–115. Rochester, VT: Bear and Company, 2008.

Masalha, Nur. *The Bible and Zionism: Invented Traditions, Archaeology and Post-Colonialism in Israel-Palestine*. London: Zed, 2007.

Masalha, Nur. *Expulsion of the Palestinians: The Concept of "Transfer" in Zionist Political Thought, 1882–1948*. Washington, DC: Institute for Palestine Studies, 1992.

Masalha, Nur. *A Land without People*. London: Faber and Faber, 1997.

Masalha, Nur. *The Palestine Nakba: Decolonizing History, Narrating the Subaltern, Reclaiming Memory*. London: Zed, 2012.

Masalha, Nur. *The Politics of Denial: Israel and the Palestinian Refugee Problem*. London: Pluto, 2003.

Masalha, Nur. "Remembering the Palestinian Nakba: Commemoration, Oral History and Narrative Memory." *Holy Land Studies* 7, no. 2 (2008): 123–56.

Masco, Joseph. *The Nuclear Borderlands: The Manhattan Project in Post–Cold War New Mexico*. Princeton, NJ: Princeton University Press, 2006.

Mazzetti, Mark. *The Way of the Knife*. New York: Penguin, 2013.

Mbembe, Achille. "Necropolitics." *Public Culture* 15, no. 1 (2003): 11–40.

McKee, Emily. "Performing Rootedness in the Negev/Naqab: Possibilities and Perils of Competitive Planting." *Antipode* 46, no. 5 (2014): 1172–89.

McKenna, Erin. "Land, Property, and Occupation: A Question of Political Philosophy." In *Philosophical Perspectives on the Israeli-Palestinian Conflict*, edited by Tomis Kapitan, 185–204. Armonk, NY: M. E. Sharpe, 1997.

McNeely, Jeffrey A. "War and Biodiversity: An Assessment of Impacts." In *The Environmental Consequences of War*, edited by Jay E. Austin and Carl E. Bruch, 353–78. Cambridge: Cambridge University Press, 2007.

Melo, Mario. "How the Recognition of the Rights of Nature Became a Part of the Ecuadorian Constitution." In *The Rights of Nature: The Case for a Universal Declaration of the Rights of Mother Earth*, 82–83. San Francisco: Council of Canadians, Fundación Pachamama and Global Exchange, 2011.

Merchant, Carolyn. *American Environmental History*. New York: Columbia University Press, 2007.

Merleau-Ponty, Maurice. *Nature*. Translated by Robert Vallier. Evanston, IL: Northwestern University Press, 2003.

Merleau-Ponty, Maurice. *Phenomenology of Perception*. Translated by Donald A. Landes. London: Routledge, 2014.

Merleau-Ponty, Maurice. *The Visible and the Invisible*. Translated by Alphonso Lingis. Evanston, IL: Northwestern University Press, 1997.

Miéville, China. *Between Equal Rights: A Marxist Theory of International Law*. Chicago: Haymarket Books, 2006.

Mikdashi, Maya. "What Is Settler Colonialism? (For Leo Delano Ames Jr.)." *American Indian Culture and Research Journal* 37, no. 2 (2013): 23–34.

Miller, Marilyn T., and Patrick Jones. "Crime Scene Investigation." In *Forensic Science: An Introduction to Scientific and Investigative Techniques*, edited by Stuart H. James, Jon J. Nordby, and Suzanne Bell, 41–66. Boca Raton, FL: CRC Press, 2014.

Milroy, Gladys Idjirrimoonya, and Jill Milroy. "Different Ways of Knowing: Trees Are Our Families Too." In *Heartsick for Country: Stories of Love, Spirit and Creation*, edited by Sally Morgan, 22–42. Fremantle, Australia: Fremantle Arts Press, 2010.

Morgan, Monica, with Eve Vincent. "We're Always Pushing the Boundaries for First Nations' Rights." In *Unstable Relations: Indigenous People and Environmentalism in Contemporary Australia*, edited by Eve Vincent and Timothy Neale, 301–16. Perth: University of Western Australia Publishing, 2016.

Moughrabi, Fouad. "Israeli Control and Palestinian Resistance." *Social Justice* 19, no. 3 (1992): 46–62.

Mowaljarlai, David, and Jutta Malnic. *Yorro Yorro: Aboriginal Creation and the Renewal of Nature*. Rochester, VT: Inner Traditions, 1993.

Muecke, Stephen. "Wolfe Creek Meteorite Crater: Indigenous Science Queers Western Science." *Ctrl-Z New Media Philosophy* 7 (2017): n.p.

Muir, John. *My First Summer in the Sierra*. 1911. Reprint, New York: Dover, 2004.

Naveh, Danny, and Nurit Bird-David. "Animism, Conservation and Immediacy." In *The Handbook of Contemporary Animism*, edited by Graham Harvey, 27–37. Abingdon, UK: Routledge, 2014.

Navy and Marine Corps Public Health Center. *Public Health Report for Camp Justice*. Portsmouth, VA: Navy Marine Corps Public Health Center, 2016.

Netzel, Linda R., Terrence F. Kiely, and Suzanne Bell. "Evidence: Origin, Types, and Admissibility." In *Forensic Science: An Introduction to Scientific and Investigative Techniques*, edited by Stuart H. James, Jon J. Nordby, and Suzanne Bell, 23–36. Boca Raton, FL: CRC Press, 2014.

New Weapons Research Group. "Gaza Strip Soil Has Been Contaminated Due to Bombings: Population in Danger." *New Weapons Research Group*, December 17, 2012. http://newweapons.org/?q=node/110.

Nietzsche, Friedrich. *The Birth of Tragedy and The Case of Wagner*. Translated by Walter Kaufmann. New York: Vintage: 1967.

Nietzsche, Friedrich. *On the Genealogy of Morals*. Translated by Walter Kaufmann. New York: Vintage, 1969.

Nietzsche, Friedrich. *The Will to Power*. Translated by Walter Kaufmann. New York: Vintage, 1969.

Nixon, Rob. *Slow Violence and the Environmentalism of the Poor*. Cambridge, MA: Harvard University Press, 2011.

Nuttall, J. William, Constantine Samaras, and Morgan Bazilian. "Energy and the Military: Convergences of Security, Economic, and Environmental Decision-Making." *University of Cambridge Energy Policy Research Group*, EPRG Working Paper 1717 (2017): 1–19. https://www.eprg.group.cam.ac.uk/wp-content/uploads/2017/11/1717-Text.pdf.

Omer, Mohammed. *Shell-Shocked: On the Ground under Israel's Gaza Assault*. Chicago: Haymarket Books, 2015.

Orwell, George. *Animal Farm*. Harmondsworth, UK: Penguin, 1973.

Pappé, Ilan. *The Biggest Prison on Earth: A History of the Occupied Territories*. London: Oneworld, 2017.

Pappé, Ilan. *The Ethnic Cleansing of Palestine*. London: Oneworld, 2007.

Pappé, Ilan. "Revisiting 1967: The False Paradigm of Peace, Partition, and Parity." In *The Settler Complex: Recuperating Binarism in Colonial Studies*, edited by Patrick Wolfe, 207–20. Los Angeles: American Indian Studies Center, 2016.

Pappé, Ilan. "Shtetl Colonialism: First and Last Impressions of Indigeneity by Colonised Colonisers." *Settler Colonial Studies* 2, no. 1 (2012): 39–58.

Pappé, Ilan. "Zionism as Colonialism: A Comparative View of Diluted Colonialism in Asia and Africa." *South Atlantic Quarterly* 107, no. 4 (2008): 611–33.

Parlati, Marilena. "Memory in T/Rubble: Tackling (Nuclear) Ruins." *CLCWeb: Comparative Literature and Culture* 21, no. 1 (2019): 1–9.

Patterson, Charles. *Eternal Treblinka: Our Treatment of Animals and the Holocaust*. New York: Lantern Books, 2002.

Perera, Suvendrini. "Dead Exposures: Trophy Bodies and Violent Visibilities of the Nonhuman." *Borderlands e-journal* 13, no. 1 (2014): 1–27.

Perera, Suvendrini. *Survival Media: The Politics and Poetics of Mobility and the War in Sri Lanka*. New York: Palgrave Macmillan, 2016.

Perera, Suvendrini. "'What Is a Camp . . . ?'" *Borderlands e-journal* 1, no. 1 (2002): 1–13.

Perera, Suvendrini, and Joseph Pugliese. "Dgadi-Dugarang: Talk Loud, Talk Strong: A Tribute to Aboriginal Leader Uncle Ray Jackson, 1941–2015." *Borderlands e-journal* 14, no. 1 (2015): 1–6.

Perera, Suvendrini, and Joseph Pugliese. "Parks, Mines and Tidy Towns: Enviro-panopticism, 'Post' Colonialism, and the Politics of Heritage in Australia." *Postcolonial Studies* 1, no. 1 (1998): 69–100.

Perugini, Nicola, and Neve Gordon. *The Human Right to Dominate*. Oxford: Oxford University Press, 2015.

Plumwood, Val. *Environmental Culture: The Ecological Crisis of Reason*. London: Routledge, 2002.

Plumwood, Val. *The Eye of the Crocodile*. Canberra: Australian National University Press, 2012.

Poulantzas, Nicos. *State, Power, Socialism*. London: Verso, 2001.

Puar, Jasbir K. *The Right to Maim: Debility, Capacity, Disability*. Durham, NC: Duke University Press, 2017.

Puar, Jasbir K. "The 'Right' to Maim: Dismemberment and Inhumanist Biopolitics in Palestine." *Borderlands e-journal* 14, no. 1 (2015): 1–27.

Puar, Jasbir K. *Terrorist Assemblages: Homonationalism in Queer Times*. Durham, NC: Duke University Press, 2007.

Pugliese, Joseph. *Biometrics: Bodies, Technologies, Biopolitics*. New York: Routledge, 2010.

Pugliese, Joseph. "'Demonstrative Evidence': A Genealogy of the Racial Iconography of Forensic Art and Illustration." *Law and Critique* 15 (2004): 287–320.

Pugliese, Joseph. "Drone Casino Mimesis: Telewarfare and Civil Militarisation." *Journal of Sociology* 52, no. 3 (2016): 500–521.

Pugliese, Joseph. "Identity in Question: A Grammatology of DNA and Forensic Genetics." *International Journal for the Semiotics of Law* 12, no. 4 (1999): 419–44.

Pugliese, Joseph. "Prosthetics of Law and the Anomic Violence of Drones." *Griffith Law Review* 20, no. 4 (2011): 931–61.

Pugliese, Joseph. "Reflective Indocility: Tariq Ba Odah's Guantanamo Hunger Strike as a Corporeal Speech Act of Circumlocutionary Refusal." *Law and Literature* 28, no. 2 (2016): 1–22.

Pugliese, Joseph. *State Violence and the Execution of Law: Biopolitical Caesurae of Torture, Black Sites, Drones*. Abingdon, UK: Routledge, 2013.

Pugliese, Joseph. "'Super Visum Corporis': Visuality, Race, Narrativity and the Body of Forensic Pathology." *Law and Literature* 14, no. 2 (2002): 267–94.

Pugliese, Joseph, and Susan Stryker. "Introduction: The Somatechnics of Race and Whiteness." *Social Semiotics* 19, no. 1 (2009): 1–8.

Qato, Danya M., and Ruhan Nagra. "Environmental and Public Health Effects of Polluting Industries in Tulkarm, West Bank, Occupied Palestinian Territory: An Ethnographic Study." *Lancet* 382 (2013): S29.

Qumsiyeh, Mazin B. "Environmental Justice and Sustainability in Palestine: Chal-
lenges and Opportunities under Colonization." Fourth International Conference on
Energy and Environmental Protection in Sustainable Development, ICEEP IV, Pales-
tine Polytechnic University, April 6–7, 2016. https://www.researchgate.net/profile/S
_Samhan/publication/301205157_Dr_Subhi_Samhan_represent_Palestinian_Water
_Authority_as_steering_committee_member/links/570ca2dc08aea660813b2dc9.pdf.

Qumsiyeh, Mazin B. "Nature and Resistance in Palestine." *Palestine Institute for Biodiversity and Sustainability of Bethlehem University*. Accessed August 21, 2018. https://
www.palestinenature.org/research/.

Ram, Uri. "The Colonization Perspective in Israeli Sociology: Internal and External
Comparisons." *Journal of Historical Sociology* 6, no. 3 (1993): 327–50.

Ramahi, Sawsan. "The Environmental Impact of Israeli Settlements on the Occupied Palestinian Territories." *Middle East Monitor*, May 11, 2014, 1–15. https://www
.middleeastmonitor.com/20140511-the-environmental-impact-of-israeli-settlements
-on-the-occupied-palestinian-territories/.

Reynolds, Henry. *With the White People: The Crucial Role of Aborigines in the Exploration
and Development of Australia*. Ringwood, Australia: Penguin, 1990.

Rilke, Rainer Maria. *The Poetry of Rilke*. Translated and edited by Edward Snow. New
York: North Point, 2009.

Rival, Laura. "The Materiality of Life: Revisiting the Anthropology of Nature in
Amazonia." In *The Handbook of Contemporary Animism*, edited by Graham Harvey,
92–100. New York: Routledge, 2015.

Rizzo, John. *Company Man: Thirty Years of Controversy and Crisis in the CIA*. New York:
Scribner, 2014.

Roberts, Adam. "Environmental Issues in International Armed Conflict: The Experience of the 1991 Gulf War." In *Protection of the Environment During Armed Conflict*,
edited by Richard J. Grunawalt, John E. King and Ronald S. McClain, 222-77. New-
port, Rhode Island: U.S. Naval War College International Law Studies, 1997.

Rose, Deborah Bird. *Dingo Makes Us Human*. Cambridge: Cambridge University Press,
2009.

Rose, Deborah Bird, with Nancy Daiyi, Kathy Deveraux, Margaret Daiyi, Linda Ford,
and April Bright. *Country of the Heart: An Indigenous Australian Homeland*. Canberra:
Aboriginal Studies Press, 2002.

Sacoby, M. Wilson, Roland Richard, Lesley Joseph, and Edith Williams. "Climate
Change, Environmental Justice and Vulnerability." *Environmental Justice* 3, no. 1
(2010): 13–19.

Safi, Ahmad Saleh. *2014 War on Gaza Strip: Participatory Environmental Impact Assessment*.
Ramallah: Heinrich Böll Stiftung, Palestinian Environmental NGOs Network, and
MA'AN Development Centre, 2015.

Said, Edward. *The Question of Palestine*. New York: Vintage, 1992.

Saif, Atef Abu. *The Drone Eats with Me: A Gaza Diary*. Boston: Beacon, 2016.

Saif, Atef Abu. *Sleepless in Gaza: Israeli Drone Wars on the Gaza Strip*. Rosa Luxembourg
Stiftung, 2014. Accessed February 3, 2015. http://www.rosalux.de/publication/40327
/sleepless-in-gaza.html.

Salaita, Steven. *Inter/Nationalism: Decolonizing Native America and Palestine*. Minneapolis: University of Minnesota Press, 2016.

Salih, Sara. "The Animal You See." *Interventions* 16, no. 3 (2014): 299–324.

Santana, Déborah Berman. "Resisting Toxic Militarism: Vieques versus the U.S. Navy." *Social Justice* 29, no. 2 (2002): 37–47.

Sayegh, Fayez A. *Zionist Colonialism in Palestine*. Beirut: Palestinian Liberation Organization, 1965.

Sayigh, Rosemary. "Silenced Suffering." *Borderlands e-journal* 14, no. 1 (2015): 1–20.

Sayre, Robert F. *Thoreau and the American Indians*. Princeton, NJ: Princeton University Press, 1977.

Scahill, Jeremy. *Dirty Wars*. New York: Nation Books, 2013.

Scahill, Jeremy, and the staff of the *Intercept*. *The Assassination Complex: Inside the Government's Secret Drone Warfare Program*. New York: Simon and Schuster, 2016.

Schmitt, Michael N. "War and the Environment: Fault Lines in the Prescriptive Landscape." In *The Environmental Consequences of War: Legal, Economic, and Scientific Perspectives*, edited by Jay E. Austin and Carl E. Bruch, 87–136. Cambridge: Cambridge University Press, 2007.

Sekula, Allan. "The Body in the Archive." *October*, no. 39 (1986): 3–64.

Shalalfeh, Zayneh Al-, Fiona Napier, and Eurig Scandrett. "Water Nakba in Palestine: Sustainable Development Goal 6 versus Israeli Hydro-Hegemony." *Local Environment: The International Journal of Justice and Sustainability* 23, no. 1 (2018): 117–24.

Shalhoub-Kevorkian, Nadera. "Criminality and Spaces of Death: The Palestinian Case Study." *British Journal of Criminology* 54, no. 1 (2014): 38–52.

Shalhoub-Kevorkian, Nadera. "Human Suffering in Colonial Contexts: Reflections from Palestine." *Settler Colonial Studies* 4, no. 3 (2014): 277–90.

Shalhoub-Kevorkian, Nadera. "Palestinian Children as Tools for 'Legalized' State Violence." *Borderlands e-journal* 13, no. 1 (2014): 1–24.

Shalhoub-Kevorkian, Nadera. "Trapped: The Violence of Exclusion in Jerusalem." *Jerusalem Quarterly* 49 (2012): 6–22.

Shalhoub-Kevorkian, Nadera, Sarah Ihmoud, and Suhad Dahir-Nashif. "Sexual Violence, Women's Bodies, and Israeli Settler Colonialism." *JADMAG* 4, no. 1 (2016): 37–41.

Shamir, Eitan. "Rethinking Operation Protective Edge: The 2014 Gaza War." *Middle East Quarterly* (Spring 2015). Accessed May 6, 2019. https://www.meforum.org/5084/rethinking-operation-protective-edge.

Sharoni, Simona. "Homefront as Battlefield: Gender, Military Occupation and Violence against Women." In *Women and the Israeli Occupation: The Politics of Change*, edited by Tamar Mayer, 121–37. London: Routledge, 1994.

Shaw, Martin. "Palestine in an International Historical Perspective on Genocide." *Holy Land Studies* 9 (2010): 1–24.

Shaw, Martin, and Omer Bartov. "The Question of Genocide in Palestine, 1948: An Exchange between Martin Shaw and Omer Bartov." *Journal of Genocide Research* 12, nos. 3–4 (2010): 243–59.

Shea, William L. "Virginia at War, 1644–1646." *Military Affairs* 41, no. 3 (1977): 142–47.

Shehadeh, Said. "The 2014 War on Gaza: Engineering Trauma and Mass Torture to Break Palestinian Resilience." *International Journal of Applied Psychoanalytic Studies* 12, no. 3 (2015): 278–94.

Sherwin, Richard. *Visualizing Law in the Age of the Digital Baroque*. Oxford: Routledge, 2011.

Shihade, Magid. "Settler Colonialism and Conflict: The Israeli State and Its Palestinian Subjects." *Settler Colonial Studies* 2, no. 1 (2012): 108–23.

Shkolnik, Michael. "'Mowing the Grass' and Operation Protective Edge: Israel's Strategy for Protracted Asymmetric Conflict with Hamas." *Canadian Foreign Policy Journal* 23, no. 2 (2017): 185–89.

Shomar, Basem. "Water Scenarios in the Gaza Strip, Palestine: Thirst, Hunger and Disease." *International Journal of Environmental Studies* 68, no. 4 (2011): 477–93.

Short, Damien, ed. *Redefining Genocide: Settler Colonialism, Social Death and Ecocide*. London: Zed, 2016.

Short, Damien, and Haifa Rashed. "Palestine." In *Redefining Genocide: Settler Colonialism, Social Death and Ecocide*, edited by Damien Short, 68–92. London: Zed, 2016.

Shukin, Nicole. *Animal Capital: Rendering Life in Biopolitical Times*. Minneapolis: University of Minnesota Press, 2009.

Smith, Heather A. "Disrupting the Global Discourse of Climate Change: The Case of Indigenous Voices." In *The Social Construction of Climate Change: Power, Knowledge, Norms, Discourses*, edited by Mary E. Pettenger, 197–216. Aldershot, UK: Ashgate, 2007.

Smith, Ron J. "Graduated Incarceration: The Israeli Occupation in Subaltern Geopolitical Perspective." *Geoforum* 42 (2011): 316–28.

Spence, Mark David. *Dispossessing the Wilderness: Indian Removal and the Making of the National Parks*. New York: Oxford University Press, 1999.

Spillers, Hortense J. "Mama's Baby, Papa's Maybe: An American Grammar Book." *Diacritics* 17, no. 2 (1987): 64–81.

Stauffer, Robert C. "Haeckel, Darwin, and Ecology." *Quarterly Review of Biology* 32, no. 2 (1957): 138–44.

Steiner, Gary. *Animals and the Limits of Postmodernism*. New York: Columbia University Press, 2013.

Steiner, Gary. *Anthropocentrism and Its Discontents: The Moral Status of Animals in the History of Western Philosophy*. Pittsburgh: University of Pittsburgh Press, 2005.

Stone, Christopher D. *Should Trees Have Standing?* 1972. Reprint, Oxford: Oxford University Press, 2010.

Strand, Trude. "'Meeting with the Dietician': Israel's Institutionalised Impoverishment of Gaza." *Theory and Event* 18, no. 1 (2015): 1–7.

Stryker, Susan. "(De)Subjugated Knowledges: An Introduction to Transgender Studies." In *The Transgender Reader*, edited by Susan Stryker and Stephen Whittle, 1–17. New York: Routledge, 2006.

Stryker, Susan. "My Words to Victor Frankenstein above the Village of Chamounix: Performing Transgender Rage." *GLQ: A Journal of Lesbian and Gay Studies* 1, no. 3 (1994): 237–54.

Svirsky, Marcelo, and Ronnen Ben-Arie. *From Shared Life to Co-resistance in Historic Palestine*. London: Rowman and Littlefield, 2018.

Todd, Zoe. "An Indigenous Feminist's Take on the Ontological Turn: 'Ontology' Is Just Another Word for Colonialism." *Journal of Historical Sociology* 2, no. 1 (2016): 4–22.

Tofakji, Khalil. "Settlements and Ethnic Cleansing in the Jordan Valley." *Palestine-Israel Journal of Politics, Economics and Culture* 21, no. 3 (2016): 81–87.

UN Environment Program (UNEP). *Desk Study on the Environment in the Occupied Palestinian Territories*. Nairobi: UNEP, 2003.

UN Human Rights Council. "Report of the Detailed Findings of the Independent Commission of Inquiry Established Pursuant to Human Rights Council Resolution S-21/1." June 23, 2015. https://www.ohchr.org/Documents/HRBodies/HRCouncil/CoIGaza/A_HRC_CRP_4.doc.

UN International Law Commission, *Preliminary Report on the Protection of the Environment in Relation to Armed Conflict*. Accessed June 3, 2014. http://legal.un.org/docs/?symbol=A/CN.4/674.

UN Office for the Coordination of Humanitarian Affairs Occupied Palestinian Territory. "Gaza Emergency Situation Report." September 4, 2014. https://www.ochaopt.org/content/occupied-palestinian-territory-gaza-emergency-situation-report-4-september-2014-0800-hrs.

UN Office for the Coordination of Humanitarian Affairs Occupied Palestinian Territory. "Gaza Initial Rapid Assessment Report." August 27, 2014. https://www.un.org/unispal/document/gaza-initial-rapid-assessment-ocha-report/.

Veracini, Lorenzo. *Israel and Settler Society*. London: Pluto, 2006.

Veracini, Lorenzo. "The Other Shift: Settler Colonialism, Israel, and the Occupation." *Journal of Palestine Studies* 42, no. 2 (2013): 26–42.

Veracini, Lorenzo. "What Can Settler Colonial Studies Offer to an Interpretation of the Conflict in Israel-Palestine?" *Settler Colonial Studies* 5, no. 3 (2015): 268–71.

Vialles, Noëli. *Animal to Edible*. Translated by J. A. Underwood. Cambridge: Cambridge University Press, 1994.

Vincent, Eve, and Timothy Neale, eds. *Unstable Relations: Indigenous People and Environmentalism in Contemporary Australia*. Perth: University of Western Australia Publishing, 2016.

Viveiros de Castro, Eduardo. *Cannibal Metaphysics*. Edited and translated by Peter Skafish. Minneapolis: University of Minnesota Press, 2017.

Von Uexküll, Jakob. "A Stroll through the Worlds of Animals and Men." In *Instinctive Behaviour: The Development of a Modern Concept*, edited and translated by C. H. Schiller, 5–80. New York: International Universities Press, 1957.

Voyles, Traci Brynne. *Wastelanding: Legacies of Uranium Mining in Navajo Country*. Minneapolis: University of Minnesota Press, 2015.

Wadiwel, Dinesh Joseph. *The War against Animals*. Leiden: Brill Rodopi, 2015.

Watson, Irene. *Aboriginal Peoples, Colonialism and International Law: Raw Law*. Abingdon, UK: Routledge, 2016.

Watson, Irene. "Buried Alive." *Law and Critique* 13, no. 3 (2002): 253–69.

Watts, Vanessa. "Indigenous Place: Thought and Agency amongst Humans and Non-humans (First Woman and Sky Woman Go on a European World Tour)." *Decolonization* 2, no. 1 (2013): 20–34.

Weill, Sharon, and Valentina Azarova. "The 2014 Gaza War: Reflections on *Jus ad Bellum, Jus in Bello*, and Accountability." In *The War Report*, edited by Annyssa Bellal, 360–87. Oxford: Oxford University Press, 2015.

Weinthal, Erika, and Jeannie Sowers. "Targeting Infrastructure and Livelihoods in the West Bank and Gaza." *International Affairs* 95, no. 2 (2019): 319–40.

Weizman, Eyal. *Forensic Architecture: Violence at the Threshold of Detectability*. New York: Zone, 2018.

Weizman, Eyal. "The Geometry of Occupation." Centre of Contemporary Culture of Barcelona (2004), 1–21. Accessed May 30, 2019. www.urban.ccb.org.

Weizman, Eyal. *Hollow Land: Israel's Architecture of Occupation*. London: Verso, 2012.

Weizman, Eyal. *The Least of All Possible Evils*. London: Verso, 2011.

White, Rob. *Crimes against Nature: Environmental Criminology and Ecological Justice*. London: Routledge, 2008.

White, Rob, ed. *Environmental Crime: A Reader*. Cullompton, UK: Willan, 2009.

Whyte, Kyle Powys. "Indigenous Experience, Environmental Justice and Settler Colonialism." In *Nature and Experience: Phenomenology and the Environment*, edited by Bryan E. Bannon, 157–73. London: Rowman and Littlefield, 2016.

Whyte, Kyle Powys. "Is It Colonial Déjà Vu? Indigenous Peoples and Climate Change." In *Humanities for the Environment: Integrating Knowledge, Forging New Constellations of Practice*, edited by Joni Adamson and Michael Davis, 88–105. London: Routledge, 2017.

Wildcat, Daniel R. *Red Alert! Saving the Planet with Indigenous Knowledge*. Golden, CO: Fulcrum, 2009.

Wilden, Anthony. *System and Structure*. London: Tavistock, 1980.

Wilson, Sacoby M., Roland Richard, Lesley Joseph, and Edith Williams. "Climate Change, Environmental Justice and Vulnerability." *Environmental Justice*, vol. 3, no. 1 (2010): 13–19.

Wolfe, Cary. *Animal Rites*. Chicago: University of Chicago Press, 2003.

Wolfe, Patrick. "Introduction." In *The Settler Complex: Recuperating Binarism in Colonial Studies*, edited by Patrick Wolfe, 1–24. Los Angeles: UCLA American Indian Studies Center, 2016.

Wolfe, Patrick. "Settler Colonialism and the Elimination of the Native." *Journal of Genocide Research* 8, no. 6 (2006): 387–409.

Wolfe, Patrick. *Settler Colonialism and the Transformation of Anthropology: The Politics and Poetics of an Ethnographic Event*. London: Cassell, 1999.

Wolfe, Patrick, ed. *The Settler Complex: Recuperating Binarism in Colonial Studies*. Los Angeles: UCLA American Studies Center, 2016.

Wolfe, Patrick. *Traces of History: Elementary Structures of Race*. London: Verso, 2016.

Wright, Ronald K. "Death Investigation." In *Forensic Science: An Introduction to Scientific and Investigative Techniques*, edited by Stuart H. James, Jon J. Nordby, and Suzanne Bell, 111–43. Boca Raton, FL: CRC Press, 2014.

Yalat and Oak Valley Communities, with Christobel Mattingley. *Maralinga: The Aṉangu Story*. Crows Nest, Australia: Allen and Unwin, 2012.

Young, Elise G. "The Case of Palestinian Women under Israeli Occupation, 1979–1982." In *Women and the Israeli Occupation: The Politics of Change*, edited by Tamar Mayer, 159–76. London: Routledge, 1994.

Zierler, David. *The Invention of Ecocide: Agent Orange, Vietnam, and the Scientists Who Changed the Way We Think about the Environment*. Athens: University of Georgia Press, 2011.

Zreik, Raef. "When Does a Settler Become a Native? (With Apologies to Mamdani)." *Constellations* 23, no. 3 (2016): 351–64.

Zureik, Elia. *Israel's Colonial Project in Palestine*. London: Routledge, 2016.

Aamer, Shaker, 132–33, 144–49
ABACUS (Adversary Behavior Acquisition Collection), 171–72
abattoir, zoopolitical practices of, 52–53, 69, 77
Aboriginal and Torres Strait Island peoples, 8, 17, 33, 64–65, 215. *See also* Australia
Aboriginal peoples: Nunga, 33; Palyku, 33; Yarralin, 65
absent referents, 27–28, 79, 160, 198, 200
Abu Ali, Salah, 116
accountability jurisprudence, 37, 41–42, 168
actor-network theory (ANT), 72, 73, 180
Adams, Carol, 27, 200
Adamson, Rebecca, 25
Adayfi, Mansoor, 147
Adorno, Theodor, 73
aeropolitics, 86, 96–99, 212
aesthetico-political art of the kill, 37, 183–87, 196, 201
aesthetic resistance, 70, 229–30n133
aesthetics, "science of," 184
affect, 5, 15, 25, 33, 36, 42, 48, 91, 137, 195–96, 218n18, 221n95; embodied, 15, 53, 144–45, 160; plants, relationship to,

116, 120–22, 204; relational ethics of finitude, 204–5
afforestation, 109, 112–15, 239n147
Afghanistan, 124, 127; *Our Condolences, Afghanistan* report, 200–201
Afghanistan, Pakistan, Somalia, and Yemen, 36–37, 166–68, 182, 194, 196, 200, 202
Africa, London Convention (1900) and, 9–12
African Americans, solidarity with Palestinians, 59
aftermath, forensic ecologies of, 14, 41, 47–49, 75, 91, 122, *122*–23, 201; attritional violence, 100–103; drone strikes, 166–67, 188, 191, 193, 197–98; "slow violence," 97–101, 182. *See also* forensic ecologies
Agamben, Giorgio, 36, 64
agency: algorithmic, 178–79; of more-than-human entities, 3, 22, 25, 29, 34, 119–20, 136–38, 141, 177, 215; of plants, 119–20
Agent Orange defoliant, 12, 219n38
Ahuja, Neel, 5, 64
al-Assad, Bashar, 209
Alatout, Samer, 84
Al-Ghawi, Hala, 88, 117–21, *118*

algorithms, 168–71, 196; as agents, 178–79; algorithmic war, 175; approximative and schematizing logic of, 176–78, 183–85; biases of, 180; biopolitical transduction switch points, 171–73; risk probability, 176–77. *See also* metadata

bin Ali Jaber, Abdullah Salim, 167

Al-Khader (occupied Palestinian territories), 85, 93

alliances with Palestinians, 7–9, 59, 82, 218n18

"all our relations" ethics, 31–32, 76, 88

Al-Muslimi, Farea (Yemeni citizen), 191

Alommor, Ali, 90, 91

al-Qaeda, 174

al-Qahtani, Mohammed, 154–55

al-Qawli, Mohamed, 199

al-Shabwani, Ibrahim, 182

alterity, 3, 29, 114, 139, 193

al-Zawahiri, Ayman, 175

Amendments to the Constitution: Fourth, 131; Fifth, 131

Ameziane, Djamel, 153

Amir, Merav, 55

Amoore, Louise, 175

analogue, analysis of, 78–79

Anderson, Nicole, 137

Andoni, Ghassan (resident of Beit Sahour), 203, 204, 205

Anghie, Antony, 11–12

Anglocene, 31

animal, the, 200; as homogenous, 138; as irreducible, 106, 154, 156; in Israeli popular discourse, 58, 67, 226n62; as "live tissue," 78–80, 151–53; no word for in Native languages, 138; a priori politicality of, 63–64; putting to death of as denegation of murder, 6; question of, 6–7, 35–36, 40–41, 64; as sign and semiotic inscriptor, 155; speciation of the Palestinian as, 55; through kinesthesia, 155; transcendence in, 135–40; *Umwelt* (phenomenal world or self-

world) of, 144; use of definite article, 55, 138; vertical descent toward purely immanent biologism of, 7, 155; *zōon*, 60, 63. *See also* human/animal binary

animal biologism, 7, 67, 155

animal capital, 11, 190

Animal Enterprise Terrorism Act (United States), 207–8

animal property, law of, 187–91

animal/property nexus, 10, 207–8

animal rights groups, 35, 40, 145; Animal Enterprise Terrorism Act and, 207–8; and greenwashing effacements, 76–77; and Israel, 75–77, 231n157

animals: as chattel, 190, 207; indiscriminate killing of, 89–91; and insects as torture weapons, 149–56; as "live tissue," 152–53; posttraumatic stress, effects on, 40, 49, 91; as property, 10–11, 187–91, 207–8; as speaking subjects, 145–46; welfarism model, 10–11. *See also* more-than-human entities

animism: creed of, 28; forensic disavowal of, 17–22, 47; "grammar of animacy," 76

Anthropocene, 3–4, 206, 212–13; as always already racialized, 30–31; and the generalized state of war, 105; military role in climate change, 29–30, 201, 213; as state/s of war, 214–15

anthropocentrism, 1–2; criminal anthropology, 67–68; as metasystem, 79; as war by other means, 7, 87, 213–14. *See also* Euro-anthropocentrism

anthropo-homonationalism, 110

anthropologism, 62, 154

anthropomorphism, 19, 114, 118–19, 206; deconstruction of, 62–63; of dehumanization, 61–62; hegemonic schema of, 62, 155, 212; no zero degree of, 24; violent effects of dehumanization category, 62

anti-Blackness, 59

"anticipatory self-defense," 173–74

anticolonialism, intersectional nature of, 84–85
antithanatological drone art, 187
anti-Zionist activists, 59
ants, at Guantánamo Bay prison, 140–49
Aotearoa–New Zealand, 32, 211. *See also* Indigenous cosmo-epistemologies
aporias, 81–83, 155–56, 214
aquapolitics, 86–87, 92–96; gendered impact of, 101; water restricted to bare minimum, 94–95; wells and sewer systems targeted, 93, 95–96
archaeology, forensic, 167
architecture and built environment, 16; control and, 53; of laboratory, 70–73; lethality of, 50–51, *51*; zoo as, 70
archives, plants as, 113
Aristotle, 32, 64
arms manufacturers, Israeli, 70–73
ars haruspicina (art of entrails divination), 152–53
"art form," drone kills as, 183–87
assemblages, biopolitical, 14, 79–80; dead as arrested fragments, 48–49; homonationalism as, 109–10; imperialism, settler colonialism, and extractive capitalism, 31
Assi, Anwar Abu, 99
atavism/throwbacks, 67
atmospheric violence, 182
atomic weapons, 12, 215
atomization of biopolitics, 35–36, 99–103
"attentive living," 18, 27
attritional violence, 97, 99–103, 121
Aufhebung (analog negation), 79
Australia: absent referents, Indigenous peoples scripted as, 27; national parks and reserves, 110, 111, 206; offshore asylum seeker and refugee prisons, 153–54. *See also* Aboriginal and Torres Strait Island peoples
autoimmunity, 29, 207, 212–13; transboundary biopolitics of, 36, 103–7, 212
Avelar, Idelber, 64

Babich, Babette, 177
Bacon, Francis, 44
Baker, Stewart, 169
Ball, Patrick, 170–71
Barak, Ehud, 58
Barakat, Rana, 83
Baratay, Eric, 58, 70
Bardenstein, Carol, 111
Bar-Tal, Daniel, 67
Bashmilah, Mohamed, 148–49
Bauer, Edmund, 193
beast/sovereign binary, 60–65, 152–54
being-in-the-world, 18, 23, 192
Beit Sahour, West Bank, 203
Belcher, Oliver, 30
Bell, Suzanne, 14, 15
Benally, Ruth, 25
Ben-Arie, Ronnen, 70
Ben Eliezer, Benjamin, 71
Bennett, Jane, 24–28
Bentham, Jeremy, 43
Benzaken, Avner, 71
"bestiary," 52–53, 61–62, 68
"beyond reasonable doubt" standard, 170–71
Bigger, Patrick, 30
binary categories, 78–79, 233n6; aggressor/victim, 103; beast/sovereign, 60–65, 152–54; culture/nature, 10, 20, 33–34, 63, 164–65, 205; human/inhuman, 62; Indigenous/animal, 206; "in/human" couplet, 62, 154–55; inside/outside nexus, 72, 102–3, 106; jungle/culture binary, 58–59; Palestinian/Israeli, 105–6; science/art nexus, 183–84; slave/culture distinction, 58; subject/object, 23, 62. *See also* human/animal binary
bin Fareed, Sheikh Saleh, 191, 193, 199
biocultural history, 113
bioinformationalization of life, 37, 168, 171–82, 184–86, 195, 201; bioinformational stereotyping, 172–73; US drone-kill chain and, 173–76

"biological threats," 52–53, 159

biophilia, 204

biopolitical modalities, 81–123; aquapolitics, 92–96; atomized biopolitics of attritional violence, 35–36, 99–103; bodies of forensic evidence and testimony of forensic remainders, 122–23; corpus delicti of phytopolitical destruction, 115–17; ecocide, facilitating, 88–92; ecocide and biopolitical interlacement of settler colonialism, 83–86, 98; interlocking, 4–7, 51–52, 69, 86–88, 97–100, 122; lemon tree example, 117–21, *118*; nucleic level, 101–3; pedonpolitics and aeropolitics, 96–99; phytopolitics, 107–9; phytopolitics of forensic trace evidence, 112–15; settler colonial paradigms and aporias, 81–83; settler phytopolitics of national parks and reserves, and the war on Palestinian trees, 109–12; social sorting and capture, 173; transboundary biopolitics of autoimmunity, 103–7; twinned, atomized and transboundary, 106–7. *See also* assemblages, biopolitical; biopolitics

biopolitical transduction switch points, 171–73

biopolitics: anthropocentric frame of, 1–2; definition of, 2; differential and interlocking elements of, 4–7, 138; massifying effects of, 5–7; as superordinate category, 6–7, 40–41, 86–87. *See also* biopolitical modalities; zoopolitics

biopower, 7, 87, 215–16

bios, 64, 105

biospherical (earth ecosystems) domain, 213

Birch, Tony, 31, 222n111

Black, C. F., 34

Black Elk, 144

Black people, 57, 59, 72; anti-Black racism, 59

Blanchot, Maurice, 148

Bobb, Scott, 122

bodies: as aggressor-victim, 103–4; as bio-machines, 78; decomposition, 159, 161, 179, 193, 197; denied to animals, 55; disembodied of corporeal legal status, 129–31; of forensic evidence, 122–23; as "screen territories," 182; terminal theft of, 55; theft of time from, 55–56

Boer War, 21

borders, 106, 151–52; limitrophy, 53–54

Bosselmann, Klaus, 207–8

Boumediene, Lakhdar, 126

Boycott, Divestment, Sanctions movement, 8

Braverman, Irus, 50, 56

British Raj, legal system of, 189

Bromberg, Gideon, 104, 106

Broswimmer, Franz, 85–86

Bruch, Carl, 12

Bryant, Brandon, 185

Buffalo Nations, 33, 223n144

Bureau of Investigative Journalism, 174

Bush administration, 127

Bybee, Jay, 149–50, 154

Cage, the: Gaza as, 35, 49–61, 69–70, 74, 105; Guantánamo Bay military prison, 36; nested series of, 49–50, 56–57, 59–60; Sri Lanka war as, 69; Wall as expansion of, 61; zoopolitics of, 49–56. *See also* Palestine, occupied

Cajete, Gregory, 15, 20, 22–23, 25, 28, 65, 206–7; on "animal" in Native languages, 138; on body memory, 120; ensoulment, concept of, 116

Calais refugee camp, as "The Jungle," 58

Calarco, Matthew, 75

calorie regulation, 61, 94

Camp Justice. *See* Guantánamo Bay military prison (Camp Justice)

capital: animals as, 11, 190; commodity form, 10–11, 132–33

capitalism, toxic, 125, 201

captivity, 49–56, 60, 126, 148–49, 155–56, 165; multiple geographic scales of, 50

carbon emissions, 30, 202, 213

carcass, as undifferentiated realm, 43–44, 199–200

carceral logic, 50, 55, 57–58, 128, 133. *See also* checkpoints, Gaza; Guantánamo Bay military prison; prison

Carlson, Bronwyn, 67–68

casino and gaming practices, 177–78

catachresis, 24

cell phones, human targets coextensive with, 169–70, 176–79, 184

Central Intelligence Agency (CIA), 148, 169, 175

checkpoints, Gaza, 35, 50–58; as abattoir, 52–53, 69, 77; as "animal pens," 50–56, *51, 54*; asphyxiation in caged corridors, 50–51; as biopolitical management, 50; as delegates of Israeli state, 51–52; "dirty sector," 52–53; expropriative nature of, 55–56; as "forcing pens," 52–55; infant deaths at, 55; as mineralogical barrier, 51–52; policing at, 53; theft of time/spatiotemporal logics of, 51–52, 55–56; vestibularity of, 55, 56–60, 105. *See also* Gaza, occupied

Chen, Mel Y., 68, 229n123, 231n160

civil disobedience, 207–8

civilians, killing of: by drones, 173–82, 187; by IDF, 46; "non-combatant deaths," 175–76

civilizational narrative, 110–11

Clear Heart program, 171

climate change, 29–31, 213, 215–16

Cloke, Paul, 120

cognition: contradictions, 20; distributed, 14, 25, 42, 47, 52, 63, 115, 180, 221n95; of plants, 113, 119

Colebrook, Claire, 214

colonialism, 82; environmental, 111; genealogy of, 11–12, 26, 163–64; Guantánamo Bay prison as emblem of, 163. *See also* settler colonialism

commodity form, 10–11, 132–33

consanguinity, 42, 44, 75, 123, 192–93, 203; fused flesh as, 192–93

considerability, 206

corpses, 43; carcasses versus, 199; double death of, 45, 46

cosmology, Native American view, 25

cosmopolitics, 20, 27, 64

counterforensics, 16

country, Aboriginal understandings of, 215

Coyle, Sean, 11

crime scene, 2, 18–19, 22, 41, 164–67; of drone kills, 199–200; Guantánamo Bay prison as, 164; microscopic, 166; *modus operandi* (criminal repeat behavior), 8, 41, 167; Mukalla, Yemen as, 166–68; Shujai'iya, Gaza as, 41; taphonomic context, 41

criminal anthropology, 67–68

criminalistics, 18

"criminaloids," 67

critical animal studies, 9, 24

Cuba, 163–64

Cullinan, Cormac, 31, 33

culture/nature binary, 10, 16, 20, 33–34, 164–65, 205; animal as already political, 63

Dahan, Eli Ben, 58

Dahir-Nashif, Suhad, 57

Dajani, Muna, 94

Dana, Tariq, 82

Da'Na, Seif, 85

Defense Advanced Research Projects Agency (DARPA), 150

Darwin, Charles, 64

data crush, 180–81. *See also* algorithms; metadata

Davis, Uri, 112

"dead meat," 74–76, 152

deanthropocentrizing approaches, 7–9, 27, 88

death: civilian, by drone-kill program, 173–82, 187; denied to animal, 80, 200; double, of disinterred corpses, 45, 46; forensic ecologies of drone death, 166–68; infant deaths at checkpoints, 55; life–death continuum, 4; management of, 2, 44–45; mechanism of, 167; by metadata, 37, 168–71, 177, 181, 193; "non-combatant deaths," 175–76; politicization of, 45; putting to death as denegation of murder, 6; "verification procedure," 46

decolonizing practices, 7–9, 82–83, 85, 87–88, 232n6; deanthropocentrizing practices linked with, 26–27, 88

decolonizing scholarship, Indigenous, 82

decomposition, 159, 161, 179, 193, 197

deconstruction, 62–63

deficit theories of more-than-human entities, 3, 10–11, 155

defoliants, 12, 86, 219n38

dehumanization, 61–62, 153–55

Deir Yassin forest, 66

DeLanda, Manuel, 89

Deleuze, Gilles, 44, 56–57

Deloria, Vine, Jr., 28, 29, 33, 145–46, 192, 207

denegatory logics, 6, 19–20, 24, 47, 131, 175–76, 205; of bestiality, 63, 153–56; "universalization" of, 26, 154

Department of Defense (DoD), 171; AR 15-6 Investigation and Report, 133–37, 140, 157–59; drone program, 37, 167

Department of Homeland Security, 151

Department of Justice, 207–8

Der Derian, James, 78

Derrida, Jacques, 6, 11, 29, 74, 133, 214, 231n57; on autoimmunity, 105; limitrophy, 53–54; on link between sovereignty and the animal, 60–61, 63–64; on trace, 113

Despret, Vinciane, 11, 41

detainees, Guantánamo Bay prison: double externality of, 132–33; as non-

persons, 36, 129–33; as package, 132–33; as plants, 163. *See also* Latif, Adnan Farhan Abdul (detainee)

Dichter, Avi, 183

DiMento, Joseph, 212

dingo, 65

"dirty sector," 52–53

disavowal, 2–3, 6, 15, 24, 154, 189, 206; of animism, 17–22; of violence, 62–65, 76

disease, due to military contamination, 95, 97–98, 100–101

dispossession/displacement, 109–12, 121; interaction between Hala Al-Ghawi and the lemon tree, 115–21, *118*

distributed cognition, 14, 25, 42, 47, 52, 63, 115, 180, 221n95

"drone casino mimesis," 177–78

"drone disposition matrix," 181–82

drone kills, 14, 36–37, 166–202; animal property law and, 187–91; as "antiseptic," 178; approximative and schematizing logic of, 176–78, 183–85; "art of" (necropoeisis), 183–87, 201; biopolitical transduction switch points, 171–73; cameras, 187; containment screen, 197–98; divination, 152–53, 184–85, 187; "double tap," 198; "enemy kills," 175; extrajudicial killing and violence, 168, 173–76, 178–79, 181, 187, 201; F3 (Find, Fix, Finish), 181; forensic ecologies of drone death, 166–68; geobiomorphologies of, 191–95, 198, 201–2; Geo Cell tracking program, 170; geopolitically dispersed assemblage of, 196; GILGAMESH program, 170, 183, 185–86; marketing of as "field-tested," 71; operator comments, 167, 169–70, 175, 178–81, 183–85, 199–200; a priori and a posteriori logics of, 178–82, 196; responsibility absolved, 196–97; signature strikes, 167, 173, 178; SKYNET program, 170; *sparagmos*, 37, 195–98; "suspect" categories, 127, 168–72,

178–79; as system effect, 177–78; tracking technologies, 167–68; Yemen strike numbers, 174

earth: body of, 23; challenges to human exceptionalism, 215; as enemy, 109; vibrant land, 24–25

Earth jurisprudence, 31–32, 204, 213

East Jerusalem, occupied, 14; evictions of families, 117, *118*; removal and obliteration of Palestinian graves in, 45–46

ecoapartheid, 96

ecocide, 13, 207, 219n38, 234n30; aquapolitics, 86–87, 92–96; corpus delicti of phytopolitical destruction, 115–17; facilitating: "no rules of engagement," 88–92; IDF perpetration of, 83–86, 108, 115–16; land-clearing practices, 31, 84, 86, 94, 236n71; multiperspectival vision, 99; "no rules of engagement," 88–92; pedonpolitics, 96–99; phytopolitical, 107–9, 209–10; polity of nature, 213; "slow violence," 97–101; as term, 85–86; US perpetration of, 194, 200–202

"Ecocide Convention" proposal, 13, 213

ecological compact, 206–7

ecologies of unrequited justice, 29–34

ecology, as term, 16–17

economy, sovereignty over, 60–61

EcoPeace Middle East, 104

ecosystems, 17, 34, 84–85, 96, 202, 213

Ecuador, constitution of, 32

Eid, Kassem, 209

Eitan, Rafael, 58

Elbit (drone manufacturer), 71

Elders Council Statement (Lakota Nation), 216

El Ghoul, Deema, 50

El-Haddad, Laila, 69

Elzanin, Elham, 229n133

embodied affects, 15, 22–23, 53, 144–45, 160

Endangered Species Act (United States), 135

engagement, rules of lacking, 88–92

ensoulment, 116

environment, as term, 16

environmental colonialism, 111

epidemiological warfare, 95

epistemologies of scent, 41–42

erasure, acts of, 25–26, 45–46, 84–85, 109, 111–15, 181, 239n137

Erez Checkpoint, Gaza Strip, 50–51

Errachidi, Ahmed, 140–49

ESC BAZ arms company, 71

Esposito, Roberto, 131–33

ethical exchanges, 36, 113–14, 203–5, 208–9

ethico-jural standing of more-than-human entities, 8, 76, 189

ethics of care, interspecies, 148, 203

ethnic cleansing, 66, 110, 228nn114–15; afforestation as, 112, 239n137

ethnicity, as unreliable descriptor, 172

ethnocentrism, 58

Euro-anthropocentrism, 7–12, 42, 76, 114, 164, 189; dehumanization and, 153, 155; Earth jurisprudence as alternative to, 213–14; Indigenous cosmo-epistemologies versus, 32–34; Indigenous legal challenges to, 211; of international law, 9–12; of law, 11, 33, 204; new materialisms and, 24–29; the Open and, 137; as embedded in Western thought, 62; relational ethics versus, 203–4. *See also* anthropocentrism

evidence, 2; articulation of, 18–19; bodies of, 122–23; categories of, 16; circumstantial, 167; *forensis* as type of, 14; geobiophysical, 16, 123, 202, 215; inscribed in landscape, 20, 48–49; as "mute witness" to speech, 18, 20; physical, 16, 18–19, 40–42, 47; textual documents, 16. *See also* trace evidence

evidentiary truth, 14–15, 18–19, 22–23, 47

excendence, 139–40; entomology of, 140–49

expert witness, 14–15, 49

extinction, serial species, 31

extra-colonial histories, 29

extrajudicial killing and violence, 37, 67, 132–33, 201; drone-kill program, 168, 173–76, 178–79, 181, 187, 201

extraordinary rendition, practice of, 148

Falk, Richard, 12

Fallon, Mark, 126–28

Fanon, Frantz, 52, 60–62, 182

Ferguson, Missouri, protests, 59

figure and ground, obliteration of, 23, 198

fingerprint identification, 21

finitude, relational ethics of, 204–5

First Nations peoples, alliances with Palestinian people, 8, 82, 218n18

First Peoples Worldwide, 25

flesh: abstract metadata transliterated to, 37, 186–87, 194–97, 201; processual connection with metadata, 194; thickness of, 192

flesh of the world, 4, 14, 22–24, 99; consanguinity, relations of, 42, 44, 75, 123, 192–93, 203; fused/entangled, 4, 123, 188, 191–93, 210; intercorporeality of, 22–23; interspecies relations and, 126; land as, 168; vegetal life as, 116, 119

fold, topology of, 56–57

Forensic Architecture, 16

forensic ecologies, 13–14; anthropocentric frames, 1–2; bodies of, 122–23; of Camp X-Ray, 161–65, 162; contours of, 7, 86–87, 121, 123, 177; crime scene, 41; of drone death, 166–68; flesh of the world, 4, 22–24; living ecologies transmuted into, 200–201; of military livestock, 73–80; more-than-human valorized by, 4, 23; survivor testimony modality, 48. See also aftermath, forensic ecologies of

forensic pathology, 22

forensics: attentive listening in, 18; colonial origins of, 21–22; counterforensics, 16; definition, 2; disavowed animism of, 17–22, 47; exchange principle, 22; forensis, 14; Indigenous, 20–21; narratological procedures, 15, 17, 19; remnants/proxy data, 15; semantic boundaries of, 3, 16; as type of legal evidence, 14

Foucault, Michel, 2, 4–5, 57, 172–73, 215; on anthropologism, 62; killing, as weakening, 100–101; "switch point," 171; unintended effects of power, 45

fractal logic, 89, 99, 106

Francione, Gary, 10–11, 190

Frazer, Ryan, 67–68

freedom: checkpoints limit, 51–53; "difficult," 138; of movement, 51–53, 148; the Open and, 139; predicated on unfreedom of others, 125; right to, 50

freedom/security nexus, 171

friendship, interspecies, 147

frontier geography, 83

Fuad (father of family), 117

funerals, US bombing of, 198

Galston, Arthur W., 85

Gans, Eric, 196–97

Gasteyer, Stephen, 94

Gaza, occupied, 1–3, 14; Ariel (illegal Israeli settlement), 93; as "Cage," 35, 49–61, 69–70, 74, 105; creeping annexation, 117; Deir Yassin (village), 109; economic sovereignty of Israel over, 60–61; as "experimental laboratory," 35, 70–73; focus group discussions, 97; as geolocation of crime, 41; Jabalia neighborhood, 44; Juhar al-Dik, 108; Khuza'a, 74–75, 77, 89, 99; as prison, 50; school bombing, 47–49; as "trap," 69–70; as "zoo," 35, 49–56. See also Cage, the; checkpoints, Gaza; Operation Protective Edge (Gaza, 2014); Palestine, occupied; Palestinians; zoopolitics

Gaza Children Cinema, 229n133

Gaza City: Shujai'iya neighborhood, 39–41; zoo, 49–50, 56

Gaza Power Plant (GPP), 97–98
gender, 68, 101; dimensions of violence, 55, 57, 225n55
Generelle Morphologie (Haeckel), 16–17
Geneva Convention, 13, 188; "Fifth," 213
genocide, 6, 13, 30–31, 61, 218n18; against animals and trees, 33, 223n144; national parks on lands of Indigenous owners, 110; US military as instrument of, 201
Genocide Convention, 13
geobiomorphologies, 191–95, 198, 201–2; defined, 194
geobiophysical prism, 16, 123, 202, 215
geocorpography, 194
geolocation technology, 176–78, 184
geophysical (forces of nature) domain, 213
geopolitical ecology, 30–31, 105
geopolitics, 9, 11–13, 16, 26, 42, 82, 164; drone killing and, 187, 189, 194, 196–97, 201–2; need for reconceptualization, 210–15, 213
Ghabsiyah (Galilee), 112–14
Ghanim, Honaida, 44–45
Giannacopoulos, Maria, 140n 223
Gibson, Jennifer, 174
GILGAMESH (drone program), 170, 183, 185–86
Greenwald, Glenn, 175
greenwashing effacements, 76–77, 109–12
Gregory, Derek, 109, 182, 195, 252n136
grieving: collective, for olive trees, 116; corporeal marks of, 120; inventory of mourning, 47; over "dead meat," 75; of violated natality, 55
Grindle, Donald, 9, 17
Guantánamo Bay military prison (Camp Justice), 14, 36, 124–65; Alpha block, 128; ants, interspecies relations with, 140–49; AR 15-6 Investigation and Report, 133–37, 140, 157–59; as cage, 36, 125–26, 128–29; Camp Echo, 140–41, 144; Camp Six, 125–26; Camp X-Ray,

126, 129; Camp X-Ray, forensic ecology of, 161–65, *162*; Code Yellow, 158; as crime scene, 164–67; detainees as non-persons, 36, 129–33; Emergency Reaction Force (ERF), 141; hunger strikes, 130, 147; Immediate Reaction Force (IRF) teams, 128–29; isolation, 141–44; journalists as military captives, 125–26; management at, 134–35; material toxicity of, 124–25; the Open in, 135–40, 142–43, 146–49; "pumpkin patch," 163; razor wire fence, 162–63, 165; Torture Memos, 149–51, 154, 169; zoopolitics of torture practices, 149–56
Guernica (Picasso), 43, 89
"guilt by association," 176, 178
Gulf War, 12–13

Hadaeid, Abu, 75
Haeckel, Ernst, 16–17
Haitians, 163–64
Hammami, Rema, 50
haptic exchange, 20–21, 136
Haraway, Donna, 136
Hardouin-Fugier, Elizabeth, 58, 70
Hass, Amira, 70, 231n152
Hassan, Emad, 159–60
Hayden, Michael, 169
Hayles, N. Katherine, 178
health, as gendered concept, 101
Health Risks Assessment for the Israeli Population Following the Sanitary Crisis in Gaza, 104–5
Hearne, Vicki, 42
Hegel, G. W. F., 119
Heidegger, Martin, 29, 173, 200; death, anthropocentric view of, 80; Open, the, 36, 136–37, 139
Hellfire missiles, 166
herbicides, toxic, 86, 98–99
hierarchies: of life, 10–11, 37, 57, 61–63, 67, 75–78, 119–20, 125–26, 130, 133, 135, 147, 152, 155, 163, 168, 188–93, 206, 225n35; Palestinian/Israeli binary, 105–6

Hillal, Jane, 94
Hiroshima and Nagasaki, 12
Hobby Lobby Supreme Court decision, 129–31
Hogan, Linda, 18, 23, 24–25, 28, 40, 147–48, 192, 217n5
Holdbrooks, Terry, 129
holding pens. *See* checkpoints, Gaza
homonationalism, 109–10
Hoque, Imran Mohammad Fazal, 153–54
hospitality, 36, 141, 143, 147, 156
Hulme, Karen, 13
"human, the," 3–4, 24, 26, 62, 64, 126, 129, 138, 152, 155, 200
human/animal binary, 54, 57, 189; inversion of, 6, 61–62, 126; onto-epistemological ground for, 6–7, 10, 35, 133, 145; parallel qualities, 63; those designated as "mere animals," 6, 68; UN Convention against Torture and Other Cruel, Inhuman or Degrading Treatment or Punishment, 36. *See also* animal, the
human exceptionalism, dogma of, 3, 11, 24, 205, 211; animals interrupt, 43, 147–48; earth's challenges to, 215–16; reductionism of, 7, 155
human rights frameworks, 75, 131, 188–89, 231n157
hunger strikes, 130, 147, 209
Hussain, Qari, 175
Hutchins, Edwin, 14
hydrocarbon logistical infrastructure, 30, 202, 213
hyperseparation, 205–6

Idir, Mustafa Ait, 126
Ihmoud, Sarah, 57, 66
"imminent threat," 174, 194
imperialism, US, 198–202
inanimal, as term, 36, 155
inanimality, 6–7; violence of, 7, 36, 149–56; as zoopolitical phantom, 7, 155
Inbar, Efraim, 100

incarceration, microgeographies of, 50
Indigenous cosmo-epistemologies, 3, 7–9; "all our relations" ethics, 31–32, 76, 88; constitutive power of animals in the production of humans, 64–65; distributed cognition antedated by, 14, 25, 63; ethical obligations to more-than-human entities articulated in, 32–33; more-than-human entities as speaking subjects, 145–46; of relationality, 17–22; settler colonial erasure of, 25–26; spatiotemporal anteriority of, 14, 25–28, 210–11; vegetal life, views of, 119
Indigenous peoples: as absent referents, 27; as "animal," 205–6; Aruacos, 164; Cuba, 164; ecology embodied as lived practice, 17; as eliminable, 5; epidemiological warfare against, 95; as non-existent, 31; no word for "animal," 138; replacement of, 5, 29, 83, 232n6; undiminished resistance of, 5; US role in appropriation of lands, 201
Indigenous-Place Thought, 27
Indigenous plant epistemologies, 113
Indigenous theories and alliances, 7–9, 218n18
Indigenous trackers, 20–21
Industrial Revolution, 31
infrastructural normativities, 172
"inhuman": complicity in denegated forms of lawful violence, 156; Guantánamo indoctrination of guards, 129; killability/violence against nonhuman animals, 2, 4, 36, 41–42, 56, 78, 151–56; thingness, 131–32. *See also* nonhuman
"in/human" couplet, 62, 154–55
"inhumanity," 154
injustice: greenwashing of, 76–77, 109–12; testimony against, 161
insects, weaponized, 149–50
inside/outside nexus, 72, 102–3, 106
Institute for International Law (University of Cologne), 174

"intent-based threat assessments," 171

intercorporeality, 22–23, 76, 136, 139, 144–45, 156–57, 193

International Criminal Court, 91–92, 188

International Environmental Law, 10; London Convention (1900), 9–10, 11–12

International Humanitarian Law, Rule 1, 175–76

international law: anthropocentric focus of, 9–12, 188–89; colonial genealogy of, 11–12; enforceability of, 13; freedom of movement as right, 50; juridical equality and unequal violence assumed by, 212–13; Rule 89 against murder, 90; US drone-kill program and, 175–76. *See also* law

intersectionality: of anticolonialism, 84–85; ecocide and biopolitical interlacement of settler colonialism, 83–86; of Israeli settler colonialism, 8, 35, 88, 107

interspecies relations, 5, 23–24; ethical exchanges, 36, 113–14, 203–5, 208–9; ethics of care, 148, 203; in Guantánamo Bay military prison, 36, 126, 134–49; "responsive," 136; zone of the political, 64

inversion, 135, 189, 197, 207–8; of human/ animal categories, 6, 61–62, 126

invertible logic of zoopolitics, 44–45, 61–62, 75, 103, 126, 197, 231n157

Isaac, Jad, 84, 94

Islamophobia, 110

Israeli Civil Administration, 93

Israeli Defence Forces (IDF), 1; campaign against Palestinian ecologies of life, 43; contingent obligation to kill, 89–90; illegal ordnance used by, 96; livestock, testing on, 73–80; no accountability for actions, 56; school bombing, 47–49; "sterile zone" designation, 53; *This Is How We Fought in Gaza* report, 88; "turkey hunt" metaphor, 56; weapons testing on nonhuman animals,

72–73. *See also* Operation Protective Edge, July–August 2014, Gaza

Israeli settler colonialism, 232–33n6; consolidation and expansion of occupation, 8; debilitation as goal of, 100; erasure of graves coextensive with logic of, 45–46; Indigenous decolonizing and deanthropomorphizing cosmo-epistemologies applied to, 7–9; instability of, 83; intersectional nature of, 8, 35, 84–85, 88, 107; sexual and gendered violence of, 57, 226n63. *See also* Israeli state

Israeli state, 4; anti-Black racism in, 59; biopolitical regime, 5; biopolitical war by other means, 7; checkpoints as delegates of, 51–52; creeping annexation, 117; "deterrence" strategy, 39; ecocide committed by, 201; ethnic cleansing by, 66; Gaza, occupation of, 1–3; graves, violation of, 45–46; green-pinkwashing as progressive, 109–10; international law and, 13; "managed attrition" strategy, 39; massacres at foundation of, 66; popular culture statements and stereotypes, 58, 67, 226n62; racism permeates, 58; recurrent wars waged by, 59; Shin Bet secret service, 183; as "the culture," 58, 60; "Wall," 51, 61, 76, 106, 108, 227n90; weapons-testing on Palestinians, 70–723. *See also* Gaza, occupied; Israeli settler colonialism; Palestine, occupied

Israeli State Comptroller, 95

Israel's Colonial Project in Palestine (Zureik), 58

Israel's Wars of Attrition (Kober), 100

Jabalia neighborhood, Gaza, 44

Jaber, D. A., 85, 93

Jaber, Faisal bin Ali, 175

Jackson, Ray (Uncle), 218n18

Jarbawi, Ali, 82

Jewish National Fund (JNF) afforestation, 109, 111–15
Jha, U. C., 12–13, 30, 85
jirga (traditional gathering of male elders), 179
Jochnik, Chris af, 211
Johansen, Bruce, 9, 17
Johns Hopkins University debate, 169
Joint Special Operations Command (JSOC), 170, 181
Joint Water Committee (JWC), 93
Jones, Owain, 120
Judeo-Christian viewpoints, 10
Juhar al-Dik (Gaza), 108
jungle metaphor, 58
jural life, 33
jurisprudence, 218n22; accountability, 37, 41–42, 168; of animals as property, 11, 187–91; Earth, 31–32, 213–14; Euro-anthropocentric, 211; Indigenous, 34
justice, 3; for "all our relations," 31–32, 76, 88; ecological, unrequited, 29–34; endless deferral of, 128; Euro-anthropocentric conceptualizations of, 32; as experience of the impossible, 214; individual acts of as provisional, 211; intergenerational and global, 215; placed on hold, 213–14; rule of law distinct from, 207–8; for victims of Guantánamo, 163
just law, 53, 179–80, 210

Kaye, Jeffrey, 133–34
Keenan, Thomas, 16
Kennedy, Henry H., Jr., 127–28
Kennelly, Cara, 30
Khalidi, Rashid, 50, 59–60
Khalidi, Walid, 112
Khan, Dost Muhammad, 187–90
Khan, Kareem, 182
Khan, Mahvish Rukhsana, 135
Khan Younis, Gaza, 95
Khdeir, Mohammed Abu, 65–66

Khdeir, Tariq Abu, 35, 65–69, 73, 79–80, 228n121
Khuza'a, Gaza, 74, 77, 89, 99
Khyber Pakhtunkhwa region (Pakistan), 187
"kill chains," 173–74, 178–79, 197
Kimmerer, Robin Wall, 76, 113, 114
kincentric worldview, 24–25, 32–33, 153
kinship, 24–25, 114, 116, 193, 205
Kirk, Paul Leland, 18–19
knowledge: abstracted, used for torture, 151; olfactory sense as metonymy for, 42; schematizing versus, 176–78, 180–81, 183–85; truth/knowledge nexus, 177
Kober, Avi, 100
Kohák, Erazim, 119
Konishi, Shino, 29
Kotef, Hagar, 55
Krome detention center (United States), 164
Kurnaz, Murat (detainee), 135
Kwaymullina, Ambelin, 17, 33, 221n83
Kwaymullina, Blaze, 17, 33, 221n83

laboratory, zoopolitics of, 70–73; inside-outside interface, 72, 102–3
LaDuke, Winona, 33, 88, 201
land, as system of reciprocal relations and obligations, 85
land-clearing practices, 31, 84, 86, 236n71; aquapolitics and, 94; national parks and reserves, 110–11
landscape, 33, 40, 181; devastated, 84, 91, 112–13; of erasure and amnesia, 114–15; evidence inscribed in, 20, 48–49; of massacre, 69
Langton, Marcia, 111
language: anthropomorphic view of, 136–37, 155; phytosemiotics, 23–24; zoosemiotics, 23–24, 145
Latif, Adnan Farhan Abdul (detainee), 36, 125, 126–29; AR 15-6 Investigation and Report, 133–37, 140, 157–59; death

of, 140, 156–61; death of as manslaughter, 158; feeding of animals in
recreation yard, 134–40; last flight of,
156–57; letter to attorneys, 128; obituary for, 159–60

Latif, Muhammed Farhan, 161

Latour, Bruno, 18–19, 28, 52, 105, 221n95;
distributed nature of interaction, 121,
180; on inhumanity, 62; speed bump
analogy, 51–52

law, 9–14; animal property, drone kills
and, 187–91; animal welfarism, 10–11; of
armed conflict and the environment,
41; British Raj legal system, 189; complicit in toxic militarism, 125; dispute as
central to, 10; Euro-anthropocentrism
of, 9–12; failure of Western, 207–9; instrumentalist, 204–5; just, 53, 179–80,
210; machinic effects of anthropocentric, 208; more-than-human as
lawfully killable, 4, 36, 126, 151–56,
207–8; "Raw Law," 223n147; standing,
questions of, 8, 33, 42, 76, 189, 218n22;
unequal coercion and, 11; validity
of, 208; of war, 9, 41, 211; Western as
"Law," 21. See also international law

law, Indigenous, 9, 21, 32–33, 210–11

learned helplessness, 150–51

Leichhardt, Ludwig, 21

lemon tree, occupied Palestine, 117–21, 118

Lentin, Ronit, 55, 228n115

Leroy, Justin, 59, 72

Levinas, Emmanuel, 29, 138

lexico-discursive logics, 36, 151

LGBT rights, 109–10

Lieberman, Avigdor, 60

life: bioinformationalization of, 37, 168,
173–76, 186; as biological substrate, 178,
185; conditions of possibility, 17, 52, 64,
78, 84; digitized, 178; hierarchies of,
10–11, 37, 57, 61–63, 67, 75–78, 119–20,
125–26, 130, 133, 135, 147, 152, 155, 163, 168,
178, 188–93, 206, 225n35; instrumentalization of, 54, 78–80, 79–80, 109, 116,
150, 153, 169–70, 181–82, 187, 190, 195,
204–5; surplus affirmation of, 204

life–death continuum, 4

limitrophy, 57, 5354

listening, 209–10

Little Bear, Leroy, 25

livestock, 10, 188–90, 190–91; forensic
ecologies of military, 73–80; military
testing on, 73–80; Palestinians treated
like, 55; politics presupposes, 74

"live tissue" training, 78–80, 151–53

Lloyd, David, 233n11

Locard, Edmond, 22

Lockwood, Jeffrey, 150

Lombroso, Cesare, 67

London, Fritz, 194

London Convention Designed to Ensure
the Conservation of Various Species
of Wild Animals in Africa, Which Are
Useful to Man or Inoffensive (1900),
9, 11–12

Looking Horse, Arval, 216

Lorber, Ben, 96

Ludueña, Fabián, 64

Machold, Rhys, 72, 73

MAMs (military-aged males), 179–81, 185

mana (authority), 32

Māori people, 32, 211

Marder, Michael, 116

Marks, Drew, 71

Masalha, Nur, 108, 114–15

massacres, foundation of Israeli state
and, 66

materialisms, new, 9–10, 24–29

material semantics, 48–49, 113, 120, 159

matter: animated particle exchange, 22,
25; vibrant, 24–25

mauri (life force), 32

Mazzetti, Mark, 169

Mbembe, Achille, 60

McKee, Emily, 109

McKenna, Erin, 93

"meat is murder" slogan, 76

Megged, Eyal, 77
Mehsud, Baitullah, 175
memes, neocolonial, 67–68
memorial, trace evidence as, 112–15
memoricide, 66
memory: of the present, 122; trace as arche-phenomenon of, 113
Merleau-Ponty, Maurice: on flesh as general thing, 198–99; flesh of the world concept, 4, 22–23, 99, 119, 192–93, 195–96; transcendence, view of, 138–39
metadata: bioinformationalization of life, 37, 168, 173–76, 186; content superseded by, 169–70; data crush, 180–81; death by, 37, 168–71, 177, 181, 193; "enemy combatants," 170–71; "patterns of life," 171, 178–79, 195; processual connection with flesh, 194. *See also* algorithms
metaphors, 24, 58, 67, 178, 184
metaphysics, 19, 29, 60, 71, 73, 133, 200
microecologies, 99–100, 103, 106, 121
microgeographies, 50, 82–84, 99–102; site-specific, 86–87
Miéville, China, 13
Mikdashi, Maya, 218n18, 233n6
militarism, toxic, 124–25; ordnance, pollution by, 86, 96–97
military: exempt from environmental protection legislation, 30; "live tissue" training, 78–80, 151–53; "organized chaos," 89
military-industrial-prison-surveillance complex, 213; "field-testing" for Israeli arms companies, 70–73; Israeli, 35, 52–53; scientifico-military regimes of experimentalism, 71
Military Orders 1015 and 1039, 107
Milroy, Gladys Idjirrimoonya, 33
Milroy, Jill, 33
minoritarian practices, 210
mnemonics of law, 53
Moadamiya, Syria, 209–10

modus operandi (criminal repeat behavior), 8, 41, 167
Mohamad, Ismael, 70
Montreal Protocol on Substances That Deplete the Ozone Layer, 211–12
moral obligations to "nonsentient" entitities, 32–33
moral rectitude of evidence, 18–19
moral theory, 10
more-than-human, 3; as ethically preceding the human, 210–11; interlocking biopolitical modalities of, 86–88
more-than-human entities: as agentic, 3, 22, 25, 29, 34, 119–20, 136–38, 141, 177, 215; context dependent in networked relations of power, 51; deficit theories of, 3, 10–11, 155; ethical exchange with, 36, 113–14, 203–5; ethico-jural standing of, 8, 76, 189; as lawfully killable, 4, 36, 126, 151–56, 207–8; moral obligations to, 32–33; physical remains of, 1–3, 14; as a priori political, 8; survival attempts by, 5; takeover of Camp X-Ray, 161–63, *162*; transboundary biopolitics of autoimmunity and, 36, 103–7; as victims, 1, 23, 24, 41–43. *See also* animals; architecture and built environment; other-than-human; plants
Morris, Benny, 59
Morrow, Karen, 11
Moughrabi, Fouad, 67
Mount Taranaki (Aotearoa–New Zealand), 211
Mowaljarlai, David, 20
multiperspectival vision, 99
murder: aesthetico-political art of the kill, 37, 183–87, 196, 201; double killing, 45, 46, 174–75; of Mohammed Abu Khdeir, 65–66; putting to death as denegation of, 6; Rule 89 of international humanitarian law, 90; *sparagmos* (ritualized dismemberment and dispersal of bodies), 37, 152–53, 168, 196, 201
Muscogee Nation, 17–18, 217n5

Nabil (farmer), 116
"nakba," environmental, 96
Nakba massacre (1948), 66
naming practices: affective labor of, 160; dispossession and, 112
nationalism, 82, 109–10
national parks and reserves, 109–12, 206; afforestation, 109, 112, 239n147
"national security," 30, 105, 154
National Security Agency (NSA), 168–70, 196
National Security Council, Principals and Deputies Committees, 196
Native American and Indigenous Studies Association, 8
Native American nations and tribes: Cherokee, 25; Chickasaw, 18; Euchee, 17–18, 217n5; Lakota, 144, 216; Muscogee Nation, 17–18, 217n5; Navajo, 17, 23, 124; Potawatomi, 76, 113, 114, 120; Red River Métis, Otipemisiwak, 26; Siksika (Blackfoot) Nation, 223n144
Native American paradigm, 25
Native Americans: cosmopolitics, 20, 27, 64; militarization of Indian country, 201; perspectives on science, 15; solidarity with Palestinians, 8–9, 82; US sovereignty over, 151–52. See also Indigenous cosmo-epistemologies
Navy and Marine Corps Public Health Center, 124
Nayaka people, 119–20
necrogenesis, 55
necropoesis, 183–87
necropolis, Palestinian, 45
necropolitics, 46, 84, 91, 100–101, 179, 187, 194–96; civilians, categorization of, 176; Gaza as "cage," 50, 55, 60; in Guantánamo Bay prison, 125, 158, 160; racio-gendered dimensions of, 55; US, 200–201; zoopolitics, aquapolitics, phytopolitics, aeropolitics, and pedonpolitics, interlocking, 86–87

necropsies, 41, 167
Neimark, Ben, 30
Netanyahu, Benjamin, 61, 77, 227n90
neutralization: legal logic of, 130–31; of Palestinian subject, 53; "verification" of, 46, 90
new materialisms. See materialisms, new
Nietzsche, Friedrich, 177, 180, 183, 185
Nixon, Rob, 97
"noble savage" trope, 17
"non-combatant deaths," 175–76
noncriminal violence, 10–11, 67, 79, 154, 185, 210–11; at checkpoints, 52–53
nonhuman: as deficit model, 3; killability of, 2, 4, 36, 41–42, 56, 78, 126, 151–56; Palestinians framed as, 41. See also "inhuman"; more-than-human
non/normative identities, 68
nonpersons, Guantánamo detainees as, 36, 129–33
Normand, Roger, 211
North Waziristan, 182
#NotABugSplat (artist collective), 187
Not a Bugsplat art installation, 187
nucleic level of biopolitics, 101–3

Obama, Barack, 168
Obama administration, 127–28, 130–31; drone-kill program escalation under, 168–69, 175, 176
obligatory contingency, 89–90
Oikonomia, 60
οἶκος (household), 16
olfactory sense, 41–42
olive trees, bulldozing of, 87, 115–17
Omer, Mohammed, 91–92, 230n133
onto-epistemological ground for human/ animal binary, 6–7, 10, 35, 133, 145
Open, the, 36, 135–40, 142–43, 146–49; denial of to Latif, 156–57, 159; Heidegger's understanding of, 136–37, 139
Operation Pillar of Defense, November 22, 2012, 122, 122–23

Operation Protective Edge, July-
August 2014, Gaza, 1, 34–35, 39–80,
57, 123, 204, 212; African American
opposition to, 59; biopolitical practices of ecological destruction, 35–36;
croplands, destruction of, 108; ecocidal effects of, 36; engagement, rules
of lacking, 88–92; reports on, 49–50;
scenes of destruction, 35; as weapons-
testing laboratory, 70–73. *See also* Gaza
Orwell, George, 68
other-than-human, 3–4, 7–10, 18, 23–24,
31–33, 145–46, 217n5. *See also* more-
than-human; more-than-human
entities
Our Condolences, Afghanistan report,
200–201
ozone depletion, 211–12

Padilla, José, 151, 154
Pakistan, 170, 174, 175; Constitution,
Article 199, 188; Khyber Pakhtunkhwa
region, 187; Peshawar High Court,
187–89
Palestine, occupied, 4–5; architecture
and built environment, 16; counterforensics to document state violence, 16;
ethnic cleansing of, 66, 110, 228nn114,
115; Ghabsiyah (Galilee), 112–14; Imwas,
Yalu, and Beit Nuba bulldozed and
turned into national parks, 111; Indigenous theories and alliances and, 7–9,
218n18; as "jungle," 48; Midya (village),
116; Mujaydial (village), 114; as pollutable space, 95–96; resource extraction
from, 81, 82, 86–87, 92–95; Sheikh-
Jarrah village, 117; villages, catalog of,
112. *See also* Cage, the
Palestine/Israel binary, 106
Palestinian Authority, 91–192
Palestinians: alliances with First Nations peoples, 8, 218n18; as "biological
threats," 52–53, 159; identity papers,
53–54; Nakba massacre of (1948), 66;

"neutralization" of, 53; as outside legal
category of human personhood, 41; a
priori criminality of, 53, 67–68; speciation of as nonhuman-animal other,
35, 41, 55, 67; trees, affective relations
with, 36; as vegetal form of life, 41;
weapons-testing on, 70–73
Palestinian species body, 54–55
Panetta, Leo, 177
Pappé, Ilan, 59, 66, 228nn114, 115
partial actors, 19
pathophysiologies of slow violence,
100–103
"patterns of life," 171, 178–79, 195
pedonpolitics, 86–87, 96–99, 212
Perera, Suvendrini, 65, 69, 163–64, 229n133
performative rhetoric, 14–15, 19, 116
performatives, 19, 121, 211; of ritualized
murder, 37, 152–53, 160, 196, 201
performative speech acts, 116
personhood: corporeal status, 129–31;
gendered, 68; Palestinians framed as
outside, 41; of Te Urewera National
Park, 32, 211; thingness, transition to,
131–32
Peshawar High Court (Pakistan), 168,
187–89
phenomenology, 22, 192. *See also*
Merleau-Ponty, Maurice
physical evidence, 16, 18–19, 40–42, 47
physiognomy, "criminal," 67–68
phytopolitics, 36, 86–87, 107–9, 212;
chronotopes, trees as, 115; corpus
delicti of destruction, 115–17; diachronic, synchronic, and protentive
dimensions, 115, 121; of forensic trace
evidence, 112–15; at Guantánamo Bay
prison, 163; phytocide, 209–10; settler,
of national parks and reserves, 109–12.
See also plants
phytosemiotics (plant languages), 23–24,
113–17, 120, 209–10
Picasso, Pablo, 43
pig, figure of, 65–69, 228n121

pigs, military testing on, 73–80
pinkwashing, 109–10
plants: as arboreal archives of Palestinian history, 113; biophilia for, 204; bulldozed by Israeli military, 43; bulldozing of, 108–9; cognition of, 113, 119; detainees as, 163; as embodied agents, 119–20; as forensic witnesses, 114; "grass-mowing operation" as frame for violence, 39, 100; lemon tree example, 117–21, *118*; memorial, trace evidence as, 112–15; neurobiology of, 119; Palestinians as "vegetal form of life," 41; phytocide of, 209–10; takeover of Camp X-Ray, 161–63, *162*; trees as family, 8; vegetal life as life, 116; as victims of military violence, 1; as weapons of dispossession, 109. *See also* phytopolitics
Plumwood, Val, 206
police, colonial, 20, 21
political, in animal societies, 63–64
polity of nature, 64, 213
posthuman, 3–4
posttraumatic stress, nonhuman animals affected by, 40, 49, 91
Potawatomi language, 114, 120
power: context dependent networked relations of, 51; redistribution of, 141; techniques of, 172; trophy photographs, 65; zoopolitics of, 40–41
"Preliminary Report on the Protection of the Environment in Relation to Armed Conflicts" (United Nations), 12
Presidential Policy Guidance (PPG), 168–69, 176
Pretty Shield (Native American), 145
Procedures for Approving Direct Action against Terrorist Targets Located outside the United States and Areas of Active Hostilities, 168–69
progressive narrative, 109–10, 205–6
property: animals as, 10–11, 187–91, 207–8; lexico-legal subsets, 188–89;

"moveable," 190; as superordinate category, 189–90
property law, 2, 168
propositions, 152; articulation of, 18–19, 115
proprietorial categories, 76, 111, 190–91, 207
prosopopoeia (personification), 24, 114
"protection" of environment, 9–10
Protection of Victims of International Armed Conflicts (Protocol I), 8 June 1977, 12
Protocol Additional to the Geneva Conventions of 12 August 1949, 12, 219n42
Puar, Jasbir, 50, 100, 109–10, 131

Qawasmeh, Hussam, 65
quartering, 52, 58–62, 135, 161
Qudeh, Raghad, 74
Qumsiyeh, Mazin, 96

race, 9, 21, 172, 226n63, n67, 228n115, 229n123, 233n6; anti-African race riots, 59; biopolitics, 5–6, 60; capitalism, 201; denegated a priori raciality of whiteness, 26; postracial, 3; "race struggle," 6
racialization, 30–31, 59, 96, 132, 172, 181; of Anthropocene, 30–31
racio-speciesism, 35, 54–55, 68, 80, 156, 185; biological-racist degeneracy, discourses of, 6; checkpoints and, 57–60; combinatory possibilities of, 57; drone kills and, 199–200; gendered, 55, 57; Guantánamo Bay prison and, 164; laboratory, history of, 71–72; new materialisms reproduce, 25; "patterns of life," 171, 178–79, 195; subspecies, 173; white status produced by, 57
racism, environmental, 31, 201, 215
Raghavan, Sudarsan, 229n127
Ramadan, 46; in Guantánamo court case, 129, 130
Ramstein Air Base, Germany, 160–61, 196

Rashed, Haifa, 85
Rau, Jacinta, 211
"Raw Law," 223n147
razor wire: as sign of absolute excess and overkill, 56; vegetation's use of, 162–63, 165
reductionism, 28; of human exceptionalism, 7, 155
referents, absent, 27–28, 79, 160, 198, 200
refugee centers, 50
refugees, environmental, 105
Reitman, Janet, 125–26
relationality, 2–4, 217n5; consanguinity, 42, 44, 75, 123, 192–93, 203; ethics of, 203–4; forensic ecologies of, 47; Indigenous cosmo-epistemologies of, 17–22; inextricable systems of, 4, 7, 17, 31, 40–41, 57; interspecies, 5, 23–24, 36; joint selves, 120; limits and possibilities of animal-human, 137; nucleic level, 42; phytosemiotic, 113–17
Religious Freedom Restoration Act (RFRA), 129–31
Remes, David, 128
remnants/proxy data, 15, 48, 110–11
reports, official: AR 15-6 Investigation and Report, 133–37, 157–59; on Operation Protective Edge, 49–50; *Our Condolences, Afghanistan*, 200–201; Reprieve, 174–75; Senate Intelligence Committee Report on CIA Torture, 148; *This Is How We Fought in Gaza*, 88
Reprieve report, 174–75
reserves, 110–11, 206
resistance, 96; aesthetic of, 70, 229–30n133; "everyday," 69–70; by Native peoples, 82–83; Palestinian and African American solidarity, 59; replanting of olive trees, 87
resource extraction: settler colonialist, 81, 82, 86–87, 92–95; by US military, 124
responsibility, 29, 196–97; as nonnegotiable, 209

rhetoric, 15
Rida, Abu, 95
rights frameworks, 75–78, 131, 231n157; Euro-anthropocentricism of, 76; ex/inclusion mechanism, 75
Rilke, Rainer Maria, 137, 139
"risk index," 53
risk probability, 176–77; "drone disposition matrix," 181–82
Rizzo, John, 169
rogue state, United States as, 156, 174, 179
Rose, Deborah Bird, 65
Royal National Park (Australia), 110, 111
Rule 89 of international humanitarian law, 90
rule of law, 207–8

sacrifice, 11, 138–39, 146, 152–53
Safar, Abeer, 84
Safi, Ahmad Saleh, 96–97, 99, 102, 103
Saif, Atef Abu, 1, 2, 39, 43–45, 123, 204, 205; school bombing, depiction of, 47–49
Salamanca, Omar Jabary, 83
Salfit Council, 93
Same, imperialism of, 24, 29
Santana, Déborah Berman, 124–25
satellite imagery, 88, 196
Sayegh, Fayez, 232n6
Sayigh, Rosemary, 117
Scahill, Jeremy, 178–79, 191
schematizing, 176–78, 180–81, 183–85
Schiffler, Björn, 174
science, 14–15; abstracted knowledge used for torture, 151; as "art form," 183; exploitation of the known, 177; "metaphysical illusion," 184; Native American perspectives, 15, 20; positivist, 173, 183; scientifico-military regimes of experimentalism, 71; as superordinate, 185; veridictional status, 15, 46, 183
science/art nexus, 183–84
"screen territories," 182, 195

secularized sacred concepts, 11, 138, 152–53, 183–85

securitization, 87, 110–11, 125–26, 151–53; freedom/security nexus, 171; of self, 189; thwarted, 106–7

Seligman, Martin, 150–51

semantics, 64, 207–8, 214; boundaries of forensics, 3, 16; of dehumanization, 153–54; material, 48–49, 113, 120, 159

Senate Intelligence Committee Report on CIA Torture, 148

sentience, 14, 26, 43

September 11, 2001, 110, 197

settler colonialism, 5; anachronic status of, 28; biopolitical practices of ecological destruction, 35–36; civilizational narrative, 110–11; as compartmentalized world, 60; double subjugation, 111; ecocide and biopolitical interlacement of, 83–86; epidemiological warfare, 95; erasure, acts of, 25–26, 45–46, 84–85, 109, 111–15, 181, 239n137; failure of obliterative process of, 29; as form of environmental injustice, 84; frontier geography, 83; "incompleteness" of, 70, 82–83; Israel-US connection, 201; macroframe of, 82; microgeographies of, 50, 82–84, 87, 99–102; new materialisms leave intact, 27; paradigms and aporias, 81–83; punitive economies of, 53; resource extraction, 81, 82, 86–87, 92–95; sexual and gender violence of, 57, 226n63; sovereignty and, 151–52; teleology of disrupted, 28; territorial expropriation and expansion, 35. *See also* Israeli settler colonialism; Israeli state; United States

"Settler Colonialism and Ecocide" (Jaber), 85

settler state: astructurality of structure of, 106–7; elimination and replacement of Indigenous people, 5; sovereignty of, 151–52, 154; totalization, fissured, 107

al Shabaab, 175

shadow archive, 65, 73, 79–80

shadow wars, 197

Shaked, Ayelet, 226n62

Shalhoub-Kevorkian, Nadera, 45–46, 57, 117–21

Shamir, Eitan, 100

Shamir, Yitzhak, 58

Shell-Shocked (Omer), 92

Sherwin, Richard, 205

Shihade, Magid, 229n133

Shin Bet secret service (Israel), 183

Short, Damien, 85

Shujai'iya neighborhood, Gaza City, 39–41

Shukin, Nicole, 11

signification, 113

slaughterhouse, 44, 69–70, 77

slavery, 31; modern-day Israeli market in Palestinians, 59; United States, 57; vestibule metaphor and, 58

"slow violence," 97–101, 182

Smith, Ron, 50, 81–82, 87

Snowden, Edward, 169

Social Darwinism, 67–68

social sorting and capture, 173

soil, pollution of, 86, 97

Somalia, 175

somatechnics, 169–70, 172–73, 187, 247n18

South Africa, 21

sovereign, beast versus, 60–65, 152

sovereignty: reserve system and the national park system as enactments of, 111, 206; of settler state, 151–52, 154; "theological phantasm," 11

Sowers, Jeannie, 104

sparagmos (ritualized dismemberment and dispersal of bodies), 37, 152–53, 168, 196–97, 201

spatiotemporal dimensions, 15, 28, 56, 91, 115, 121–22, 149, 194; Guantánamo Bay prison and, 164–65; of indetermination, 214 speaking subjects, animals as, 145–46

"Speaking to Trees" (Kohák), 119

speaking with, 42, 119–20

species: emergence of, 173; government of, 5, 173; theory of, 193–94

species body, 54–55

speciesism, 5–6. *See also* racio-speciesism

speech, of more-than-human entities, 23–24

Spence, Mark David, 240n145

Spillers, Hortense, 55, 57–59

spirit/energy waves, 25–26, 28, 141

Sri Lanka, 69

standing, 8, 33, 42, 76, 189, 218n22

starvation: of animals and humans, 90; calorie regulation, 61, 94

state: biopolitical power of, 2–4; objectives to foster life or disallow it to the point of death, 4, 84; security, as biopolitical ruse, 125; structure of, 22n10, 58, 70, 81, 106–7

statist operation, tributaries/capillaries of, 7, 86–87, 101, 117

stereotyping, bioinformational, 172–73

"sterile zones," 53

Stimson, Adrian, 223n144

Stone, Christopher, 189

structure of state, 22n10, 58, 70, 81, 106–7; coconstitutive astructurality, 107

Stryker, Susan, 68, 194, 251n130

subject/object binary, 23, 62

subspecies, 173

suffering: communal dimensions of, 23; invertibility of, 44; material and temporal dimensions of, 47–48

supremacism, human, 206, 215

Supreme Court, 128; *Hobby Lobby* decision, 129–30

surplus affirmation, 204

surplus violence, 56, 225n55

surveillance: military-industrial-prison-surveillance complex, 35, 52–53, 70–73; totality of drone, 184

survival media, 229n133

survivance, 29, 48, 83, 114, 115, 122

"suspect" categories, 127, 168–72, 178–79

"sustainability," 9–10, 92, 143, 206

Svirsky, Marcelo, 70

"switch point," 171

Syria, 209–10

Tait, Robert, 42–43

taphonomic context, 41, 166

targeted destruction of ecologies, 29–30; Gaza Power Plant, 97–98; well and sewer systems, 93, 95–96

targets of drone strikes, 168; cell phones, human targets coextensive with, 169–70, 176–79, 184; as somatechnical, 169–70, 187

technicity, automated, 168, 172, 196

technologies of war: death by metadata, 37; semiautomated, 36–37, 182, 201; technicity, automated, 168, 172, 196; used against US Black populations, 72. *See also* drone kills

tele-techno-mediations, 184, 187, 194, 198

terra nullius narrative, 31, 67–68, 94, 107–8, 205

territorial expropriation and expansion, 35

terror: "animal enterprise," 207–8; of animals, 79, 89, 207–8; by Immediate Reaction Force (IRF) teams, 128–29

testimony, forensic, 16, 32, 34, 87, 91–92; by bones of Palestinian dead, 45; incarnate, 161; of more-than-human entities, 47–49; as relational assemblage, 22; speaking with as evidence, 42; survivor modality, 48

Te Urewera National Park (Aotearoa-New Zealand), 32, 211

thanatopolitics, 44–45, 122–23

theological concepts, 10, 184; sacrifice and, 11, 138–39, 146, 152–53; secularized sacred, 11, 152–53, 184–85

theo-onto-epistemological view, 10–11

theory/praxis nexus, 82
thickness of flesh, 192
thingness, 190; transition to, 131-32
This Is How We Fought in Gaza report, 88
threats: "biological," 52-53, 159; "imminent," 174, 194; "intent-based threat assessments," 171
time, reinscription of, 146
Todd, Zoe, 26, 27
topography, 112-13, 115, 195
torture: experiments on military livestock, 73-80; at Guantánamo Bay military prison, 36, 127-31, 133; learned helplessness, 150-51; as "trauma training," 151-53; vertical descent through, 154-55; weaponized insects, 149-50; zoopolitics of, 36, 126, 149-56
Torture Memos (Guantánamo Bay military prison), 149-51, 154, 169
toxicity: at Guantánamo's Camp Justice, 124; as proxy agent of biopolitical state, 103; wastewater from Israeli sources, 93
toxic militarism, 86, 96-97, 124-25
toxic waste dumping by Israel, 93, 95-96
trace evidence, 1, 15, 18-20, 164-65; drone kills and, 199; Indigenous trackers, 20-21; phytopolitics of, 112-15. *See also* evidence
trans, figure of, 68-69, 106, 194, 229n123
transboundary biopolitics, 36, 103-7, 212
transcendence, 135-40; within immanence, 139
transgender studies, 68
transhuman-animal entities, 44, 68
transliteration, 37, 186-87, 194-97, 201
transnational colonial frame, 232n6
"trap," 69-70
"trauma training drill," 151-53
trophy photographs, 65
Trump, Donald, 176
truth: evidentiary, 14-15, 18-19, 22-23, 47; more-than-human entities as speaking, 23-24; truth/knowledge nexus, 177

Tulkarem, Ephraim/Tabeh checkpoint, West Bank, 51
Turgeman, Meir, 67
2014 War on Gaza: Participatory Environmental Impact Assessment (Safi), 96-97, 99, 102

Uexküll, Jacob von, 144
Umwelt, 144
United Nations: Abu Hussein school, 43; complicity in Gaza as prison, 50; Food and Agriculture Organization, 108; report on Gaza, 88
United Nations Charter, 188
United Nations Convention against Torture and Other Cruel, Inhuman or Degrading Treatment or Punishment, 36, 151, 153, 155
United Nations Convention on the Prohibition of Military or Any Other Hostile Use of Environmental Modification Techniques (ENMD) (1976), 12
United Nations Declaration on Permanent Sovereignty over Natural Resources, 94
United Nations General Assembly Resolution, 188
United Nations International Law Commission, 13, 213
United Nations UNITAR-UNOSAT, 88
United States, 4-5; absent referents, Indigenous peoples scripted as, 27; "anticipatory self-defense" as ruse, 173-74; carbon emissions, 31; casino and gaming practices in drone-kill program, 177-78; complicity in Israeli settler colonialism, 218n18; court power, concern with, 127-28; drone kills as murder, 174; extraordinary rendition, practice of, 148; hydrocarbon logistical infrastructure of imperialism, 30, 201, 213; international law and, 13;

United States (continued)
  military purchases from Israeli manufacturers, 72; national parks, 110–11; as
  rogue state, 156, 174, 179; sovereignty
  over Native Americans, 151–52; "victim" status, 197, 252n136. See also drone
  kills; Guantánamo Bay military prison
  (Camp Justice)
United States Coast Guard, 151
United States military: Immediate
  Reaction Force (IRF) teams, 128–29;
  as instrument of genocide, 201; as one
  of largest polluters, 124; single largest
  landowner, equipment contractor
  and energy consumer in the world,
  124. See also Guantánamo Bay military
  prison (Camp Justice)
Universal Declaration of the Rights of
  Mother Earth/Pachamama, 32
unmanned aerial vehicles (UAVs). See
  drone kills
US District Court, Washington, DC,
  129–31
US Senate Judiciary Committee, Subcommittee on the Constitution, Civil
  Rights and Human Rights, 191

Venkatasubramnian, Suresh, 180
vestibularity, 62, 67, 126, 155, 164; of
  checkpoint holding pens, 55; of Israel's
  "animal kingdom," 56–60; jungle/
  culture binary, 58–59; refugee concern
  and, 105; slave/culture distinction, 58;
  US slavery and, 57
Vialles, Noëli, 52, 69
Vibrant Matter (Bennett), 25–28
victims: aggressor-victim, 103–4;
  more-than-human entities as, 1,
  23, 34, 41–43; sparagmos inversion,
  197; United States' claim to, 197,
  252n136
Vietnam War, 12, 85
violence: atmospheric, 182; attritional,
  97, 99–103, 121; disavowal of, 62–65,

76; forensic insignia of sovereign-
  imperial, 198–202; gendered dimensions of, 55, 57, 225n55; of inanimality,
  6–7, 36, 149–56; macro-operations of,
  69–70; noncriminal, 10–11, 52–53, 67,
  79, 154, 185, 210–11; question of the animal and, 6–7, 35–36, 40–41; relational
  genealogies of, 66; saturated, 2, 48, 91,
  122, 128–29, 162, 193–94, 210; sexual and
  gendered, 57, 226n63; "slow," 97–101,
  182; surplus, 56, 225n55; targeted
  destruction of ecologies, 29–30, 93–98;
  zoopolitical, 36
Virtuous War (Der Derian), 78
visuality, regimes of, 65–69; drone kills
  and, 178, 179, 183–84; shadow archive,
  65, 73, 79–80
Viveiros de Castro, Eduardo, 20, 64

Wadiwel, Dinesh, 189, 190
Wall, the, 51, 61, 76, 106, 108, 227n90
Walsh, Sean, 94
war: algorithmic, 175; by other means,
  anthropocentrism as, 7, 87, 213–14;
  state/s of, 214–15
war, law of, 9, 211; environmental law-of-
  war treaty, 213; inadequate protections for environment, 12–13; rules of
  engagement, 88–92
war crimes, 13–14, 91–92, 188, 198–99,
  202; drone-enabled, 198; hidden by
  afforestation, 112; SKYNET and,
  170–71
waste: animal carcasses, 90; biopolitical,
  128, 159, 178; immaterial, 55; military
  ordnance, 213, 215–16; Native American communities bear brunt of, 201;
  Pacific as dump, 206; toxic, 30, 93,
  95–96
wastelands/wastelanding, 93, 95–96,
  98, 103–4, 229n127; phytopolitical,
  107–9
water policies, Israel's impact on
  Palestinians, 85

Watson, Irene, 33, 223n147

Watts, Vanessa, 27, 34

weapons technology, "field-tested" on Palestinians, 70–73

Weinthal, Erika, 104

Weizman, Eyal, 16, 72, 83

West Bank, occupied, *51*, *54*, 55, 59, 71, 87, 203; aquapolitics of Israel and, 92–94; creeping annexation in, 117

Whanganui river (Aotearoa–New Zealand), 211

"What is the Anthropocene-Political?" (Colebrook), 214

White, Rob, 31

white phosphorus, 96

whiteness: colonialism and, 21, 31; denegated a priori raciality, 26; paternal protectionism of, 240n144; slavery and, 57

Whyte, Kyle Powys, 84, 85

Wildcat, Daniel, 17–18, 204, 217n5

Wilden, Anthony, 78–79, 132

witnesses, more-and other-than-human, 47–49

Wolfe, Patrick, 27, 70, 81–84, 107

World War I, 12

World War II, 12

Yazzie, Robert, 23

Yellowstone National Park (United States), 110–11

Yemen, 14, 127, 161; Al-Majalah (village), 191; Al-Shihr (village), 192–93; Mukalla (village), 166–68; US drone strikes against, 166–68, 174, 182

Young, Elise, 101

Yusufzai, Mushtaq, 198

Zierler, David, 85

Zionism, 82, 85, 108, 109

zoē, 64, 105–6

zoo: Gaza as, 35, 49–56; Guantánamo Bay as, 126; as microcosm of racio-speciesism, 58; as term, 70

zoo, Gaza City, 49–50, 56. *See also* Cage, the

zōon, 60, 63

zoopolitics, 7, 35, 212; animals as fungible/replaceable matter, 11, 55, 132, 138, 152, 168, 190, 207; beast/sovereign binary, 60–65, 152–54; "bestiary," 52–53, 61–62, 68; of the Cage, 49–56; "dead meat," 74–76, 152; invertible logic of, 44–45, 61–62, 75, 103, 126, 197, 231n157; of laboratory, 70–73; practices of confiscation, 11; regimes of visuality, 65–69; of torture practices, 36, 126, 149–56. *See also* biopolitics; Gaza

zoosemiotics (animal languages), 23–24, 145

Zubaydah, Abu, 149–50

Zureik, Elia, 58